WERTHEIM PUBLICATIONS IN INDUSTRIAL RELATIONS

POTENTIALS OF THE AMERICAN ECONOMY

Selected Essays of Sumner H. Slichter

Sumner H Slichter

Potentials of the American Economy

Selected Essays of

Sumner H. Slichter

Edited by John T. Dunlop

CAMBRIDGE, MASSACHUSETTS

HARVARD UNIVERSITY PRESS

1961

Distributed in Great Britain by
Oxford University Press
London

Library of Congress Catalog Card Number 61–5577

MANUFACTURED IN THE UNITED STATES OF AMERICA

Notes and Acknowledgments

The twenty-eight selections from the writings of Sumner H. Slichter here reproduced have been chosen from the almost five hundred items listed in the bibliography at the end of this volume. The sifting and final choices were made with the following criteria in mind. They should be representative of his full career and, insofar as possible, show the development of his ideas in the changing times of the past forty years. The selections should reflect the major fields of his interests and illustrate the wide range of audiences to which he spoke and publications for which he wrote. They should treat problems and issues of continuing interest. They are drawn exclusively from articles, statements, and speeches rather than from his books.

The selections are organized into four parts. Part One, The American Economy, comprises five pieces treating the changing character of the American economy and its interactions with the larger community. Part Two, The Economic Outlook, consists of eight papers analyzing business conditions and public and private policy proposals appropriate to the diagnosis. Part Three, Industrial Relations, includes eight articles which reflect Slichter's continuing interest in industrial workers and their organizations, labor-management relations, and the role of government. Part Four, Economic Analysis and Policy Issues, contains seven papers largely concerned with wages and the economic consequences of setting the price of labor through collective bargaining.

The concentration of the selections on these major themes has the merit of showing the development of Slichter's ideas and highlighting a series of penetrating comments on the economic history of his times. While these themes provide a degree of unity to this volume, they have precluded some of his stimulating pieces in other fields, such as his reply to attacks upon the foundations ("Undermining the Foundations," *Atlantic Monthly,* September 1954), and more of his concern with retirement policies, social security and foreign economic policies. The plan of the volume also necessarily excludes some longer pieces, such as the *Governor's Labor Management Committee Report* (1947) and all but the introduction and conclusion of "Postwar Boom or Collapse" (*Harvard Business Review,* Autumn 1942). All of the other selections have been reprinted here in full. There is thus involved some duplication of ideas, but each article or essay is always seen as a whole and the elements of repetition help to identify the persistent themes of his thought.

The title of this collection of articles has been selected to reflect the closing thought of his presidential address to the American Economic Association, "The possibilities of modern technology are tremendous. If these possibilities can be realized, no one can doubt that we are on the threshold of gaining a far better standard of living than man has ever known. Nothing can prevent us from realizing the possibilities of modern technology except unwillingness to place a high valuation upon certain common interests —particularly our interests in enterprise, experimentation, innovation. Never have the rewards of a broad view of common interests been more attractive. Never has the folly of narrowly pressing special claims been greater. The economic future of our country and of the world depends upon the clarity with which this is seen."

Mr. Thomas Wilson, Director of Harvard University Press, suggested the volume, and Mrs. Ada Pence Slichter graciously gave her consent and cooperation and selected the photograph which appears as the frontispiece. The photograph is reproduced with the permission of the Harvard University News Office. The drawing on the jacket by Miss Irene Burns originally appeared in the *Harvard Business School Bulletin* (February 1960) and is reproduced with the permission of the *Bulletin*. The original publishers of the articles here reprinted have all kindly granted permission to reprint them here.

The original articles have been edited only to provide a measure of uniformity in spelling, punctuation, tabulation, and notation. Some substantive footnotes in the originals have been incorporated in the text.

Mrs. Esther Brine and Miss Mary Watson, who served as secretaries to Mr. Slichter for many years, have been of invaluable assistance in reviewing his files and papers and in helping to prepare the bibliography which appears at the end of this volume.

October 1960

CONTENTS

SUMNER HUBER SLICHTER

Professor Slichter wrote two brief memoranda about himself and his work (apparently in the fall of 1952) which were found in his files. It is well to quote them both, for he was a dispassionate and penetrating observer not only of his time but even of himself. These two statements provide his own views of the major influences on his thought, some of his principal accomplishments, and the more significant positions he had taken on issues of his times.

Some Things That I Think and How I Got That Way

I grew up in a university community and come from a family with a university background. My father was professor of mathematics at the University of Wisconsin, and later dean of the Graduate School there. He was a man of tremendous erudition and imagination. He carried his knowledge lightly, but was ready at a moment's notice to discuss the latest developments of science in a wide variety of fields. Although I am the only social scientist in a family of men interested in the natural sciences, I do not know much science. One of my brothers is director of the Geophysical Institute at the University of California. One studied chemical engineering but went into business and became vice president of the Northwestern Mutual Life Insurance Company; another studied geology and also went into business. He now owns his own steel foundry in Milwaukee. My wife's father was a civil engineer and a member of the engineering board that conducted the valuation of the railroads for the Interstate Commerce Commission. My two sons are both in the natural sciences—one a chemical physicist at the Bell Laboratories in New Jersey, and the other assistant professor of physics at the University of Illinois. Although my association with natural scientists and engineers has taught me little science, it has helped me appreciate the great economic significance of science and industrial research.

I began my university work more or less accidentally at the University of Munich when the family was abroad. I think that growing up in the Middle West where the future is more important than the past, and particularly at Wisconsin in the days of the LaFollette reform movement, were important influences in my outlook. I do not know how I happened to become interested in economics. Certainly my interest in the subject, and particularly in labor problems, was greatly stimulated by John R. Commons, one of the pioneers in developing labor economics. But I was interested in these matters before I got into college.

Commons placed strong emphasis on field work and fact-gathering. My interest in labor problems was stimulated by C. W. Price, Safety Manager of the International Harvester Company, who came to Madison to head the accident prevention work of the Wisconsin Industrial Commission. Largely through the influence of Price, I spent a summer as a machine hand in the Deering Works of the International Harvester Company in Chicago, and began a study of the then-new subject of the turnover of factory labor. This summer was 1912. The piece on the turnover of factory labor was published in 1919.

My first job was with the Federal Commission on Industrial Relations, established early in the Wilson Administration to take a look at labor problems. Along with a good many other members of the staff, I was fired in the spring of 1915 because the Commission was divided over how to spend its money. The majority favored spending the money on public hearings rather than on more research. I had become interested in law and was undecided for about two years whether to go into economics or to go into law. During this period of indecision I took about two thirds of a law course at the Law School of the University of Wisconsin, the University of Chicago, and New York University.

I finally decided in favor of economics. After a year of teaching at Princeton in 1919–1920, during which time I was the assistant to Professor David A. McCabe, I went to Cornell. There I soon got started on an extensive study of the shop rules and policies of trade unions. This study was sponsored by the Brookings Institution at Washington, and I spent three alternate years, 1925–26, 1927–28, 1929–30, in Washington and in the field gathering material on union shop rules and policies. I was particularly interested in the experiments in union-management cooperation in the shops of the Baltimore and Ohio and Canadian National, and in the men's clothing industry, and in the Cleveland market of the women's garment industry. Material for this work was gathered by visits to shops and by field work in the several clothing markets, particularly Chicago, Cincinnati, and Cleveland. The work was published in 1941 by the Brookings Institution under the title *Union Policies and Industrial Management.*

The problems of the economy during the great depression following 1929 led me to become interested in the problems of business enterprise. I became one of the early critics of the policies of the Roosevelt Administration. It seemed quite plain to me that the attack of the Roosevelt Administration on the great depression was unduly narrow and based in considerable measure on false premises. The depression indicated, above everything else, the need for encouraging business enterprise and particularly for developing sources of venture capital. The Roosevelt Administration never adequately understood these needs. In particular, I dissented vigorously from the New Deal view that the economy had become mature and was threatened with stagnation. Although I did not know much science, my association with natural scientists had been sufficiently close to make it clear to me that the industrial revolution had a long way to go. The assumptions of economic maturity accepted by the New Deal economists and politicians reflected their unfamiliarity with the potentialities of science and technology, and their inability to envisage the capacity of technological discovery to develop great new investment and employment opportunities. My views on these issues were expressed in several articles in the *Atlantic Monthly* during the depression period and particularly in my presidential address before the American Economic Association in December 1941, under the title "Conditions of Expansion."

When the Committee for Economic Development was formed in 1942 by a group of forward-looking businessmen who believed that economic expansion could be successfully encouraged and that the encouragement of economic expansion was the best way to meet the postwar economic problems, I was glad to join the Research Advisory Board and to become its chairman. I ceased to be chairman of the Research Advisory Board about a year ago, but I am still a member of the Board.

During the war I challenged the widely prevalent view that the immediate aftermath of the war would be a great economic depression accompanied by severe unemployment. The country was still so depression-minded that it accepted as inevitable a severe depression following the great drop in military expenditures. My view that the war could be followed by a boom rather than a depression is embodied in a book entitled *Present Savings and Postwar Markets,* published by the McGraw Hill Company. This book consists of articles appearing in the *Harvard Business Review* during the war.

During my first five years at Harvard I was almost exclusively associated with the Harvard Business School. Thereafter my work became divided between the Business School and the Department of Economics and the newly formed School of Public Administration.

About 1940 I became interested in the Trade Union Fellowship Project—a plan for giving work in economics and administration to experienced trade-union officers on leave of absence from their unions. This plan was originally suggested by trade-union leaders themselves and is still in operation. During the last eleven years about one hundred and fifty trade unionists have been sent to this course and some of them now occupy important places in the trade-union movement. The Trade Union Program at Harvard gives real education. It does not attempt to indoctrinate; it attempts to develop independent thinkers—the kind of men who can make difficult policy decisions when they have to do it on their own.

The great rise of the trade unions made it clear to me that the policy of encouraging unions would have to be supplemented by the policy of regulating some aspects of trade-union activity. In 1947, I served as chairman of a tripartite committee appointed by the Governor of Massachusetts to recommend changes in the labor laws of Massachusetts. Most of the unanimous recommendations of this committee were adopted by the Legislature in a law which is now somewhat misleadingly referred to as "The Slichter Act." The recommendations are particularly important in protecting the rights of individual members within trade unions and in giving the government of the Commonwealth ways and means for dealing with strikes or lockouts that would imperil the public health or safety.

In 1947 and 1948, I served as associate chairman of the Advisory Council on Social Security of the Finance Committee of the Eightieth Congress. This committee reached unanimous recommendations on various changes in the Old Age and Survivors Insurance Act. The substance of most of these changes has recently been enacted into law. Work on this committee led me to challenge the prevalent view that the solution of the problem of old age security is to be found mainly in pensions or old age assistance. During the last several years I have been challenging the practice of automatically retiring employees at the age of sixty-five.

Some Positions I Have Taken

1. That the American economy is not in danger of stagnation.

   See my presidential address before the American Economic Association in December 1941, entitled "The Conditions of Expansion," and my piece, "Business Looks Ahead," in the *Atlantic Monthly,* November 1939, and my earlier piece in the *Atlantic Monthly* entitled "The Great American Experiment."

2. That the Second World War would not be followed by a depression, but by a boom.

   See my piece, "The Outlook for Private Enterprise," in the February 1942 issue of *Commerce Magazine,* Chicago, Illinois, and my article in the *Harvard Business Review,* Autumn Issue, 1943, entitled "Present Savings and Postwar Markets," and my talk at the University of Pittsburgh entitled "After the War: Prosperity or Depression?"

3. That the country is gradually becoming a laboristic economy in which the value judgments of the community as a whole are more and more reflecting the value judgments of the employee class in America, by far the largest class.

   See my paper, "Are We Becoming A Laboristic State?" *New York Times Magazine,* May 16, 1948.

4. The view that the strategic point at which to attack the problem is to encourage more risk taking and to encourage more people to make a living by giving jobs instead of holding jobs.

   See my piece, "More Job Givers Wanted," *Fortune,* October 1945.

5. The view that trade unions have attained such power that public policy should endeavor to regulate their use of power.

   See the Report of the Governor's Labor-Management Committee in Massachusetts which resulted in the enactment of the so-called Slichter Law, and my *Trade Unions in a Free Society,* presented at the Bicentennial Conference of Princeton University. See also my piece, "The Great Question in

Industrial Relations," *New York Times Magazine,* April 1947; also my article, "The Taft-Hartley Act," *Quarterly Journal of Economics,* February 1949; and "Some Basic Issues Raised by Trade Unions," a paper read before the American Philosophical Society on November 21, 1947.

6. The view that the obsolete accounting methods of American business have caused profits to be substantially overstated.

   See "Business Profits Exaggerated!" testimony before the Joint Committee on the Economic Report of the President, reported in the *Commercial and Financial Chronicle,* December 9, 1948.

7. The view that the retirement policies of American business are producing great wastes of labor and introducing great hardships among older people.

   See my piece, "The Pressing Problem of Old Age Security," *New York Times Magazine,* October 16, 1949.

8. The view that the expansion possibilities of the American economy are considerably underestimated.

   See my paper, "How Big in 1980?" *Atlantic Monthly,* November 1949.

9. The view that small savers are entitled to as much protection against inflation as wage earners receive through escalator clauses.

   See my paper, "Curb Inflation with Purchasing Power Bonds," *Commercial and Financial Chronicle,* March 15, 1951, and my paper, "The Integrity of the Dollar," *Proceedings of the Academy of Political Science,* May 1951.

10. The view that there is a conflict between maximizing employment and keeping prices stable.

    See my article, "How Bad Is Inflation?" *Harper's Magazine,* August 1952, and my correspondence with the *Journal of Commerce.*

II

Slichter was born in Madison, Wisconsin on January 8, 1892. The ties to his family were very close throughout his life; he maintained an active correspondence with his father and mother until their deaths at advanced ages, and part of each summer from his first years of teaching was spent at a cottage on Lake Mendota in close proximity to family and old friends.

In the autobiographical quotations above, Slichter emphasizes that his associations with natural scientists, particularly his family, had helped him to appreciate the great economic significance of science and industrial research —one of the major persistent themes of his writings. It is interesting to compare an address of Slichter's father—professor of mathematics and Dean of the Graduate School—delivered on June 12, 1911, before the Madison Literary

Club, on "Industrialism" [1] with the first essay reprinted in this volume. The natural scientist said: "Industrialism is merely science in action, or militant science. . . . Science dominates industrialism. Science corrects the evils it itself creates. . . . It has spread through humanity a spirit of optimism. . . . Perhaps the greatest contribution of science and industrialism to our era is the removal of controversy from human progress." When Slichter was invited to address the Annual Engineers' Day Dinner at the University of Wisconsin on May 3, 1957—designated Slichter Day that year—his subject was "Technology and the Great American Experiment." On the home ground of those who made famous the passing of the old frontier, he stressed the new frontiers created by science. In the spirit of his father, Slichter said: "An outstanding contribution of technology, and of science as well, to the values that guide our lives is their influence upon the sense of social responsibility. . . ."

Slichter's father spent many of his summers in the West doing consulting work with the U. S. Geological Survey or the railroads on the flow of underground waters, his own specialty. It may be that this early experience contributed to Slichter's becoming a "railroad bug" with detailed knowledge of schedules, division points, and railroad lore. In the 1920's, and again in the last years of his life, he was to study intensively railroad labor-management cooperation and work rules. In the days before air travel became general, Slichter said he enjoyed nothing better than sitting in the last seat of the last coach on a slow train and spending the day writing.

Slichter's mother, Mary Louise Byrne, was the youngest of nine children of parents who emigrated from Ireland to Wisconsin in 1848. She was principal of one of Madison's largest elementary schools at the age of twenty, after attending the University for two years. On his father's side, the first member of the family to emigrate to the United States, around 1780, was Christian Slichter, born of a Mennonite father and a French Huguenot mother. Professor Mason in recounting these facts has observed that "one fancies he saw in Slichter the embodiment of that sturdy Huguenot individualism and the propensity to dissent so obviously characteristic of his ancestors." [2] Professor Trumbower, eleven years Slichter's senior and a lifelong correspondent, recounts that they first met in 1908. "Sumner was an unusually interesting young fellow, mature in his interests and serious in his outlook on the world.

[1] Charles S. Slichter, *Science in a Tavern, Essays and Diversions on Science in the Making* (Madison: The University of Wisconsin Press, 1958), pp. 109–126.

[2] E. S. Mason, "Sumner Huber Slichter, 1892–1959," American Philosophical Society, *Year Book for 1960*, 1961.

He was an individual with a fine sense of humor and a non-conformist attitude. A bit eccentric as to dress, he wore no overcoat in the coldest winter weather in Madison and always wore a cap instead of a hat."

Slichter completed his B.A. in 1913 and his M.A. a year later at the University of Wisconsin. As his autobiographical note indicates, he worked in the Deering Works of the International Harvester Company in Chicago during the summer. He was keenly perceptive of the reactions of his fellow workers. He quotes the remarks of the old lathe hand who ran the machine next to his in an article published seven years later (see p. 172, note 3). In the summer of 1914 he joined the staff in Chicago of the U. S. Commission on Industrial Relations, 1912–15, of which Professor John R. Commons was a member.[3] He roomed with Edwin E. Witte, then also on the staff.

When the research staff of the Commission was curtailed, Slichter decided to complete the doctorate at the University of Chicago. He took work with J. M. Clark, and his dissertation on *The Turnover of Factory Labor* was written under the direction of Professor H. A. Mills. The preface to the published version states that the preliminary work had been done at Madison in the seminars of Professor J. R. Commons (who wrote an introduction to the volume) and that Professor William M. Leiserson had supervised the collection of data for the Commission. In June, 1918, Slichter was awarded his Ph.D. degree, enlisted in the field artillery, and married Ada Pence.

They had been in the same class in high school and in college; their fathers were both professors at the University of Wisconsin, one in mathematics and the other in civil engineering, and their families were close friends. Ada Pence taught English and Latin in high school in Madison and later in Chicago, to which she had moved when her father became a member of a board to make a valuation study of the railroads for the Interstate Commerce Commission. As the prefaces of his books acknowledge, Mrs. Slichter regularly read and suggested changes for style and expression in his manuscripts. During the period he was writing his elementary textbook in Economics, *Modern Economic Society,* Mrs. Slichter audited his classes and worked over the manuscript as the "students' friend."

Slichter came out of the army as a second lieutenant in December 1918. In the summer of 1919 he was anxious to gain further factory experience and was hired in Chicago for a machine operation (see page 177, note 6). He

[3] For a discussion of the Commission see Mark Perlman, *Labor Union Theories in America, Background and Development* (Evanston, Ill.: Row, Peterson and Company, 1958), pp. 279–301.

joined the Machinist Union in the plant, but before he reported for work, the plant was involved in a strike and he never did go to work there. In the fall of 1919 an opening developed rather suddenly at Princeton, and Slichter became an Instructor in Economics, assisting Professor David A. McCabe. The following year he joined the Department of Economics at Cornell as an Assistant Professor; in 1925 he was promoted to Professor. In 1930 he was called to Harvard School of Business Administration, on the initiative of Dean Donham, as Professor of Business Economics. The appointment is a tribute to the foresight and initiative of the Business School. A comparison of Slichter's career before 1930 and at Harvard after 1930 indicates that he was a relatively late starter and suggests that Cambridge was a stimulating community and an effective platform for his talents.

During the years 1931–1933 Slichter gave a course of lectures under the auspices of the Wertheim Committee under the general topic of "Industrial Relations in the United States Today." This appointment had been a factor in attracting him to Cambridge. Slichter was invited in 1935 to join the Department of Economics and, with its creation, the faculty of the Littauer School of Public Administration. In 1940 he was appointed Lamont University Professor, the first University professor at Harvard, and moved his office from 210 Morgan Hall to 229 Littauer Center. Throughout the almost thirty years of his career at Harvard he maintained an active interest in both the Business School and the Department of Economics. In the Business School he taught courses on "Problems of Industrial Relations" and "Problems of Economic Balance" from his arrival in Cambridge through World War II. For some years he planned to write a book with the title of this second course. In the postwar era, in the Business School he taught a course on the "Economic Aspects of Public Policy" until 1954.[4] In the Department of Economics he gave a full year graduate course on trade unionism, collective bargaining, and public policy until 1957, and he presided over the Littauer Seminar in Collective Bargaining attended by students from all schools of the University and addressed by leaders of labor, industry, and government, from its inception in 1938 until his death on September 26, 1959.

In 1940 Slichter took the leadership in the establishment of the Trade Union Program at Harvard for officers and representatives of labor organizations. The project grew out of discussions with Robert Watt, the International Representative of the AFL, who complained that Harvard was doing so much to educate business leaders and so little for labor organiza-

[4] Charles A. Bliss, "Sumner Slichter, An Appreciation," *The Harvard Business School Bulletin*, February 1960, pp. 14–19.

tions. Slichter sought from Robert Watt and other labor leaders what they thought the University should do and what the unions would be willing to do. Slichter maintained an active interest both in this program and in the Advanced Management Program at the Business School for business executives.

III

Slichter was a complex person, and his career had many facets. Some indication of the range of the interests and activities of the man is an essential introduction to these essays.

(1) He was pre-eminently a scholar with an insatiable desire to find out the facts, to understand how men and organizations make their decisions, and to discern the trends and tendencies of the times. He was a strong believer in field work, and he practiced the art throughout his career. Three years of the 1920's were spent entirely in field work, and after 1955 he was intensively involved in field work for his second Brookings Institution study. He visited thousands of business executives and labor leaders. He believed in the intensive questioning of a wide range of people involved in a situation after a careful review of the available documents and statistics. He was never fully satisfied with the available data or replies, and he would return again and again to a situation seeking new nuances and subtleties. He sought ever new statistical breakdowns and series.

The two volumes which best reflect this method are likely to remain classics for many years in the field of labor economics: *Union Policies and Industrial Management* (1941) and *The Impact of Collective Bargaining on Management* (1960), published posthumously in collaboration with two former students and colleagues in the Business School, Professors E. Robert Livernash and James J. Healy. As these titles reflect, throughout his career he was interested in the interrelations between workers and supervision and between labor organizations and management, particularly in their consequences for the enterprise and the economy. As early as the preface to his first book he said, "although nominally a study of the labor turnover, the work is fundamentally a study of the methods of handling men." He was equally interested in analyzing collective bargaining as a system of industrial jurisprudence and as a method of setting the price of labor.

He was distrustful of formal models and closed systems in theoretical or econometric terms. He was critical of manuscripts or dissertations which started with elaborate theoretical schemes. He was not interested in system building. He favored short chains of reasoning, and he was fond of addressing to the facts a long series of relatively discrete questions. His files on any topic are full of detailed questions scribbled on all types and manner of paper.

It would be a mistake to classify Slichter as an institutionalist as that term is ordinarily used, although he was unrivaled in analyzing the complex interrelations between the economy and the larger community, and few men have had more faithful understanding of how business organizations and labor unions operate in policy making and administration. He knew these institutions intimately without falling in love with them like so many others who have studied them. The questions he addressed in field work and to statistical data were not random; they reflected keen theoretical interests. Rather than starting with explicit and comprehensive theoretical propositions, he sought gradually in any one area to develop a body of propositions appropriate to a particular problem. He was readily prepared to discard these ideas if they did not appear useful in another context and begin all over again. Where other men tended to become wedded to their ideas, more than others he had a detachment which permitted him to shed a cherished view. It may be surprising, but he did not find the case method of teaching entirely congenial, even in Business School courses. He used cases as illustrations and he developed extensive statistical material for his classes, but he was more comfortable in exposition of a problem area. Neither "institutionalist" nor "theorist" describes his interests and methods; he was a general economist concerned to apply economic principles to a specific problem and to modify these results in the setting of the whole society.

Slichter was primarily an economist; he did not find other disciplines such as sociology or political science congenial for his problems, but he tended to analyze particular situations by treating as variables those dimensions which economists often regard as given in their formal analysis—technological conditions, consumer tastes, income distribution, policies of managements and labor unions, political developments as well as public policies. While Slichter's analysis may not always have been entirely elegant or rigorous, it was often the more insightful and penetrating.

(2) Slichter was a keen observer of business conditions, an unusually successful prognosticator of the business outlook, and a fearless critic of private and public policies. He was a commentator and pamphleteer extraordinary. While he was not ordinarily regarded as a popular teacher in the classroom, he was an extraordinary and effective teacher of economics in the American community. The bibliography at the end of this volume reflects

the wide variety of platforms from which he spoke and the periodicals in which he wrote. He addressed business, banking, and trade-association groups; civic audiences, university conferences, Congressional committees, public forums, and some union meetings. He spoke typically from a prepared manuscript which was then printed in a house organ or reprinted in a magazine with wide distribution. Moreover, he wrote for the widest range of popular and professional journals. He reprinted these addresses and articles and mailed them regularly to a list of approximately three thousand names. Each year he declined more invitations to speak or write than he was able to accept.

From November 1952 until his death he prepared every month a regular analysis of the business outlook in the United States for the *Nihon Keizai Shimbun* of Tokyo which he also reproduced and mailed to a selected list of over three hundred leaders of business and finance, economists, and public figures. He joined the Board of Directors of Standard and Poor's in 1955, and after 1946 he was economic advisor to Incorporated Investors. He was a trustee of Teachers Insurance and Annuity Association from 1952 to 1956.

Slichter was undoubtedly the best-known economist of his day to the American community generally, although it is hard to imagine anyone less a publicist. For the general audience he used a great many facts and statistics. He carefully cultivated the faculty of compressing a wide-ranging analysis within a few pages. He was intolerant of economic nonsense; at times he was even caustic. The following excerpts are illustrative of his comments on public and private policies in recent years:

> Certainly the program of supporting the prices of farm products is one of the most ridiculous ventures ever undertaken by any government anywhere—truly Alice-in-Wonderland economics. The Federal government is undertaking to prevent the great technological revolution in agriculture from depressing the relative prices of a few favored crops—and the American people are docilely permitting themselves to be taxed to support this madness. . . . Much intervention on behalf of the government is simply a way of protecting the old from the new.
>
> The policies and institutions originally created to reform free private enterprise are in many cases themselves in need of reform. Certainly this is true of the progressive income tax law, the interstate commerce commission, the industrial relations policy of the Federal government represented in the main by the Taft-Hartley Act, and the farm program. Who will undertake the task of reforming, not free private enterprise, but the institutions established to reform free private enterprise?
>
> Today the process of exploitation in capitalist America is diametrically op-

posite to the process described by Karl Marx. Marx thought that capital exploited labor, but in America today, labor exploits capital, science, and engineering.

The oil quotas are an unwarranted act of economic aggression on behalf of a few oil states against the nation as a whole and against the free world. . . . The action of the President in curbing petroleum imports is sordid politics at its worst.

The decision to place a stable price level ahead of growth is the most important economic decision that has been made in this country since the Roosevelt administration by passing the Wagner Act challenged the traditional interpretation of the commerce clause and the fifth amendment.

By and large, the top executives of American enterprise have rather limited familiarity with problems of industrial relations and spend relatively little time trying to understand these subtle and difficult problems. Progress is being made. . . . Nevertheless, this interest is far less than it should be in view of the enormous possibilities of saving capital expenditures simply by improving employee-management relations.

The Institute of Life Insurance has launched an ambitious campaign to persuade people to spend less and save more. . . . A sudden reduction in consumer spending and a sudden increase in savings as advocated by the Institute of Life Insurance, would not produce a higher rate of investment. On the contrary, it would simply produce unemployment.

In the role of commentator and critic of economic policies of his times he was unique. He was nobody's man and he belonged to no group or school. In the variety of activities in which he engaged, he will be most sorely missed as economic prophet, analyst, and critic.

(3) From time to time throughout his career Slichter accepted a variety of assignments from governmental agencies. As has been noted, the first such assignment was in 1914–15 as a junior staff member of the U. S. Commission on Industrial Relations. During World War II he served as a part-time public member of the Boston Regional War Labor Board, and he was chairman of a special panel appointed by the national board to study wartime policy problems created by the widespread organization of foremen. In 1947 he became chairman of a tripartite committee appointed by Governor Bradford of Massachusetts to examine labor-management legislation. In contrast to the national conflict of the period, the unanimous report led to the enactment of legislation popularly known as the "Slichter law."[5]

[5] See George P. Shultz, "The Massachusetts Choice of Procedures Approach to Emergency Disputes," *Industrial and Labor Relations Review*, April 1951, pp. 359–374.

In 1947 and 1948 Slichter was associate chairman, with Stettinius as chairman, of the Advisory Council on Social Security to the Finance Committee of the United States Senate. The unanimous report of the Committee became a basis for the liberalization of the Social Security Act in 1949.

Slichter appeared before a number of Congressional committees, including the Joint Economic Committee and the Senate Finance Committee.

(4) Slichter's activities included service in a wide range of professional organizations and committees. He selected for emphasis the fact that he was Chairman of the Research Advisory Board of the Committee for Economic Development from its inception in January 1943 until June 1951. He devoted considerable time to the work of the CED and played a significant role in its activities of this period. He served for extended periods on the Labor Advisory Committee of the Twentieth Century Fund and the Labor Market Committee of the Social Science Research Council.

Slichter was elected president of the American Economic Association in 1941, and in 1949 he became the second president of the Industrial Relations Research Association, following his old friend, Edwin E. Witte. He was the recipient of five honorary degrees, including awards from Wisconsin and Harvard.

These facets of his career do not entirely portray Slichter the person. Many who knew him only casually no doubt had the impression he was somewhat formal, reserved, and preoccupied. There is no doubt that he was busy; he worked long hours and drove himself with a demanding schedule. However, he was quite willing to take time for serious discussion with students, colleagues, or visitors. But he remained an individualist. In going through Harvard Yard he was apt to stop to collect a couple of fallen sticks to take home for the fireplace. Or he could tell the number of haircuts he had during the year. He kept meticulous and detailed account of expenses that were to be charged to others.

In the circle of his family or intimate friends, he was a somewhat different person. He had a keen sense of humor and a sparking wit. When his volume, *What's Ahead for American Business,* was reviewed in a Soviet journal, Slichter circulated a translation saying, "Some of my friends may not realize that I am a venal war-monger." He carried on an extensive correspondence in his handwriting with his family and with a number of close friends. He often wrote on stationery that he had collected on various trips throughout the country. For his close friends he made each year a number of Christmas cards composed of slogans and signs he had clipped from magazines and newspapers. He was greatly interested in his garden and spent considerable time on its care. He was a generous and kindly person who would drop a note, send some flowers, or give a call.

Slichter was able to develop a detachment in the analysis of institutions and business conditions that was extraordinary. In the language of his colleague, Professor Schumpeter, he was not one of those economists who fell in with the humors of his age. He seemed to have little difficulty in separating his diagnosis of a problem from his valuations or prescriptions. The times can ill afford to lose the independent spirit and detached judgment exemplified by the selections in this volume.

Part I

THE AMERICAN ECONOMY

INTRODUCTION

"It is one of the glories of American Institutions that they give unrivaled opportunities to innovators and critics of all kinds. The large output of criticism of all aspects of American life is a healthy protection against complacency. In the field of economics it is a useful reminder that industrial institutions can still stand much improvement. It has the effect, however, of causing many Americans to understimate the substantial merits of their economic institutions." *

Sumner Slichter was pre-eminent as an observer and an analyst of the American economy; he was keenly perceptive of changes in economic institutions and in the dynamic interactions between the American economy and its larger community setting. It was not the formal analysis of given economic institutions that primarily interested Slichter. But the process of change in the economy and the subtle interactions between the economy and the society were his unrivaled domain. He was equally concerned with short-term fluctuations and longer-run transformations.

The five selections which constitute Part I illustrate Slichter's insights into the dynamic elements reshaping the American economy and the larger community. These essays reflect no parochial economic orientation; rather they demonstrate a profound understanding of broad social processes. The training and intellectual habits of an economist, guided by a wide-ranging and independent spirit, are applied to illuminate social change.

Foremost among the dynamic factors stressed by Slichter are science, research, and technology. In an address at the Annual Engineers' Day Dinner at the University of Wisconsin, May 3, 1957—reprinted here as the first selection—he said: "But historians have paid too much attention to growth of population and to geographical expansion and too little to the development of technology. During the last hundred years technological progress has surpassed geographical expansion as a creator of opportunity and social fluidity."

The other four chapters in this part indicate that Slichter placed emphasis upon a number of other factors transforming the American economy over the long term. Among the most significant are: the improvement in the

* Sumner H. Slichter, *The American Economy, Its Problems and Prospects* (New York, 1948), p. v.

art of business management, the changing character of competition, the effects of economic stabilizers such as unemployment compensation and pension plans, the changing use of leisure, the growing proportion of the work force comprised of working wives, the increasing importance of education, the impact of strong trade unions, the growth of the middle class and the elimination of social extremes, the dynamic role of the consumer and consumer credit, and the influence of ideas that have their roots in changing economic conditions upon the whole community.

On the whole, Slichter strongly approved most of the long-term changes these factors were creating in the American economy. He was concerned, however (Chapter 5), lest able executives were not provided with sufficient incentives to start new concerns of their own; he sought revision in tax laws that discriminate against investment in risky projects, and he was concerned with the inflationary bias in the economy. But on balance he felt that the American economy was tending to be more dynamic, with ever higher standards of living and more leisure, which provided wide opportunity for the development of individual and cultural growth. He believed that the American community was becoming less sensitive to political uncertainties. "Today, we realize that even if we cannot solve a problem completely, we can at least do something about it. . . . Thus, by giving us new powers, . . . science and technology contribute to the advancement of morals."

1

Technology and the Great American Experiment

Address at the Annual Engineers' Day Dinner, University of Wisconsin, May 3, 1957.

I

THE cultural history of America needs to be rewritten to take proper account of the impact of technology upon life and thought in the United States, especially upon social and political philosophy. Technology is a major influence in molding thought in the modern world, but its influence is in the main indirect. Karl Marx, whose inquiry into the effects of technology is still the most famous of all such studies, thought that the principal influence of technology would be to sharpen the class struggle. As technological change increased the capital needed per worker, the savings of the community would be less and less sufficient to provide the jobs needed by the growing labor force, unemployment would increase, and deepening misery would eventually produce revolution and the introduction of socialism. Marx misjudged the effects of technology mainly for two reasons—he failed to see that changing technology would increase the demand for skilled labor, and he failed to see that rising productivity would raise wages. Hence, Marx failed to see that technological change, instead of increasing the spread between the haves and the have-nots would greatly expand the middle class.

Thorstein Veblen has made the most ambitious attempt by an American scholar to examine the effects of technology upon thought. He believed that the habits of thought engendered by the technological disciplines undermined respect for property and other traditional rights and thus created a demand for changes in the control of industry. He also believed that technology tended to create the kind of industrial system that could be properly run only by engineers. He hinted strongly that sooner or later the engineers would displace the businessmen as directors of industry. But Veblen eventually saw that he was wrong. In his last book, *The Engineers and the Price System,* he abandoned his earlier view that people who work closely with technology lose their respect for various traditional rights, and he conceded that engineers as a group are a rather conservative lot and have no desire to seize control of industry from the businessmen.

The failures of Marx and Veblen warn us that the effects of technology upon society are easily misjudged. It can be shown, however, that technology today is a principal influence (probably the most powerful single influence) keeping strong and vigorous the philosophy of democracy that has led the United States to embark upon one of the most magnificent experiments in human history. The American experiment is the attempt to make available to all members of the community (not simply to a privileged few limited by birth or wealth) the opportunity to lead the good life and to acquire the physical comforts of life. It is this bold and magnificent democratic philosophy which insists that all can and should have the good life that makes the American experiment something truly new in the history of mankind. The objective of the American experiment, as I have noted, has been twofold—to give people the opportunity to develop themselves and also the opportunity to acquire goods—but America has not sought to advance one of these objectives at the expense of the other.

Closely related to the American experiment and influenced by it has been the social and political revolution that has been going on in Europe for the last two hundred years. The two movements, however, are more or less distinct. Both the American experiment and the European revolution have the same basic philosophy—making the good life and the good things of life available to everyone. But the European movement has been occurring in old societies in which institutions of privilege were well established, in which resources were limited, and in which many people doubted the feasibility of opening the good life to all members of the community. Hence, the European movement has had to be revolutionary and it has, quite naturally, been accompanied by much philosophizing aimed at justifying the destruction of old institutions.

The great American experiment, developing among the settlers of a vacant continent, has had to do only limited tearing down of institutions of privilege. The American experiment had its beginning among the earliest settlers in New England, who sought opportunity to lead the good life, as they saw it, not by overthrowing institutions, but by escaping from them. The earliest settlers in New England were definitely seeking the good life, not the good things of life. The experiment developed as the natural response to conditions under which men in this country lived—not as the result of a carefully reasoned philosophy, though some philosophers and political theorists have affected American ideals. The rise of the democratic philosophy was accelerated by the Revolution. The fact that the people had to fight for their rights increased their self-assertiveness, and the large exodus of British loyalists at the end of the Revolution facilitated the replacement of institutions of privilege that had grown up in some colonies with institutions of democracy. But the most important condition that has produced and kept alive the kind of thinking that characterizes the American experiment is abundance of opportunity. Never in the world's history had men known opportunity in such abundance, and they came from Europe in millions to seize this great chance. Some sought primarily freedom from the restrictions and disabilities of stratified societies; others were mainly interested in the chance to make a living.

It is not surprising that men who were enjoying unprecedented abundance of opportunity should develop a more or less distinctive philosophy of life. No single great document fully expresses the philosophy of the American experiment, though the Declaration of Independence and the Bill of Rights contain much of it, and no philosopher has provided a comprehensive statement of the philosophy, though much of it is found in Emerson and John Dewey. Conditions of life in the United States have produced pretty general agreement among Americans, at least in the north, on three crucial propositions. One proposition is that economic, political, or social privileges are bad and should be prevented from arising and eliminated where they exist. At present the country is trying rather halfheartedly to apply this philosophy to the multitude of economic, political, and social discriminations against Negroes. A second proposition is that steps should be taken to make opportunity even more abundant. The best manifestation of this belief is the development of tax-supported free or almost-free public education, extending through the college and graduate school level. Even as early as 1860 the country had seventeen state universities. It has always been somewhat of a struggle to implement the idea of free public education, and it is still a struggle today when many question the wisdom of investing heavily in our young people. But slowly the idea of free public education is making progress. A third proposition is acceptance of the idea that it is practicable as well as right that *all* members of the community, not merely a privileged few, should have the opportunity to develop themselves and to live well—that attainment of this ideal is not beyond our resources.

What role has modern technology played in the American experiment? Its influence has been indirect, but nevertheless of great importance. The abundance of opportunity that has been the most important single influence in producing the philosophy is usually explained by the rapid settlement of the vacant continent. Undoubtedly, occupation of the continent had much to do with creating opportunity—particularly until the Civil War and a little after. But historians have paid too much attention to growth of population and to geographical expansion and too little to the development of technology. During the last hundred years technological progress has surpassed geographical expansion as a creator of opportunity and social fluidity.

It is easy to demonstrate the great influence of technology upon the kind of thinking that is producing the great American experiment. When the geographical frontier closed, more than two generations ago, many people thought that opportunity would diminish, that class lines would become sharper and class conflict more bitter, and that America would lose its buoyant faith in the future that had always stimulated its expansion. In short, it was feared the United States would gradually take on the characteristics of the stratified European societies. But nothing of the sort has happened. Opportunity has remained abundant, society has become even more fluid, and confidence in the future has remained strong. Indeed, instead of America's becoming more like Europe, Europe, which is also under the influence of modern technology, is slowly becoming more like the United States.

The reason that the passing of the frontier turned out to be a far less momentous event than might have been expected is that technological change rather than geographical expansion has been the principal source of opportunity. An examination of the process by which opportunity has been created makes plain the superior influence of technology. Rapid occupation of the vacant continent, it is true, helped people who were already on the ground to rise in the economic and social scale. But growing opportunity for the community as a whole—a chance for *all* members of the community to live better-rounded lives, to obtain a better education and more leisure than their fathers had, and to live better than their fathers lived—requires gains in average per capita incomes and, therefore, in productivity.

Mere filling up of the vacant continent does not necessarily bring about much increase in productivity—it does so in the main only to the extent that new resources are richer than old ones. The increase in productivity that kept opportunity abundant and growing has been principally the result of technological change. As the rate of technological change has increased, the gain in per capita incomes has accelerated. This gain was about twice as large in the second half of the nineteenth century as in the first half, and it has been faster in recent years than in any previous years.

But the effect of technology upon opportunity is not adequately described by showing in a general way that gains in productivity are the principal source of opportunity. Technological change *might* have diverted the gains of productivity to the property owners and *might* have produced abundant opportunities for property owners but not for workers. But that has not happened. Perhaps the course of technological development has been pretty much a happy accident—though I do not think so. At any rate, technological change has channeled most of the gains of productivity into the hands of workers rather than into the hands of property owners, so that the share of property owners in the national product today is far less than it was a hundred years ago. This has happened in large part because technological change has limited the need for unskilled workers and has increased the need for skilled and professional workers. The number of common laborers in the country today is considerably less than it was forty-five years ago, and the number of skilled and professional jobs has been growing far faster than the labor force. Indeed, today the shortages of skilled and professional workers are greater than ever.

Not only has technological development created opportunity by increasing productivity, but it has also increased opportunity by preventing the successful from entrenching themselves in positions of power and privilege. Technology has done this by bringing into existence one new industry after another. Many of these new industries have grown in large measure at the expense of old industries. Thus profits have not been allowed to flow year after year through the same channels into the hands of a given group of lucky investors. As the pattern of industry has changed, the flow of profits has shifted, and many well-yielding securities of yesterday (the securities of the turnpike companies of a century and a half ago, the canal companies, many railroads, many street railway lines, interurban lines, bus lines, coastwise steamship lines, some locomotive manufacturers, New England textile mills, Pennsylvania hosiery mills, Connecticut hat factories, many automobile manufacturers, automotive parts manufacturers, and many movie houses) have become the cats and dogs of today.

II

That modern technology has been much more than a provider of goods, that it has been a powerful influence upon thought and upon the values and the social organizations that determine the quality of thinking in the community is clearly seen by the critics of technology who fear its effects upon our civilization. Let us look at a few of the principal problems that critics of technology believe it imposes upon society.

The oldest charge against technology, that it degrades the workers by robbing them of skill and responsibility, is heard far less frequently today than it was heard a generation or more ago. The reason is that this charge is now pretty generally recognized to be false. There are, of course, many instances in which technology does reduce the need for skill and responsibility, but a look at the jobs in industry shows that the usual effect of technology is to increase the demands on the worker. The work of the common laborer, which could formerly be done by managing a few simple tools and bits of apparatus (picks, shovels, wheelbarrows), is now largely done by power-driven apparatus. As apparatus is made more and more automatic, the number of machine-tending jobs diminishes and the number of maintenance and repair jobs increases. Modern apparatus also increases the need for planning and scheduling jobs. Finally, and most important, the fact that technology is in a state of flux increases the need of a whole range of nonroutine jobs. The early views of the effect of technology upon men have turned out to be wide of the mark.

A recent charge against technology is the assertion that technology, by giving us more and more leisure and income, is weakening higher education by creating a strong and insistent demand for college work by persons not capable of doing it. Now it is clear that technology is indirectly responsible for the rapidly growing demand for higher education, and it is also clear that some students are capable of doing much better work than others. Naturally, a rapid influx of students with widely differing abilities creates difficult problems for colleges and universities. But I do not think that the facts state a problem for the community as a whole. Certainly we are not going back to a nondemocratic philosophy of higher education—to regarding it as something suitable for only a few prospective clergymen, lawyers, doctors, and persons of leisure. It is a good thing, not a bad thing, that a growing proportion of the population wishes to continue in school until past the age of twenty. The growing demand for college work is more of an opportunity for educators than it is a problem, and professors and others who see it only as a problem are lacking in vision and in a proper philosophy of education.

Quite contradictory to the notion that technology is creating an excessive demand for higher education is the charge by Edward Heimann, Reinhold Niebuhr, and others that technology is ruining our standards of value and our taste by producing an excessive interest in *things* at the expense of interest in personal development and human welfare.[1] This result is said to follow from the extraordinary productivity of industry.

The essence of Heimann's and Niebuhr's argument is that the cultural interests of man are too narrow and his altruistic impulses too weak to enable him to make proper use of the flood of goods produced by modern technology. Lacking adequate desire to improve themselves and lacking proper standards of generosity, men are led by the ever-growing flood of goods to attach undue importance merely to living well or better—to acquiring the comforts and conveniences of life. And in a society in which many men have very limited ambitions with respect to developing themselves and limited concern for the plight of others (especially foreigners), the easiest way to sell goods in large quantities, it is said, is to build up bad standards of value and taste. In order to sell the "orgy" of goods turned out by modern technology, salesmanship and advertising must exploit all manner of mean and ignoble motives. In the words of Reinhold Niebuhr, our culture is the first in the world's history to become "captive to its economy." Unless we buy without regard to moral and esthetic qualities, he says, the industrial system will break down.[2]

Certainly, Heimann, Niebuhr, and others are right that abundance of goods as well as scarcity can create problems, and that ours is the first *major* civilization at least that must wrestle with the problems of abundance. Abundance creates the danger that men will become interested merely in living better rather than in living better lives. Nor can there be doubt that the excesses of salesmanship and advertising are among the more unlovely products of our civilization and that modern technology is responsible at least for the scale of salesmanship and advertising.

But the indictment by Heimann and Niebuhr goes much too far. There is an enormous interest in self-improvement and self-development, rather than in the mere acquisition of goods, as is made plain by the complaint that too many people seek to go to college. And when one looks at the kind of goods that people are acquiring, one's fear that the country is building up false standards of value takes a considerable drop. One notes an enormous increase in admirable uses of income—the purchase of millions of owner-occupied homes, a rapidly climbing demand for education, sharply growing outlays for medical care and for insurance of various kinds, fast-growing expenditures on vacation and travel, and a sensational expansion in spending

[1] Edward Heimann, "The Economy of Abundance," *Social Action* (January 1957), pp. 6–11, especially pp. 8–9.

[2] See his comment on Heimann's article in *Social Action* (January 1957), pp. 12–14, especially p. 12.

on drudgery-reducing household appliances. Nor is bringing news and entertainment into the home a bad idea.

Related to the criticism of Heimann and Niebuhr is the charge made by many artists that technology is debasing taste by making it far more profitable for artists of various kinds to cater to the uneducated many rather than to the cultured few. The charge that modern methods of communication stack the rewards in favor of products intended for the mass markets is undoubtedly correct. But this is only part of the story. Technology, by giving the artist command of new media, has created new forms of art and has invigorated old forms. Furthermore, while technology, by raising per capita incomes in the community and increasing leisure, makes immense rewards available to those who cater to the mass markets, it also enables the serious artist to make a better living than he could have gained in a poorer society. Indeed, modern technology, for all of the stimulus it has given to production for mass markets, has not prevented a great growth of art and writing that are often drastically introspective and subjective, and intended only for the initiated.

A bit of reflection will produce the conclusion, I think, that the charge that modern technology stacks the rewards in favor of the commonplace states a challenge as much as a problem—a challenge to every artist, every writer, every educator. Here is a new kind of society—a society in which leisure is broadly distributed in the form of a short work week rather than concentrated in a small class of the very rich; in which literally millions of people have gone to college and possess incomes that permit them to buy pictures and books in modest amounts and to travel. It is a society in which, thanks to technology, leisure, education, and incomes are growing. Here obviously are the makings of a cultural revolution, if artists can create broad interest in serious work. The opportunity is theirs, such opportunity as artists have never had. If they fail to produce the cultural revolution, perhaps the fault will be with the artists. One observation may be safely made. If serious art is to play a significant role in a society with such powerful democratic traditions as ours, where cultural developments and public policies alike are made by the whole community rather than by a small aristocracy or ruling class, artists must address themselves not solely to a small audience of the initiated; they must touch in a significant way the lives of the many.

An oft-repeated charge against modern technology is that it converts men into conformists and robs them of their individuality. It is said to do this because it exposes us to enormous pressures from media of mass communication—newspapers, magazines, billboards, radio, and television in which we are said to see or hear the same ideas or slogans endlessly repeated—and because it requires us to make our living as members of groups or teams in which our individualities are more or less suppressed.

These charges leave me unimpressed. Modern methods of communication are a good way of acquainting people with a multitude of conflicting points of view. How can conformity be encouraged if one is at a loss what to conform to? And if organizations suppress individuality, they do it quite inefficiently. Every organization that I have had a chance to observe has been full of strong-willed individuals, and the problem of the organization is to get a reasonable amount of teamwork.

All history has been a sort of struggle between man and his institutions. Organizations of various sorts, mainly governments and churches, have attempted to regiment their members—to suppress their individualities, to make them conformists. The most complete control of the group over the individual is found in primitive societies. Sometimes the conflict between individuals and institutions swings in favor of the individuals and sometimes in favor of the institutions, but the trend through the centuries shows individuals winning release from institutions. Certainly modern man in western Europe and America is more individualistic and more disposed to challenge authority than was medieval man.

The great enemies of conformity and the great sources of individualism have always been communication, travel, and education. Modern technology is steadily strengthening each of these sources of individualism. Education, especially higher education, is the strongest influence in our culture for individualism because it encourages the habit, dreaded by all regimenters, of thinking for oneself. The fight to keep institutions and organizations in their place and to build a community of strong, inquisitive, and independent individuals is far from won, but technology, through helping men afford travel and education and by bringing them better instruments of communication, is helping to win the day for individualism.

An outstanding contribution of technology, and of science as well, to the values that guide our lives is their influence upon the sense of social responsibility. Strangely enough, this effect has escaped the attention of the moralists who worry about the effects of technology upon our ethical standards. Before the rise of modern science and technology, man lived in an environment which was pretty much beyond his control. When he had tough problems, he could do little about them. But as science and technology have given him insights into his environment, this feeling of helplessness has been slowly disappearing. Today, we realize that even if we cannot solve a problem completely, we can at least do something about it. The result is a growing sense of social responsibility—a growing disposition to make planned attacks on our problems. No longer can we ignore human suffering or misery by taking refuge in the comfortable excuse that conditions are beyond our control, and that all we can do is to provide charity. Thus, by giving us new powers, science and technology also give us new responsibilities and foster a new willingness to act on those responsibilities. In this way science and technology contribute to the advancement of morals.

III

Technology will play an even greater role in our lives than it has played up to now. The reason is that each advance in science and technology increases man's capacity to make additional discoveries. Hence, the great American experiment will receive ever-growing support from science and technology. The outlook for the experiment looks bright.

In spite of this favorable outlook, however, the time has come to provide the American experiment with a comprehensive and well-considered statement of its objectives and its significance. To produce such a statement would require the work of men with great insight in the fields of history, philosophy, politics, and social institutions. Too long our great experiment has been merely the product of conditions without the stimulus and guidance that can be provided only by a well-expressed philosophy. We shall accomplish more effectively what we are trying to do if we have a greater awareness of our objectives. Furthermore, a well-expressed and well-understood philosophy will help us to see more clearly the deficiencies in our accomplishments. It will force us to consider whether we are giving too much attention to acquiring things and too little attention to developing men. It will give us tests by which to appraise institutions and policies. It will help overcome selfish obstacles to the experiment. Most important of all, it will enhance the significance of the lives of each and every one of us by giving us a sense of the magnificence of the great enterprise in which we are participating and of the worthwhileness of the goals for which we are striving.

2

The Growth of Moderation

The Atlantic Monthly, October 1956.

THE demand for moderation that all observers note as a growing characteristic of American politics is not merely attributable to current prosperity. Behind this demand are impressive changes in American economic and social conditions that have escaped general attention because they have been occurring so gradually. In the last forty or fifty years, however, these changes have produced a near revolution in the economic and social structure of the country.

Three principal long-run developments account for the slowly growing demand for moderate policies:

1. The traditional middle-class occupations have been growing faster than other kinds of jobs.

2. The composition of the middle class and the economic connections of its members have changed. As a result, the attitudes of members of the middle class toward economic issues have changed.

3. Great changes have occurred in the distribution of family incomes, enabling a considerable proportion of wage earners to adopt pretty much the same standard of consumption as professional and technical workers and as many administrators.

It is evident from these changes that the evolution of American society has followed a course very different from that frequently predicted a generation or so ago. At that time it was widely believed that technological change, the rise of big business, and the struggles between the classes would slowly wipe out the middle class. It was also widely predicted that, as the United States became older and more industrialized, class lines would sharpen and conflict between the classes would become more severe. But class lines have been becoming more and more blurred, and the demand for moderation in public policies appears to be coming from all groups in the community.

Let us see how the changes in economic and social conditions that have stimulated the demand for moderation have come about, and then let us consider briefly the broad implications of these changes—not only their effect upon politics but also their effect upon the economy and upon the culture of the country.

The growth of middle-class occupations. The traditional middle-class occupations are those of self-employed business owners (farmers, shopkeepers), professional and technical workers (some self-employed and others employees of business concerns and the government), salespeople, and clerical workers. In 1910 the workers in these occupations constituted 39.6 per cent of employed persons; in April 1956 they formed 45.8 per cent—in spite of a big drop in the number of self-employed farmers from 17.3 per cent of employed persons in 1910 to 6.1 per cent in April 1956. In the borderland between the traditional middle class and the laboring class are the skilled craftsmen. If these are counted in the middle class, the middle-class workers constituted 51.3 per cent of the labor force in 1910 and 59.1 per cent in April 1956.

Behind the growth of middle-class employments lie changes in methods of business management, changes in technology, and changes in the kinds of goods and services demanded by consumers. About fifty years ago American business concerns began to discover the uses of staff executives. These are experts in various fields, such as engineering, accounting, marketing, personnel, industrial medicine, public relations, who advise the line or operating executives in making decisions and who, in some cases, help line executives carry out policies. There has been an enormous growth in these occupations and in the clerical workers to help the staff officers. For example, about the year 1900 business began to discover that record keeping pays. At that time there was no cost accounting in American industry—indeed, very little accounting of any kind. The entire country had only 250 C.P.A.s; today there are over 40,000. Other kinds of staff experts, such as time-study men, market analysts, personnel men, industrial physicians and nurses, who were virtually unknown fifty years ago, are today numbered by the thousands. Engineers, who were fairly well established in industry by 1900, have increased twenty times in the last half century—from 41,000 in 1900 to about 850,000 today. The latest development has been the addition of industrial research departments which employ over 200,000 research scientists and technologists and which industry is expanding just as rapidly as the colleges and universities can turn out trained men.

Technological change is another influence that has increased the relative importance of the middle class. Not only has it increased the demand for engineers, chemists, physicists, time-study men, and other technical and semi-technical workers, but cheap mobile power, made possible by the gas engine and the diesel, has drastically cut the demand for wielders of picks and shovels and for unskilled farm laborers. As a result, the number of common laborers has dropped from 8.9 million in 1910 to 5.9 million in April 1956, and from one fourth of the employed persons to one eleventh.

Finally, rising family incomes have helped the middle class to grow because they have increased the number of families that can afford the services of professional workers—teachers of all kinds, doctors, dentists, writers, and entertainers.

From business owner to employee. During the last forty years the proportion of the middle class who are self-employed (farmers, business owners, independent professional workers) has dropped and the proportion who are employees has risen. Naturally employees, even well-paid employees, tend to see many matters from the point of view of the employee rather than from the viewpoint of the business owner or of top management. Thus far middle-class workers who are employees have shown only limited interest in unionism, but airplane pilots, actors, train dispatchers, and yardmasters are well organized, and there is some unionism among engineers doing routine work, and among teachers, draftsmen, journalists, salespeople, and office workers.

Part of the change in attitudes among middle-class workers comes from changes in their economic connections. The proportion of them who are employed by business is diminishing. Most teachers work for the government, and so do an increasing proportion of administrators, engineers, accountants, lawyers, and scientists. These employees are concerned with serving the public rather than with helping enterprises make money, and in some cases they are concerned with regulating private industry. Still others are trade-union officers or employees and represent the interests of wage earners in dealing with business. Since the middle class is increasingly composed of employees rather than self-employed persons, and since a growing minority of the middle class do not work for business enterprises, it is not surprising that the interests of business owners carry less and less weight in the thinking of the middle class.

The sense of belonging. The narrowing of the differences in incomes during recent years has been almost sensational. Between 1935–36 and 1950 the average income among the one fifth of the families at the bottom of the income scale gained 78 per cent in purchasing power but the average income of the 5 per cent of the families at the top of the income scale gained only 17 per cent in purchasing power.

Two influences have been mainly responsible for cutting the differences in family incomes. One has been the strong ambition of people to improve their lot. This ambition, together with the availability of free or almost-free public education, has greatly increased the reluctance of many persons to accept unskilled jobs and has increased the number of persons qualified for skilled or technical jobs. As a result, the wages of unskilled workers have risen faster than the wages of skilled and professional employees—in spite of the fact that industry has less and less need for common labor and more and more need for skilled and technical workers.

The second influence narrowing the differences in family incomes has been the entrance of women (particularly wives) into industry. In 1940, one out of eight married women worked in industry; at present the ratio is about one out of four or less. Married women are most likely to work when the income of the husband is low. Among nonfarm families in which the husband earned $3,000 a year or less, the proportion of wives in the labor force was about twice as large as among the families in which the husband earned $5,000 a year or more. Most of the family incomes of $6,000 to $10,000 are made possible because the wife works—for in two out of three such families the wife is a wage earner.

Because the gap between the wages of the unskilled and those of skilled and technical workers is narrower than formerly, and since one out of four wives is a wage earner, the nature of the husband's occupation no longer determines family income. For example, one out of five families of skilled craftsmen has an income of more than $7,000 a year. But among professional and technical workers the proportion is one out of six, and among sales and clerical workers, only one out of seven. About 72 per cent of the families of managers and nonfarm business proprietors have incomes of less than $7,000. Hence one out of five skilled craftsmen and their families are able to live better than more than seven out of ten managers and business owners. In such a society class lines naturally become quite blurred. Many a wage earner has just as much cause to worry about how government spending affects his income tax as does the typical manager, doctor, or lawyer.

It is not surprising that skilled or semiskilled workers, whose children go to high school or college, who own homes, drive cars, have television sets, and who in general live as well as a large proportion of lawyers, doctors, salesmen, foremen, and teachers, do not think of themselves as belonging to a class apart. They feel very much members of the community and are inclined to adopt pretty much the same variety of viewpoints on most public issues (money for schools, higher taxes on gasoline, stricter zoning laws, foreign aid, publicly owned water power, defense spending, general tax cuts, help for agriculture) as other members of the community.

Middle-of-the-road voters. It is becoming clearer every day that these economic and social changes are strengthening the demand for middle-of-the-road policies, and the most astute present and recent leaders of both parties —President Eisenhower, Adlai Stevenson, Lyndon Johnson, Thomas Dewey —have been quick to note it. The movement toward moderation during recent years has come from both the right and the left. Much of the middle class has moved from a position of great conservatism to a middle-of-the-road position. Since many middle-class workers are employees and are also identified with management, their views of issues reflect a mixture of the employee viewpoint and the management viewpoint. Wage earners, too, have been moving toward a middle-of-the-road position—the result of their increasing ability to live in the same way as other parts of the community.

The shift toward the middle of the road is reflected, on the one hand, in the success of the Republicans in increasing their share of the labor vote as the party has become more liberal and, on the other hand, in the success of the Democrats in holding a good part of the managerial and professional vote acquired during the depression of the thirties, as these groups have gradually become less business-minded. In 1952 the Republican and Democratic parties each had a large part of the vote of the skilled and semiskilled workers—45 per cent for Eisenhower, 52 per cent for Stevenson, and 3 per cent for other candidates. The proportion of trade unionists preferring Republican presidential candidates increased from 20 per cent in 1936 to 39 per cent in 1952 and to 56 per cent in May 1956. On the other hand, in 1952, 32 per cent of the professional and managerial workers, traditionally a conservative group, preferred Stevenson and 2 per cent preferred minor candidates.

The result of these two movements from the right and the left toward the center has been a demand for the welfare state, but for a rather mild form of welfare state. Most people wish the government to give help to various groups in the country—considerable protection to employees and to farmers against economic hazards, considerable help to small business, retired persons, disabled workers, and fatherless children. But there is no strong demand for drastic changes in economic institutions or policies—for radical changes in the control of industry or in the relations between government and industry. If either party were to offer an extreme program, it would quickly find itself with only a handful of supporters. There is nothing for the two parties to do except to compete for the votes of the moderates.

A more rapidly growing economy. The economic and social changes of the last generation have had profound effects, not only upon politics but also upon the economy of the country, and they raise important questions for the future of American culture. The principal effect upon the economy has been to make consumers play a more active role in determining the demand for goods, and thus to make the economy more dynamic. Competition in consumption has always been keen in the United States, but it has been made keener in recent years by the rise of low incomes relative to large incomes and by the consequent weakening of class lines. The growing competitiveness of consumption is clearly shown by the rapid growth of consumer credit. One of the great uses of consumer credit is to enable families to buy things that their neighbors do not yet possess. Another use is to enable families to keep up with their neighbors by buying without further delay things that their neighbors already have.

Keen competition in consumption helps the economy grow since it causes demand to expand ahead of personal incomes. Obviously such an economy grows more readily than one in which the volume of consumption is almost completely determined by the size of personal incomes. Many economists have seriously underestimated the capacity of the American economy to grow because they have believed that consumers play only a passive role in determining the demand for goods—merely spending their incomes rather than initiating increases in demand more or less independently of changes in their incomes.

Challenging cultural issues. The recent economic and social changes in the United States also raise very fundamental questions about the future of our civilization. Many people of high ideals are concerned lest a philosophy of moderation interfere with the ability of a country to improve the condition of its people. Is a country that loves moderation, that wishes to enjoy its prosperity, that strives for peace of mind, capable of having the aspirations and the ambitions and the determination that great advances in civilization require? These advances demand strong dissatisfaction with some aspects of things as they are and strong resolution to change those conditions. Will the habit of being moderate prevent the people from adopting high ambitions and developing a stubborn determination to achieve them?

I suspect that a spirit of moderation is usually favorable to progress. So far, the greatest obstacle to progress has not been disagreement about objectives or ideals, but division among the supporters of widely accepted ideals as to how best to achieve them. Time and again noble causes have been discredited because their supporters have insisted on moving ahead rapidly with untried methods. Willingness to proceed slowly step by step and to experiment on a small scale with ways and means (a spirit of moderation) would have produced more progress.

As for the danger that a spirit of moderation will weaken our ambitions and aspirations, protection will come from the growing influence of science upon men's thinking. Science is a spur to progress because it forces new responsibilities upon us. It does this because it gives us far more control over our environment than any previous age has possessed. Incomplete as our control still is, it is sufficient to rob us of the comfortable excuse that we might as well ignore a condition or a problem because, as men used to think, not much can be done about it anyway. Today, for the first time in history, men must face the fact that they have the capacity, if they have the will, to do something about most problems that confront them. With science forcing new problems on our attention and showing us that we can probably do something about them, we are well protected from the danger that a spirit of moderation will prevent the community from seeing the faults in existing institutions and from entertaining strong ambitions to make the world a better place.

3

Our Economy—Is It Politics-Proof?

New York Times Magazine, December 4, 1955.

How much political uncertainty can the American economy stand without perceptible effect on the volume of production and employment? Put in another way, how susceptible is economic activity to more or less purely psychological influences?

Last March, when the stock market was being investigated, Secretary of the Treasury Humphrey told the Senate Banking and Currency Committee that "confidence in this country's economy is such a fragile thing that it can be lost in a day." He added: "Since most American families are able to buy a good many things that they do not need, they are in a position to postpone or cancel a great many of their ordinary purchases. Whenever they lose enough confidence to do either, business must dip."

Since President Eisenhower became ill, spokesmen for the Administration have been taking a very different view of business confidence. Confidence is now represented as a hardy plant that will be affected little or not at all by the political uncertainties created by the probable retirement in 1957 of a political leader in whom the business community puts extraordinary trust.

Which view of confidence is correct—the one advanced by Secretary Humphrey or the one put forth by the Administration? This question is one of more than passing interest. It involves the basic question of whether our economic institutions can be expected to work well under democratic conditions. It is in the nature of democratic institutions to produce political uncertainty. Indeed, it is part of the merit of such institutions that they make it easy for the people to change the government and its policies whenever they feel so disposed.

It would be foolish to deny that public policies have often profoundly affected the operation of many economies. History abounds with examples of countries that have made themselves rich or made themselves poor by their choice of economic policies. Indeed, one can easily cite countries in the world today that are keeping themselves poor by discouraging the accumulation of capital, the entrance of foreign capital, and the adoption of modern technology. Today the American people are having an opportunity to observe how satisfactorily their economy stands the psychological shock of a drastic and unforeseen change in the political outlook.

I believe that during the last twenty years the American economy has been developing characteristics that make it far less sensitive than ever before to political uncertainties and that give it a considerable capacity to expand even in the face of somewhat unfavorable public policies. Furthermore, I believe that the development of the economy has been bringing about social and economic changes of historic importance that are reducing the differences between the political parties and are making quick and drastic shifts in public policy quite unlikely.

I

To begin with, let us see what has been happening to make the economy less sensitive to political uncertainties and more capable of going ahead in the face of them. There have been four principal developments that tend to make business rather independent of changes in the political outlook: (1) the growth of built-in stabilizers; (2) the improvement in the art of business management; (3) the rapid growth of the new industry of discovery; and (4) the great improvement in the position of consumers.

The growth of built-in stabilizers. The growth of pension plans (public and private), of unemployment compensation (including supplementary benefits), the large volume of expenditures by the federal, state, and local governments (amounting to over a sixth of the purchases of goods and services), and the high personal and corporate income-tax rates all work to limit the effect of a setback in business upon incomes after taxes.

Incomes will, of course, drop if production and employment fall, but no drop in production today can produce the decrease in incomes after taxes that would have been caused by the same decrease in production twenty-five years ago. This means that the economy is less sensitive than it used to be to unfavorable developments of all kinds—including, of course, political uncertainties.

The improvement in the art of business management. The art of business management has been improving rapidly for the last fifty years or more, but the progress achieved in the last twenty-five years has been particularly impressive. The great problems suddenly thrust on managers by the great depression of the thirties, the rapid rise of unions, the Second World War and the Korean War have all contributed to the development of administrative skills and to the improvement of administrative practices.

Since the art of management consists largely in knowing how to get things done, progress in the art of management means that men are gaining in control over their environment and are learning better how to achieve their objectives in the face of obstacles. Our skill in the art of management in the United States today is a far more valuable national resource than it was twenty-five years ago—in fact, our knowledge of the art of management is one of our most productive resources.

Of what has progress in the art of management consisted? I can mention only a few of the most important recent gains. One of the most important, for which the pioneer thinking seems to have been done at General Motors, has been a realization of the desirability of a partial separation of the two functions of making policies and of executing policies. The result has been an improvement both in policy making and in policy execution because it has meant that both policy makers and policy executors have had more time to do their jobs.

A second important gain has been a growing realization of the importance of plenty of staff work to assist both policy makers and policy executors. The growth in the number of staff executives (who make studies, gather information, and give service and advice) as distinguished from the line executives (who are responsible for the day-to-day running of the business) has been going on for fifty years, but the expansion of staff has been particularly rapid in the last twenty-five years.

But even today staff officers have failed in many enterprises to attain the influence to which they are entitled by reason of their knowledge of various fields, such as markets, credits, technology, industrial relations, and by reason also of the fact that as a rule they have greater opportunity than line officers to think about the long-run problems of the concern. The enormous increase in staff means that business is far better prepared than ever before to deal with its problems, to make plans, to develop policies—in short, to overcome difficulties and to attain its objectives.

A third important gain in the art of management has been the rather general raising of the horizons of business concerns. It is increasingly common for managements to attempt to work out more or less definite plans for the development of the enterprise over a period of five or ten years.

True, these plans have to be revised from year to year and the changes are often important. The significance of the new horizons of business, however, consists in the fact that today's decisions are to a growing extent being affected by long-range considerations and that the uncertainties of the moment and other short-run matters have less influence than they once had on the decisions of executives.

The rapid growth of the industry of discovery. It helps one to appreciate the profound economic significance of technological research to think of it as a separate industry, producing its own distinctive product, new knowledge. It is true that much research is not motivated by the desire to help anyone make money and is carried on in universities or government laboratories where it does not directly contribute to profits. But much technological research is definitely intended to produce commercial results and, even though most of it is done in captive plants that are intended to serve only their owners, technological research is an industry.

Unquestionably, it is by far our most productive industry and, though it is still small, it is growing rapidly. As late as 1946 it had about 122,000 research engineers and scientists; today it has over 200,000 and its demand for men is far greater than the universities and engineering schools can supply.

The rise of the industry of discovery makes the economy less sensitive to political changes and political uncertainties for the simple reason that it enormously increases the influence of technological change and prospective technological change upon the policy decisions of business. What the politicians may do remains important, but of growing importance is what the engineers and scientists are about to discover. Thus, as the industry of discovery expands, the scientist and engineer gain in influence and, relative to them, the importance of the politician shrinks.

The great improvement in the position of consumers. In his statement of March 1955, Secretary Humphrey pictured the American consumer as quite ready to throw the economy into a recession because most American families buy much more than they need and because confidence in this country's economy is "a fragile thing."

This picture of the American consumer has no resemblance to reality. It is true that the American consumer buys far more than he (or she) needs to sustain life or even, in many cases, to live in modest comfort. But this does not mean that the American consumer does not have an urgent desire to possess what he purchases or that he is quite ready at the slightest cloud on the economic horizon to cut his spending.

As a matter of fact, most consumers strongly aspire to a higher standard of consumption than they are enjoying, and they have demonstrated again and again that they are ready to cut their saving and often to go into debt in order to get what they want. For example, between the first quarter of 1954 and the third quarter of 1955, when personal incomes after taxes grew by $18.6 billion a year, personal consumption grew by $23.8 billion—a fact which incidentally cannot be reconciled with theories of consumption widely held among economists.

Possibly there was a time in the history of the country when the American consumer was the timid sort of person pictured by Secretary Humphrey but, if so, there is no statistical evidence of it. American consumers have repeatedly shown a strong willingness to buy consumption goods even in the face of falling incomes and growing unemployment. Invariably, in a period of general contraction, consumption expenditures drop far less than personal incomes.

During recent years the economic position of American consumers has been enormously strengthened. Many millions of long-service and medium-service workers have been given by seniority rules virtually complete protection from layoff, and short-service workers have been given considerable protection (though inadequate) by unemployment compensation.

Private pension plans supplementing the federal scheme have spread to 13,000,000 workers, and there has been an enormous spread in insurance against sickness. An interesting and important change has been a rise in the number of families with two or more income earners—from one out of four in 1950 to three out of ten in 1954. There has been a further increase in 1955 because employment has risen by 3,000,000, but the number of families has increased by only 700,000 to 800,000.

In the early months of the recession of 1953–54, American consumers demonstrated in a dramatic fashion that their confidence is not a fragile thing. In the face of a rise of one million in unemployment between October and December 1953, consumers substantially increased their buying of goods (over and above the usual seasonal rise) and they increased their short-term indebtedness by nearly $1.2 billion—mainly to buy automobiles and Christmas presents.

II

What are the social and economic changes that are reducing the differences between the political parties and that are making radical changes in public policy quite unlikely? Here we are encountering some of the most important transformations in the Western world—transformations that extend far beyond the United States to Britain, Sweden, Denmark, the Netherlands, and are introducing drastic changes in the political life of those countries.

The essence of the matter is that a more or less accidental combination of circumstances—the adoption of policies designed to promote full employment, the nature of modern technology, the spread of education, the rise of trade unions, the spread of social legislation, the growing practice of wives working in industry, the availability of cheap consumer credit and cheap real-estate credit, the institution of progressive taxation and other changes—are all combining to build up a large middle class that is becoming the dominant class in the community.

The social and economic transformation that has been going on in the United States and northern Europe during the last generation is one of the most dramatic in all history and its consequences are many and profound. A similar transformation of economic and social institutions may be occurring in France, Italy, and many Latin American countries, but the evidence from these countries is scanty and conflicting.

In the United States the rise of the middle class is reflected in the sharp drop in the number of common laborers in the community (from 29 per cent of the labor force in 1910 to 11 per cent in 1950). It is also reflected in the rise in the proportion of professional workers (from 4.4 per cent of the labor force in 1910 to 7.2 per cent in 1950); in the rise in the proportion of craftsmen and foremen (from 11.7 per cent of the labor force in 1910 to 12.9 per cent in 1950); and in the proportion of clerks and salesmen (from 10.2 per cent in 1910 to 19.0 per cent in 1950).

As a result of the spread of education, the achievement of full employment, and the wage policies of trade unions and the government, the salary and wage structure has been compressed. Thus, between 1939 and 1954 the median income of common laborers outside of agriculture rose by 253 per cent, but the median income of professional workers increased by only 182 per cent. Since 1951, when the consumer price index has increased only about 3.3 per cent, the proportion of spending units (members of the same family living together who pool their incomes to meet major expenses) with incomes of $3,000 to $7,500 increased from 47 per cent to 52 per cent in 1954.

Particularly interesting is the sharp increase in spending units with incomes of over $5,000 a year—from 21 per cent of all spending units in 1951 to 32 per cent in 1954. In part this sharp increase is due to a rise in the proportion of married women at work. The rapid increase in spending units with incomes of $5,000 or more goes far to explain the surprisingly large and persistent demand for houses and automobiles.

As the middle class becomes larger relative to the very poor and the very rich, political parties that cater primarily to the right or the left find the going tougher. Success in politics becomes more and more a matter of catering to the middle classes and of playing down appeals to the extreme right or the extreme left.

In Sweden the necessity of appealing to the middle groups is marked by a diminishing of differences between the Socialists and the Liberals. In Britain the rise of the middle class has produced a crisis in the Labour Party. Bevan's effort to rekindle a radical spirit in the party and to win support for a broad program of nationalization has been crushed, and it has become clear that Bevan is an outdated man.

In the United States the rise of the middle class is reflected in the Republican Party in the rise of the Eisenhower wing at the expense of the right-wingers, and in the Democratic Party in the decline in influence of old Roosevelt "New Dealers" and in the desire of Democratic politicians to avoid connections with organizations such as Americans for Democratic Action.

A severe depression would undoubtedly sharpen the differences between the parties in the United States and would accentuate the influence of the left-wingers in the Democratic Party, but the days when this country can experience anything worse than moderate or possibly mild depressions are gone forever. In the meantime, both the great parties will have to devote themselves more assiduously to cultivating the favor of the dominant and growing middle class.

The Republicans and Democrats have their differences on foreign aid, tariffs, tax policy, military spending, and perhaps on industrial relations and farm aid, but their differences are not wide and often are not clean-cut. Since both parties will be asking the support of the same middle body of voters, their programs are bound to be pretty much alike—just as the programs of the Conservatives and Labour in Britain and the Socialists and Liberals in Sweden are not far apart and are becoming more and more alike.

III

The trends in the economy which have been reducing its sensitiveness to political conditions (the growth of built-in stabilizers, the improvement of business management, the growing importance of technological change as a determinant of business decisions, and the improving economic position of consumers) show no signs of ceasing. Furthermore, the growth of the middle class that is forcing the political parties to pay less and less attention to right-wingers and left-wingers will continue. Modern technology has less and less use for the common laborer and more and more need for the high-school and college graduate.

As all political parties are forced to appeal more and more to the dominant middle class, each will nominate middle-of-the-road candidates whose differences on economic issues, though significant, will not be of first importance to American industry. In short, the United States is making good progress in achieving the kind of political institutions and the kind of economic conditions that are favorable for steady growth.

4

The Growth of Competition

The Atlantic Monthly, November 1953.

I

ONE of the most widely held misconceptions about the American economy is the belief that competition is gradually diminishing in vigor and is being supplanted in many industries by various forms of monopoly. The belief that competition is dying is probably accepted by a majority of economists and certainly by a large part of the general public. Probably no single belief has done more to undermine confidence in the future of the economy and to convince many people that socialism or central planning is inevitable.

If competition in fact were dying out, the matter would be most serious. Competition quickly and severely punishes managements that are stupid or lazy or that get out of touch with conditions. In the tough struggle between communism and private enterprise, business needs the spur and the discipline of stiff competition to keep it dynamic and well managed.

But as inquiry will show, competition is not dying out; it is steadily spreading, taking new forms, and growing in vigor. Granted that in some industries it is not as strong or as pervasive as it should be. Granted that the business world is full of groups that wish strong competition for the other fellow but desire restraints on rivalry among their own members. Granted that some of the groups wishing to limit competition (the high-tariff advocates and the "fair-trade" advocates) have strong influence within Congress, and that there is danger that this businessman's Administration may weaken the foundations of private enterprise by supporting curbs on competition. But the fact which overshadows all others in significance is that competition over the years has been gaining, not losing, in vigor, and there is good reason to expect it to continue to grow. What steps can we take to encourage it?

The belief that competition is dying owes its broad acceptance mainly to the rise of big business. People quite understandably but wrongly confused big business with monopoly. It was discovered that in most industries half to three fourths of the output was concentrated in the hands of four or five firms or less. The conspicuous growth of large companies led to the belief that concentration of economic power was growing. Books expounding this theme were widely read, and one by Berle and Means became famous. The Roosevelt Administration appointed a special commission to study the alleged concentration of economic power.

Within the last few years, however, it has become clear that the public's ideas about the concentration of economic power were wrong. Two facts in particular stand out. One is that a considerable degree of concentration is found in many forms of activity. For example, more than half of the members of Protestant churches are found in five denominations out of more than two hundred and twenty; half of the candidates for Ph.D. in economics are found in four institutions, and half of the physicists with Ph.D.s received their degrees in one of ten large institutions. Similar concentration occurs in other fields of learning—though the institutions that give the most degrees vary. Consequently, when consumers concentrate their buying of cars or cigarettes or soap, they are behaving in a normal fashion—in the same way that people do in selecting their churches or schools. Hence, concentration of production does not mean that sellers are dominating buyers. It simply reflects the fact that there is frequently a great concentration of people's choices.

The second fact is that the degree of concentration of production has not appreciably changed in the last fifty years. Measurement of concentration is difficult—some studies show some increase, others show some decrease in recent decades. The only safe conclusion is that there has been little change in the degree of concentration. Insofar as the belief that competition is declining rests upon the assumption that concentration of production is growing, it rests upon a fictitious foundation. Incidentally, even a growth in the concentration of production is not conclusive evidence that competition is becoming less vigorous, because a few large concerns may battle strenuously for larger shares of the market.

II

The evidence that competition has been spreading, taking new forms, and growing in vigor is abundant. This evidence falls into five principal parts: (1) the disappearance of various conditions that have limited competition; (2) the rise of new business methods and new types of business organizations that increase competition; (3) the increase in the number of products, services, and processes, broadening the range of buyers' choices and intensifying the struggle for the buyers' trade; (4) changes in conditions which intensify old forms of competition; and (5) the growing efforts of business to improve its products and to meet the desires of consumers.

The disappearance of various conditions that have limited competition. The holders of the belief that competition is declining look back to an imaginary age when the country was made up of many thousands of small concerns all vigorously competing with one another. As a matter of fact, these conditions never existed. Population was sparse and transportation was poor and expensive. Most communities could afford few business concerns and were pretty completely cut off from other places by the poorness of roads. It is plain that such conditions limited competition.

What a transformation has occurred! The growth of population has made possible several competing stores or dealers in many places where formerly there was room for only one. Far more important has been the effect of better transportation. The automobile and good roads have given extraordinary mobility to consumers. With two out of three families owning cars and with good roads covering the land, buyers are able to switch their custom from one seller to another, indeed from one town to another, to take advantage of any attractive buying opportunities within a radius of fifty miles or more. Never in the history of the world has such a large body of consumers been so well provided with good transportation and thus been so independent of the merchants of any particular town or place.

Improved transportation has also stimulated competition by exposing producers to competition from new and distant sources of supply. Of special interest are refrigeration and pipelines. Refrigeration in vessels and railroad cars has put the winter fruits and vegetables of the South and the tropics in competition with the canned and preserved fruits and vegetables of the North; coal from West Virginia and Pennsylvania must compete in the East with gas piped halfway across the continent from Oklahoma and Texas.

The rise of new business methods and new types of business organizations that increase competition. One of the most stimulating competitive developments of the last century has been the rise of mail-order selling, because it has brought vigorous competition into thousands of communities, no matter how isolated. Mail-order selling has been a fairly recent growth. Back in the days of Adam Smith—a time when many people uncritically assume that competition was more pervasive than it is today—there was no selling by mail. The great mail-order houses got their start in the last quarter of the nineteenth century. But mail-order selling is by no means confined to the mail-order houses, and it is constantly being extended to new products. One may buy by mail not only any article of apparel or food or furniture, but trailers, boats, insurance, and prefabricated houses.

Mail-order selling was soon followed by two other types of distributor—the chain store and the supermarket. Each is based on the discovery that cutting traditional retail markups produces rapid turnover of stocks and good profits. The grocery chains and supermarkets have little respect for the conventional boundary lines of business and are selling cigarettes, toys, phonograph records, hardware, underwear. Today about half of the supermarkets are carrying nylon hosiery. A year ago the proportion was one out of four. Three out of four supermarkets now handle houseware items such as cutlery, cake pans, butter dishes, and many others, and their sales of these items are estimated at more than $135 million a year. The supermarkets are even invading the fields of the drugstore, the great disregarder of business boundary lines. In many communities more tooth paste and shaving cream are sold in supermarkets than in drugstores. But the drugstores have retaliated by selling groceries, so that in some places more coffee is sold in drugstores than in grocery stores.

New kinds of business are constantly arising to threaten the markets of old businesses. The motel competes with the hotel, the drive-yourself companies with taxis and even with owning one's own car, the outdoor movie with the motion-picture theater, the book clubs with the retail bookstores, the vending machine with the retail store. Self-service drugstores have recently come into existence. Another new type of business is the renting of tools to persons who wish to build their own houses or to do other construction work for themselves. Savings banks, within the last fifty years, have had to meet stiff competition for the savings of individuals from life-insurance salesmen, credit unions, mutual funds, and even government savings bonds; in some states savings-bank life insurance competes with the ordinary life companies. Of particular importance in increasing the competitiveness of the economy are the recently developed venture-capital companies. These concerns help promising new companies get started in business by putting capital into them and in some cases giving them managerial assistance.

The increase in the number of products, services, and processes. The competitiveness of the economy is constantly being intensified by new products, services, and processes. It is true, of course, that the making of new products (and the plant and equipment to produce them) increases the demand for goods as well as the supply of goods because it brings into existence jobs and incomes. But the new products can get a share of the expanding market which they create only by competing vigorously with old products for the incomes of consumers.

In the period 1940–1951, when the output of the economy as a whole increased by about 5 per cent a year (faster than the long-trend growth) and population was growing less than 1.5 per cent a year, output and sales of television sets grew 113 per cent a year, freezers 71 per cent, dishwashers 21 per cent, frozen foods 19 per cent, kitchen cabinets nearly 15 per cent, water heaters 14 per cent, electric shavers 8.5 per cent, cigarettes 7.6 per cent, washing machines 7.5 per cent. Unfortunately two of the fastest-growing industries have been parimutuel betting, on which people spent over $269 million in 1952—thirty-three times as much as in 1929—and the gambling coin-machines, on which $150 million was spent in 1952—nineteen times as much as in 1920. New industries which grow faster than the average are a constant threat to the established industries. The new industries force the old ones to keep prices down and values up in order to retain their share of the market and to keep their sales from shrinking.

Many new commodities and services meet essentially the same need as some old product or service. When this happens, two or more products or services battle for the same market. The advance of technology is constantly increasing the number of commodities and services that are in direct competition with each other. Consider some of the many cases of intercommodity competition that have developed during the last fifty years. Today oil competes with coal, and gas in turn competes with oil. Cotton and wool meet the ever-growing competition of artificial fibers, paper competes with glass and cloth, the bus and the privately owned automobile with the railroad, frozen food with canned food, the telephone with the telegraph, the movies with the legitimate theater, and television with the movies, the radio with the newspaper, oleomargarine with butter, the trailer with the apartment or dwelling house. Five years ago the volume of detergents sold was one eighth the volume of soap. Today sales of detergents by weight exceed the sale of soap.

Changes in conditions that intensify old forms of competition. Competition is being stimulated by the growth of leisure and by the fact that people own much larger stocks of goods than they formerly possessed. Within the last fifteen years the five-day week has become fairly universal outside of agriculture. The spread of the five-day week has intensified the ancient competition between home work and industry and has caused the home to win back part of the lost ground. Largely because Saturday is no longer a workday in industry, people are painting and papering their own houses, even building their own houses in all or part, and are making increasing quantities of furniture and clothing. In one community the building of additional bedrooms in attics is so great that a course in night-school instruction is offered to help owners do a better job. The result has been a rapid growth in sales of paints, patterns, hand tools, and semiprefabricated houses to individuals. Industry, of course, continues to strive for work that might be done in the home. One of the most interesting recent efforts of industry to compete with the home is the launderette—the self-service laundry.

The great increase in personal possessions in itself intensifies competition between the new and the old. In the early days of the automobile industry, for example, there was little competition between new cars and old ones—nearly all of the cars purchased were new ones. Today most prospective buyers have the choice of buying either a good secondhand car or a new one. Indeed, the purchases of old cars in 1952 were considerably more than half again as large as the purchases of new cars. That means that unless the new cars are sufficiently more attractive than the old, the owners will use their old cars a year or two longer. Despite this, about three out of five purchasers of new cars trade in a car that is less than five years old.

What is true of automobiles is true of other forms of durable goods—refrigerators, vacuum cleaners, radios, even television sets. A large proportion of the possible buyers of new articles already possess an earlier model which serves the essential purpose and is not discarded until the new models are sufficiently superior. The secondhand market flourishes. The fact that American families are already well stocked with a wide variety of durable consumer goods is additional reason why producers place so much emphasis upon improving the quality of their goods rather than simply reducing the price.

The expansion of technological research. The expenditure of huge sums on improving old products and developing new products is a recent change in industry which has attracted surprisingly little attention. Half a century ago industry depended for inventions and discoveries largely upon enterprising and daring individuals (a Morse, McCormick, Bell, Goodyear, Edison, Marconi, or Ford) who went ahead on their own with such resources as they had or could beg or borrow.

During the last thirty years (and especially the last twenty) a revolutionary change has occurred. The search for new and better products and for better methods in many enterprises is becoming a normal part of business operations and is being financed out of the current revenues of business concerns. The result has been a startling growth in the scale of research and the support given to it. In 1950, private industry spent about $1.1 billion on technological research—nine times as much as in 1930. More than four times as many scientists were employed in industrial laboratories in 1950 as were employed twenty years before.

Industrial research is competition at its best because it means that the producer is making systematic efforts to reduce his costs or to improve his product. Hence, the spectacular growth of research and the huge sums now spent every year on improving products and cutting costs refute effectively the assertion of those who argue that the economy is becoming less competitive. Never in the world's history have existing products and methods encountered a greater challenge from new products and better methods. Better fabrics, better methods of insulation, better methods of preserving food are among the many changes that will soon be ready. Furthermore, the kind of competition represented by research tends to spread and to grow more intense. The very fact that one enterprise is using research to cut its costs or to improve its products means its rivals must do the same thing or be left behind. One laboratory leads to others and to further competition. Although industrial research has been spreading rapidly, even today only a few managements appreciate its possibilities. Hence there is room for an enormous expansion of research during the next few years.

III

Even though the economy has been growing more competitive, the country would be wise to encourage competition still further. So important is keen business rivalry that we should not trust to chance that it will continue to gain in vigor. There are a number of ways in which it could be encouraged:

Avoid reimposing the excess-profits tax except in time of war. This tax hits hardest the very person who needs to be encouraged—the successful innovator. He will become a more formidable and effective competitor if he is permitted to plow back a large part of the profits of his successful innovation instead of turning most of them over to the government.

Forbid agreements by which manufacturers control the prices which retailers charge for the manufacturer's product. Such agreements prevent the more efficient retailers from attempting to gain volume by underselling their less efficient rivals and thereby limit competition. Experience proves that the margins which manufacturers give to retailers are far greater than efficient retailers require.

Encourage enterprises to install new and better equipment by giving managements greater discretion over the rate at which they are permitted to charge depreciation for tax purposes. More rapid replacement of equipment would be encouraged by permitting larger write-offs in the first several years of the life of an asset.

Withdraw undue protection to American industries against foreign competition. A large part of American manufacturing industries are protected by such high duties that they have virtually no foreign competition. Although they are exposed to all kinds of competition in the American economy, some direct competition from abroad would be stimulating.

Encourage able young executives to go into business for themselves. This is a difficult and complicated problem. Many thousands of new enterprises are started in the United States each year, but about half of them are sold or liquidated within two years. One of the difficulties is that the persons best qualified to start new enterprises—namely, successful young executives in established concerns—usually have such good prospects for advancement with their present employers that they are little inclined to take the enormous risks inherent in striking out on their own or in accepting an offer from a struggling new company.

The venture-capital companies that have come into existence within the last few years are an important step in the direction of encouraging able executives to start out on their own. These concerns, as I have pointed out, are especially important because they put capital into new enterprises—enterprises which have no earnings record but which appear to be promising. Thus the venture-capital companies help able men obtain much-needed funds.

Changes could be made in the corporate income-tax laws that would make working for a new and struggling concern a more attractive gamble for executives than it is today. An executive who gives up a secure job with an established enterprise is now compelled to sacrifice the pension rights he has earned during his service. This is unfair and, in addition, it is bad for the economy as a whole. When an executive who shifts from one company to another sacrifices his pension rights, pension rights become a form of industrial serfdom and discourage competition among concerns for executives. Company contributions to pension plans should not be permitted to be counted as an expense in computing tax liability unless the plan vests with any employee of, say, ten years' service or more the right to claim all premium payments made on his behalf.

Help small companies with an earnings record obtain the capital needed for growth. Next to the scarcity of capital for new companies, the most serious lack in the capital market is the scarcity of funds for small but growing companies—companies which need medium-term or long-term loans but which are too small to go to the bond market and which represent too great a risk for life-insurance companies and other institutional investors. Hence there is need for more venture-capital companies and also for more of the similar industrial development companies, such as the Industrial Development Bank of Canada and the Maine Development Corporation. If small concerns find it easier to grow, competition is bound to be brisker.

Expand the government's support of research. There are limits on the kind of research that private industry can support because the results of much research soon become available to everyone. Therefore, much of the support of research should come from the government. There has been an enormous increase in government support in the last fifteen years, and the federal government is spending over $1.3 billion on research. Unfortunately the availability of the results of much government-supported work is unduly restricted by sincere but ill-conceived efforts to protect national security, and the government is now disposed to cut instead of increase its grants for research. But government support of research not only aids defense but helps make the national economy both more productive and more competitive.

The growing competitiveness of the economy causes one to be confident that industry will continue to be progressive and that it will adapt itself successfully to changing conditions. The development that gives most reason for confidence is that the support of invention and discovery has become a normal part of business operations. There is, however, a paradox about competition in the making of innovations. Each innovator is attempting to discover something unique—in other words, to become a sort of monopolist. But the public need not fear this sort of monopoly. Each of the would-be monopolists is limited in his power by the fact that he has many rivals who are also attempting to discover acceptable innovations. America is fortunate that its economy in the last generation or so has developed to such an unprecedented degree this best of all kinds of competition. Rivalry in efforts to discover new products and to improve old ones assures us that our fund of technical knowledge will grow rapidly and that the economy will be tough, adaptable, and pretty well prepared for any emergency. The daily necessity of meeting new threats to their markets will keep managements keen and alert and will assure that only the most resourceful and progressive managements will survive.

5

Strong Points and Weak Points in the American Economy

Address before the Citizens' Advisory Committee of the New York Public Library, February 10, 1953.

I

IN DEMOCRACIES, where the ultimate responsibility for policies rests with the people, the various members of the community need to have more or less definite opinions about the points of the economy that they consider good and about the points that they consider bad. My remarks here will deal with a few of the more important aspects of the economy that seem to me to be good and a few others that seem to me to be bad. I shall skip a discussion of the important question of the yardsticks by which one decides that a given feature of the economy is good or bad. In general, the points that I have classified as good are conditions (1) that help bring about rapid growth in output per capita; (2) that cause the gains of growing productivity to be widely distributed; and (3) that cause the growth of the economy or productivity to be little retarded by adverse conditions, such as severe depressions or bad public policies. There are, of course, other important yardsticks.

There is general awareness that productivity per capita has been growing fairly rapidly. Indeed, output per man-hour has doubled during the last thirty-five years. Much less well known is the fact that the fruits of greater productivity are widely distributed and that the American economy stands out because of its success in building up a large middle class. Half of the money income before taxes, or 53 per cent after taxes, goes to the middle three fifths of the income receivers. Likewise, it does not generally seem to be realized that the economy has demonstrated an extraordinary capacity to function well under unfavorable conditions, such as a bad tax system with stiff rates. These bad and drastic taxes have not prevented capacity production, a record-breaking rate of investment, or even a high rate of saving.

Among the many conditions that are responsible for the good showing of the economy, I have selected eleven for brief discussion.

The value of labor and capital in many industries has been kept higher than their market prices by education and technological progress. This has not been true all of the time, but it has been true most of the time. And it has happened in most industries and has been of great importance. When the value of labor (or any other resource) exceeds its market price, employers buy more labor (or the other resource) and the economy expands. Thus a growing labor force is easily absorbed. There are countries in the world, however, in which education is so meager, technology is so stagnant, and savings are so low that additions to the labor force can be absorbed only by depressing the rate of remuneration.

The capacity to make technological progress seems to be increasing, for the proportion of resources devoted to research is growing. For example, total expenditures on public and private research, exclusive of research on atomic energy, were seven times as large in 1947 as in 1930.[1] I am not sure, however, that in the future education and technological progress will be able to keep labor worth a little more than its wages. The rise of unions has brought an important new element into the economy. Unions may tend to limit expansion by keeping wages too high in relation to the worth of labor. In that event, fiscal or credit policy may have to be used to offset the influence of unions and to keep labor worth more than its wages.

The community is pretty generally committed to the desirability of small, rather than large, families. The great dread of the classical economists was that the increase in population would swallow up the gains of technological progress. The plight of India, Egypt, Ceylon, China, Puerto Rico, and many other parts of the world reminds us that the fears of the classical economists were far from groundless. The growth of population can easily offset the gains of technology. If the birth rate in south and southeast Asia remains high for another generation, the resulting misery and lack of hope will give the communists an excellent chance to capture those parts of the world. Indeed, a high birth rate is the best ally of communism. Limitation of population is so much taken for granted in this country that we easily forget that it is an essential condition to our high output per capita.

The community is production-minded. By this I mean that the community has faith in production as a way of solving problems. This faith is in

[1] The President's Scientific Research Board, *Science and Public Policy* (Washington, 1947), I, 9, 12.

contrast to well-established attitudes in Europe. The Organization for European Economic Cooperation, in its fourth annnual report, takes notice of the lack of productivity-mindedness in Europe and recommends an intensive drive that will make all sections of the community more productivity-minded.[2] The preoccupation of Europe with the division of wealth rather than its production is of long standing. Evidence of it is found a hundred years ago in John Stuart Mill who said: "It is only in the backward countries of the world that increased production is still an important object; in those most advanced, what is economically needed is a better distribution."[3]

The economy has considerable capacity to control the volume of expenditures by making technological discoveries which lead to new or better articles of consumption or new investment opportunities. It is important that an economy be able to expand by raising the expenditures for goods as rapidly as productive capacity grows. This means that at least part of the community must be willing to spend more than their recent incomes. There are two principal ways of inducing them to do this—by offering them better goods at more attractive prices, or by creating new investment opportunities through the development of new processes and new types of equipment.

The rapid growth of industrial research to which I have referred has substantially raised the capacity of industry to increase the demand for goods as the productive capacity of the economy expands. Furthermore, the growth of industrial research probably on balance reduces the tendency of production and employment to fluctuate. Some economists explain fluctuations in production and employment by the tendency of the volume of investment spending to be determined by changes in the size of recent incomes. But insofar as investment expenditures are determined by technological discoveries, they are not responsive to changes in recent incomes. Hence, in an economy such as that of the United States, in which a large part of the investment spending is determined by technological discoveries, changes in recent incomes have only a limited tendency to introduce fluctuations into production and employment.

Decision making is broadly decentralized. There are almost four million enterprises outside of agriculture and between five and six million in agriculture. This means that there are millions of places where policies are made or where experiments may be tried out. When there are many enterprises, there is a better chance that the executives with originality and imagination will become heads of concerns where they are best able to give expression

[2] OEEC, *Fourth Annual Report,* "Europe, The Way Ahead" (Paris, 1952), pp. 23, 193–196.
[3] John Stuart Mill, *Principles of Political Economy* (New York, 1908), II, 338.

to their originality. Furthermore, when there are many enterprises instead of a few, there is a better chance that some original and imaginative subordinate will succeed in winning the approval of his superiors for bold and worthwhile experiments. A large number of enterprises, therefore, helps make the economy dynamic and adaptable.

New enterprises are not difficult to start—at least in most industries. New enterprises are a way in which new ideas may be tried out. Hence, it is an element of strength in an economy if new enterprises are easily started. In the United States new concerns are fairly easily started—as is evidenced by several hundred thousand business births each year. There are also opportunities to start in business by acquiring firms. Perhaps new concerns are *too* easily started—at least in most parts of the economy. This is suggested by the high infant mortality among new concerns. About half of the new firms established started between 1946 and 1951 were sold or liquidated within two years.[4]

Executives and technicians are not above doing manual work. In many countries of the world, perhaps most countries, the development of technology and the efficiency of operations have been hindered by the unwillingness of engineers and supervisors "to get their hands dirty." Even in the United States routine office or selling jobs are regarded as more genteel than routine jobs in the shop. But this preference of routine workers for white-collar jobs has not been accompanied by the tradition that engineers and supervisors should keep out of the shop as much as possible and should refrain from doing manual work when their help is needed to locate trouble or to demonstrate a new method. The development of enginering and production methods has been greatly helped by the fact that engineers and executives are not simply office men.

A high proportion of production is in the hands of concerns owned by many stockholders rather than in the hands of family enterprises. Well over half of the output of the economy, or about three fifths of the privately produced output, is turned out by corporations, and most of the corporate-produced output is turned out by corporations open to investment by the general public and operated by professional managers. Family-owned and managed enterprises are not particularly important outside of agriculture and retailing. The United States is fortunate that second, third, and fourth generation family-managed concerns are not particularly numerous in its economy.

It is hard, I concede, to surpass in zeal and efficiency the management of

[4] *Survey of Current Business* (December 1952), p. 12.

the founders of enterprises. Furthermore, the founders are usually willing to plow back a large proportion of the earnings. After a generation or two, however, there is frequently a considerable change in the management of family-owned concerns. The members of the family wish to withdraw a high proportion of the earnings, and the operating heads are likely to be family members who did not gain their jobs by merit and who may even have been pushed into carrying on the business out of a sense of duty to the family. Such enterprises do not help to make the economy progressive and efficient.

In the United States family management has not been perpetuated by family loyalties. If the next generation is not particularly interested in the business, the enterprise is sold or professional management is brought in. Professional management may be less aggressive than founder management, but it is usually more aggressive than second or third generation family management and it is interested in seeing that the concern grows rather than in providing plenty of income for the leisure activities of the owners.

The proportion of professional and skilled workers in the labor force has been rising and the proportion of common labor has been falling. This is important because it makes for more equality of incomes—it tends to increase the number of professional and skilled workers, who are in the middle income groups, and to reduce the number of common laborers, who are at the bottom of the scale. The economy has not been behaving as Karl Marx said capitalism would develop. Instead of producing a small class of very wealthy and a large class of very poor, it has been building up a large and ever-growing middle class.

The increase in the number of professional and skilled workers relative to common laborers may be regarded as a sort of victory for science and technology over the common laborer. By embodying their skills in machines and apparatus of various sorts, the scientists and engineers force more and more common laborers to become machine operators—sometimes rather skilled operators, as in the case of much of the earth-moving machinery that replaces pick-and-shovel men; sometimes semiskilled factory workers. A big market, such as now exists in the United States, helps the scientists and engineers win out in competition with common labor. A big market is good for machines, which means that it is good for the scientists and engineers who invent them, the skilled workers who maintain them, and the skilled or semiskilled workers who operate them. But since common laborers cannot run or repair machines, the big market limits the employment opportunities of common laborers and forces them to acquire skills.

The possibility of substituting labor and capital for one another has not been particularly high, and willingness to use present income to buy sources of future income seems to be strong. That is a nontechnical way of saying that the elasticity of substitution between capital and labor seems to be less than one and that the demand for future income in terms of present income does not seem to have elasticity of much greater than one. These two conditions account for the rather surprising fact that a rapid rise in capital per worker has been accompanied not by a rise in the share of the national income going to property, but by a fall. This is an important development because it helps explain why inequality of incomes has been diminishing. Since capital and labor are not easily substituted for one another, a tendency for the supply of capital to increase faster than the supply of labor produces a substantial drop in the returns on capital. But since the demand for future income is strong in at least a part of the population, the drop in the return on capital does not reduce the proportion of incomes that are saved—and the supply of capital continues to increase much faster than the labor force. What seems to have happened is that between the seventies of the last century and the twenties of this century, capital per worker (expressed in dollars of constant purchasing power) grew about threefold, but the share of property in the national income dropped from around one fourth to about one fifth.[5] Since the twenties there has been another great drop in the proportion of the national income going to property, but this later drop is due to public policies as well as to economic conditions.

There is a strong desire to make more money rather than to enjoy the income of accumulated wealth. This fact is closely related to the absence or weakness of class lines in the country and the competitiveness of consumption here. The strong desire to make money has far-reaching consequences. Some of its effects on the culture of the community may not be good, but its economic consequences seem to be desirable. It makes competition keener; it is partly responsible for the rapidly growing support of research by industry; it explains why industry remains progressive and enterprising in the face of extraordinarily stiff tax rates; it makes the division of income more even.

The strong desire to make money is an important reason why competition is vigorous. This is a matter of great importance. Competition among sellers gives a range of choice to buyers; competition among buyers gives a

[5] Simon Kuznets, "Capital Formation, 1879–1938," in *Studies in Economics and Industrial Relations*, University of Pennsylvania Bicentennial Conference (Philadelphia, 1941), p. 67; and Simon Kuznets, *National Income, A Summary of Findings* (New York, 1946), p. 50.

range of choice to sellers. Hence pervasive competition is necessary to assure that freedom of choice is widely distributed. Many economists believe that competition has been gradually getting weaker and less pervasive, but the facts do not support this belief. When Adam Smith and the classical economists first began to explain economic behavior in terms of competition, the vigor of competition was limited by many conditions—by the fewness of sellers in many markets, by the high cost of transportation, by the lack of standard grades to describe the quality of commodities. Competition has steadily been getting more pervasive and keener. It is being made more intense by the cheapening of transportation; by the increase in the size of markets, making possible more enterprises; by the spread of industrial research, increasing the competition between industries, between materials, and between processes; by the growing importance of stocks of durable goods, which makes more intense the competition between the old and the new; and by the rise of large chain stores and mail-order houses which offer ready-made nation-wide distribution facilities to new manufacturers and which seek to make money by large turnover at low margins rather than by high margins at the cost of slow turnover.

The strong desire to make money partly explains the keen interest of business in research. Industrial research is a form of competition. Its rapid expansion reflects both the desire of enterprises to outdo their rivals and the fear of each concern that its rivals may outdo it. At any rate, the spectacular growth of research has been one of the most important recent developments in industry. In 1900 there was one engineer to every two hundred and fifty industrial workers; in 1940, one to every eighty industrial workers; today, there is one to every sixty industrial workers.[6] The growth of industrial research, as I have pointed out, greatly improves the capacity of industry to control the level of investment opportunities and the volume of consumption.

The strong desire to make money goes far to explain why the economy has performed so well in the face of stiff taxes and bad public policies—why, indeed, high and bad taxes have, to some extent, actually *encouraged* efficiency and enterprise. Many people take it for granted that every advance in taxes is discouraging. Everyone agrees, however, that competition stimulates efficiency. The effects of higher taxes are similar to the effects of competition. When several concerns are competing, each is threatening to take away business from the others and thus to reduce the profits of the others. This constant threat to the profits of each enterprise, whether the threat is produced by competition, by higher taxes, or by demands for higher wages,

[6] Paul Cohen, "Shortage of Engineers," *Technology Review* (February 1952), p. 168.

encourages efficiency. But the only reason it does this is that the demand for a good profits record is a very stubborn one—in the language of economics this demand, when measured in terms of the time and effort expanded by managers, is an inelastic one. This means that the more effort required to achieve a certain level of profits, the more time and effort managers will spend in trying to achieve that level.

The demand for a good profits record could conceivably be an elastic demand. If it were, the economy would behave very differently. As profits became harder to win, managers would spend *less* (not more) time and effort trying to make a good record. Hence, competition would discourage efficiency—and so also would higher taxes or demands for higher wages.

II

What are the principal weak points in our economy? There are, of course, many weak spots, but I have picked out six which seem to me to be particularly important: (1) the economy is still subject to recessions; (2) the ownership of corporate industry is not sufficiently broad; (3) able executives are not provided with sufficiently powerful incentives to leave established concerns and start new concerns of their own; (4) enterprises have strong reasons for raising capital by going into debt rather than by selling stock; (5) the tax laws discriminate against investment in risky projects; and (6) the economy has an inflationary bias.

The economy is still subject to recessions. The economy has a tendency to grow at a faster rate than can be sustained. Hence its growth is interrupted by recessions. Much progress has been made in the last twenty years in reducing the tendency of the economy to contract severely as a result of several years of too-rapid growth. For example, the danger of forced and large-scale liquidation, such as occurred between 1929 and 1933, has been virtually eliminated by the Banking Act of 1935. Furthermore, unemployment compensation and pensions limit the extent to which a drop in production carries with it a drop in personal incomes and hence in the demand for goods. But although considerable progress has been made in reducing the susceptibility of the economy to recession, the problem of preventing interruptions to growth is far from solved.

The ownership of corporate industry is not sufficiently broad. Although corporations turn out more than half of the nation's output, corporations open to investment by the general public (publicly owned corporations) have only about 6 million stockholders. In addition, there are around 1.5

million persons who own stock in family corporations but no stock in companies open to investment by the general public. About 8 per cent of the 47 million families of the country contain at least one owner of stock in publicly owned corporations.[7] The number of real-estate owners is about twice as large as the number of stockholders in publicly owned companies, and the number of persons owning at least $1,000 of so-called liquid assets (government bonds, checking accounts, savings accounts, shares in saving and loan associations and credit unions) is four times as large as the number of stockholders.[8]

In a community made up predominantly of employees, the ownership of corporate industry by a small part of the community must be regarded as representing a condition of instability. It creates the danger that the proper interests of the owners of corporations will receive inadequate consideration in the making of public policies. That this danger is real is proved by the fact that corporate stockowners have been singled out to bear enormous special tax burdens not imposed on other parts of the community. Thus far the attempts to impose large special burdens on the owners of corporations have not produced disastrous results because corporations have been able to shift most of the corporate income tax to the general public. The history of the last twenty-five years, however, should be a warning that the owners of corporations are in danger of unjust treatment unless the number of corporate owners is greatly increased. Furthermore, the community itself has an interest in increasing the number of shareholders because the policies that satisfactorily represent the interests of the country toward corporations are not likely to be achieved if the political influence of shareholders is weak.

Able executives are not provided with sufficient incentives to leave established concerns and start new concerns on their own. Successful executives usually have such favorable prospects in the concerns for which they work that they have little incentive to assume the hazards of starting enterprises of their own. And yet the economy needs to have some of its ablest young executives try their hand at starting new businesses. Enterprises started by competent and ambitious men would have a better-than-average chance of surviving and growing. A larger number of well-managed new concerns would make industry more productive and more progressive. Consequently, the community needs to encourage able executives to start their own companies or to make it easier for new concerns to hire the best executive talent.

Unfortunately, our economic arrangements place substantial obstacles

[7] *Federal Reserve Bulletin* (September 1952), p. 11.
[8] *Ibid.*, p. 6.

in the way of the starting of new concerns by successful executives. During the last few years there has been a rapid spread of pension plans for executives. Almost none of these pension plans permits the employee who leaves the concern to retain the credits built up on his behalf. Hence, an executive who leaves an enterprise to start a new business must ordinarily sacrifice his pension. The government should remove this obstacle to the starting of new enterprises by experienced executives. The law should provide that employer contributions to pension plans shall not be a deductible expense in determining income-tax liability unless the plan vests with any employee of, say, ten years' service or more all past service payments and current premium payments made on his behalf.

Enterprises have strong reasons for raising capital by going into debt rather than by selling stock. More than half of the outside capital raised by corporations between 1946 and 1951 was obtained by going into debt and only about one eighth by the sale of stock. The tax laws virtually subsidize the raising of capital by going into debt because interest on debt is a deductible expense for income-tax purposes. The main reason why external capital has been obtained by going into debt, however, has been the lack of a broad market for equities—another aspect of the fact that only a small proportion of savers invest in stocks.

The market for stock is gradually being broadened by laws permitting insurance companies and savings banks to invest limited amounts in equities, by the rapid growth of pension funds, by the growth of investment trusts, and by the educational campaigns of brokers and stock exchanges. Some of the bad results that might be expected to accompany the lack of a broad market for stocks have not occurred. Confronted with a relatively unfavorable market for equities, corporations in recent years have reinvested about half of their earnings. They have obtained far more money from reinvested earnings than from going into debt and have thus preserved a well-balanced capital structure. Nevertheless, the economy would be less susceptible to recession if corporate debt were smaller than it is—even though the problems created by corporate debt are less serious than those created by noncorporate mortgage indebtedness and consumer debts. But part of the corporate debt carries substantial annual repayments. These, together with repayments on noncorporate debt, are bound to be a deflationary influence whenever there is a substantial drop in new investment.

The tax laws discriminate against investment in risky projects. In a progressive and dynamic economy someone must take chances. Furthermore, someone must own the less-desirable business concerns—not all of us can restrict our investments to the "blue chips." The government should not ordinarily subsidize the taking of chances or the ownership of the weaker and less-promising concerns. On the other hand, it should not penalize the taking of chances or the ownership of the less-desirable securities.

And yet the tax laws of the country do discriminate against risky investments. This result is produced by inadequate provisions for offsetting capital losses against general income. When capital gains exceed capital losses, the excess of gains is taxed, but when capital losses exceed capital gains, only nominal relief is given. A tax law which is neutral between risky and nonrisky investments would give equal treatment to gains and losses.

The influences making for expansion have been so powerful since the end of the Second World War that even bad tax laws have not prevented rapid growth of industry. But the time may come when the influences making for expansion are less powerful than they have been since 1946. Under such circumstances the discrimination in our tax laws against risky investments could be serious.

The economy has an inflationary bias. By this I mean that the various institutions of the economy make it easier for the price level to go up than to go down or to remain unchanged. Perhaps it would be too much to expect a perfect balance in the institutions of the economy so that those which tended to make prices go up were precisely offset by those tending to make prices go down. Certainly it is not surprising that there is not perfect balance.

Many people believe that technological change, which has been raising output per manhour about 2.5 per cent a year, tends to make prices drop. I do not believe that this is true because technological change tends to increase spending as well as to raise the supply of goods. Its net effect on the price level is probably small and may change from time to time. I suspect that the usual effect of technological change is to raise prices. Other influences tending to raise prices are supports to the prices of farm products, absence of effective controls over consumer credit, the policy of vigorously fighting recessions with the result that prices do not fall enough during a recession to offset all of the rise of the preceding boom, and powerful trade unions.

Earlier in these remarks I pointed out that technological progress in the past had tended to raise the value of labor and capital above their market prices and that this difference between worth and price encouraged expansion. Perhaps the rise of powerful unions is causing this characteristic of our economy to be lost. Unions seem to be powerful enough to raise wages even when prices are falling. For example, between September 1948 and December 1949, when the consumers' price index fell by 4 per cent and the index of wholesale prices by 11.5 per cent, hourly earnings of factory workers rose by 3.4 per cent, or a little more than the gain in output per manhour. The hourly earnings of other nonagricultural workers rose by about the same amount. And between March 1951 and November 1952, when wholesale prices of commodities other than food and farm products dropped 3.8 per cent and the consumers' price index rose by 3.6 per cent, average hourly earnings of nonagricultural workers rose by 9.5 per cent. This was over twice as fast as the rise in output per manhour. More unemployment than the community is willing to tolerate seems to be required to prevent unions from raising labor costs by pushing up wages faster than the rise in productivity.

Slowly rising labor costs will not produce a runaway inflation, but they are likely to produce other problems. They may make it harder for industry to absorb the annual increment in the labor force. Certainly they will sooner or later compel upward adjustment of prices.

At present there is no satisfactory way of preventing a creeping rise in labor costs. The ability of employers to resist union demands is weakened by the strong preference of most employers for bargaining separately. This causes the wage pattern in each industry to be set, or at least strongly influenced, by the employer who is willing to make the biggest concessions. Industry-wide bargaining, which has disadvantages of its own, might stiffen the resistance of employers to wage demands, but it might not. It might lead employers to make concessions and to pass on the costs to consumers.

Up to now it has been considered good public relations by the large employers, whose wage settlements have great influence upon the pattern of wages, to grant fairly generous wage advances in periods of high employment. If the time ever comes when these large employers decide that it is better public relations to resist the demands of unions, the tendency for wages to rise faster than output per manhour will be altered and the country will have a good chance of achieving a stable price level. Perhaps employers could be induced to do a better job of bargaining if there developed a strong public opinion against raising wages, except in specific circumstances, by more than the approximate rate of increase in output per manhour, which is about 2.5 per cent per year.

III

What should we do to improve the economy? If one compares our economy of today with the American economy of 1900 or 1920 or 1929 or any other date, one finds, I think, that the economy of today is definitely superior—it has greater capacity to control the volume of expenditures by creating new investment opportunities, or by developing new products; it is more competitive; it has been supplied with various arrangements which make it less susceptible to severe ups and downs. Some of the improvements have been definitely planned; others, such as the greater capacity of the economy to create investment opportunities, cannot be said to have been planned—they are a result of the progress of science and technology.

The community needs good arrangements for improving its economy. Fortunately, the community can count on fairly rapid progress in the social sciences. The quantity of work is growing quite rapidly and the quality is improving. Research of great promise is under way on the economics of growth, the behavior of consumers, the sources and uses of incomes and funds, and the economics of saving.

But the discoveries of the social sciences are not automatically applied. The community needs many men of affairs, business executives, trade-union officials, lawyers, farmers, who are sufficiently interested in the problems of economic policy to give considerable thought and attention to them. But the influence of isolated individuals is limited. Hence the community needs organizations that have the principal purpose of studying problems of economic policies and making specific policy suggestions.

These organizations should meet several specifications. They should be nonpolitical and nonpartisan; their recommendations should be based on research and should reflect the insights of both social scientists and men of affairs. There are at least two organizations in the United States which more or less meet these specifications. One is the Committee for Economic Development and the other is the National Planning Association. Each organization is concerned with problems of public policy; each is nonpartisan; each bases its policy recommendations upon research; and each draws upon the scientific knowledge of social scientists and the practical experience of men of affairs. There are other organizations, such as the Foreign Policy Association and the League of Women Voters, which are primarily engaged in the study of policy problems but which do not combine practical and theoretical skills as do the CED and the NPA, or which do not take definite positions.

The great cloud over the future of our economy is, of course, the possibility of a world war. Perhaps after stockpiling atomic bombs for fifteen or twenty years both the United States and Russia will decide that a war would be intolerably destructive. Given the condition of peace, one cannot avoid being optimistic about the future of our economic institutions. I believe that the process of policy making is bound to improve at least slowly—as it has done during the last several generations. This will happen partly because the social sciences will add to our understanding of men's behavior and partly because in colleges, in adult education, and perhaps even in secondary schools we shall learn to teach men to do the kind of thinking that responsible policy making requires. The case system of instruction, which is the method best adapted to that purpose, is still used on only a limited scale, but its use is bound to spread.

Finally, the outlook for improvement in our institutions is made more favorable by the sense of social responsibility for which the rise of science and technology is largely responsible. Primitive man, living in a world that he did not understand, could do little about what happened to him and was concerned mainly with propitiating nature or his gods. Religion under such circumstances could give rise to no movements of human betterment or reform. Science and technology, however, are bringing about a moral revolution because they are teaching us that we can do something about our own condition and the condition of our fellows. Consequently, we can no longer escape the responsibility of trying to make the world a better place. We cannot plead ignorance or incapacity—we know enough now so that we might be successful in eliminating bad conditions. Thus the rise of science has thrust new responsibilities on us—responsibilities which previous ages did not feel able to accept but which the community now seems ready to assume.

I close these remarks, therefore, on a hopeful note. The improvement of our economic institutions during the first half of the century, in large part unplanned, was considerable—undoubtedly greater than anyone would have dared to predict. Progress in the second half of the century will, to a greater extent than ever before in human history, be the result of deliberate policies. And businessmen will not sit on the sidelines. They have already shown in the CED and the NPA that they will participate in research and planning, that they will cooperate in combining practical experience with theoretical insight. If the great calamity of war can be avoided, can anyone doubt that, with the great gain in scientific knowledge of the last fifty years to build on, with the heightened sense of social responsibility, and with the broader participation of the community in policy making, we shall make far more progress in improving our economy in the second half of the century than in any previous period?

Part II

THE ECONOMIC OUTLOOK

INTRODUCTION

SUMNER SLICHTER was most widely known in the American community for his continuing analysis of the economic scene and the business outlook. He developed his views in hundreds of speeches before business and professional groups, testimony before Congressional committees, articles in leading magazines, and after November 1952 in a regular news letter prepared for the *Nihon Keizai Shimbun* of Tokyo. These papers were in turn often reprinted and widely distributed.

The eight papers in Part II have been selected from a very large collection. They have been chosen to reflect Slichter's analysis of economic conditions and his policy recommendations at critical points since his interests were turned in this direction by the Great Depression. The first paper (Chapter 6) was presented on November 11, 1932, at the very bottom of the depression. The following selections were written from the vantage point of the downturn of 1937, the prospects in the fall of 1942 of "Postwar Boom or Collapse," the outlook in early 1948, the problems in the fall of 1952 of the post-Korean War adjustments, the recession of 1958, and the economic questions of the spring of 1959. This sequence of selections provides a form of history of the economic developments and issues of economic policy that occurred over the last generation.

The final selection of Part II (Chapter 13) reprints the letter to the *Nihon Keizai Shimbun* for January and the first half of February 1959. Slichter wrote eighty-three such letters, the first in November 1952 and the last for September 1959. These letters discussed the major economic indicators, provided an interpretation of recent developments and general projections of the future; often they contained critical comments on private and public policies and suggestions for new policies by government, the banking system, business managements, and labor organizations.

These eight papers on the economic outlook reflect well Slichter's habits of mind and methods of presentation. They discuss both immediate developments and long-run structural changes impinging on business conditions. They use detailed statistical series—Slichter was always probing existing series and writing for new breakdowns and tabulations—and they make broad generalizations derived from wide contacts, experience, and insights. They detail the past and often boldly forecast the future. They contain much analysis of economic developments and institutions and many policy proposals and judgments. They concentrate upon the economic aspects of events, but they also recognize the decisive role of psychological and political factors.

Slichter always developed his ideas with clarity and directness. As Professor Charles A. Bliss has said, "Uniformly well written and persuasively phrased, they were never negative and commonly set forth some proposal he wished to advance." He sought to challenge and to stimulate each audience, and none escaped without some doubts having been raised concerning at least one cherished idea or policy. Slichter in these papers was more than analyzing the economic past and projecting the outlook; he was engaged in the economic education of leaders of various segments of public opinion.

Slichter designed no formal econometric model of the economic system, and he developed no single theory of business fluctuations. Yet he scrutinized statistical materials and never tired of addressing new questions to the facts. He seemed to distrust rigid models and in each situation sought to discover the strategic and decisive factors that were most likely shaping current economic developments. But the search for these factors was not random or aimless; he was guided by theoretically relevant relationships suggested by others and by his insights and experience. The diversity of events and the variety of combinations reflected in economic developments fascinated him. He was always willing to take another look, to examine new facts and statistical evidence, and he was willing to change his mind and admit readily that he had a new view. Perhaps it was these qualities that resulted in the record of such accurate forecasts of the economic outlook.

6

The Immediate Unemployment Problem

The Annals of the American Academy of Political and Social Science, January 1933. This paper was presented on November 11, 1932.

My discussion of the immediate unemployment problem will fall into two parts. First, I wish to focus attention upon the problem which will confront us between now and next summer. Then I wish to shift attention to the problem that we shall face during the next two or three years and perhaps longer.

The number of unemployed now approximates eleven million, or about one fourth of the population normally in gainful employment. In addition, roughly half of the employed are working only part time. It is inconceivable that between now and the end of the winter there will be a sufficient revival of business to absorb a large fraction of the unemployed. This is particularly true in view of the fact that a substantial expansion of demand could be met simply by increasing the working hours of the men on part time. Despite all that we might do to make jobs by promoting business revival, it is plain that the problem which immediately confronts us is primarily one of providing relief.

I

Extent of the relief burden. How great is the relief burden likely to be? The number of the *totally unemployed* is at least one fourth greater than a year ago, and the volume of *unemployment* is at least one third greater. The proportion of the unemployed who have exhausted their resources and the resources of their friends and relatives is rapidly rising. This is demonstrated by the fact that nearly half of the persons now seeking relief from welfare agencies in New York City have never before sought such help.

The record of relief throughout the depression indicates that expenditures have roughly doubled each year. Perhaps this geometric progression will not continue. Nevertheless, it is well to remember that forecasts of the relief burden have almost invariably been too low.[1] December 1932 is not far away, and it should be possible to estimate with some accuracy the probable load for that month and to compare it with that of a year ago. Last December the number of families receiving relief in Chicago was 99,293. For December 1932 the number is estimated at 164,000. In Cleveland, in December 1931 there were 18,978 families on relief; this December it is estimated there will be 34,775. In Cincinnati, 13,203 families were aided in December 1931; for the coming December, the estimate is 24,975. In New York, where 46,500 families are now under the care of the Home Relief Bureau, it is estimated that approximately 46,000 additional families, as a minimum, will have to be provided for during the winter of 1932–33. On the basis of this and other evidence it seems safe to conclude that the relief needs of this winter will be approximately twice those of last winter.[2] They may be much more.

When I point out there is bound to be a large increase in the relief load, let me remind you that the standards of relief have been shockingly low. Shoes and clothing are given only in extreme cases, and in most cities rent is paid only on eviction. Allowances for a family rarely average more than five dollars a week, and allowances of three and four dollars a week are common. In many rural communities the standards are lower. Some counties in Illinois are giving no more than six or seven cents a person per day. Many persons in dire need obtain no relief whatever—partly because false pride prevents them from making application, and partly because inadequate resources compel the welfare agencies to refuse thousands of worthy cases. For over a month last spring, the New York City Home Relief Bureau accepted no new cases. At that time the Bureau had a waiting list of over 19,000.

Resources of local agencies diminishing. Up to the summer of 1932, prac-

[1] A fairly typical experience is that of Chicago, which late in 1931 undertook to raise $10,500,000 with the expectation that it would last until the fall of 1932. The fund was exhausted early in February 1932.

[2] Other estimates indicate that this general conclusion is conservative. In Dayton, Ohio, for example, the number of relief families in December 1931 was 5,083; for December 1932 the number is estimated at 11,000. In Columbus, Ohio, 4,136 families were aided by the principal relief agencies in December 1931. The same agencies estimate that they will have 12,600 families on their relief rolls this coming December. In Stark County, Ohio (which includes the cities of Canton, Massillon, and Alliance), the families on relief are expected to increase from 5,692 in December 1931 to 10,799 in December 1932. The reports to the Children's Bureau of the U. S. Department of Labor, covering the relief activities of 748 agencies or divisions of departments in 125 cities, show an increase in the number of families aided from 333,720 in August 1931 to 731,394 in August 1932.

tically all the relief was provided by local agencies, either public or private. The proportion of the burden borne by public and private agencies has varied widely among different communities, but totals from many cities indicate that about three fourths of the relief has come from public agencies and about one fourth from private. Only eight states had given help in substantial amounts, and the assistance by the federal government was negligible. The ability of the local agencies, both public and private, to bear the burden is steadily diminishing. Shrinking private incomes and heavy increases in income taxes are reducing both the willingness and the ability of individuals to contribute to charity. Noteworthy is the fact that the Gibson Committee in New York, which last year raised $18 million, is this year attempting to raise $15 million. Last year Cook County raised $10.5 million from private donations; this year the goal is $7.5 million. As a general rule the goals of community chests in 1932 are below those in 1931.

The financial difficulties of the private agencies are compelling them to withdraw as far as possible from pure unemployment relief work. This increases the burden on the public agencies. But the ability of the cities and the counties to raise funds by taxation is shrinking, because about nine tenths of their income is derived from the taxation of real estate which, even before the depression, was heavily overtaxed relative to other sources of income. Falling rents and a rising percentage of vacancies are steadily reducing the ability of real estate to bear the burden of relief. The decrease in rents varies from place to place, but it is rare to find a city in which rents are not at least 20 per cent below those of 1929. The drop in rental income is, of course, much greater.

All this is reflected in the mounting tax delinquencies. Last year Detroit imposed a levy of $76 million, of which it failed to collect $18 million. Pittsburgh had a levy of $22.59 million, of which over $3 million was delinquent. In Cleveland nearly 19 per cent of the county taxes and about 56 per cent of the special assessment taxes are delinquent. Particularly important is the fact that ability to give relief has diminished most of all in precisely those communities where unemployment is greatest. For a few months, relief may be financed by borrowing; but city after city has now reached the point where further borrowing is impossible.

This, then, is the situation that we face this coming winter: relief needs, even on an inadequate basis, will double those of a year ago. Local resources will be no greater, and in the very places where unemployment is worst and the need is greatest, they will be much less. How should this problem be met?

Expansion of public works. Throughout the depression it has been urged that unemployment be relieved by the expansion of public works. Shortly after the stock-market crash, President Hoover urged this policy upon the states and municipalities, and the federal government has practiced it on a modest scale. In the fiscal year 1930–31 the outlay for federal construction was about one third more than in 1929. In 1931–32 there will be another increase, so that in this year the total outlay for *federal* construction may be approximately double that of 1929. Federal construction, however, has normally been only a small part of all public building, and the cities and states, on the whole, have failed to heed Mr. Hoover's advice to expand construction. On the contrary, in 1931 they reduced their building so much that, despite the increase in federal construction, the total outlay for all public works in the country was substantially less than in 1930. (In 1930 the figure was $3.632 billion. The preliminary estimates of Mr. Arthur D. Gayer for the National Bureau of Economic Research put the expenditures for 1931 at about $3 billion.) In 1932 came the collapse in the bond market which has practically prevented municipal financing. Simultaneously there has developed an economy drive which in some communities has amounted to hysteria. As a result, nonfederal public works have dropped from about $2.5 billion to about $800 million; and *all* public construction, local, state, and federal, is not more than half the level of 1931. Thus, instead of reducing unemployment by expanding public construction, we find ourselves increasing unemployment by curtailing public works.

Undoubtedly many cities could achieve substantial savings by building now, when costs are low, rather than waiting until several years later when costs will be higher. Nevertheless, a bond issue today would mean higher taxes to the extent of the interest and amortization charges, and few communities, no matter how low their ratio of indebtedness to property values, are willing to impose any new burdens on the taxpayers. Furthermore, the market for municipal securities, though much stronger than formerly, is none too good.

To meet these two obstacles to an increase in public works, Congress has given the Reconstruction Finance Corporation $1.5 billion for loans on certain types of "self-liquidating" public or semipublic projects. The Corporation has been accused of being dilatory and unduly technical and meticulous in requiring that the letter of the law be observed. Whether or not these criticisms were once true, I do not believe that they are true today. Naturally it has taken a little time for the Corporation to build up an organization. This task, however, has been done rather quickly.

By the end of October, the Corporation had received one hundred and forty-nine fairly complete applications for "self-liquidating" loans. Many of the applications were not eligible under the terms of the law or were not accompanied with proper supporting data. Indeed, a recent tabulation indicated that approximately half of the applications were not eligible and that many others were of doubtful eligibility. (The Corporation attempts to "salvage" projects which appear to have merit but which are not eligible in the particular form presented.) Up to November 1, the Corporation had made twenty-four "self-liquidating" loans totaling $135,433,500. Not one cent of this amount, however, had been spent and not a man had been put to work by it. This is not a criticism of the Corporation. On the contrary, to some extent it reflects the fact that the Corporation has granted loans faster than the communities have been prepared to use them.

But even if work were instantly started on all the projects for which the Corporation had authorized loans up to November, the number of jobs *directly* provided would be less than twenty-five thousand. The number of jobs that would be indirectly created is conjectural, but it would not bring the total up to one hundred thousand. *But there are eleven million unemployed.* Possibly by next summer or a year from this winter, the loans of the Corporation may have a perceptible effect on employment. During this winter, however, they will have virtually none. They leave the relief problem practically unaltered.

Spreading the work. Another proposal for relieving unemployment which has attracted much attention is "spreading the work." More or less organized support for this plan goes back to the beginning of the depression, but last September a greatly intensified drive began under the leadership of President Teagle of the Standard Oil Company of New Jersey. Mr. Teagle announced that the plan might put a million men back to work, and expressed the hope that it might eventually give jobs to two million.[3]

Spreading work has two aspects which should be carefully distinguished. Work may be divided as business drops, in order to prevent layoffs; or it may be divided in order to give jobs to persons who are now unemployed. Most instances of spreading work which have been reported in the newspapers are of the former variety.[4] The normal seasonal shrinkage in em-

[3] *New York Times*, September 2, 1932, p. 1.

[4] In San Francisco, where the "spread-work" movement has been carefully organized and vigorously pushed, incomplete returns indicate that four thousand more people are working today than would have had jobs if work had not been spread during the last few months. But about *three out of four* of these persons are workers who were saved from being laid off by spreading work, and *only about one fourth* are persons who were unemployed and who were given jobs that were created by dividing the work. For this information I am indebted to Mr. Paul Eliel of the Industrial Association of San Francisco.

ployment may be expected to increase the number of idle during the winter by at least a million. There is reason to hope that, by spreading work, a large proportion of these prospective layoffs will be prevented.

But what prospect is there that spreading work will positively reduce the eleven million unemployed? In manufacturing, the work has already been spread remarkably thin. For example, in twenty-one industries during August 1932, the National Industrial Conference Board reports an average working week of only 32.2 hours, with average weekly earnings of $15.35. Only four industries averaged 40 or more hours a week. With hours and earnings in manufacturing so low, how much thinner should work be spread?

Full-time employment appears to be most prevalent in banking, insurance, wholesaling, retailing, and public utilities. Consequently, these industries furnish the best opportunities to spread work. But despite the fact that the sacrifice is mainly borne by the workers, most employers are strongly opposed to taking work from their present employees for the purpose of giving jobs to men who are now unemployed. One reason is that managements are reluctant to incur the ill will which this step might arouse among their men. Another reason is that many enterprises, even after three years of cutting and economizing, are still carrying more employees than they really need. The low scale of compensation which prevails in both retailing and banking is a serious obstacle to spreading work, particularly in view of the fact that many workers who have full-time jobs are supporting relatives. It is a serious matter to reduce the working hours (and hence the compensation) of a fifteen-dollar-a-week clerk who may be the sole member in her family who has a job. In this connection it is interesting to observe that several of the Standard Oil companies, in cutting the hours of employees to forty a week, are not reducing the compensation of employees receiving less than $100 a month.

At any rate, after careful inquiry I have found relatively few banks, insurance companies, stores, or public utilities that have divided work in order to make room for additional employees. In view of the obstacles to spreading work any thinner than it is spread today, we shall be fortunate if the movement to share the work succeeds in preventing an increase in unemployment this winter. It will be a miracle if the movement creates as many as a million new jobs before spring. But even such an unexpected accomplishment would leave ten million men unemployed, which would be about one fourth more than last winter. It is important to remember that much relief is necessary even for men who have part-time jobs. When a man is reduced to two or three days a week, any unusual expense means that he must have help from somewhere.

National aid inadequate. Public works, self-liquidating loans, and spreading work promise little help toward meeting the relief problem of this winter. What are we to do? Additional help is imperative. Where is it to come from?

One possibility is national aid. The Reconstruction Finance Corporation has been given $300 million to "lend" to the states and the local communities. How far will this go? At the Relief Conference in Washington during September, Mr. Pomerene, chairman of the Corporation, announced that he interpreted the law to mean that the $300 million should be made to last two years. As a device for encouraging the local communities to draw generously on their own resources, this statement is unobjectionable. But is there any real prospect that the $300 million will last two years? Last spring the Bureau of the Census made a study of relief expenditures by governmental and private organizations in certain communities during the first quarter of 1931. The communities included all of the larger cities and contained 60 per cent of the country's population. They undoubtedly included a much larger fraction of the unemployed. During the first three months of 1931, these communities spent $73,757,300 for relief to families outside of institutions and for homeless men. At the rate of increase which seems to have occurred, these communities must have spent about $140 million during the first quarter of 1932. During the first quarter of 1933, they will probably need about $280 million.

Let us assume that the local communities are able to raise as much for relief this year as last; if the increase in expenditures were to fall entirely upon the funds of the Reconstruction Finance Corporation, nearly half those funds would be exhausted during the first three months of 1933. These will probably be the worst three months of the year. Nevertheless, the evidence points to the conclusion that even if the local communities could maintain their expenditures undiminished, substantially all of the Reconstruction Finance Corporation's $300 million would be required before June 30, 1933 merely to meet the *increase* in the relief needs of these communities representing only 60 per cent of the country's population. But the local communities as a whole will not be able to maintain their relief expenditures on the same scale as last year, and considerable relief must of course be provided in the rural communities from which returns of relief expenditures are not available. Unless the standards of relief, already dangerously low, are to be substantially reduced, much more help must be given the local communities before next July than the $300 million which the Reconstruction Finance Corporation has available.

The states must act. Where is this help to come from? The bodies which have been most delinquent in meeting the unemployment problem thus far have been the states. Only eight states have given relief in substantial volume. It is true that these states include many of the industrially important ones—New York, New Jersey, Pennsylvania, Ohio, and Wisconsin—but the record of the states as a whole is not good. The states can tap many sources of revenue which are not open to the cities, because it is exceedingly difficult for cities to raise money by any method other than taxing real estate. Furthermore, participation of the states in the relief work is particularly important because they are the logical bodies to raise the standards of local relief, to supervise the establishment of proper relief agencies in each city and county, and especially to see that small cities and rural communities, which have no organized charities and which have been exceedingly backward in extending help, are provided with organizations.

I am aware of the political difficulty in getting states to act. Unemployment is concentrated to a great extent in the cities; and the rural communities, hard hit by the drop in agricultural prices, are reluctant to permit the state's taxing power to be used to meet the need in the cities. This difficulty is accentuated in some states by long-standing differences between the cities and the rural communities over the use of the taxing power and by differences in the party control of state legislatures and municipal administrations. Finally, the economy movement may make the states reluctant to participate in unemployment relief.

Nevertheless, the states must be induced to act. How to get them to act is perhaps the most important aspect of the unemployment relief problem at this moment. The Emergency Unemployment Relief Act provides that federal relief funds shall not be in lieu of money made available by the various states and their political subdivisions, but rather shall be supplementary thereto. The Reconstruction Finance Corporation has followed the policy of making grants for short periods and in limited amounts only, and of insisting that the states and the local communities make a real effort to help themselves.

For example, the Corporation has declined to grant further loans or assistance to the local communities of the State of Michigan unless the state contributes some money of its own. Temporary aid of $2.5 million to Detroit and to other communities until the first of December was granted on the understanding that additional funds will not be provided unless the state legislature makes an effort to raise funds within the state. The Corporation has insisted that the Government of Illinois call a special session of the legislature to provide for relief. On November 4, in granting a loan of $5,462,265 to Pennsylvania, the Corporation urged in strong terms the need for further action by the state and its political subdivisions at the earliest possible moment, and announced that it would "hesitate" to provide further funds "until the State and/or its various political subdivisions have taken action to meet the emergency needs of the people."

Whether the Reconstruction Finance Corporation succeeds in stimulating the states to act must depend upon public opinion. The policy of the Corporation is bound to arouse intense criticism from diverse sources—from those who feel that relief should not be delayed or limited while governmental units battle over the allocation of the burden, and from many interests which oppose any increase in state taxes or any diversion of state funds from their present uses. Possibly the volume of criticism will be so formidable that the Corporation will capitulate before it. I hope, however, that the public in the main will support the Corporation in its efforts to induce the states to assume more responsibility for unemployment relief. Relief will be better organized and more efficiently administered, and the unemployed will be more adequately provided for, if each state establishes a relief board and provides it with some funds. Furthermore, if the states refuse to act, Congress will naturally be more reluctant to grant federal aid for relief during the winter of 1933–34.

II

I have said that the immediate problem confronting us is primarily one of giving relief rather than of creating jobs by assisting the revival of business. But naturally it is important to do everything possible to accelerate revival. There is an enormous amount of postponed spending which will begin once revival is fairly under way. And even though revival could not greatly alter the relief burden this winter, it might substantially reduce the burden during the coming summer and the following winter. But so great is the lack of confidence, and so readily, in the present state of psychology, are proposals misinterpreted and misunderstood, that it is necessary to be exceedingly judicious in planning assistance to business. Nevertheless, there are several steps which the government might take.

Aid through distribution of cotton. Let me begin with a modest suggestion which would be at once a relief measure and a help to business revival. The purchasing power of many millions of Americans depends on the price of cotton. The price is low partly because of the enormous carry-over of approximately 12 million bales. The faster we reduce this carry-over, the more rapidly will the price of cotton recover and the greater will be the purchasing power of a large part of the country. Last summer Congress gave 500,000 bales from the holdings of the Cotton Stabilization Corporation to the Red Cross for distribution in the form of cloth or garments for the unemployed. The Red Cross reports that its cotton will not suffice for more than one quarter of the requests from its local chapters, and that the supply will be exhausted by about January 1933. The Cotton Stabilization Corporation still has about 400,000 bales of "stabilization cotton," and the cooperatives have an even larger amount. Surely it is ridiculous for the government to hold cotton in the hope of ultimately recovering part of the purchase price, when millions of people are urgently in need of clothing and *when the very retention of the cotton retards the recovery of business.* Surely the least which the federal government can do to help the unemployed is instantly to give all of the cotton acquired in the course of "stabilization" operations to the Red Cross for distribution to the unemployed.

The original transfer of 500,000 bales permitted some of the cotton to be used to pay for the fabrication of the rest into cloth and garments. This greatly limited the relief to the unemployed, because far more cotton has been needed to pay for the cloth and the garments than is contained in the cloth and the garments themselves. I suggest, therefore, that the government not only give its cotton to the Red Cross without delay, but also appropriate a sufficient sum to pay for the fabrication of the cotton. The fabrication should be done as work relief, subject to the restriction that the manufacturer should make no profit and that the hours of labor for the individual workmen should not exceed thirty-two a week. This arrangement would greatly increase the relief afforded by the cotton, and it would also accentuate the effect on the carry-over; because when part of the grant is used to pay for fabricating the remainder, the movement of cotton into consumption is greatly reduced. In making the original grant, Congress stipulated that the cotton should be used only to purchase cloth or garments made entirely of cotton. It would be wise to relax this restriction and to permit some of the cotton to be traded for wool.

The British debt. The two most important steps which the government could take to accelerate the revival of business are (1) to revise the British debt settlement and (2) to settle its own budget problem.

One of the principal reasons why business enterprises are postponing commitments is because of uncertainty over price movements in the immediate future. A major reason for uncertainty over prices here is uncertainty over the future value of the British pound. Depreciation in the pound, which reduces the buying power and increases the selling power of Great Britain and all countries that base their currencies on the pound, tends to lower prices in all gold currencies. The present weakness in the pound is not entirely attributable to the prospective debt payment which falls due on December 15. It is partly seasonal and partly attributable to prospective settlements with foreigners who elected not to convert their holdings of the British war loan. Nevertheless, resumption of payments on the debt by Great Britain could not continue without putting the pound under pressure and thus threatening our own price level. Not only are the British payments large (about $190 million a year), but since they are in gold, the drop in prices has greatly increased the burden of making them. Exports of approximately 50 per cent more commodities would be required for the British payments today than were needed when the settlement was negotiated. In addition, Great Britain's receipts from her debtors have been greatly diminished by the cessation of reparations payments from Germany and by the fact that her claims upon her allies are payable in pounds instead of gold.

Much silly talk has recently come from members of Congress and others to the effect that if our debtors do not pay, the American taxpayer must. So far as the British payments are concerned, this is ridiculous. Far more accurate would be the statement that for every dollar received from the British, the whole American people will pay many times over. In particular will American debtors and American cotton growers and wheat raisers pay—debtors because the drop in our price level will make their debts more burdensome, and cotton growers and wheat raisers because the prices of those commodities are likely to be dragged down more than others by further depreciation of the pound.

Probably the most important single step we could take to guard against a further drop in prices and thus to smooth the road to recovery would be to negotiate promptly a generous revision of the British debt settlement. Since negotiations and ratification take time, the moratorium should be extended until June 1934. If this is not done, at least Great Britain should be given the option of paying in goods or pounds instead of in dollars.

Reducing the deficit. The government's budget problem arises from the disappointing yield of the new taxes. Apparently the deficit for the current year will be well in excess of a billion dollars. Let me say emphatically that I am not in favor of attempting to balance the budget in the midst of depression. An enormous amount of nonsense has been talked on this subject during the last year. The government deficit in a period of depression is valuable because government borrowing is likely to produce inflation—or at least to offset in some measure the deflationary effect of the liquidation of private indebtedness. *But if the deficit is too large and excites too much alarm, its net effect may be deflationary rather than inflationary,* because apprehension over the fiscal policy of the government may cause many business enterprises to postpone buying and, insofar as possible, to avoid commitments.[5] The unexpectedly large deficit which is developing this year seems to be having this effect. In order to gain the maximum inflationary benefit from the deficit, it is necessary, therefore, to reduce the deficit.

It makes a great deal of difference, however, how the deficit is reduced. Burdening the country with new taxes, at a time when taxation is already taking one fifth or more of the national income, is not likely to help business. This is particularly true of taxes which are likely to fall temporarily or permanently on the working capital of business enterprises.[6] Consequently, the deficit should be reduced in the main by cutting expeditures rather than by imposing new taxes. The obvious exception is, of course, a tax on beer. If the industry is legalized, it can bear a fairly heavy tax and should bear it. But most estimates of the probable immediate yield from a tax on beer are much too high.

Suggested government savings. Time does not permit an analysis of the intricate problem of how expenditures might most advantageously be reduced. Approximately $150 million might be saved by transferring the post office to a public corporation, operated by a general manager subject to a board of directors who possessed authority to set whatever rates were necessary to cover costs.[7] But undoubtedly the country is not yet prepared to

[5] This is likely to be particularly true of enterprises which have loans that are about to mature and which fear that large flotations by the government may prevent private enterprises from floating loans on favorable terms.

[6] Here is the principal objection to a sales tax. Under present market conditions most sales and excise taxes cannot be promptly shifted by producers to consumers, and consequently they fall upon working capital. Most enterprises are already operating at a loss or making only small profits. As everyone knows, nothing is more effective in inducing managers to postpone every possible repair and replacement, to let inventories fall to the very minimum, and to lay off every man who can possibly be spared than to see their working capital steadily being consumed by sales below cost.

[7] This would mean abolishing the position of postmaster general. It would also mean that postmasters would no longer be political appointees. They would be selected and promoted from small offices to large ones on the basis of efficiency and performance, just as the managers of chain stores are appointed and promoted.

insist upon this step. Some savings could be achieved by bureau reorganizations and by conducting the operations of the government more efficiently, but the amount which could be saved without sacrificing valuable work is small in relation to the deficit.

Undoubtedly the greatest opportunity to reduce expenditures would be to cut the payments to veterans for disabilities not incurred in service. These payments should never have been made in the first place. They now approximate $450 million a year, or nearly one fourth of the expenditures of the federal government. Nothing would do more to eliminate the fear caused by the deficit and to improve public sentiment toward national finances than for Congress to reduce by $250 million or $300 million the payments to veterans not disabled in service. Indeed, I venture the assertion that $250 million taken from the veterans would do more to inspire confidence in the national finances than $750 million of savings achieved in other ways, because it would demonstrate that Congress had the courage and the vision to rise above petty politics in dealing with budget problems. This statement illustrates how largely the problem presented by the deficit is a psychological one. The problem is not to eliminate the deficit, but to reduce it sufficiently and to administer national finances in such a manner as to eliminate the fear caused by it—and thus to derive the maximum inflationary benefit from the deficit.

The dole system. Thus far I have arbitrarily defined the immediate unemployment problem as that which must be met between now and next summer. But unemployment will probably be severe during the winter of 1933–34 and possibly much longer. I make this statement in full realization of the fact that a rapid and spectacular business revival would not be at all surprising. So great is the amount of postponed buying by both consumers and business enterprises that a change in the trend of prices (brought about by the revision of debts, the application of the domestic allotment plan, or the world's steadily growing gold stocks) might soon initiate a spectacular upward spiral of buying and investing. It is merely conservative, however, to assume that the revival will be slow and to plan unemployment relief accordingly. Let us face these facts squarely and ask frankly what they mean.

To begin with, they probably mean that we must have the dole on a large scale for at least two more years. It has been said that our present dole system is the worst in the world. Since, whether we like it or not, we must have a dole, is it not sensible to make our dole system the best in the world?

What kind of an organization is required? A substantial proportion of the relief funds for at least the next year must come from the federal government. The task of administering federal aid and of furnishing leadership to the states and the local communities in organizing relief is too big to be handled permanently by a division of the Reconstruction Finance Corporation. An emergency board of unemployment relief is needed in Washington. In addition, state boards are needed, such as those in New York and Illinois; and in many communities subsidiary local boards should be established. The federal board should cooperate with the state boards in organizing and perfecting local relief agencies, and should grant financial aid to the states where, in the judgment of the federal board, local conditions warrant it. But the federal board should be definitely instructed by Congress to refuse federal aid to any state or locality which, in the judgment of the board, fails to make a reasonable effort to help itself.

Work relief. Because relief must continue for a long time, as much of it as possible should be work relief. Unfortunately the tendency in most communities has been to reduce the amount of work relief. In some places, particularly in large cities, difficulty has been experienced in finding enough suitable work-relief projects. Often the administration of work relief has been unsatisfactory, and this has had unfortunate effects upon the morale of the holders of work-relief jobs. Most important of all, the expense has been too large in comparison with home relief.

None of these disadvantages is insurmountable. Imagination and careful search will reveal a surprising number of opportunities for work relief even in the large cities. The projects, of course, need not be manual labor, and the need for work relief for the "white-collar" unemployed is great. Many useful surveys and investigations might be made by white-collar unemployed. Furthermore, with a state or national relief organization, it would be possible to transfer some city unemployed to projects outside of the cities. Proper administration is largely a matter of proper planning. The hours of employment can be so adjusted that this form of relief does not cost substantially more than home relief. In order to stimulate the development of work relief, a bureau of work relief should be established under the direction of the federal unemployment relief board. This bureau should have a substantial appropriation to be used in financing approved projects in cooperation with the states, the cities, or the counties.

Limiting working hours. Finally, and most important of all, the prospect of two or more years of unemployment on a large scale means that much more drive should be put behind the movement to spread work. It should be a drive, however, not to spread work thinner than it is now being spread, but to prevent hours from being increased too much when business picks up. The subcommittees which have been established by the Teagle Committee can scarcely be expected to do this. They are not likely to remain in existence long enough and they lack authority to prevent recalcitrant employers from increasing hours rather than hiring more men. The responsibility for preventing a too-rapid increase in working hours might well be combined with the administration of unemployment relief. The title of the semipermanent board established in Washington should be the Emergency Board of *Employment* and of Unemployment Relief, and the board should be authorized to establish in the various industries committees with the function of determining at frequent intervals what working hours, in view of the unemployment situation in the industry, are reasonable. Note that the restriction on hours would relate to the *working* hours of the *men* —not the *operating* hours of the *plants*. The plants might work twenty-four hours a day, seven days a week, provided they worked no man more hours than permitted. Violation of these orders should be punished by suitable penalties.

Probably the government could not constitutionally exercise this authority except for the period of the emergency. During the emergency, however, there can be no question that Congress possesses the authority to limit working hours by reasonable methods for the purpose of giving more men an opportunity to earn a living.

It is a most grave situation—this one of prolonged unemployment which seems to confront us—and one which we cannot meet unless we are willing to do some things which we have never done before. Perhaps we shall be saved from it by the spectacular revival which the large volume of postponed buying makes possible. Obviously, however, it would be rash to gamble on such a revival. We must prepare to deal with the absorption problem by creating efficient machinery for controlling the increase in working hours and for compelling universal division of work as business picks up.

7

Safeguards Against Depressions: An Analysis of Depression Cures

Address before the Special Session for Business Executives, Department of Economics and Business Administration, Westminster College, New Wilmington, Pa., November 19, 1937.

I

BETWEEN the summer of 1936 and the summer of 1937 the cost of living advanced by 4 per cent. The income of industrial workers, including factory, railroad, and mining employees, advanced 12 per cent, and the cash income of farmers by 12 per cent. Industrial production increased 5 per cent. Productions of consumers' goods did not increase at all. Despite the fact that consumer purchasing power was outrunning production, the country is plunged into a depression. A similar experience preceded the recession of 1923–1924.

These experiences remind us that a pronounced recession in business may occur even when consumer purchasing power is growing faster than industrial production. The reason is plain. The immediate determinant of the state of business, as every businessman knows, is the outlook for profits. When the outlook for profits improves, business enterprises expand their expenditures, employment and production increase, and the standard of living of the entire community rises. When the outlook for profits is uncertain or dark, enterprises postpone commitments and reduce expenditures, the volume of employment and production falls, and the standard of living drops. The state of consumer purchasing power is only one of many variables which affect the outlook for profits. That is why profit prospects may grow less favorable even while consumer purchasing power is growing.

Although consumer purchasing power is only one of the many variables affecting the outlook for profits, the prospect for profits is the dominant factor in determining consumer purchasing power. It is easy to see why this is true. The incomes of four out of five families are nothing but the expenditures of business enterprises. Hence, before a drop in consumer incomes can occur, business enterprises must decide to spend less, and before an increase in consumer incomes can occur, business enterprises must decide to spend more. Consequently, when one examines the monthly figures on industrial production and retail sales, one finds retail sales lagging from three to six months behind industrial production. In periods of depression industrial production always starts upward while retail sales are still going downward, and in periods of boom industrial production starts downward while retail sales are rising.

This brief analysis indicates the nature of the problem of fighting depressions. Reduced to its simplest terms, it is a problem of inducing an increase in business spending. Since the volume of business spending depends upon the outlook for profits, the essential thing is to improve this outlook. The increase in business spending must not be confined to items on current account. It must include a sufficient volume of new investment to absorb that part of the individual savings of the community which the government does not absorb, for obviously if individuals and enterprises save more than they invest, the turnover of bank deposits will continue to drop and so will the demand for goods.

II

Before I discuss the role of the government in dealing with depressions, permit me to comment briefly on the responsibilities of private enterprise. The extraordinary difficulties of the last depression compelled us to look so much to the government for help that we have tended to overlook the role of private resourcefulness and initiative in producing revival. Recovery from depression, as I have pointed out, can come about only by an expansion of business spending. Every businessman knows, however, that profitable changes in methods, equipment, and product have to be discovered. They are the result of a systematic search for ways of cutting costs and increasing sales. This indicates the all-important contribution that private enterprise must make to fight depressions. Its job is to discover new profitable opportunities for increasing business spending. The government can help by assisting in various ways the removal of maladjustments which stand in the way of private business. No government aid, however, can take the place of efficient, resourceful, ingenious, and courageous management struggling to find new ways of making money. Private enterprise needs to keep itself prepared at all times to fight depression (1) by keeping a large backlog of industrial research work in process so that projects can be brought to completion within a relatively short time and (2) by accumulating sufficient reserves in good times to maintain research work in bad times.

Four principal government policies have been advocated for fighting depressions. They are:

(1) Relief to debtors

(2) Encouraging reductions in the price level by deflationary policies

(3) Encouraging increases in the price level by inflationary policies

(4) Attempting to maintain or increase consumer purchasing power by various methods.

Let me comment briefly upon each of these policies.

(1) In its mildest form, assistance to debtors has involved maintaining easy money conditions which facilitate either the funding or the renewal of short-term debts and the refunding of long-term debts at lower rates of interest. The funding of short-term debts is undoubtedly helpful, because it releases for expenditure on commodities income which might otherwise have to be devoted to the repayment of indebtedness. Likewise, the refunding of long-term indebtedness is helpful because it improves the credit position of enterprises and permits them to pursue more liberal budget policies. Whether the renewal of short-term loans, which is an inevitable accompaniment of easy credit, is helpful or harmful is a disputed question. Enterprises naturally wish to avoid forced sales, but distress selling which reduces prices below replacement cost is one way of creating a price structure in which businessmen have confidence and which, therefore, serves as a safe foundation for forward planning and advance commitments.

In case of extraordinarily severe depressions, such as in 1929–1933, aid to debtors may take the form of government loans. The proper limits of this policy are not entirely clear. The strongest case is in favor of loans to banks because nothing is so deflationary as banking difficulties. There is also a strong case for government loans to home owners and farm owners. The alternative social unrest would have been in itself seriously detrimental to business. Furthermore, this aid usually represented a scaling down of the debtor's fixed charges and, therefore, both improved his credit condition and increased his ability to purchase commodities or to pay off other debts. Of doubtful wisdom was the aid extended in the last depression to the railroads. What was needed was prompt reorganizations which would have reduced fixed charges and improved the buying power and credit of the roads. Government aid seems to have delayed or prevented the needed reorganizations and, therefore, to have reduced the buying power of the roads.

(2) Italy and pre-Nazi Germany furnish the principal recent instances of attempting to fight depression by forcing down prices. Germany and Italy decreed price cuts largely for the purpose of meeting competition of the depreciated British pound.

What is the theoretical argument in favor of general price reductions? If the general price level is lowered, and if the bank deposits of the country are not reduced, and if the deposits are spent at the same rate, it is obvious that expenditures of the country will buy more goods than they would buy at the higher price level. There are three principal weaknesses to this argument. One is that the drop in prices may bring about a drop in demand deposits by making it possible for many enterprises to get along with smaller bank loans. A second is that the very drop in prices may reduce the turnover of bank deposits by creating lack of confidence in the price structure and thereby inducing postponement of commitments. A third weakness arises from maladjustments in the price structure, and a proportionate drop in all prices does nothing to eliminate these maladjustments.

Much seems to depend upon how price reductions occur. The success of small cuts may do harm rather than good by arousing the expectations of further cuts and thus inducing postponement of commitments. On the other hand, a quick and drastic cut in prices of goods to a level substantially below production costs may convince buyers that prevailing prices are too low to last and thus effectively move inventories into consumption and pave the way for a rise in prices and expansion in production. It is illuminating to contrast the decline in prices following 1929 with the decline following 1920. After 1929, prices moved downward gradually by small cuts, which had the effect of inducing postponement of commitments. In 1920, the drop in prices was far more precipitous. Inventories were dumped on the market so much below replacement costs that businessmen considered it safe to buy and an upturn in business soon followed.

Is it helpful in periods of depression to reduce the price of labor? From the standpoint of labor income, it does not seem to make much difference whether the price of labor is reduced or not. At any rate, comparison of the period 1920–1921, when the price of factory labor was reduced about 20 per cent, with the period 1929–1931, when the price of factory labor was scarcely reduced at all, shows that payrolls held up slightly better in relation to the volume of industrial production in the former period than in the latter. One of the principal arguments against the reduction of wages is that such reductions are likely to arouse the expectations of cuts in finished products, thus inducing postponement of commitments. The country which employed wage cuts most successfully during the last depression is Australia, where wage reductions were coupled with an inflationary policy which tended to support prices at the time that wages were being cut. At the present moment a general spiral of wage cuts would not facilitate recovery, but reductions in a few specific instances (especially in the building trades) would be desirable because they would increase the number of investment opportunities.

Instead of a general reduction in prices, what seems to be needed is a change in price relationships. Since a depression is a time when businessmen are finding difficulty in discovering enough new investment opportunities, what is particularly needed is a drop in the cost of investment—that is, a drop in the prices of industrial equipment, building materials, construction labor, and interest rates. The ideal development would seem to be a cut in the costs of investment combined with a temporary and drastic reduction in the prices of finished goods sufficient to clean out inventories and to produce a subsequent rise in the prices of finished goods. When the costs of investment have been reduced and the prices of raw materials and finished goods are so much below replacement costs that they begin to rise, the stage is set for recovery.

(3) One of the most widely advocated cures of depression during recent years has been an increase in the general price level. The expectation of rising prices does, of course, encourage forward planning and a certain amount of business expansion. Nevertheless, a proportionate increase in all prices would not remove the maladjustments in the price structure that limit the volume of investment. However, an expectation that prices are going to rise relative to costs of production will produce an expansion of investment. This is what most persons who talk loosely about a rise in the price level have in mind. They are not thinking about a rise in interest rates or in the price of labor, but rather of a rise in commodity prices.

The proposal that commodity prices be raised encounters the problem of ways and means. Price increases do little good unless they are brought about by increases in demand. This is why price increases achieved by controlling the supply or conditions of production are likely to be ineffective. Here we see one of the principal difficulties with the NRA. Many economists have advocated easy credit as a device for raising the demand for goods. Experience indicates that lower interest rates are useful in a limited way but that their effect is small, particularly in severe depression. During the last depression currency depreciation was effective in halting the decline or raising the price level of many commodities. The early currency depreciations were not planned—they occurred despite the struggles of governments to prevent them. Only late in the depression was this device voluntarily employed. It is doubtful whether it will be employed in the future.

The most promising device for raising prices or halting their decline seems to be government spending—or more strictly speaking, deficit financing. It requires some courage at the present moment to advocate this device in the United States. After increasing the government debt by approximately $20 billion during the last four years, we find ourselves with another depression on our hands as soon as we eliminate the deficit. Nevertheless, I hope to convince you that this device, properly employed, is one of the most useful ways of combating depressions and, indeed, an essential method of offsetting drops in business spending.

(4) Many persons have advocated combating depression by increasing consumer purchasing power. In itself an increase in consumer purchasing power is obviously useful. It helps to eliminate excessive stocks, to reduce short-term indebtedness, to correct maladjustments in the price structure, and to increase profitable investment opportunities. The crucial question is whether the methods employed to increase consumer purchasing power do more harm than good.

The Roosevelt Administration has endeavored to increase consumer purchasing power by (1) raising the price of labor, and (2) by government spending. I pointed out above that a drop in commodity prices substantially below costs may induce firmness in the prices of goods and hence some forward buying on the basis of this firmness. By analogy it might be argued that an advance in wages, which are the principal element in most costs, would creat firmness in commodity prices (1) by convincing buyers that the prices of good are bound to rise in adjustment to higher costs, and (2) if the demand for labor is inelastic, by increasing the demand for consumers' goods. Experience with the NRA in the summer of 1933 indicates that to a very limited degree this conclusion is true. Nevertheless, a rise in costs relative to commodity prices is not equivalent to a drop in commodity prices relative to costs. There are two principal reasons why it is not. One reason springs from the fact that in the midst of depression business enterprises are particularly concerned with preserving a highly liquid position. A drop in commodity prices permits an enterprise to increase its inventories with only a small reduction in its cash. An artificially induced rise in wages, on the other hand, threatens the cash position of enterprises, because no concern dares count on promptly getting back the increased amounts which it spends on wages. Hence, although the advance in wages may induce some forward buying of commodities, this effect is likely to be offset by other cuts in expenditures which each enterprise makes for the purpose of protecting its cash position. The second reason why the rise in wages is less stimulating than the drop in commodity prices is because it tends to raise the cost of new plants and equipment relative to old plants and equipment. The new and the old are constantly in competition with one another—new equipment, new plants, new methods, new products are competing with old equipment, old plants, old methods, and old products. Whether business is active or depressed depends upon whether the new is winning out rapidly or slowly in competition with the old. A depression is a time when the new is winning out slowly in competition with the old, and a boom is a time when the new is winning out rapidly in competition with the old. A general rise in wages raises the cost of the new and hence limits the increase in profitable opportunities for investment. Consequently, although a rise in wages may induce a limited increase in consumer incomes, this increase does not carry over very effectively into an increase in the volume of investment. This seems to have been the experience of the United States during the last few years.

Another way of increasing consumer purchasing power is by government spending, or deficit financing. This method has the advantage of increasing consumer purchasing power without directly raising production costs. Our recent experience with deficit financing make us vividly aware of the difficulties and dangers which it involves. If deficit financing is not accompanied by encouragement to business enterprise, it has little effect upon the volume of business spending, but simply causes idle bank deposits to pile up in the possession of business enterprises. This happened to a considerable extent in 1933 and 1935. During this period government spending was producing rapid increases in bank deposits, but the turnover of bank deposits was steadily dropping until it reached a low in August 1935.

If the policy of deficit financing is pursued too long in a period of recovery and if it is not tapered off gradually as business improves, it is likely to produce an inflationary price rise and inventory speculation which in itself produces recession. Experience since 1935 indicates vividly the political difficulties in tapering off government spending. The transition from government-stimulated to privately stimulated recovery has been shown to be difficult. In order to facilitate the transition, the government must be willing to give proper encouragement to private enterprise. Unfortunately, the stimulating effect of a large deficit may conceal the real business situation and so blind the government to the need for encouraging private enterprise. Indeed, misled by the stimulating effect of deficit financing, the government may easily impose a dangerous burden of taxes and social-reform measures upon business and thus counteract the effects of deficit financing.

Finally, if too large a part of government expenditures are spent on public works, it tends to obstruct recovery by raising the prices of building materials and labor. In order that private investment may be encouraged, these prices need to be kept low relative to other prices. Certainly, government expenditures on public works during the last several years have retarded private building by raising the prices of materials and labor. Government spending should be used to support the demand for consumers' goods by being used for straight relief or for work-relief projects which consume only small quantities of materials or else the government should predicate its willingness to buy building materials or building labor upon the willingness of sellers to make concessions in prices.

Despite our recent unsatisfactory experience with deficit financing, the case in favor of it is very strong. Ours is a society in which business spending is bound to drop whenever the future looks less favorable. When business spending drops, consumer purchasing power drops also because most consumers' incomes are nothing but the expenditures of business enterprises. But when consumer purchasing power drops, business becomes still less profitable, and thus the drop in business spending feeds on itself. Plainly, a society so vulnerable to business recession as ours needs to protect itself against the drop in business spending. This is simply common sense because the people of the country are not going to tolerate a substantial drop in their standard of living whenever the prospects for profit become darker. Consequently, the government must provide consumers a source of income which does not depend upon business spending.

There is another way to put the case for deficit financing. In depression, investment opportunities shrink, and so expenditures on new plant and equipment shrinks. Individual savings, however, do not shrink in proportion to the shrinkage in investment. This means that savers hold uninvested funds which in turn means that the velocity of circulation and, therefore, the total volume of spending drop. Obviously a way is needed to absorb the uninvested savings of individuals when the volume of investment drops. Deficit financing is such a device. It is a means by which a part of the uninvested savings of the community are converted into consumer purchasing power whenever the volume of investment drops. This very conversion of saving into consumer purchasing power tends to increase the number of investment opportunities and the volume of investment.

III

The discouraging experience of the last several years has led many persons who believe in deficit financing as a sound economic theory to abandon faith in it as a practical political policy. Much can be done, however, to reduce the political dangers associated with deficit financing. For example, federal expenditures on relief and public works can easily be handled so as to reduce the pressure from cities upon the federal treasury. Nevertheless, it is true that deficits in future depressions should be kept much smaller than in the past depression, because when the deficit is large enough to arouse fears of inflations it encourages short-term planning but discourages long-term planning. Furthermore, it would be wise to provide deficit financing not entirely through the general budget, but in large measure through the medium of unemployment reserves.

Unemployment reserves have three important superiorities over a deficit in the general budget. In the first place, unemployment compensation increases automatically as business falls off and helps, therefore, automatically to halt the drop in consumer purchasing power. In the second place, and equally important, unemployment-compensation payments decrease automatically as business picks up. Thus the problem of reducing the deficit as business revives is removed from the discretion of Congress. In the third place, no part of unemployment compensation is spent for capital goods. It all goes to unemployed labor and, therefore, tends to support the prices of consumer goods—exactly the group of prices that should be supported in periods of depression.

Our present unemployment-compensation acts are far from adequate. This is to be expected because they are new. They provide payment in most instances for only fifteen or sixteen weeks of unemployment. As soon as contributions can be properly increased, the duration of benefits should be raised to at least twenty-six weeks. This may be done by the device of workmen's contributions. It has been the history of all forms of social insurance, such as group insurance and private pension schemes, that in the beginning they were noncontributory. As they become better understood and more widely desired by workmen, they became contributory. The same evolution may be expected in the case of unemployment compensation.

Many persons have questioned whether unemployment compensation can be of much help in fighting depression. This depends, of course, upon whether reasonably adequate reserves are accumulated. It was found in the last depression that a deficit of two or three billions a year gave great support to business. Unemployment reserves probably cannot be paid on this scale, but even considerably smaller payments would be of considerable help. The sales of bonds from the unemployment reserve fund would supply a much-needed outlet for individual savings that otherwise would be hoarded. Thus they would permit the consumption of one part of the community to be financed by the savings of another part at a time when savings are too large relative to investment opportunities and when the decline in consumer incomes is itself reducing the number of investment opportunities. It is not ordinarily realized that we had a system of unemployment reserves in the depression of 1920–1921. It took the form of Liberty Bonds purchased by workers during the war which they sold to support themselves when they became unemployed. The remarkable stability of retail trade during the depression of 1920–1921 must be attributed in large measure to those sales of Liberty Bonds—which was, of course, equivalent to a system of unemployment reserves.

IV

My analysis indicates that business activity is bound to drop whenever the prospects for profits become less favorable and that these downturns cannot be entirely avoided. We speak of the stock market being in a strong technical position or a weak technical position. Suppose we apply this concept to business. If business is in a strong technical position when a downturn occurs, the recession will not be prolonged and perhaps it will not be severe. Since recessions cannot be entirely avoided, the most important thing of all is to prevent their being prolonged or severe by keeping business at all times in a strong technical position.

When is business in a strong technical position? On the whole it was in a strong technical position in 1920 because the war had created large capital shortages and because consumers, instead of being in debt, held large quantities of government bonds. Consequently, the resulting depression, although severe, was very short. Keeping business in a strong technical position involves the following:

(1) Keeping the short-term indebtedness within limits because short-term debts involve mortgaging future incomes and reducing future consumer power. Concretely, this means exercising a strict control over installment buying by insisting upon substantial downpayments and by keeping the term of payment short.

(2) Keeping inventories within reasonable limits by avoiding specula-

tion in commodities. This involves carefully controlled credit policies. Even more important, it involves the avoidance of production bottlenecks in industry by foreseeing increases in demand.

(3) Building up large unemployment reserves to protect consumer purchasing power from being drastically reduced by drops in the volume of business spending.

(4) Finally, and most important of all, maintaining at all times industrial research on a large scale for the purpose of creating new opportunities for profitable investment by improving equipment and products and by developing new products. A large reserve of investment opportunities in the process of being developed is a necessary foundation to a strong technical position of business.

8

Postwar Boom or Collapse

Excerpts from Harvard Business Review, Autumn 1942.

As a result of the war, the United States is developing by far the best trained and most efficient working force in its history. Never before has training been given on a scale comparable to that of the last two years. Not only have workmen by the hundreds of thousands received formal and systematic training, but the production emergency has compelled thousands of managers to solve new problems, try new methods, and accomplish the impossible. It has made managers more resourceful, jolted them out of ruts, and compressed into several years the managerial experience of a decade. What applies to industry applies also to the Navy and the Army. Training in the industrial arts is being given on a large scale. More important, the qualities of leadership, initiative, and resourcefulness are being developed as only danger and combat can develop them. The University of Hard Knocks is an expensive institution, far too costly for most of us to attend, but in times of war millions are compelled to attend it. At great cost it does develop men.

After the war the United States will have by far the largest and best equipped plant that it has ever possessed. In 1941 expenditures on manufacturing facilities reached an all-time high, about $4.5 billion against the previous high of $3.2 billion in 1920, a year of much higher prices.[1] About half of the total expenditures were in direct war industries.[2] At the end of March commitments for war-plant expansion were about $13 billion.[3] Some of the

[1] *Survey of Current Business* (February 1942), p. 6.

[2] *Ibid.*, p. 6. Expenditures for ordnance were about $620 million; aircraft, $500 million; chemicals, $525 million; and shipbuilding, $450 million. About one fourth of the capital outlay in manufacturing went into industries producing on a large scale for both military and civilian industries—iron and steel, $520 million; nonferrous metals, $320 million; machinery, $300 million. Among the civilian industries, food and kindred products made capital expenditures of about $330 million—textiles, apparel, and related products, $180 million; automobiles, $180 million; pulp and paper, $80 million.

[3] *Victory* (May 19, 1942), p. 32. Of these projects about $10.7 billion were government-financed and $2.3 billion privately financed. The capacity of the steel industry has been increased from about 81.6 million tons to nearly 89.2 million tons in July 1942. At the end of July 1942, the War Production Board announced that it was planning to increase steel ingot

new plant, such as shipyards, powder mills, and shell-filling plants, may have little use after the war. Other plants will not be favorably located for peacetime operation. Still other plants, such as some airplane plants, will be needed by the armed forces after the war. An estimate of the "average" increase in the capacity of manufacturing plants is almost meaningless, particularly when the disparities in the increases in different industries are so great. Capacity is a matter of balance. Small expenditures at bottleneck points may enormously increase capacity. No one knows just what the war expenditures will do to industrial balance. Depressions tend to cause finishing capacity to become too large relative to primary capacity. On the whole, the war will probably raise raw-material capacity relative to finishing capacity for *peacetime* goods. One thing is quite clear, that the war will produce a particularly large rise in the kind of capacity which makes possible further increases in capacity.

The prospective increase in the nation's plant fills many people with dread. They fear that we are likely to be poor *because* we are able to produce so much. Before Pearl Harbor a *Fortune* survey found that 69.9 per cent of persons interviewed expect things to be worse after the war than before. Early in June 1942, the Gallup Poll found a slight majority of people had given up the idea of a postwar depression. Businessmen were expecting prosperity by two to one. Farmers and lower-income groups, however, were expecting depression. Is there any basis for this fear? If we really have the kind of economy in which a gain in productive capacity reduces living standards, it is high time that we changed it.

The record of the last century shows plainly that rapid growth in plant does not inevitably make the nation poor. Nevertheless, it is *possible* that too much plant may make us poor. Our economy is geared to a rate of growth which is determined by the volume of savings at different levels of national income. Unless there is enough growth or change to put to work all the savings that would be made at full employment, expansion will halt before full employment is attained. Hence too much plant may cause unemployment by limiting investment opportunities. That is why the war, by increasing the amount of plant in the community, may greatly increase the difficulties of maintaining full production and employment after the war.

---

capacity by another 10 million tons, bringing the total to nearly 100 million tons. The capacity of the aluminum industry at the end of 1943, even allowing for some high-cost capacity that cannot be economically operated in time of peace, will be five times the prewar capacity. The National Machine Builders Association estimates that the output of machine tools in 1942 will be $1.4 billion. Even in 1940, when the industry was operating at a high rate by previous standards, its output was only $459 million.

The problem of maintaining employment after the war falls into two principal parts: (1) the problem of transition, of shifting from a huge rate of government spending back to private spending, and (2) the long-run problem of keeping busy a far larger and more productive plant than ever before. . . .

. . . . . .

What general conclusions emerge from this survey?

1. The pattern of economic trends after the present war is likely to differ substantially from the pattern after the First World War, especially if price control during this war is more effective than during the previous one.

2. The problem of shifting from war production to peace production is being largely determined today by the success of price control and by the methods of financing the war.

3. The management of the transition will produce a sharp conflict between those who wish the quickest possible shift and those who wish to maintain equality of opportunity for all competitors to gain access to civilian markets at the same time.

4. The immediate aftermath of the war will be determined by whether spending will be more affected by war workers' fears of a shrinkage of income than by the desire of millions of people to make postponed purchases with surplus savings. The fears will be relatively more important after this war than after the last one unless the purchasing power of surplus savings is preserved by effective control of prices. The government should regard its responsibility as simultaneously guarding against a postwar boom and a postwar depression.

5. The longer the war, the greater is the probability that economic trends after the war will be governed by deferred demand rather than by fears of war workers of unemployment and shrinkage in their incomes.

6. The higher prices rise during the war, the less will be the danger of a postwar boom. The whole question of control of prices during the war needs to be reconsidered in the light of the effect of price control during the war upon the propensity to consume after the war. How favorable a consumption function could we stand after the war in view of the prospective great demand for industrial equipment at home and abroad? Would a moderate additional rise in wholesale prices (say about 30 per cent) be desirable in order to reduce the postwar conversion of war savings bonds into goods and, therefore, to reduce the postwar competition between the demand for consumer goods and the demand for capital goods?

7. Success in maintaining a good balance in the early stages of transition between the rise in civilian employment and the drop in war employment will almost certainly generate a large amount of optimism and will create danger of an uncontrolled boom. This danger may persist in greater or less degree for perhaps fifteen years, until surplus savings have been liquidated and production and prices have adjusted themselves to the large volume of demand deposits.

8. The threatened boom cannot be averted by traditional methods of credit control. A variety of methods, which for a short time will include rationing certain scarce articles and, for a longer time, will include price controls, will probably be necessary.

9. The problem of averting a postwar boom will be greatly mitigated if the productive capacity of industry increases during the war and in the immediate postwar years by a larger amount than has been assumed in this analysis. It would be particularly hepful if the pervasive scarcities imposed by the war should produce a large number of capital-saving inventions. The outlook is bright for faster technological change than has been assumed in the analysis.

10. The management of the shift from war production to civilian production involves many questions of timing. For example, it is important that large reductions in taxes be postponed until after the conversion of war savings bonds into goods has been pretty much completed.

11. The huge increase of demand deposits in relation to prices as a result of the war will increase the instability of the economy because small changes in liquidity preference will produce great changes in the demand for goods. The growth of physical production will gradually remedy this condition, but a substantial rise in prices during the first decade or two after the war may also be necessary.

12. The best opportunity to open American markets to foreign goods is likely to occur shortly after the war when tentative exchange rates are worked out between the dollar and foreign currencies.

13. The quantity of goods which the United States will feel disposed to supply the rest of the world for the first two or three years after the war is likely to be quite limited.

14. The prospects of a high level of employment for some years after the war will depend in large measure upon the capacity of unions and business to work together on problems of taxation and wage policy. Because taxes on profits substantially reduce the demand for labor, unions may eventually be expected to take the lead in insisting that taxes on profits be reduced to

a low rate and kept there. The interest of unions in this matter is far greater than that of business owners, because a drop of one dollar in the outlook for profits produces a drop of several dollars in the demand for labor. It may take the unions a decade or two to discover their interest in this matter, but it cannot escape their notice forever.

15. If collective bargaining in plants and industries is not conducted within the framework of a national wage policy, it may substantially reduce the marginal efficiency of capital and the demand for labor, because the parties in these cases are not interested in the effect of their bargains upon the general level of employment.

16. If unions and employers undertake to set a national wage policy, they will eventually discover that the conditions which make possible larger payrolls also make possible larger profits. This discovery will revolutionize industrial relations and will provide a new basis for cooperation between unions and business in stimulating expansion and technological improvement. Such cooperation would end the danger that the politicians may dominate industry. It would make all previous efforts to raise the standard of living seem feeble. The success of unions and business in achieving this revolution in industrial relations and in developing the new capacity to cooperate in promoting expansion will depend upon their ability to view payrolls and profits in national terms. Only when this is done does it become clear that the conditions of larger payrolls are also the conditions of larger profits.

9

Survey of Our Economy: Pluses and Minuses

New York Times Magazine, February 29, 1948.

I

DOES the recent precipitous slide in grain prices mark the beginning of the much-heralded "postwar recession"? Is the country about to experience another 1921? Can the economy shift from its postwar boom to more normal conditions without first going through a severe recession? Last May *The Economist,* London, said that "it will be very surprising, not to say unnatural, if the present feverish pace of business [in the United States] can be replaced by a rather more sober stride without an intervening adjustment of some severity." A leading weekly magazine now predicts that deflation will definitely set in by midsummer and that unemployment will be rising by July. It anticipates a decline of about 20 per cent in production and about 20 per cent in prices.

A large drop in grain prices will not precipitate a recession unless the country is ready for one anyway. Consequently the best way to judge the immediate business outlook is to examine the principal weak points and strong points in the economy. Let us, therefore, take stock, looking first at the weaknesses and then at the strong points. At no time, of course, is the economy without *some* weaknesses. What are the principal ones today?

1. The decline in the rate of saving, which has stimulated the demand for consumer goods during the last two years, cannot be expected to continue much longer. Between the fourth quarter of 1946 and the fourth quarter of 1947 the annual rate of saving declined by $2.1 billion despite the fact that incomes after taxes rose by the annual rate of $15 billion. The rate of saving is now almost as low as in 1937, when per capita real income after taxes was about 30 per cent lower than now. In fact, the rate of saving by individuals is so low that widespread fears of a recession might easily cause the rate of

individual saving to rise, weakening the demand for consumer goods and reducing incomes.

2. The abnormally high rate of expenditures on food and drink creates the possibility of a substantial drop in the demand for these goods. Before the war people were spending about 25 per cent of income after taxes for food and drink; today the proportion is nearly 30 per cent. The proportion of incomes spent on food and drink might fall to 25 per cent of incomes after taxes, particularly if people become fearful of recession.

3. Considerable progress has been made in catching up on accumulated demand. Radios, for example, are now plentiful. The number of passenger automobiles registered increased by about 2.3 million during the last year and is now at an all-time high, a million above 1941.

4. Total domestic expenditures on capital goods have been large—around $30 billion a year. During the last fifteen months there has been little increase in spending on capital goods. This indicates that no immediate increase is likely. Indeed, since the capital-goods industries are producing at capacity, no large immediate increase in spending on capital goods is possible unless prices rise. Widespread uncertainty about business prospects could easily produce some drop in these expenditures. The cost of building is high and the prices of building materials have risen more than most prices. The expectation of lower building costs, particularly lower material prices, could easily produce a considerable postponement of construction.

5. The indebtedness of business concerns to banks, though still low in relation to incomes, has grown considerably during the last year. The holdings of cash and government securities by enterprises have dropped substantially. Current assets now consist far more of inventories and accounts receivable than was true a year ago. As a result, enterprises are becoming increasingly reluctant to increase short-term indebtedness and banks to make additional loans, especially for real estate.

6. The dollar value of inventories in the last twelve months has increased by about $7 billion, or over 20 per cent. The ratio of inventories to sales, it is true, is little greater than a year ago and is well below prewar, but this does not mean that the size of inventories should be viewed with complacency. It is the relationship of inventories to *future* sales, not *present* sales, which is important. The danger that a drop in sales might precipitate considerable unloading of inventories is much greater today when inventories are in excess of $40 billion than a year ago when they were $7 billion less.

7. Net foreign investment (mainly excess of exports over imports), which was much larger in 1947 than in 1946, will not increase further and probably

will undergo some drop. Exports are not likely to rise further, and imports are slowly growing as the rest of the world recovers its capacity to produce.

8. A third round of wage increases has started and seems destined to continue. Major uncertainties in business may limit the amount of wage increases, but will not prevent them altogether. Wage advances which occur when the business outlook is uncertain or unfavorable will have an effect very different from that of wage increases in periods of expansion. In periods of expansion higher wages are assumed to mean larger consumer demand because they are not expected appreciably to reduce employment. In periods of uncertainty or contraction higher wages cause enterprises to look for ways of protecting their liquidity. This means that higher wages will produce more or less completely offsetting decreases in expenditure. In fact, the decreases in expenditures may substantially more than offset any increase in payrolls.

9. The budget of the federal government may become a powerful deflationary influence, particularly if the demand for goods levels off. The cash surplus during the next year may be in excess of $7 billion. So long as the economy is expanding, a budget surplus can easily be prevented from being deflationary by being used to pay off government debt held by the public or the banks. Thus, the money taken from the public in the form of taxes is restored to it in the form of repayments of the debt. So long as there is a good demand for investment-seeking funds, the money used to repay the debt quickly goes to work. When the demand for loans and investment-seeking funds ceases to expand, however, the funds restored to the public by paying off part of the debt no longer go quickly into circulation and the surplus becomes a powerful deflationary influence.

10. The British are determined to avoid devaluation, and so long as a strong sellers' market continues, their chances of succeeding are good. If devaluation of the pound occurs, however, it will put downward pressure on prices all over the world.

II

The above list of weaknesses, looked at alone, may seem moderately impressive. It looks far less impressive, however, when considered in connection with the many strong features of the economy. As a matter of fact, the condition of the economy is still very strong—stronger than most Americans and foreigners realize. Let us take stock of its principal strong points.

1. Although the prospect for more abundant supplies of grain is excellent,

no general weakness in agricultural prices is likely—especially not in meat and dairy products. The cattle population of the country has been dropping for several years. The pig crop this coming spring will be about 10 per cent smaller than last year. Per capita meat consumption in 1948 will have to drop nearly 8 per cent below 1947. No improvement in supply is in sight before 1949.

2. Expenditures are still low in relation to the money supply. For example, although spending on commodities and services is about 2.4 times as large as in 1940, demand deposits and money outside of banks are about 2.9 times as large. Personal holdings of currency and demand deposits have increased fourfold since 1940, but expenditures on consumer goods and on personal taxes have only increased about 2.5 times. Incidentally, although the average of *all* wholesale prices at its January peak was about the same as the peak of 1920, the prices of nonfarm and nonfood products as a whole are considerably below the peaks of 1920. Many important commodities (including some agricultural products), such as sugar, rubber, hides, copper, cotton, and even wheat, are far below their peaks of the First World War or its aftermath. Furthermore, in comparing prices now and in 1920, one should remember that hourly earnings today are twice as high as in 1920.

3. Private debt is small in relation to the national income—far smaller than in 1920 or in 1940. For example, in 1940 private debt was two thirds *larger* than the annual national income. Today it is over 10 per cent *smaller* than the annual national income. While the national income has increased more than two and a half times, private debt has increased less than one fourth.

4. Despite the progress made in meeting accumulated needs for goods, the backlog of demand is still huge. In 1947, 833,000 dwelling units were completed, but the increase in the number of families was about a million. Consequently, dwelling units were fewer in relation to the number of families than at the beginning of the year. Despite the fact that per capita real income is 30 per cent above prewar, the number of families living doubled up is more than 50 per cent greater than before the war. A strong demand for housing is in prospect for some time to come.

Although much progress has been made in meeting the accumulated demand for automobiles, the ratio of cars to families is less than in 1940, when per capita real incomes were much lower and people were less able to afford cars. Furthermore, the average age of cars today is nine years, in comparison with 5.5 years before the war. The number of passenger cars on the road is now greater than before the war, but the car supply, as measured by the remaining life of the cars now in service, is probably no more than half of prewar.

5. The accumulated needs of business for plant and equipment are enormous. During the last eighteen years the plant of American industry has been wearing out or becoming obsolete almost as fast as it has been replaced, so that the plant of industry today is little larger than in 1929. In the meantime the population of the country has increased by twenty-three million (nearly the equivalent of two Canadas) and the labor force by over ten million. Capital per worker, which ordinarily increases at about 2 per cent a year, is smaller than twenty years ago. Industry is producing nearly 70 per cent more physical output than in 1929, but it is doing it in large part with old and obsolete equipment. Iron and steel, railroads, oil, electric light and power, textiles, and many other industries are grievously short of capacity and will be for years to come. Equipment makers are commonly booked up for two or more years. Even if businessmen were definitely convinced that the country was to experience a moderate recession, they would not cancel orders for equipment. They need equipment too badly and they cannot afford to lose their priority on the books of sellers. If the banks refuse to finance purchases of equipment, enterprises will obtain the money by further sales of their government securities or by borrowing from insurance companies, which have been increasing their lending capacity by selling government securities to the Reserve Banks.

6. The accumulated needs of states and cities for streets, roads, schools, hospitals, and other public works are large, and expenditures for these purposes during 1948 will be greater than in 1947.

7. The current high level of business activity has been due in the main to consumer buying and to business buying for replacements—the two most stable types of buying and the kinds least sensitive to unfavorable developments in business. Spending on long-range investment plans, the most sensitive type of spending, has been small. For example, in 1947, one dollar was spent for capital goods for every $5.50 spent on consumer goods. This was the same as in 1940, when the total national income was much lower and when expenditures for capital goods might be expected to be lower relative to expenditures for consumer goods than now. The fact that most of this business spending for capital goods has been for replacements is indicated by the small volume of business construction. This was less than 2.5 per cent of the national income in 1947 in comparison with nearly 5.4 per cent in 1929.

8. The capacity of consumers to expand their demand for goods is still large. They have huge holdings of cash and bank deposits, and consumer in-

debtedness is abnormally low in relation to consumer incomes after taxes. For example, in the fourth quarter of 1947 incomes after taxes were 2.4 times as large as the average for 1940, but consumer credit had increased only 46 per cent. In fact, consumer indebtedness at the end of 1946 was even smaller in relation to incomes after taxes than at the bottom of the depression in 1933. The next six months will see many wage increases, and these will add to consumer incomes because under present conditions they will not cause unemployment.

An important element of strength in the economy is that a high level of production has been maintained in the face of stiff taxes and a large surplus in the federal budget. This means that the government has the powerful instrument of tax reduction to use, if necessary, in halting a recession. There is some danger that the government will use this instrument prematurely.

III

The many strong features in the economic situation do not assure that the country will not escape an early recession, but they make an early recession unlikely and indicate that, if one occurs, it will be mild. It is too soon to judge whether or not the United States will be able to shift from the postwar boom to more or less normal conditions without sooner or later going through a sharp and severe readjustment. Thus far the country has succeeded in achieving and maintaining a high level of employment and even in going through a 50 per cent rise in wholesale prices within two years without developing a large amount of speculative buying. That is encouraging. The postwar boom in the stock market never got very far. Speculative accumulation of inventories has not become widespread. There has been considerable buying of real estate at high prices and on thin margins, but real-estate speculation has not yet gone to the fantastic extremes of some previous booms.

The drastic drop in grain prices has greatly strengthened the economy and has improved to a small extent the prospect that the country can get back to normal activities without experiencing a bad recession. Grain prices, of course, are still high and will sooner or later drop some more. Both corn and wheat are still substantially higher than they were a year ago. The drop in grain prices, however, has occurred at a time when it is not likely to be contagious. It has undoubtedly put an effective damper on speculation in grains. Furthermore, it has given the country a vivid example on a small scale of the aftermath of inflation. This will promote a spirit of caution among businessmen and, if at some later time the rapid rise in bank credit is resumed, perhaps this example will cause the public to insist on a more vigorous policy of control by the Federal Reserve Banks than was pursued in 1947. Thanks to the recent drop in grain prices, every businessman can today view the immediate future with definitely greater optimism than would have been warranted a month ago.

10

How Stable Is the Economy?

Address before the Kentucky Bankers Association, Louisville, Ky., Oct. 20, 1952; The Commercial and Financial Chronicle, October 23, 1952.

In about two years or less one may expect the outlays of the government for defense and foreign aid to begin to drop. The decrease will be around $5 billion to $10 billion a year, and will continue for two or three years. The ability of the country to adjust itself to the drop in the demand for defense goods will depend upon the capacity of the economy to grow. If the drop in defense spending comes in one of the periods when the economy is expanding, the adjustment will probably be made quite smoothly. On the other hand, if the drop is superimposed on a more or less normal period of recession, the resulting contraction could be substantial and painful.

In these remarks I wish to examine in a fairly concrete fashion some of the weak spots and strong spots in the economy. I have two purposes in mind. In the first place, I wish to shed light on the problem of adjusting the economy to a drop in defense expenditures. In the second place, I wish to indicate some policies that would help make the adjustment come easier.

I

As a foundation for this analysis, I wish to look briefly at the movements of output and prices over the last sixty years. During most of this period the economy was growing. Its output, expressed in dollars of constant purchasing power, increased about 115 per cent in the twenty years from 1889 to 1909; 112 per cent in the twenty years from 1909 to 1929; and 80 per cent in the twenty-one years from 1929 to 1950. Part of the rise has been due to the growth of the labor force, but most of the gain in production has been due to the rise in output per manhour. In fact, during the last twenty years or so, about 73 per cent of the gain in total production was due to more output per manhour, and about 27 per cent to more men at work.

Although the expansion of the economy has been rapid, with physical output growing from 80 per cent to more than 100 every twenty years, the growth has not been steady. In fourteen of the sixty-one years from 1889 to 1950, the physical output of the economy dropped. In other words, the economy has been contracting during about 23 per cent of the time and expanding during about 77 per cent of the time. Expansions and contractions of physical production correspond quite closely to booms and recessions in employment or in the *dollar* volume of output, but not exactly. For example, some recessions, such as 1924, 1927, or 1949, were not accompanied by any drop in the *annual* figures for production.[1] Furthermore, there have been some periods of boom, such as 1920, 1945, and 1946, when the annual figures for output were below those of the previous year. Most of the drops in physical production have been small—in nine out of the fourteen cases the drop was less than 5 per cent. The largest drop was fourteen per cent. It occurred between 1931 and 1932.

The movement of prices during the last sixty years has, in general, been upward. In 1950 the wholesale price level was over 180 per cent above 1889—in other words, it had almost trebled. But the rise of prices has been far from steady. In twenty-one years out of the sixty-one, the average wholesale price level was lower than in the preceding year. In other words, prices were falling about one third of the time and rising about two thirds of the time. The drops in prices, however, were much greater than the drops in output. Some of the price declines ran for more than a year, so that the twenty-one years in which prices dropped were concentrated in thirteen declines of four years or less each. In two of these declines the drop in wholesale prices was over 30 per cent; in another it was nearly 20 per cent; in still another, over 10 per cent; in two more, between 5 and 10 per cent.

Periods of expanding production have usually (but not always) been accompanied by rising prices. Between 1889 and 1950 there were nine periods during which physical output rose without interruption, at least as shown by annual figures. One of these periods was three years in length; three were four years, one was five years, one was six, one was seven, one was nine. The present period of expansion has already run six years without interruption except for a slight one in 1949.[2] In seven of these nine periods of expanding production the price level rose and in two of them it fell. Some of the rises in the price level were quite large. In three periods the price level advanced

[1] There may have been a drop which did not show up in the annual figures.

[2] Physical output in the year 1949 as a whole was the same as in 1948. There was a small drop within the year.

over 30 per cent and in one of them (the period of the First World War) nearly 100 per cent. In still another period of expanding output (1894 to 1903) the price level increased 24 per cent.

The fact that the growth of output is interrupted every now and then by periods of contraction and that some of these contractions are accompanied by substantial drops in the price level has always been an important influence on business thinking and has limited the willingness of managements to expand their enterprises. If the danger of general drops in demand could be substantially mitigated, there is little doubt that most business concerns would plan more ambitiously for expansion. The result would be a more rapid growth in output and in the country's standard of consumption.

II

The success of the economy in adjusting itself to a drop in defense spending will depend upon the weaknesses and strengths in the economy. What are these weaknesses and strengths? The great weaknesses are: (1) the large increase in automatic savings brought about by the enormous increase in private pension funds during the last six years; (2) the large rise in corporate and personal indebtedness during the last six years; (3) the fact that the maturities of E bonds will be considerably smaller in 1955 and 1956 than in 1953 and 1954; (4) the fact that a high rate of expenditures on plant and equipment for nearly five years has pretty well supplied the country with new and efficient producing capacity; and (5) the fact that the number of new housing starts has for several years been substantially outrunning the increase in the number of families. The large rise in debt and the large expenditures on plant, equipment, and housing are characteristic of the later phases of a boom and suggest that the drop in defense spending will more or less coincide with a normal contraction after a boom and may greatly aggravate that contraction.

The principal elements of strength in the economy are: (1) a large volume of liquid resources; (2) fairly well-developed arrangements for partly maintaining many personal incomes in periods of contraction; (3) some backlog of unmet needs, particularly in the field of public construction; (4) recent important gains in the capacity of industry to create new investment opportunities and new and better consumer goods; (5) the strong spirit of caution that dominates decision making by managements and consumers. Let us examine first the weak spots in the economy and then the strong spots.

(1) *The large increase in automatic savings brought about by the recent*

increase in private pension funds. It is estimated that the receipts of private pension funds are exceeding their disbursements by over $2 billion a year. This excess of receipts over disbursements will change rather slowly. It will be somewhat affected by business recessions because receipts are partly based on the size of payrolls and because recessions will bring about some retirements that have been deferred and thus increase disbursements from pension funds. Nevertheless, for some time to come, private pension funds will be taking in considerably more than they are paying out in pensions. These investment-seeking funds may prove quite deflationary in periods when the demand for investment-seeking funds is dropping.

(2) *The large increase in corporate and personal indebtedness.* Corporations and individuals have been going into debt much too fast. The increase of net private debt was $30.8 billion in 1951, $36.4 billion in 1950, and $136.4 billion since the end of 1945. Between the end of 1945 and the end of 1951, net private debt virtually doubled, while the money value of the national product increased about 53 per cent. In 1945 the country had about 65 cents of private debt for every dollar of annual product; in 1951, it had almost a dollar of private debt for every dollar of annual product.

Between the end of 1945 and the end of 1951, state and local governments increased their indebtedness by nearly $10 billion. Only the federal government has been reducing its debt. By the end of 1951, the gross debt of the federal government stood about $22 billion below the end of 1945—a drop of about 8 per cent. The federal debt has recently begun to rise and will probably continue to rise for several years to come. In view of the large amount of uninformed discussion one reads and hears about federal finances these days, it is worth noting that while business, individuals, and state and local governments have been increasing their debts, the federal government has been cutting its debt.

It is important to see clearly just how and why the volume of debt creates problems. There is no doubt about the capacity of the country to pay the interest on its present debts, or even on a much larger volume of indebtedness. As a matter of fact, despite the rapid rise in business and personal debts, the *total* indebtedness of the country, public and private, is smaller in relation to the net national product than it was at the end of the Second World War. While the money value of the national product has been rising about 53 per cent (as it did between 1945 and 1951), the total indebtedness of the country, public and private, has increased only about 30 per cent.

The problem created by debt arises from the effect of annual repayments of the debt on the demand for goods during periods of business contraction.

This problem occurs primarily in connection with private indebtedness, not public indebtedness, since public bodies can avoid the deflationary effects of repayments in periods of contraction by incurring new debts to pay off old ones. But business concerns and consumers cannot as a rule meet repayments out of new borrowings—or, at least, they are unwilling to do so. This means that in periods of contraction repayments of private indebtedness by some firms and individuals will accentuate the drop in the total demand for goods unless these repayments are offset by new borrowings by other firms and other individuals. Some new borrowing, of course, goes on even in years of contraction. Once private debts become quite large, so that the annual repayments also become quite large, it becomes extremely difficult in periods of contraction to persuade other firms and other individuals to borrow enough to prevent a net drop in the volume of indebtedness and, therefore, to prevent repayments from producing a net drop in the demand for goods.

This brief analysis shows you the yardstick that should be used in determining whether the volume of indebtedness has become too large. It is not enough that the interest can be easily paid or that the principal can easily be repaid when due. The test is whether the repayments have become so large that they exceed the amount of new borrowing that is likely to occur in a period of contraction. After that point is reached (and perhaps even *before* it is reached), further increases in private indebtedness should be regarded with considerable disfavor and should be discouraged.

No one knows, of course, just how much new private borrowing can be induced in a period of contraction. That depends, among other things, upon the severity of the contraction. Hence one can only make a rough guess as to when the repayments on private indebtedness have become large enough to aggravate seriously the problem of controlling recessions. It is obviously not essential that repayments of private indebtedness be offset solely by private borrowing—new public borrowing will do just as well, provided the borrowed money is promptly spent. But the amount of public borrowing which the community is willing to do and the amount of borrowed money it can promptly spend in a period of recession are limited. At the present time, there are many people who are concerned about the size of the federal debt and who would be disturbed at seeing it rise very rapidly in a period of recession. The more reluctant the country is to see a rise in public borrowing and spending in periods of recession in order to offset repayments of private debts, the more the country should be willing to limit the increase of private indebtedness in periods of boom.

The annual repayments on the present volume of private indebtedness have become large enough so that it will be difficult to offset them in a period of moderate or even mild recession. Consequently, the time has come to discourage vigorously any further increases in net private indebtedness—not indefinitely, but for at least several years until the country has had time to grow up to its present debts. I cannot offer a precise estimate of the volume of annual repayments, but they must be quite large—particularly in view of the many term loans providing for annual repayments over ten years or less, the large volume of mortgages which are being amortized over a twenty-year period or less, and the large volume of consumer indebtedness outstanding. One of the figures that is badly needed in the statistics issued by the Department of Commerce is an estimate of annual debt repayments.

Of special interest is the problem created by consumer indebtedness, which many retailers and others argue is not too large. The holders of the view that the present volume of consumer indebtedness is not too large labor under the mistaken belief that the question of the safe size of consumer indebtedness depends mainly on the ratio of such indebtedness to disposable incomes and on other tests that determine the soundness of individual credits. At the present time installment loans alone are so large that repayments on them are running well over $8 billion a year. New installment loans are running slightly larger than this, so that the total is still increasing. It is not likely, however, that new installment loans could be made at the rate of $8 billion a year in a period of recession. In the year 1948, new installment loans made by the principal types of lenders were $5.9 billion; in 1949, $6.5 billion; in 1950, $7.6 billion. Hence a fairly substantial contraction in the outstanding volume of installment loans is likely to accompany a recession. Consequently, during the next year, when the level of business will be high, every effort should be made to prevent a further rise in the volume of consumer credit. Such an increase would simply lay the foundation for trouble in a year of recession.

Repayments on real-estate loans can also be troublesome. It is argued that the payments on these loans (plus taxes on the house) are not much larger than the amounts that people would be paying in rent had they not become home owners. Hence, it is said that the effect of repayments on mortgages is negligible. This is not quite true. Payments of rent, of course, are often used to pay interest and to repay part of the principal of a mortgage on the house, but to a considerable extent rental payments are a return on the owner's equity. To that extent they are likely to be regarded as current income and to be currently spent by their recipients. Repayments of the principal on real-estate loans, however, are regarded by their recipients as repayments of capital. They do not form the basis for current expenditures, but the basis for new investment-seeking funds. Hence, if a drop in the general level of business produces a shrinkage in investment opportunities, repayments of real estate loans will be deflationary. Consequently, the next year or so is the time when further increases in the total outstanding volume of real-estate loans should be vigorously resisted.

(3) *The fact that the maturities of E bonds will be considerably smaller in 1955 and 1956 than in 1953 or 1954.* During 1953 and 1954, when defense expenditures are at their peak, business will be sustained to a substantial extent by the large maturities of E bonds which will rise from about $3.3 billion in 1952 to about $5.1 billion in 1953, and $5.7 billion in 1954. In 1955 and 1956, however, just when defense spending is expected to be dropping, the E bond maturities will also drop. Of the E bonds now outstanding, there are maturities of $4.4 billion in 1955 and $2.2 billion in 1956. To the extent that the owners of maturing E bonds continue to hold E bonds or reinvest their money in the new H bonds, K bonds, or in other securities, or use it to pay off debts, the timing of maturities creates no problem. To the extent, however, that the owners use the money from their maturities to buy houses or consumer goods, the timing is unfortunate because it tends to increase the demand for houses and consumer goods at the peak of defense spending and to reduce this demand at just about the time defense spending drops.

(4) *The fact that a high rate of expenditures on plant and equipment has pretty well supplied the country with new and efficient producing capacity.* Ever since the end of 1945 the country has been experiencing one of the biggest booms in the construction of industrial plant and equipment in its history—perhaps the biggest boom. I use the word "industrial" in the broad sense to include agricultural as well as nonagricultural industries. Total outlays on plant and equipment from the end of 1945 through the first half of 1952, expressed in dollars of 1952 purchasing power, were about $214 billion. At the end of 1945 the reproducible plant and equipment of all American industry represented an investment less depreciation of about $244 billion, expressed in dollars of 1952 purchasing power. This figure does not include inventories or undeveloped natural resources. Hence the expenditures on plant and equipment during the last six and a half years have been about 88 per cent as large as the total investment in plant and equipment less depreciation at the beginning of the period.[3]

The recent huge expenditures on plant and equipment have followed a

[3] The estimate of investment in plant and equipment that I have used, which is made by bringing down to date the estimate of Kuznets for 1938, is probably somewhat too large. At any rate, this seems to be indicated by later research which has not yet been published.

sixteen-year period marked by the Great Depression and the war during which time the plant and equipment of American industry were being replaced only about as rapidly as they were wearing out—in some years not even that rapidly. As a result, the investment in plant and equipment less depreciation when expressed in dollars of constant purchasing power was scarcely any larger at the end of 1945 than at the end of 1929—though in the meantime the population of the country had increased by 18 million, or nearly 15 per cent, and the civilian labor force by 4.7 million, or over 9 per cent. As a result of the high average age of industrial plant and equipment at the end of the war, nearly 59 per cent of the expenditures on plant and equipment during the last six and a half years have been needed to offset depreciation and obsolescence. The investment in plant and equipment less depreciation expressed in 1952 dollars has increased from $244 billion at the end of 1945 to $335 billion in the middle of 1952, or about 37 per cent.

Population and the civilian labor force, of course, have been increasing too. Between the end of 1945 and the middle of 1952, when investment in plant and equipment rose 37 per cent, population increased almost 13 per cent and the civilian labor force a little more than 13 per cent. If one compares the prewar year of 1939 with the middle of 1952, one finds that the investment in plant and equipment less depreciation expressed in dollars of constant purchasing power has increased nearly one third, while population has increased nearly 20 per cent and the civilian labor force nearly 14 per cent. The most important comparison is between the years 1929 and 1952 because this comparison shows the effect of *both* the depression and the war. It shows that the large outlays on plant and equipment during the last six and a half years have just about restored the relationship between plant and equipment, on the one hand and population and, on the other hand, labor force that existed twenty-three years ago. Investment in plant and equipment less depreciation has increased by about 34 per cent, when expressed in dollars of constant purchasing power, population by nearly 30 per cent, and the civilian labor force by 28 per cent. The growth of plant and equipment has been little more than the growth in population and labor force.

Since there is a long-run tendency for plant and equipment to grow relative to population and the labor force, plant and equipment per capita of population and per member of the labor force are probably still a little below long-term trends, but not very much. At any rate, it will not be easy for the scientists and the engineers to develop enough new investment opportunities to bring about a net increase in plant and equipment of $13 billion or $14 billion a year. That would be a rise of about 4 per cent. The labor force is growing at roughly 1 per cent a year. Of course, with the consumption of plant and equipment running at the rate of about $20 billion a year, the demand for plant and equipment will always be large. Nevertheless, we shall do well after the defense plants have been built to keep the total expenditures for plant and equipment (new and replacements) much above $30 billion a year. It is now running about $36 billion a year.

(5) *The fact that the number of new housing starts has for several years been substantially outrunning the increase in the number of families.* Residential construction was low during the depression and the war, so that the wartime and postwar marriages created an acute housing shortage. The shortage was aggravated by the high level of employment and incomes and by rent controls. Between the beginning of 1947 and the end of 1951, however, the number of dwelling units increased by over 6 million, while the number of families increased by about 4.3 million. In 1952, the increase in the number of dwelling units will be about 50 per cent greater than the increase in the number of families.

A high demand for houses may be expected to last for a considerable period of time because many people have a strong preference for living in detached dwellings that they own, because more and more people prefer to live outside congested districts, and because the monthly out-of-pocket cost of living in one's own home and paying installments on a mortgage is little greater than paying rent. Nevertheless, now that the housing shortage in most cities is no longer acute, it will not be easy to find a market for 1.1 million or 1.2 million dwelling units a year. One dare not expect the experience of 1949 to be repeated. At that time the demand for houses was so great that it was affected very little by the small drop in employment, and for the year as a whole more residences were started than in the previous year. From now on, the demand for houses will be considerably more sensitive to any drop in employment and incomes that may accompany a contraction of defense spending.

III

What are the principal elements of strength in the economy?

(1) *The large volume of liquid resources.* The Second World War, as is well known, saw an enormous expansion in personal holdings of liquid assets. These holdings, exclusive of trust funds, increased from about $45.1 billion at the end of 1939 to $138.6 billion at the end of 1945. They have con-

tinued to increase since the end of 1945, and at the end of 1951 stood at $156.8 billion. In the two years since the outbreak of fighting in Korea, personal holdings of currency and bank deposits grew by $6.7 billion, and holdings of savings and loan shares by $4.1 billion. These gains were partly offset by a drop of $2.1 billion in personal holdings of U. S. government securities. During the last two years there has been a fairly sizable rise of $6.5 billion in semiliquid assets, such as corporate securities, state and local government securities, credit-union shares, and other semiliquid assets. Individual holdings of liquid assets are smaller in relation to personal incomes than they were at the end of 1945, but they are still very large. They are an important stabilizing influence because the possession of substantial liquid assets tends to make persons keep up their expenditures in the face of falling incomes.

(2) *Fairly well-developed arrangements for partly maintaining many personal incomes in periods of contraction.* During the last twenty years the country has greatly improved its arrangements for assuring that any drop in incomes from production is partly offset by other forms of income, such as unemployment compensation, pensions, old-age assistance, or general relief payments. Such forms of income come into existence only because of contraction, and they fall substantially short of offsetting all of the loss of income from production. Hence, these forms of income can only mitigate a recession—they cannot prevent one. Their mitigating influence, however, is important. The arrangements that have been added to the economy in the last twenty years to provide income to persons who lose their jobs assure that the loss of income from a recession would be offset to a greater extent than ever before.

Of special interest is the spread of pension plans. In the event of a moderate recession, I suspect that many firms will adjust their work forces to a drop in demand by retiring older workers who have now passed the pensionable age rather than by laying off younger workers. I am not sure that this will be a desirable arrangement. Certainly it will introduce many new problems. The fact that fairly liberal pension arrangements now exist in a great many plants, however, is bound to cause managements to make greater use of retirements as a method of cutting the labor force when the demand for labor drops.

(3) *Some backlog of unmet needs.* The great deferred demand of individuals and business enterprises that accumulated during the Second World War has been pretty completely met. There is no reason to expect that deferred demand for automobiles, houses, and even industrial equipment will mitigate a new recession, as it did in 1949. In the field of public construction,

however, roads, schools, hospitals, water supply, sewage, and other public works, the unmet needs are still enormous. In fact, they are probably larger today than they were a few years ago. Certainly the car and truck population has been increasing faster than the capacity of roads. At the end of 1950 there were 50 per cent more passenger cars and trucks registered than at the end of 1940. Likewise, the population of school age has been increasing faster than schoolroom space. It takes time to make expenditures on public works because there usually is more or less disagreement about just what to do and where to build the new roads or new schools. The process of planning and reaching agreement has been going on steadily. It seems certain that for several years more, at least, states and localities will spend increasing amounts on various kinds of public works. These will help offset the drop in defense spending.

(4) *Recent important gains in the capacity of the economy to create new investment opportunities and new and better consumer goods.* Perhaps the most important thing that has been going on in the American economy in recent years is the enormous boom in science and technology. This boom goes back at least fifty years, but it has been particularly strong in the last twenty years. It is indicated by the fact that the number of scientists, technicians, and engineers in industrial and government research laboratories is nearly five times as large today as in 1930. The country is doubling the number of chemists every fifteen years and the number of physicists every eight years. Total expenditures on private and governmental research (not counting the large outlays on atomic energy) were seven times as large in 1947 as in 1930, and they are much larger today than in 1947. Technological research has, of course, been enormously stimulated by the Korean War, the defense program, and the keen military competition with Russia—despite the fact that the bad personnel policies of the armed services have aggravated the shortage of scientific and technical personnel by unnecessarily interrupting the training of many men.

No other country, except perhaps Russia and Canada, has experienced such a vigorous boom in science and technology as has the United States. This boom has greater economic significance than you might expect. Not only does the larger volume of industrial research mean that industry is better able than ever to increase the output of goods—it also means that industry is better able than ever to increase the demand for goods. Research increases the demand for goods in two ways. In the first place, it increases directly the number of investment opportunities by developing new and superior kinds of equipment, new processes, new ways of making things. In the second place, it helps industry offer consumers new and more attractive goods, thereby helping industry induce individuals to spend a little larger proportion of their incomes on consumption.

A rise in the proportion of incomes spent on consumption is quite important. Not only does the resulting rise in consumption increase the number of investment opportunities, and thus raise the amounts spent on investment goods, but it also raises the secondary effects on demand of every dollar spent on investment goods. It is obvious that the increase in demand that results from someone's decision to invest a dollar is not limited to the one dollar of additional demand for investment goods which is thereby created. The recipients of the dollar spent on investment goods spend most of the dollar on consumption, and the recipients of the part of the dollar spent on consumption spend most of their additional income on consumption, and so on indefinitely. It is plain that the larger the proportion of any increase in income which each recipient spends on consumption, the larger are the secondary effects of the original rise in spending which created the original increase in income. Hence, the success of industry in persuading people to spend a larger part of their income on consumption raises the secondary effects on demand of every dollar spent on investment.

The rise of applied science and technology in the last twenty years places American industry in a far better position than ever before to fight recessions because it puts the demand for goods to a greater extent than ever before within the control of industry.

(5) *The strong spirit of caution that dominates decision making by managements and consumers.* Both managements and consumers wonder what will happen when defense spending drops, and both fear a recession. This makes them cautious. The caution of managements is reflected in the reduction of inventories during the last year in retailing, in wholesale trade, and in the manufacture of nondurable goods—in short, in all branches of business except the manufacture of durable goods where the rise in inventories during the last year is explained by the expansion of military production. In August 1952, retail inventories were 10.4 per cent below a year ago, wholesale inventories 7 per cent below, and inventories in the manufacture of nondurable goods 1.5 per cent below. Part of these drops was attributable to the small decline in the wholesale price level, but most of it represented a drop in the physical volume of inventories.

Caution among consumers is much less pronounced than among businessmen. Nevertheless, personal savings are still fairly high in relation to incomes after taxes. It should be noted, however, that during the last fifteen or eighteen months there has been a marked rise in the disposition of consumers to buy. Between the second quarter of 1951 and the second quarter of 1952, the annual rate of personal incomes after taxes increased by $8.3 billion, but personal consumption expenditures increased by an annual rate of $10.4 billion. The diminishing caution of consumers is reflected also in the sharp rise in consumer credit during the last year. Consumers show no disposition to reach for goods, but the tendency for people to raise their spending for consumption faster than their incomes go up should be discouraged, at least during the next year or so.

IV

The foregoing analysis makes it plain that the drop in defense spending is likely to begin when normal business trends are downward and is likely to aggravate the contraction. Consequently, the country needs to make careful and ambitious plans to prevent or limit these effects. Furthermore, the country needs to begin making these plans and executing them at once and without regard to whether this or that special interest group likes the plan. Next only to the problem of working out a satisfactory foreign policy for the country, the problem of how to prevent or to mitigate a recession when defense spending drops will be the biggest problem of whoever shoulders the terrific responsibilities of the presidency next January. Indeed, the development of a satisfactory and successful foreign policy and the avoidance of recession as defense spending drops are closely related because even a moderate recession in the United States would have far-reaching repercussions throughout the world and would be a serious setback to our foreign policy.

What can the United States do to limit or prevent a general recession in business as defense spending drops? Some of the steps can best be taken by government; others can be taken by business. I shall not attempt to list the two kinds of steps separately, but I shall indicate briefly some of the most important ones.

Keep the plateau of defense spending as low as national security permits. The country badly needs arrangements by which the defense program can be critically reviewed from time to time in a responsible fashion by Congress. Throughout the last two years the executive branch of the government, including the armed services, has been far from frank. Production goals and schedules for defense goods have been proclaimed and the country has been told that national security would be imperiled if these schedules were not met. The schedules proclaimed in the early or middle months of 1951 have not been even remotely met. In July 1951, the country was informed by the Council of Economic Advisers that defense spending would be at the annual rate of $64 billion in the first quarter of 1952. In that quarter defense spending was at the annual rate of $46 billion—$18 billion less. And yet, no matter how far reality fell short of the schedule previously announced as necessary for security, the country has always been told in the quarterly reports of the Director of Defense Mobilization that the defense program was going fine, and that the security of the country was being built up at a satisfactory rate. In view of the lack of frankness which has characterized the setting of defense goals and schedules, I do not hesitate to ask whether the plateau of defense spending (including foreign aid) which has now been set as necessary, namely, between $60 billion and $65 billion a year, really is necessary. Perhaps it is, but the country has not been told why.

The advantages of a lower plateau (say around $55 billion a year) are substantial. The lower plateau would mean that the ultimate drop in defense spending would come later and be smaller. It would mean buying less equipment that will almost immediately become obsolete. It would mean that the cash budget for the present fiscal year would be in balance, or virtually in balance. Since a major problem of the new Administration will be averting or limiting a recession when defense spending drops, it is appropriate that the new Administration address itself quite promptly to the plateau problem and decide whether a lower and longer plateau is not compatible with our national security and our foreign policy.

In discussing the problem of averting a recession, however, I shall continue to assume that the drop in defense spending begins late in 1954 or early in 1955, and that the plateau is about $60 billion a year.

Liberalize unemployment compensation and pension plans. I do not suggest across-the-board liberalization because there are many cases where the ratio of benefits to customary earnings is too high. But there are also many cases in which it is too low. Such cases are found among the higher-paid workers. In order to get the maximum stabilizing effect from unemployment compensation and pension plans, the benefits should be as high relative to customary earnings as will not undermine the will to work.

Resist strongly for the next year or two further increases in the total volume of corporate and personal indebtedness. I have already explained why a pause is needed in the rise of private indebtedness. During the next year the rise in the indebtedness of the federal government will probably be sufficient to provide the country with the increased money supply required by the growth of the physical production. Some rise in private indebtedness may be inevitable, particularly if unions raise labor costs by pushing up wage rates faster than the increase in output per manhour. A rise in labor costs and prices will increase the need for working capital. Corporations can mitigate the tendency for the repayments of debt to aggravate recessions by replacing part of their indebtedness with equity securities and funding part of their short-term debts. The tremendous demand for capital during the last several years has pretty much precluded such replacement or funding. If, as seems likely, there is a drop in investment over the next two years, the opportunity should be used to pay off debts with funds from new equity issues or to fund short-term debts.

Plan a large program of toll roads and start and expand construction of them as defense spending drops. The nation is now wasting huge sums on a poorly planned road program. Because of failures to distinguish between the needs of local traffic and through traffic, roads which should serve through traffic are permitted gradually to be converted into congested business streets by allowing business establishments to grow up on the sides of the road. This has happened on such a large scale that the nation lacks an adequate system of through roads. The nation needs business streets and it also needs through roads, but where traffic is heavy the two uses do not mix—they conflict. Furthermore, the nation has too long uncritically followed the socialistic principle of the government's constructing roads and offering them free to whoever cared to use them. That method is inevitable in the case of local traffic, but it is not inevitable in the case of through traffic.

The strong and growing demand for roads well adapted to through traffic means that sufficient toll revenue could be collected on a considerable mileage of new limited-access highways in the East, Northeast, and parts of the Middle West, South, and Far West to pay maintenance costs and to amortize bonds issued to pay for the highways. Hence the demand for through-traffic roads creates an investment opportunity which can do much to offset the drop in defense spending. The new Administration should lose no time in planning a substantial expansion of toll roads to be under construction on a large scale early in 1955.

Step up industrial research to increase the volume of investment opportunities and to induce consumers to spend (or to attempt to spend) a larger proportion of their incomes on consumer goods. This is the principal contribution that business can make toward averting a recession as defense spending drops. It is by far the most important of all the possible antirecession steps. It may seem strange to suggest that research be stepped up when it is already being quite generally conducted under considerable pressure and is being hampered by lack of personnel. Furthermore, research has to be planned well in advance and it cannot be expected suddenly to produce new products, new methods, or new materials in response to a demand or need for them. Nevertheless, there is some good in its being known that late in 1954 or early in 1955, or even before, there will be a considerable need for new markets and that enterprises which are prepared to offer important improvements in their products or important new products will profit greatly. A general attempt to get ready for buyers' markets will go far to prevent buyers' markets from coming into being.

Cut taxes. This is the biggest contribution that the government can make toward averting or limiting a recession. In the present fiscal year the cash budget of the federal government will probably be in the red by a moderate amount. It will probably still be in the red in the fiscal year 1954–55—the year in which the drop in defense spending is expected to begin—unless the plateau of defense spending has been lowered or other cuts have been made in government spending. Let us assume that the prospect for the fiscal year 1954–55, with the defense expenditures dropping after January 1, 1955, is no better than a balance in the cash budget—or perhaps even a defict in the cash budget. Do I still suggest cuts in taxes? Some cuts in taxes will probably have taken effect about January 1, 1954.

The answer to the question must depend, of course, upon how large are the tax reductions effective in 1954. Unless tax cuts effective in 1954 are quite large, additional cuts will be needed when defense spending drops. Since the government will be spending less, the public must spend more, or total demand will drop. But the public will be able to spend more provided the government reduces its tax take from the incomes of the public. Furthermore, the public, with larger incomes after taxes, will be willing to spend more.

What kinds of taxes should be cut? If the excess-profits tax, or any part of it, is still on the books, it should certainly be cut because it penalizes just the kind of enterprise that can do most to increase employment. Except for the excess-profits tax, however, corporation taxes should not be touched. An attempt to stimulate investment in a period of possible recession by cutting the normal corporate income tax is not likely to be successful. The tax cuts most likely to stimulate employment are (1) reductions in excise taxes on those products for which demand is quite sensitive to price, so that a lower total of price plus excise tax would raise total consumer expenditures for the article; and (2) reductions in the personal income tax. Cuts in the personal income tax are roughly equivalent to increases in income and should produce pretty much the same rise in the demand for goods that higher incomes bring about. Since the income tax is already steeply progressive, the cuts should apply to all income brackets.

Tax reductions which accompany the drop in defense spending will probably mean that the cash budget of the federal government will be in the red during the period when defense spending is dropping. Unless private business shows signs of vigorous expansion, a period of falling federal spending is a time when some deficit in the budget is needed. As business later expands, the rising yield of federal taxes will probably soon put the budget in balance.

V

This analysis of the problem of averting a recession when defense spending drops shows that the problem is tough. Our analysis also shows that the instruments available for dealing with this tough problem are powerful. Certainly the possibility exists that the powerful instruments available will be used so wisely and effectively that no recession will occur. Human beings, however, do not usually show such wisdom, and will probably not do so in formulating policies when defense spending drops. Hence *some* recession is likely. But with industrial research continuing on a large scale and with the government and banks discouraging further net increase in private indebtedness, and with the government making cuts in taxes to take effect in 1954 or 1955, the recession can be kept mild. The development of policies to deal with the reduction in defense spending should be the major concern of business for the next two years and, next to the development of a satisfactory foreign policy, it should also be the principal concern of the new Administration.

11

The Financial Condition of the United States

Statement before the Finance Committee of the United States Senate, Washington, D. C., April 18, 1958.

My remarks will fall into six parts. In the first place, I wish to look briefly at the long-run prospects for the economy, which have been little affected by the current recession; in the second place, I wish to discuss the general nature and extent of the recession; in the third place, I wish to explore the causes of the recession; in the fourth place, I wish to examine briefly the prospects for recovery; in the fifth place, I wish to discuss what might usefully be done to promote recovery by business and government; and, finally, I shall comment briefly on some aspects of the problem of inflation.

I

The long-run prospects of the American economy rest primarily upon: (1) the capacity of the economy to raise productivity; (2) its capacity to increase the demand for goods; (3) its capacity to finance economic expansion.

Those economies of the world which are having trouble in growing lack one or more of these essentials for growth. The current recession has not significantly altered any of these three basic capacities of our economy.

(1) *The capacity of the economy to increase productivity.* Observation of the economies of the world shows that capacity to raise productivity depends far more upon the people and their institutions than upon natural resources. Institutions are important because they determine opportunity and security, but most important of all are the qualities of the people—their desire to better themselves, their courage, their spirit of enterprise, and their know-how. In this day and age the kind of know-how that counts most in

determining productivity is that of the scientist, the engineer, the business administrator.

Both the number of technicians and the scale of research in the American economy are growing rapidly. An even faster growth would be desirable, particularly in view of the rapid progress of Russia, but know-how in American industry is growing faster today than it has increased in the past. For example, the number of scientists and engineers employed in specialized research more than doubled between 1941 and 1953, increasing from 87,000 in 1941 to 192,000 in 1953, and expenditures by industry on research and development more than doubled between 1953 and 1956.[1] The McGraw-Hill capital-expenditures survey just issued (April 18) reports that research spending by industry will increase 14 per cent in 1958 and by 1961 will be three times the level of 1953. American industry will be spurred in the years immediately ahead by the research now in progress.

Research today is an industry—and an industry that is booming right through the recession. The growth of research is broadening the basis for success in business—success depends not only upon the quality of the operating organization and of the equipment but also upon the quality of research. The growing importance of research is leading to the founding of an increasing number of new concerns (most of them of small or of modest size) whose principal assets are the brains of their research staffs and the ability of the concern to attract men with first-rate minds.

American management in the last half century has developed methods (especially in cost control and industrial engineering) much admired by visiting productivity teams, but important new improvements in the art of management may be expected. We need and are gradually getting businessmen who are also scientists and engineers and who are good at working with scientists and engineers. In addition, it is reasonable to expect that special efforts will be made to speed up staff work and to solve the problem of reconciling originality and individuality among managers with good teamwork.

Productivity per manhour apparently had a sensational spurt between 1947 and 1952, increasing by 21.7 per cent in five years. But this spurt was probably more apparent than real and seems to have reflected abnormalities in the figures for 1947. The figures for the gross private product of the econ-

[1] *Economic Report of the President* (January 1954), p. 163. The research and development expenditures of industry increased from $1.430 billion to $3.250 billion, and total research and development expenditures for the country as a whole (including government and university expenditures) increased from $4 billion in 1953 to $6.5 billion in 1956. *Statistical Abstract of the United States,* 1957, p. 495.

omy, when expressed in dollars of constant purchasing power, show considerably less output in 1947 than in 1944 and about the same gross product as in 1945. But nongovernment employment in 1947 was about 4.8 million greater than in 1944 and nearly 5.6 million larger than in 1945. The large drop in output between 1944 and 1947 is not easily reconciled with the substantial rise in employment. Productivity in 1947 was probably affected by the absorption of a large number of soldiers, but the figures for 1947 may have been affected by statistical errors. In the next five years, from 1952 to 1957, the increase in productivity was much less—12.6 per cent, and in the two years 1955 to 1957, only 2.6%. Labor productivity of agriculture in recent years has risen twice as fast as labor productivity in nonagricultural industries, as the following table shows.[2]

Percentage increase in productivity per manhour paid for:	*1947–52*	*1952–57*	*1955–57*
All private industry	21.7	12.6	2.6
Agriculture	38.7	32.5	8.3
All private nonagricultural industries	17.5	9.4	1.4
Manufacturing industries only	16.4	13.7	1.1
All private nonagricultural and nonmanufacturing	18.1	7.6	1.9

The reasons for the poor record in productivity from 1955 to 1957 are not understood. The fact that the poor showing is made by all branches of industry suggests that it may be attributable to statistical errors. At any rate, the United States is building up rather rapidly a group of technicians who specialize in changing either the products or the processes of industry.

(2) *The capacity of the economy to increase the demand for goods.* As rising productivity makes goods more abundant, perhaps we shall eventually pause and ask what all this eager striving for more output is for. Up to the present, however, few Americans have asked that basic question. Living standards in this country are highly dynamic. This is not an accident. It reflects the great capacity of changing technology to stimulate demand by making available new goods (bicycles, phonographs, automobiles, telephones, radios, television sets, refrigerators, outboard motors, movie cameras, and scores of others) that people have been eager to incorporate into their standard of consumption. People have done this by spending a more or less constant proportion of their rising per capita incomes on con-

[2] *Economic Report of the President,* 1958, p. 107.

sumption. And technological progress has also stimulated enormous investment spending by developing innumerable new kinds of capital goods. This process will continue on an increasing scale. Keynes, who was the great believer in a chronic deficiency of demand, was led into his error by his failure to grasp the effect of technological research upon the demand both for consumer goods and for capital goods.

Success in increasing the demand for goods depends in part upon the strength of the spirit of enterprise in the community and upon the number of persons who have the optimism and courage to start new concerns. The business birth rate in the American economy is high. The number of business enterprises outside of agriculture has increased from 2,995,000 on January 1, 1947, to 4,182,000 at the beginning of 1955 and to 4,332,000 on June 30, 1957. There were 341,000 business births in 1953, 331,000 in 1954, 380,000 in 1956, and 211,000 in the first half of 1957.[3]

(3) *The capacity of the economy to finance expansion.* The economy is well supplied with funds to finance the expansion of industry. In spite of the great increases in tax rates on both corporations and individuals, gross private saving in the economy is virtually as large a proportion of the gross national product as it was back in 1929 when tax rates were low. It was 15.0 per cent of the gross national product in 1929 and 14.7 per cent in 1957. Personal saving as a percentage of disposable income has risen in spite of high taxes from 5.0 per cent in 1929 to 7.0 per cent in 1956 and 6.5 per cent in 1957. Gross business saving has had a small drop as a ratio of gross business product from 12.1 per cent in 1929 to 11.3 per cent in 1956.

Though one has heard much about the scarcity of savings in recent years, interest rates have been extraordinarily low. The yield on high-grade municipal bonds in 1957, according to *Standard & Poor's,* was 3.60 in comparison with 4.27 per cent in 1929, and the yield on Aaa bonds, according to *Moody,* was 3.89 in comparison with 4.73 per cent in 1929.

Business relies much less upon short-term debt for financing its operations than it formerly did. Thus between 1929 and 1957 when the gross privately produced output increased nearly threefold (from $100.0 billion to $395.5 billion), the loans of all commercial banks increased only a little more than half as fast—163 per cent (from $35.7 billion to $93.9 billion). Both short-term corporate debt and long-term corporate debt have increased much more slowly than sales of corporations (in billions):

[3] *Survey of Current Business* (April 1955), p. 15, and (January 1958), p. 6. Discontinued businesses were 338,900 in 1956 and 176,000 in the first half of 1957.

	Corporate sales	Corporate debt	
		Short-term	Long-term
1929	$138.6	$41.6	$47.3
1950	431.9	81.9	60.1
1956	605.5	110.9	97.3
1957	—	109.5	106.0

Sales in 1929 were 3.3 times short-term debt; in 1956, 5.5 times short-term debt.

It is of some interest that the cost of small loans ($1,000 to $10,000), as reported in the *Federal Reserve Bulletin,* is less in New York City than in eleven Southern and Western cities. For example, in June 1957, the rate on loans of $1,000 to $10,000 in New York banks was 5.24 per cent; in eleven Southern and Western cities it was 5.42 per cent. During the period of credit restraint, the spread between small loans ($1,000 to $10,000) and large loans narrowed from 1.5 per cent in 1955 to 1 per cent in 1957.[4]

In spite of the large volume of investment-seeking funds, the view is often expressed that there is a shortage of capital willing to take long chances for the sake of the possibility of large profits. The high business birth rate shows that there are a large number of persons who are willing to start enterprises, and it is common knowledge that many of these persons could use more capital. But the high infant-mortality rate among new enterprises shows that a large proportion of business starters have more courage and hope than judgment or skill. Hence, the would-be supplier of venture capital has a difficult problem of choice and he must have a fair proportion of big successes to compensate for his losses. Progress in the art of judging business risks would make feasible increases in investment in new concerns, but, in view of the difficulty of sizing up risks and the high mortality rate among new concerns, the assertion that the new enterprises as a whole are failing in substantial measure to get the amount of capital which they could put to good use is unproved.

The view is also held that there is a serious shortage of capital available for intermediate term loans to small enterprises—loans too long to be suitable for commercial banks and too small to be made in the open market through banking middlemen. There is some shortage of medium-term loan capital, but there is a greater shortage of attractive risks. These facts are

[4] *Federal Reserve Bulletin* (March 1958), p. 323. The rate on small loans was 5.0 per cent in 1955 and 5.5 per cent in 1957; on loans of $200,000 or more, 3.5 per cent in 1955 and 4.5 per cent in 1957.

demonstrated by the recent growth of industrial development corporations. Each of the six New England states has an industrial credit corporation. The most striking thing about these six companies is the fact that they have grown only at a moderate rate.

The Massachusetts Business Development Corporation, the largest of the six, made or participated in ninety-nine loans totaling $13,894,500 since 1953. The importance of these loans to various firms and communities is considerable, but the modest growth of the corporation indicates that attractive risks are not numerous and underlines the conclusion that attractive investment opportunities suitable for small, medium-term loans are more scarce than investment funds. In a highly competitive economy, such as the American one, in which profit margins tend to be low, the new concern must have a product of unique merit or it must have unique operating advantages or other special characteristics in order to offer an attractive risk for a development bank.

II

Of the $16 billion drop in the annual rate of gross national product between the third quarter of 1957 (the peak quarter of the boom) and the first quarter of 1958, about $10.5 billion, or 65.6 per cent, is accounted for by a shift from the accumulation of inventories at the rate of $3 billion a year to the liquidation of them at the rate of $7.5 billion a year. Total personal consumption expenditures dropped less than 1 per cent, but outlays for durable consumer goods dropped 10 per cent and investment in business plant and equipment about 5.9 per cent—and plans for future investment had dropped much more.

The drop in output is concentrated in the manufacture of durable goods, both industrial equipment and consumer durables, in mining, in parts of construction, and in transportation. Of the drop of 2,112,000 in nonagricultural wage and salary employment (seasonally adjusted) between August and March, considerably more than half (53.8 per cent) was in durable-goods manufacturing—which ordinarily supplies less than one fifth of the nonfarm jobs. In the fields of retail and wholesale trade, government service, and miscellaneous industries, which supply more than half the nonfarm wage and salary jobs, the drop in employment between August and March was only one third as large as in durable-goods manufacturing. Although the recession has been concentrated in durable-goods manufacturing and related parts of the economy, it has been spreading slowly and has been becoming broader. For example, most of the small drop of employment in trade and in the service and miscellaneous industries has come since December.

The recession is marked by widespread and vigorous efforts of business enterprises and banks to improve their liquidity—to reduce short-term liabilities and to build up short-term assets. This strong passion for liquidity seems to have started last September. Evidence of the pursuit of liquidity is found in the liquidation of inventories for the purpose of passing off short-term liabilities, in the high level of new long-term corporate bond issues, which have the purpose in part of providing funds for the repayment of bank loans, in the reduction of the business loans made by banks which, in the case of the weekly reporting member banks, have fallen by $1.409 billion between December 31 and April 2 (in comparison with the rise of $225 million in the same period last year), in the strong preference for short-term securities resulting in a widening spread between short-term and long-term interest rates, and in the reluctance of business concerns to start new projects involving long-term capital expenditures. One reason why an easy-money policy is important in a period of recession is that it facilitates and accelerates the achievement of greater liquidity.

Once enterprises have improved their liquidity to their satisfaction, they will undertake many expenditures that they are not now willing to make. The pursuit of liquidity has at times in the past been quite disastrous, producing re-enforcing reductions in disbursements and incomes. An encouraging feature of the current recession is that the pursuit of liquidity has not produced a self-sustaining spiral of contraction. On the contrary, the recession, as I have pointed out, has been characterized by a widening gap between the rate of final sales and the rate of production. At the peak of the boom, in the third quarter of 1957, production was exceeding final sales to individuals, government, industry, and foreigners by about $3.0 billion a year. By the first quarter of 1958, however, final sales were exceeding production by $7.5 billion a year. Between the third quarter of 1957 and the first quarter of 1958, production dropped by about $16 billion a year, but final sales dropped only about one third as much, or about $5.5 billion a year.

The marked excess of final sales over production has been made possible by the failure of cuts in production to pull down buying of goods by the government or to reduce appreciably the general level of personal incomes, which in March were only 1.7 per cent below the all-time high of last August. In addition, sales appear to have been helped by a small drop in the rate of personal saving between the third quarter of 1957 and the first quarter of 1958.

III

Proper analysis of the causes of the recession must await a more thorough examination of the existing data than has been possible up to now and the collection of additional data.

One way of looking at the recession is to regard it as a normal adjustment to a slower rate of growth aggravated by some unfortunate outside events such as credit policy, the procurement policies of the defense department, and the failure of most of the 1958 cars to meet the approval of the public. The high level of investment activity attained in 1956 made the economy vulnerable to contraction, since it was natural for enterprises to slow down the increase in their investment spending. It is always true to a considerable extent that the economic activity of today is determined by the economic activity of yesterday. To the extent that this is true, the economy tends to generate cycles. Thus, the adjustment of the economy to a slower rate of growth tends to take the form of a temporary contraction, since a drop in the rate of expansion means an absolute drop in the orders to equipment makers and suppliers of raw materials.

Decisions to cut the current rate of buying of plant and equipment were made in late 1956 and early in 1957. In durable-goods manufacturing, which felt the effect of the drop in automobile sales in 1956 and the failure of the sales of durable household goods to increase, appropriations for capital expenditures, according to the quarterly survey of the National Industrial Conference Board and *Newsweek*, apparently began to be cut either in the third quarter or the fourth quarter of 1956.[5] In nondurable-goods manufacturing, where orders held up better than in the durable goods, the drop in capital-goods appropriations began to decline in the second quarter of 1957. The drop in new capital appropriations was accompanied by a drop in new orders of manufacturers. The drop in new orders began in durable-goods manufacturing in November 1956, and in nondurables in January 1957.

Important to note is the fact that actual outlays on manufacturers' plant and equipment continued to expand long after new appropriations for capital spending started to be cut. In fact, the expansion of spending for business

[5] National Industrial Conference Board, *Business Record* (March 1958), pp. 92–93. Because of possible effect of the steel strike upon appropriations, there is some doubt as to whether the drop began in the third quarter or the fourth quarter of 1956, though the evidence on the whole indicates the third quarter.

plant and equipment did not reach a peak until the third quarter of 1957 by which time new appropriations for capital spending had dropped in the reporting companies in durable-goods manufacturing to less than half the appropriations of the third quarter of 1955 and to nearly 30 per cent below the new appropriations in the third quarter of 1956.[6] The fact that new capital appropriations in durable-goods manufacturing began dropping late in 1956 and new orders began dropping early in 1957 is interesting in the light of the testimony of Mr. William McChesney Martin, Jr., before this Committee on last August 15 to the effect that "the inflation spiral . . . seems to have begun about a year ago in the summer of 1956."[7]

Now it is never true that the economic activity of today is completely determined by the economic activity of yesterday. Various "outside" events initiate new responses of consumers and businessmen. The outside events may encourage or discourage expansion. They include the acquisition of new knowledge which opens up important investment opportunities, changes in the desires of consumers, the introduction of an immensely popular consumers' good (such as the "new look" in cars in the fall of 1954), the introduction of an important new good that people do not like (such as the weird collection of headlights, fins, tails, wings, etc., that is called an automobile in 1958), or a change in credit policy or in fiscal policy. These outside events may re-enforce or dampen the cycles generated by the dependence of today's economic decisions upon yesterday's results.

Three aggravating influences in 1957. In 1957, three outside influences (credit policy, federal fiscal policy, and the failure of the automobile industry to produce cars that met favor with consumers) combined to aggravate the tendency of the economy to react to a slower rate of growth by going into a temporary contraction. Tight credit policy tended to aggravate the tendency of the economy to contract because it retarded growth in new areas which might have offset to some extent the drop of investment in business plant and equipment. For example, overdoing credit restraint undoubtedly retarded the rise in investment in housing—this rise began in the late spring of 1957. A faster rise in housing would have helped offset the plans of business to cut investment in plant and equipment, and, in addition, it would have stimulated the demand for household goods, thereby discouraging cutbacks of investment plans by the makers of durable consumer goods.

By late July 1957, when the second-quarter figures on the gross national

[6] National Industrial Conference Board, *Business Record,* pp. 92–93.

[7] *Hearings before the Committee on Finance, United States Senate,* 85th Congress, 1st session, Part 3, p. 1319.

product became available, it became evident that credit restraint was being overdone. The figures on industrial production, new orders of manufacturers, and unfilled orders had for some months been strongly suggesting that the Federal Reserve was applying the brakes too hard. The figures on gross national production showed a drop in spending on durable consumer goods from an annual rate of $35.9 billion in the first quarter of 1957 to an annual rate of $35 billion in the second quarter. The figures on industrial production in June, which became available about the middle of August, showed no gain in the seasonally adjusted index of output of nondurable manufactures between December 1956 and June 1957; a drop in the index of output of durable manufactures from 167 in December to 163 in June; a drop in the index of primary metals production from 145 in December to 132 in June; a drop in the index of output of durable consumer goods from 141 to 129; a drop in the index of output of electrical machinery from 223 to 209. New orders of manufacturers had decreased from a high of $30 billion in November 1956 to $27.1 billion in June—well below new orders in June 1956, when new orders were $27.7 billion. Deliveries had been running behind new orders for six successive months, with the result that unfilled orders had fallen from $64.2 billion in December 1956 to $60.3 billion in June.

In the face of this overwhelming evidence that the economy was not expanding, the Federal Reserve continued to tighten credit and money. The bill rate increased from an average of 3.165 per cent in July to 3.404 per cent in August and to 3.578 per cent in September; the yield of Baa corporate bonds rose from 4.73 per cent in July to 4.82 per cent in August and 4.93 per cent in September. I do not know what tests led the Reserve to continue to tighten credit after production had ceased to expand or had started to decline and after new orders were declining. Apparently, the Reserve was attaching excessive weight to the movement of the price level and insufficient importance to the movement of production and new orders. In August 1957, when the Federal Reserve made the blunder of tightening credit instead of relaxing it moderately, the index of wholesale prices other than farm and food prices had scarcely moved since February 1957. The upward movement in wholesale prices was largely a result of the rise in farm prices, and it was the policy of Congress to encourage a rise in the prices of farm products. The consumer price index was rising, but much of this represented the price of food, and the policy of Congress is to encourage rises in the price of food up to so-called "parity." Most of the nonfood part of the consumer price index is not sensitive to credit policy.

By early October it was evident that a recession was beginning, but the

Federal Reserve allowed the bill rate in October to rise to 3.591 per cent, and other interest rates rose as well. Even after the Federal Reserve finally acted to relax credit, it moved very slowly. The bill rate in November averaged well above November 1956, and even in December the bill rate averaged about 3 per cent. Not until the week ending February 12, 1958, when the recession had been in progress for about six months did the volume of Federal Reserve credit exceed the volume of the previous year.

The tendency of the economy to adjust itself to a slower rate of growth by going into a temporary contraction was aggravated by the unfortunate timing of changes in federal fiscal policies. New defense contracts were cut from about $18 billion in the first half of 1957 to $12 billion in the second half. This cutting of orders seems to have been partly the result of the debt limit and partly the result of the failure of the Defense Department to keep up to date in deciding what to buy and what not to buy. It postponed much buying in order to re-evaluate its program, and these postponements came just when they aggravated the tendency of the economy to contract.

Finally, a late influence in aggravating the recession has been the failure of most of the 1958 cars to appeal to the public. Although poor automobile sales are partly a result of the recession, the unattractiveness of the 1958 cars appears to be an independent contributing cause of the recession. In spite of the recession, the drop in the buying of houses and most household durables is much less than the drop in the buying of cars.

No rolling adjustment. Another way of looking at the recession is to regard it as the result of the failure of new dynamic influences in the economy to develop at the precise time they were needed to replace old dynamic influences that were petering out. This explanation is not inconsistent with the one previously offered, but it has a different emphasis. Whereas the first explanation stressed the dependence of today's decisions upon yesterday's results, the second explanation stresses the looseness of the connections between the ever-changing succession of dynamic influences that keep the economy growing.

The way in which a changing succession of influences produces expansion is illustrated by the period 1954 to 1957. Early in 1954, when slow recovery from the recession began, three principal influences produced expansion. They were a drop in the rate of liquidation of inventories and finally a shift to the accumulation of inventories; a rise in consumption expenditures stimulated by a drop in the rate of personal saving; and a slow rise in investment housing stimulated by an aggressively easy credit policy. In the early part of 1955 recovery reached its second phase. A falling rate of personal saving ceased to be a stimulant, and investment in inventories became erratic. But the demand for housing continued to grow, and a strong demand for durable consumer goods developed. Both of these last two sources of demand reached their peak either just after or just before the middle of 1955. But about the time these influences for expansion petered out, three new influences for expansion took over. They were growing expenditures by governments for goods and services, business outlays on plant and equipment, and net foreign investment. These three influences sustained further expansion until early in 1957.

The recession may be regarded as a failure of new dynamic influences to develop to take the place of falling outlays on plant and equipment, falling defense orders, and falling net foreign investment. Technological research, though going on at a high rate, was not ready with enough new products or investment opportunities. The electric light and power industry began a rapid expansion, and the housing industry began to grow slowly even in the face of a tight credit policy. Had there been a good rise in nondefense spending by government (say on roads and schools) to offset the drop in defense spending, had an unreasonably low debt limit not been imposed on the government in 1957, and had the 1958 cars been more popular, a new succession of dynamic influences would have kept the economy slowly expanding. The recession must be regarded not as an inevitable result of the internal operation of our economy, but as the result of a mixture of bad luck and of our failure to see the problem in time to do something about it.

Averting recession. Could the recession have been averted? In the year 1957 we did not understand the situation well enough to take the action needed to avert the recession. Today we know much more than we knew a year ago, but even today we probably do not know enough to avert the sort of recession that hit us last year. Possibly ten years hence we shall have improved our arrangements for checking recessions sufficiently so that we shall then be able to handle the problem which we failed to see last year and which is still beyond our power to handle.

The difficulty arises from the long lead time in modern industry between decisions to spend and the actual date of spending. As a result of this long lead time, decisions by business to reduce the initiation of new projects may be laying the foundations for future contraction when actual spending is still rising, and when the immediate problem is one of controlling inflation. This was true in late 1956 and early 1957, when the deflationary decisions began to be made in the durable-goods industries before the end of 1956 and in the nondurable-goods industries early in 1957. The dilemma confronting the policy makers from this situation is how simultaneously to discourage both deflation and inflation—how to discourage *future cutbacks* in spending while discouraging *present increases* in spending. The problem is aggravated by the fact that considerable time is required for the statistics to indicate a trend. Hence, before one really knows that deflationary decisions need to be combated, the contraction may be imminent.

The effect of credit restraint in a period of boom is probably to aggravate any tendency to postpone the initiation of new projects. This conclusion is not necessarily an argument against the use of credit restraint to force the stretch-out of spending on old commitments. It means, however, that special steps need to be taken to offset the bad effects of credit restraint upon future spending plans.

I see no way of simultaneously discouraging present intentions to spend and encouraging future intentions to spend. Hence, when present spending (and incidentally, future spending) is discouraged, measures to *offset* the discouraging effect of credit restraint on future spending are needed. One procedure might be to offset impending cuts in private investment with increased purchases of goods and services by the government. The authorization of these government purchases should not be delayed until recession begins. Since the government (as well as business) requires considerable time before it is ready to make contracts, the time to authorize increased government spending is immediately after the reports show that private industry is reducing the initiation of new projects—no matter how much spending on old projects may still be growing. As a result, authorization for increased government spending may occur in the midst of a boom when the monetary authorities are struggling to control the amount of demand.

IV

Four present trends in the economy may be predicted with reasonable certainty. One trend is that government spending will continue to rise, though for some months to come the rise will be moderate. The federal government, in particular, has been moving only slowly to increase its spending. A second trend is the liquidation of inventories, which will continue for some months longer. It is impossible to judge how far the current drop in inventories will go. In the current recession the drop in inventories will be stimulated by the planned cuts in outlays on plant and equipment. Up to the end of February, the drop in the book value of inventories from August was half as large as the total drop in the recession of 1953–54. In the recession of 1953–54 liquidation of inventories continued for nine months after new orders of manufacturers began rising. But the volume of new orders of manufacturers, according to the latest figures (those of February), has not begun to rise. One may expect, however, some drop from the present exceptionally high rate of inventory liquidation. Liquidation of inventories was high in manufacturing in December, so that February marked the third month of high liquidation of manufacturers' inventories. A third trend in the economy is declining expenditures on business plant and equipment. A continued drop in these outlays is indicated by the recent reports of the Department of Commerce and the Securities and Exchange Commission. A fourth trend is a fairly steady rate of investment in housing. The slow rise in investment in housing in the face of general contraction was interrupted in the winter, though spending for housing held up quite satisfactorily. New measures to stimulate housing will probably require several months to take effect.

The principal uncertainty in the economy is what consumers will do about paying their debts and spending their incomes. In the recession of 1953–54, consumers cut their rate of saving substantially and continued slowly to increase the amount of their short-term indebtedness. But today consumers owe far more than they owed several years ago, and in February consumers cut their indebtedness by moderately more than the usual seasonal amount. Decisions of consumers to cut their debts rapidly could be dangerously deflationary. We lack experience to guide judgment concerning the probable behavior of consumers, but the strong long-term upward trend in consumer indebtedness, the plans of consumers to buy more secondhand cars than they purchased last year, and the use of easy credit terms as a selling device give reason to believe that a rapid reduction in consumer indebtedness will be avoided. An encouraging fact is that there appears to have been a moderate drop in the rate of personal saving between the last quarter of 1957 and the first quarter of 1958.

Recovery prediction. The net result of these several trends will create no great change in the level of economic activity in the next several months. Rising government expenditures and reduction in the rate of liquidation of inventories will tend to pull us up, and falling outlays on plant and equipment and possibly liquidation of short-term consumer indebtedness will tend to pull us down. Spending on housing will not make much difference one way or the other. Recovery will begin slowly when the rise in government spending and the drop in the rate of liquidation of inventories will more than offset the drop in spending on plant and equipment and possibly a slow reduction in short-term consumer indebtedness. It is difficult to judge when this will be, but my guess is that it will occur in the second quarter, so that the first quarter of 1958 will mark the low point of the recession. At any rate, in the first phase of recovery the two principal expansive influences will be rising government spending and a declining rate of liquidation of inventories. Personal incomes and personal consumption expenditures will cease to fall.

In the second phase of the recovery, which will probably begin in the latter half of 1958, government spending will continue to grow and liquidation of inventories will give way to accumulation of inventories, but new expansive influences will develop. Housing will begin to expand, consumers will begin to increase their short-term indebtedness, and personal consumption expenditures will rise slowly. But business spending on plant and equipment will undoubtedly continue to decline—business already made that decision and is not likely to alter it.

Sometime in 1959 business outlays on plant and equipment will start to rise. That will mark a third phase in the recovery. A slow rise in spending on plant and equipment is preferable to a rapid rise. It should be understood that the United States does not have the instruments through which to combat a sudden upsurge in buying. For example, after the poor car year of 1958, the automobile makers may come forward with models that meet the people's fancy, and small, economical cars may become the rage. We could have in about 1960 or 1961 a rush to buy cars that would be quite as disturbing as the 7.2 million car year of 1955.

When recovery occurs, one may count on its being accompanied for the first year or so by a rapid rise in the productivity of labor. This gain in productivity will retard the absorption of the unemployed. Unemployment in June, when the graduates and schoolchildren hit the labor market, will be well in excess of 5.5 million. In no months of 1958 will unemployment drop as low as 4 million. If, by the last quarter of the year, we raise the gross national product to $445 billion a year (about $20 billion a year above the rate of the first quarter), and if efficiency in the current year rises by the normal rate of about 2.5 per cent a year, we shall have about 4.4 million people unemployed.

V

What action is indicated by this prospect—particularly the prospect that we shall have more than 4 million unemployed throughout 1958 and probably well into 1959? Unfortunately, the failure of the Administration and of Congress to move promptly against the recession last fall or early in the winter increased the danger that we shall try to overstimulate recovery. Let me discuss first the steps that business might well take against the recession and then the steps that government might take. Most discussions of anti-recession policy have neglected the important role that business might play.

(1) *Steps that business might take.* Business is at all times attempting to enlarge its markets and to sell goods. Hence, the essential contribution that business can make to mitigating the recession is to do better and more vigorously the things that it usually does. But there are three principal aspects of business activity that deserve special emphasis. One is to prepare the way for the introduction of new and more attractive products by clearing out stocks of old products. This means price cutting, but it is price cutting that will have important advantages for the price cutter since it will prepare the ground for expanding the sale of new and better products.

A second step is for business to speed up its efforts to bring out new products or new models of old products. Since years are usually required to develop new products, the amount that can be done to speed the introduction of new products is limited. But in the case of products that are to be introduced late this year or early next year some acceleration may be possible. For example, it may be feasible in the case of some articles to incorporate in 1959 models some features originally planned for 1960 models.

Part of the process of making new models attractive is to surprise the consumer with attractively low prices. The recession is giving many enterprises both the incentive and the opportunity to take stock of their operating methods and to eliminate inefficiencies and wastes. Passing on much of the savings in cost to consumers is likely to be the most effective form of advertising.

At this point let me add a special word on the prices of consumer durable goods. These are the articles that are customarily sold at so-called "administered" prices, and there has been much ill-informed comment to the effect that firms selling at administered prices had increased their prices rather freely and that these increases had been the principal cause of the recent inflation. Nothing could be further from the truth. The index of the prices of durable commodities (household appliances, furniture and bedding, floor coverings, dinnerware, automobiles, tires, radios and TV sets, durable toys, sporting goods, water heaters) in February 1958 stood at 110.3 (1947–49 = 100), whereas the consumer price index as a whole was 122.5. Between 1955 and February 1958, the index of prices of consumer durables rose by just under 5 per cent, whereas the consumer price index as a whole rose by nearly 7 per cent. Sometimes it is said that prices of consumer durables have risen beyond the reach of consumers, but in February 1958 personal incomes were more than 12 per cent above 1955.

A third principal step that business concerns might take is to review their investment programs for 1958 and 1959. Reports of the Department of Commerce show that investment programs initiated by manufacturers in 1958 will represent expenditures of about $10 billion, or 29 per cent less than programs started in 1957. The rate of $10 billion a year, after correction for the drop in the purchasing power of dollars invested in capital, is the lowest rate of investment in manufacturing in any postwar year—even about 15 per cent below the investment in manufacturing in 1946 when the gross national product in physical terms was about one third less than it is today.

The hours worked indicate that durable-goods manufacturing was operating close to capacity in each of these two months. The percentage increases in output in this period of over two and a half years fall far short of the 3 per cent rise per year that is about normal for the economy. The recent large increases in capital expenditures in America represented rising prices to a greater extent than an increase in real capital. For example, though expenditures on industrial equipment increased by 25.5 per cent between 1953 and 1957, in dollars of constant purchasing power the rise was only 8.9 per cent. So 61 per cent of the increase in expenditures on equipment was pure inflation representing no physical expansion. And while outlays for equipment in terms of constant dollars rose by 8.9 per cent, the labor force increased by 6.5 per cent. And the story of industrial construction is essentially the same—more than two thirds of the increase in expenditures on industrial construction between 1953 and 1957 was pure inflation and less than one third represented an expansion of physical plant.

Various factors have influenced the investment programs for 1958. One influence has been the desire for liquidity that I have already mentioned. Another influence has been the widespread illusion that a considerable excess of productive capacity has been created. This view is ill-founded. There are a few industries which grew too fast relative to industry as a whole, but in manufacturing as a whole there has been a very modest rise in capacity during the last several years. The best way to measure the increase in capacity in manufacturing is to compare the change in the seasonally adjusted index of output for two periods of peak production. The following table shows the changes between May 1953, when output set an all-time record up to then, and December 1956, when output set a new all-time peak.

	May 1953	*December 1956*	*Percentage increase*	*Average weekly hours* *May 1953*	*Dec. 1956*
Total manufactures	139	149	7.2	40.7	41.0
Durable	156	167	7.1	41.5	41.9
Nondurable	123	130	5.7	39.5	39.7

(2) *Steps that the government might take.* The outstanding issue in govment policy toward the recession is whether or not a tax cut would be desirable. But this question has been virtually decided. Congress has not passed a tax cut, and it has not squarely faced up to the issue of whether or not a tax cut is desirable. Nevertheless, it has passed a number of measures that will lead to substantial increases in expenditures in the fiscal year 1958–59. At the same time, the recession has been cutting the yield of existing taxes. Hence, there is good reason to expect a deficit of at least $5 billion to $6 billion in the cash budget for 1958–1959, and the deficit may well rise to $7 or $8 billion. A tax cut would increase the deficit above this amount. Furthermore, a tax cut would not begin to stimulate the economy until about the time that the steps already taken (accelerated placement of contracts and new spending measures passed by Congress) would begin having a pronounced effect.

Government spending, deficit, and tax policies. The economy will undoubtedly need a substantial budget deficit to stimulate expansion next year. The immediate question is whether the economy will need a larger deficit than will be produced by present taxes and present planned expenditures. The prospective deficit will be more than sufficient to offset the drop in the rate of investment in industrial plant and equipment below the all-time high of the third quarter of 1957. It will not be sufficient to produce full employment, but it will be large enough to give the economy all the stimulation it can stand without rapidly pushing up costs and prices. Hence, I believe that the tax cut should be confined, as I shall explain presently, to temporary reductions in excise taxes.

The government has done a remarkably poor job of speeding up its spending on goods and services. Mr. Eisenhower had announced in the middle of February that the government planned to place $13 billion of major defense procurement contracts in the first half of 1958. At the rate at which procurement contracts were being let in January and February, actual contract placing will fall far short of this goal. Furthermore, actual spending for goods and services by the federal government for the first quarter of 1958 was no greater than in the fourth quarter of 1957. It will be anti-inflationary for the government to spend as much money in the calendar year

1958 as possible, and particularly in the first half of 1958. The reason is that the economy will have more unused capacity during this period than it will have later on.

In addition to stepping up spending in the immediate future as much as possible, moderately large long-term increases in spending should also be planned. The United States is a growing country, with its population rising by about three million a year and with its output growing at a normal rate of around $14 billion a year or more. Such a growing economy needs more and better schools, roads, recreation areas, and projects for the development of its resources. If the economy were to succeed in achieving full-capacity operation by the early fall of 1959, the gross national product should be around $470 billion a year, or about $45 billion above the present rate. Certainly a substantial part of this increase of $45 billion in the gross national product should go for much-needed public works of various sorts.

There are two steps for mitigating the recession that deserve specific comment. One step is to provide the states with funds to pay extended unemployment benefits but at the same time to impose higher standards on the states. The imposition of higher standards is quite as important as producing funds for the payment of extended benefits. Unless higher standards are imposed, the states will neglect to improve their unemployment-compensation schemes, expecting the federal government to bail them out. The higher standards should include a minimum rate of contribution and should raise the ratio of benefit payments to weekly wages. In 1957 the average weekly unemployment benefit paid by the states was only 34.0 per cent of the weekly earnings of factory workers. In 1939 benefits averaged 44.7 per cent of the weekly wage of factory workers.

A second step is to suspend (or at least cut in half) until October 1, 1958, or November 1, 1958, the 10 per cent excise tax on automobiles. This tax cut would diminish rather than aggravate the long-run danger of inflation. The temporary cut would encourage many people to buy 1958 cars rather than to wait for 1959 cars. This would put thousands of idle automobile workers back to work, increase personal incomes and corporate profits, and raise the revenue yielded by personal and corporate income taxes. It would have little or no net effect on the size of the budget deficit in 1958–1959; it would limit slightly the increase in demand for goods in 1959 when demand will be large and rising; and it would increase to some extent the supply of secondhand 1958 cars on sale in 1959 and 1960 when the availability of these secondhand cars would furnish desirable competition for new cars and thus be a useful check on inflation.

Of great help would be a good supply of mortgage money, for that would stimulate housing by reducing interest rates. The desire for liquidity has temporarily been limiting the effect of Federal Reserve policy upon long-term interest rates and, therefore, upon the supply of mortgage money. The new reductions in Reserve requirements announced the morning of April 18 may soon produce some effects upon the long-term part of the mortgage market. The gradual achievement of liquidity will eventually increase the supply of long-term money and push down interest rates on mortgages and other long-term obligations. It is important, however, that this effect be achieved promptly because building is sensitive to the cost of mortgage money. If the long-term money market continues to be more or less isolated from the short-term, the Federal Reserve should consider small direct purchases of long-term government securities.

Let me digress briefly to express disagreement with the proposal made by Mr. William McChesney Martin, Jr., before this Committee on August 13, 1957, in which Mr. Martin urged that the Employment Act be amended "by a straightforward explanation and directive to all agencies of the government that anti-inflationary actions are to be taken promptly whenever the cost of living begins to rise." [8] Since the cost of living has been rising right through the recession, such an amending of the Employment Act, had it been in effect, would have forced the Federal Reserve and other government agencies to have been taking anti-inflationary actions right through the recession. The inadequacy of price movements as the sole guide to government economic policies is also illustrated by the experience of last summer, when too much attention to price movements and too little attention to production movements caused the policy of credit restraint to be carried to excess and aggravated the recession.

VI

An economy which has a great capacity, through large and expanding technological research, to increase the demand for goods and which possesses a powerful trade-union movement should not be surprised at finding itself confronted with a more or less chronic problem of inflation. The tendency for demand to outrun productive capacity can be controlled by a policy of credit restraint, though the operation of credit restraint obviously poses many problems. Far less tractable is the problem resulting from the tendency of

[8] *Hearings before the Committee on Finance, United States Senate,* 85th Congress, 1st session, Part 3, p. 1271.

trade unions to push up wages far faster than the increase in output per manhour. In the period 1947 to 1956, average hourly compensation of employees in nonagricultural industries increased 61.4 per cent while real product per employee hour increased only 26.1 per cent. The excess of the increase in compensation over the increase in productivity averaged over 3 per cent a year. The increase in compensation exceeded the rise in productivity in all but two out of the last nine years.

There is no quick and early solution to the problem of wage-push inflation. The problem can be mitigated to an important extent by inventions and administrative improvements that increase the productivity of labor without raising the demand for capital goods. But these methods can hardly be expected to raise productivity as fast as unions push up wages. So we come face to face with the essential fact that most employers are not strong enough to resist the demand of unions.

The current recession, I think, is making the problem of wage-push inflation slightly more tractable by increasing the opposition of both employers and the public to wage demands that outrun productivity. The recession is stiffening the resistance of employers to excessive wage increases because it is teaching some employers the costliness of agreeing to substantial wage increases far in advance. It is safe to say that the steel industry will long remember the wage increases for 1958 which it agreed to back in 1956. Contracts of two or three years' duration are almost a necessity in modern industry, but the experiences of 1958 will warn employers to go easy in committing themselves to large future wage increases.

More important than the effect of the recession upon the resistance of employers will be its effect upon the attitude of the public toward wage increases. The recession, however, has helped the public see more clearly than ever that rising wages are a principal cause of rising prices. The issue had been confused by the honest belief of many people that rising wages simply reflected a strong demand for goods. But wages have continued to rise throughout the recession in the face of falling demand for labor and goods. Thus the recession has given the public a clearer picture than ever of the responsibility of rising wages for rising prices. The more plainly the public sees the relationship between wages and prices, the more carefully it will appraise the demands of the unions. The public is obviously getting tired of the stiff annual rounds of wage increases that far exceed the contribution of the workers to productivity. An atmosphere is being built up in which employers who take long and costly strikes in an attempt to hold wage increases down to increases in productivity will have strong public support.

These changes do not promise an early disappearance of the problem of wage-push inflation, but they give reason for believing that the tendency of wages to outrun productivity will be less in the future than it has been during the last ten years.

12

Inflation—A Problem of Shrinking Importance

Address before the Association of Reserve City Bankers, Boca Raton, Fla., April 13, 1959; The Commercial and Financial Chronicle, April 23, 1959.

I

THE postwar world has been an age of inflation. All of the industrial countries of the free world have had rising price levels, and in the less-developed countries price levels have been rising also, in many cases faster than in the industrial countries. Accurate comparisons of changes in the price levels in different countries are not possible because of differences in the ways of measuring prices and differences in the composition of the index numbers. Nevertheless, one is justified in saying that there have been great differences between countries in the amount of price increase.

The rise in the consumer price index between 1948 and 1957 among the industrial countries outside of the Iron Curtain ranged from a low of 9.4 per cent in Switzerland to a high of 124 per cent in Austria. The United Kingdom had a rise of 50.6 per cent; Sweden, of 46.8 per cent; France, of 76.7 per cent; West Germany, of 14 per cent. No industrial country in this period had a drop in the price level.

The record of the United States during this period of inflation has been exceptionally good. Between 1948 and 1957 the consumer price index here rose 16.9 per cent. Only three of the industrial countries, Belgium, Switzerland, and West Germany, had a smaller rise in the price level during this period. But ill-informed talk about inflation in the United States has aroused unjustified fears and has given Americans an inferiority complex on the subject of prices. Few Americans are aware that this country has done a far better job of limiting the rise in the price level than have most other industrial countries. Few Americans know that the index of consumer prices has risen in the United States during the last ten years less than one third as much as in the United Kingdom, only one fourth as much as in France, one seventh as much as in Austria, only one third as much as in Norway, less than half as much as in Sweden, the Netherlands, or Denmark, and over one third less than in Italy or Canada.

Ill-informed talk about inflation has also led many Americans to overlook the fact that the rate of increase in prices is diminishing. The drop in the rate of price increase has been world-wide. In the United States, the consumer price index increased 73 per cent in the period 1939 to 1948 and only 20 per cent in the period 1948 to 1958. In the five years ending in 1953 the consumer price index rose by 11.3 per cent; in the five years ending in 1958 the increase in the index was only 7.8 per cent.

As the rise in the price level has become more gradual, talk about inflation has increased. Perhaps the reason is that people are gradually perceiving that inflation is not a temporary phenomenon, due to acute but passing maladjustments, but that it is a lasting phenomenon due to built-in characteristics of the economy that are not easily changed.

II

The causes of price movements during the last twenty years have varied from country to country and from time to time. It is a mistake to generalize from the specific causes that have caused inflation in particular countries at particular times. Each case of inflation must be examined in the light of the particular facts. Our concern should be focused especially upon the future, and we should seek to discover whether the economy has acquired characteristics that give good reason to expect the price level in the future to be stable, to rise, or to fall.

Three principal explanations of inflation in the United States have been advanced: (1) the great increase in the money supply that occurred during the war; (2) the increase in so-called "administered prices" in certain industries, particularly steel and automobiles; and (3) the effect of rising labor costs.

The effect of great increases in the money supply. The war was financed to a substantial extent by borrowing from the banks. As a result, the money supply (measured by demand deposits and currency outside of banks) by 1945 was almost three times as large as in 1939. In relation to the gross national product at current prices, the money supply was about 46 per cent greater than in 1939. The war had forced people to go without many things and had built up an enormous backlog of unsatisfied needs for goods, particularly durable consumer goods and capital equipment. It is not surprising that the combination of a huge increase in the money supply and the accumulated need for goods produced a substantial upsurge in prices once controls and ceilings were removed. The consumer price index had risen 40 per cent between 1939 and 1946; it rose another 23 per cent between the years 1946 and 1948. The rise in the index of wholesale prices was even greater.

The year 1948 may be regarded as a dividing year in the postwar economic history of the United States. It was followed by the first drop in the price level in the postwar period—for prices in 1949 were somewhat lower than in 1948. The year 1948 was close to the time when the economy reached the peak of its liquidity. In terms of current dollars, the economy reached its maximum degree of liquidity in 1946 when there was 52.2 cents of demand deposits and currency outside of banks for every current dollar of gross national product. From then on the economy rapidly lost liquidity, for the money supply increased far less rapidly than the dollar volume of the gross national product. By 1957 the money supply was down to 31.5 cents per dollar of gross national product. When the gross national product is expressed in dollars of constant purchasing power, the maximum liquidity of the economy is found to have occurred in the year 1947, when there was 36.4 cents of demand deposits and money outside of banks for every dollar of gross national product expressed in 1958 prices.

Explanations of inflation that are valid for a period when the economy was becoming more liquid are not necessarily valid for a period during which the economy was losing liquidity. Hence, though inflation up to about 1948 can be explained in large part by the increase in the money supply, that explanation is not satisfactory for the subsequent period when real national product was growing considerably faster than the money supply. For this subsequent period the money-supply theory would call for a drop in the price level, but prices continued to move upward, though at a slower rate.

The period subsequent to 1948, when output was outrunning the money supply, was also a period when public and private debts were increasing. There was a great increase in home ownership with a rapid expansion of mortgage indebtedness, a large growth in short- and intermediate-term consumer credit, a substantial rise in the gross debt and guaranteed issues of the federal government, and a large growth in state and local government debts. All in all, between 1948 and 1958 the net public and private debt of the country increased by over $324 billion, or nearly 75 per cent. And yet, in spite of this enormous growth in debt, the money supply grew less rapidly than physical output. Between 1948 and 1957 the growth in the money supply was 24 per cent, and the growth in the gross national product, expressed in dollars of constant purchasing power, was 39 per cent. The economy was becoming less liquid because much of the increase in debt was being financed out of savings. Tables 1 and 2 set forth the essential facts concerning the changing liquidity of the economy.

Table 1

Year	*Gross national product in 1958 prices*	*Consumer price index (1947–49 = 100)*	*Total deposits and currency excluding U.S. govt. deposits (billions)*	*Total demand deposits and currency (billions)*	*Total money supply per dollar of gross national product in 1958 prices*	*Total demand deposits and currency per dollar of gross national product at 1958 prices*	*Annual rate of turnover of demand deposits in 337 or 338 reporting centers*
1929	$201.0	73.3	$54.6	$26.4	27.2¢	13.1¢	—
1939	208.8	59.4	63.3	36.2	30.3	17.3	—
1945	354.1	76.9	150.8	102.3	42.6	28.9	13.5
1946	312.2	83.4	164.0	110.0	52.5	35.2	14.1
1947	311.8	95.5	170.0	113.6	54.5	36.4	15.5
1948	323.7	102.8	169.1	111.6	52.2	34.5	16.6
1950	351.6	102.8	176.9	117.7	52.3	33.5	17.2
1957	451.1	120.2	227.7	138.6	50.5	30.7	23.0
1958	437.7	123.3	241.0	143.1	55.1	32.7	22.9

Table 2

Year	*Gross national product at current prices (billions)*	*Total amount of money per dollar of gross national product*	*Demand deposits and currency outside of banks per dollar of gross national product*
1929	$104.4	52.3¢	25.3¢
1939	91.1	69.5	39.7
1945	213.6	70.6	47.9
1946	210.7	77.8	52.2
1947	234.3	72.6	48.5
1948	259.4	65.2	43.0
1950	284.6	62.2	41.4
1957	440.3	51.7	31.5
1958	437.7	55.1	32.7

The effect of so-called "administered" prices. By the ambiguous expression "administered prices" is apparently meant prices fixed by a few large concerns which are not under pressure to keep profit margins modest for fear that their customers or someone else will start in business in competition with them. There is impressive evidence that these situations exist in the case of steel and automobiles and perhaps some other industries as well, but there are not enough such situations to explain the rise in the price level. Indeed, the durable consumer goods category in the consumer price index, which would show the greatest effect from so-called administered prices, has risen less in recent years than other parts of the index (Table 3). So-called

Table 3

Year	*All items*	*Durables*	*New cars*
1939–1958	108.2%	97.0%	151.9%
1953–1958	7.9	—2.0	14.5
1955–1958	7.7	5.0	15.6

Changes in the quality of cars preclude accurate measurement of changes in their prices.

administered prices have a strong appeal to politicians as a cause for inflation because they give the politicians a chance to blame "big business," but they are not a satisfactory explanation of inflation. They apply to too few prices. A special difficulty with administered prices as an explanation of inflation is that the period 1947 to 1958 has been a time of shrinking profit margins, indicating that sellers were having difficulty in maintaining profits. This matter is discussed below.

The effect of higher labor costs. Inflation in the United States in the period from about 1947 or 1948 to the present, when the liquidity of the economy was shrinking and profit margins were narrowing, is best explained through rising labor costs. Indeed, rising labor costs seem to have played an important role in pushing up prices even during the period prior to 1948 when the money supply was growing faster than output. In the fourteen years from 1933–34 to 1946–47, hourly earnings of factory workers increased more than output per manhour in nine years and exceeded the rise in the consumer price index in eleven years. But it is in the period subsequent to 1947 that the effect of rising labor costs upon prices is particularly impressive. The following five facts stand out:

(1) The period from 1947 to 1958 was a time of decreasing profit margins. This fact is important because it shows that the initiative in raising

prices was not being taken by employers. In the four years 1947–1950 inclusive, the net income of nonfinancial corporations after taxes per dollar of sales averaged 4.45 cents. In the next four years the average net income was 4.10 per dollar of sales; and in the three years, 1955–1957 inclusive, it was about 3.3 cents per dollar of sales.[1]

(2) During the eleven-year period 1947 to 1958, the rise in hourly compensation for all workers in private industry exceeded the gain in real product per manhour in eight years. For the eleven-year period the rise in hourly compensation was almost twice as large as the rise in real product per manhour. The rise in hourly compensation was 66.7 per cent; the gain in real product per manhour was 33.6 per cent. In a consolidated income statement of American business, labor costs are by far the most important cost. In 1957 they represented about two thirds of income originating in business and about four fifths of income originating in corporate business.[2] In other words, in a consolidated income statement of American business labor costs are twice as important as all other costs combined. When labor costs are this important and when year after year the hourly compensation of employees outruns output per manhour, some increase in the price level is obviously necessary.

(3) In every one of the last eleven years without exception the average hourly compensation of workers in private industry rose more than the consumer price index. Some people have suggested that wages were simply chasing prices up, but the fact that in eleven successive years hourly earnings rose more than prices indicates that the reverse was true—that prices were chasing wages up.

(4) In every one of the last eleven years except one, the hourly compensation of workers in private industry rose by more than nonfarm wholesale prices.

(5) In every one of the last eleven years except one, the hourly compensation of workers in private industry rose by more than the wholesale price of finished goods.

Table 4 compares the change in wages with changes in productivity and in prices.[3]

[1] 85th Congress, 1st session, Joint Committee Print, *Productivity, Prices, and Incomes,* Table 26, p. 109; and U. S. Department of Commerce, *U. S. Income and Output,* p. 205.

[2] *Supplement to Survey of Current Business: U. S. Income and Output,* (U. S. Department of Commerce, 1958), pp. 134–135. In 1957, of $308.0 billion of income originating in business, $206.1 billion represented compensation of employees. Of $202.0 billion of income originating in corporate business, $161.9 billion represented compensation of employees.

[3] The changes in the year-to-year compensation of employees are computed from data in *Hearings before the Joint Economic Committee,* 86th Congress, 1st session, p. 782.

Table 4

Year	*Increases in average hourly compensation of workers in private industry*	*Change in real product of private industry per manhour*	*Change in consumer price index*	*Change in nonfarm wholesale prices*	*Changes in wholesale prices of finished goods*
1947–48	8.5%	3.6%	7.6%	8.5%	7.9%
1948–49	2.7	2.9	—0.9	—2.0	—2.8
1949–50	5.7	7.1	0.9	3.7	1.8
1950–51	9.3	2.5	8.0	10.4	9.5
1951–52	5.8	2.2	2.3	—2.3	—0.5
1952–53	5.9	4.1	0.8	0.7	—1.0
1953–54	3.5	1.8	0.3	0.4	0.3
1954–55	2.9	4.4	—0.3	2.2	0.2
1955–56	6.0	0.6	1.5	4.4	2.8
1956–57	6.0	2.7	3.4	2.8	3.6
1957–58	3.0	1.0	2.7	0.3	2.3

III

It would be an oversimplification to attribute the tendency of wages to outrun productivity solely to the unions. Even unorganized workers possess considerable bargaining power under conditions of high employment through their ability to withhold efficiency. But there is abundant evidence that unions have been successful in achieving their objectives of raising money wages.

Union membership was only a small part of the labor force until the federal government in 1933 and 1935 adopted the policy of vigorously encouraging membership. Today about half of the blue-collar workers in industry are union members, and unions are particularly strong in the large companies in heavy industry that have the highest productivity and set the pattern for wage changes. Today virtually no one works at production jobs in the coal industry, the steel industry, the automobile industry, the rubber industry, the can industry, the flat-glass industry, the railroad industry, the men's-clothing industry, the women's-garment industry, the airplane industry, the air-transport industry, and in many parts of the construction industry, the paper industry, the electric light and power industry, and the trucking industry, except on terms agreed to by some union.

One bit of evidence of the influence of unions on wages is the fact that wages have outrun productivity in the face of declining profit margins—a set of conditions that strongly suggests that wages have been pushed up much more than bid up. A second bit of evidence is that wages continued to rise in the face of falling demand for labor throughout the recession of 1958. A third piece of evidence is the fact that the rise of wages in the recession was greater in durable-goods manufacturing, where the recession was more severe but the unions stronger, than in nondurable manufacturing. A fourth bit of evidence is the success of the United Mine Workers in raising wages in the face of shrinking employment and in the success of a few unions, such as the hosiery workers, in driving nearly all union firms out of business.

Some spokesmen for unions have asserted that unions have failed in their essential purpose of raising money wages. By comparing price increases in highly organized industries with price increases in poorly organized industries, they have argued that unions have not affected prices. Such comparisons are meaningless. When labor costs are two thirds of all costs, it is impossible to isolate their effect and to judge the influence of unions by whether or not the final stages in producing a commodity happen to be highly organized or not.

IV

What about the future of inflation? The influences affecting the price level change from time to time. I am pessimistic about the possibility of halting creeping inflation largely because I am optimistic concernings the prospects of the economy and its capacity to grow. I expect that in the decades immediately ahead the movement of the price level will be affected by three principal influences: (1) the expansion of technological research; (2) the growing demand for government services; and (3) the great bargaining power of trade unions. Each of these influences will tend to produce a slow rise in the price level.

The expansion of technological research. Technological research, as everyone knows, has been growing rapidly for over fifty years. Measured in terms of the number of scientists and engineers devoting full time to research, this activity is more than five times as large as it was in 1930; measured by the ratio of research expenditures to the gross national product, it is about thirteen times as large. Technological research affects both the demand for consumer goods and the demand for capital goods. It affects the demand for consumer goods by developing new kinds and varieties of consumer goods. People acquire these additional goods by going into debt, by drawing on accumulated savings, or simply by saving a smaller proportion out of a given volume of income. Technological research affects the demand for capital goods partly by developing new consumer goods that require new plant and equipment for their manufacture and partly by developing new processes and equipment that represent new investment opportunities.

The prospect that technological research will continue to expand and that it will raise the capacity of the economy to discover and develop new investment opportunities creates the probability that we shall be living most of the time in strong sellers' markets. That means that it will be difficult to prevent the price level from rising. This prospect shows how erroneous it is to assume that inflation necessarily means that there is something wrong with the economy. A rising price level (inflation, if you will) is likely to be a sign of vigorous economic health, of an economy possessing great capacity to develop new investment opportunities.

The growing demand for government services. The strong demand for goods will be re-enforced by the growing demand for government services. As population grows and as the country becomes more crowded, as per capita incomes increase, as standards of consumption rise, the development of natural resources, the invasion of space, the efforts to control the weather, the provision of solitude and recreation, the support of science and education, the provision of transportation facilities will all make increasing demands on the government. We shall be reluctant to let the government spend a larger part of our incomes for us, but we shall also be faced with the fact that we have common needs that only the government or public corporations can satisfy. To some extent the dilemma may be met by curtailing the free services of government and expanding the service charges and fees. Such changes make for fiscal soundness, but the service charges and fees do tend to raise the price level.

The great bargaining power of trade unions. In the kind of economy that we have and may expect to have, can trade unions be expected to limit their demands to the increase in real output per manhour? Certainly under most circumstances unions will have difficulty in justifying any greater demand, for increases that exceed the gain in productivity mean that the particular group of workers is claiming the right to profit at the expense of the rest of the community. But the fact that wage increases which exceed the average rise in productivity cannot under most circumstances be justified does not mean that they will not be made. Furthermore, although some employers now declare that they will not concede increases that exceed gains in productivity, one must remain skeptical until one sees employers hold the line in the strong sellers' markets that vigorous economic expansion may be expected to create.

V

What is done about inflation depends a good deal upon circumstances, so that a complete policy cannot be spelled out in advance.

Government spending is not the heart of the inflation problem. Indeed, this year we are being given a demonstration of the rather remote relationship between the state of the budget and inflation. The federal government is experiencing by far the largest cash deficit since the Second World War. Nevertheless, in February the consumer price index was no higher than it was in June, and the wholesale price level was virtually the same as in June. But the new and important demands that are being made on the government indicate the need for the government to review carefully the many subsidies that it now grants for the purpose of determining which are meritorious and which are not and to develop a program of service charges and fees for government services that are of commercial value to special groups. Finally, in order to reduce the inflationary impact of government fiscal operations, the government should at long last take the necessary steps to build up a healthy nonbank market for long-term government bonds. There has not been such a market for over ten years. The banks and insurance companies have been liquidating their holdings and the securities thus released have been purchased, not by the general public, but by government-controlled trust funds. Building a market for long-term government bonds obviously means paying the market rate of interest. This means getting rid of the present ceiling of 4.25 per cent. The President has mentioned the desirability of eliminating the ceiling, but he has shown no disposition to make it an issue and to fight for it. But unless the ceiling is eliminated, there will not be a broad market in long-term governments—unless the government is willing to bring out a savings bond without a maturity date, paying interest equal to a fixed amount of purchasing power. The failure of either the present Administration or the previous Administration to face up to the fact that there is no broad market for long-term governments illustrates the sharp contrast between what people are willing to say about inflation and what they are willing to do.

Since the heart of the inflation problem is the tendency of wages to outstrip productivity, the central attack on inflation should be directed to limiting the economic power of trade unions. Depriving unions of some of their present extraordinary privileges, such as the use of coercive picketing to force people to join or the conscription of neutrals in labor disputes, would remove some glaring injustices, but would have little effect upon the bargaining power of most unions. Breaking up some of the large unions would have consequences that are hard to predict. Unions would lose some of their present ability to support strikes by some members while other members work and pay special assessments into a strike fund. Nevertheless, the new unions might drive hard bargains. There would be rivalries among them and each would have a strong desire to make a good showing.

Thus, if there were three or four unions in the automobile industry, each might feel a strong urge to make a better settlement than any of the others. Hence, breaking up the unions might increase their militancy and make reasonable settlements with them more difficult.

A solution to the wage-price spiral. Solutions to the problems of rising labor costs may be found to some extent in the transformation of the character of unions. There are important possibilities for men to increase their earnings through earning a bonus based upon the success of the enterprise in reducing the ratio of labor costs to sales. Experience shows that this sort of incentive is capable of evoking a powerful response from the employees and that their capacity to contribute to technological advance is surprisingly strong. It is one of the shortcomings of management that it has allowed much of the potential interest and ability of the labor force to go to waste. Enlisting the active cooperation of employees in reducing the ratio of payrolls to sales is a promising method of attacking the central cause of inflation. It has the important advantage that it does not build up class conflict. On the contrary, it helps the employee become an integral part of the process of production; it makes use of his mind as well as his muscles; and it gives him a good opportunity to share in progress by making technological change yield him an increase in pay.

Finally, for those who are deeply concerned lest inflation produce dire catastrophe, there is the remedy of reducing tariffs and eliminating quotas. This would be a good step to take even in the absence of a problem of inflation because it would expose the American economy to a more vigorous competition from abroad. Foreign competition would be good for industry because it would be a wholesome spur to efficiency and to inventiveness in industry. In addition, it would encourage capital and labor to move from industries where they are at a comparative disadvantage in this country into industries where they are at a comparative advantage.

Too much should not be expected from reducing tariffs and eliminating quotas because, as a general rule, American producers (especially manufacturers) can undersell their foreign rivals. The strong position of American manufacturers is indicated by the fact that our exports of finished manufactures in 1958 were 2.4 times our imports. Nevertheless, the reduction of duties and the elimination of quotas would make it more difficult for American firms to pass on increases in labor costs to consumers and would stiffen the resistance of American employers to wage demands, thereby retarding the tendency of rising wages to push up prices.

No single step that the government could take would do so much to discourage inflation as the reduction of duties and the elimination of quotas. I suggest that the President begin the attack on inflation by withdrawing the recently imposed quotas on oil. These quotas are not even remotely connected with national defense. His willingness to do this will be a good test of his willingness to come to grips with the problem of inflation. I suggest, furthermore, that Congress provide for immediately starting a program that would gradually eliminate all duties and quotas within the next ten years. Willingness to support the elimination of duties and quotas is a good test of one's interest in inflation. People who are not willing to support the elimination of duties and quotas cannot claim to be strong opponents of inflation.

VI

A discussion of the consequences of inflation must distinguish between the effects of the rising labor costs and the effects of rising prices.

(1) Rising labor costs are not likely to produce a cost-price squeeze. The reasons for this conclusion are twofold. In the first place, rising wages will be accompanied most of the time by a high rate of technological innovation which facilitates translation of higher labor costs into higher prices. In the second place, higher labor costs under most circumstances tend to generate income, thereby facilitating the translation of higher labor costs into higher prices.

(2) If labor costs rise, higher prices are needed to protect the community against possible adverse effects of higher labor costs. For example, higher prices are needed to prevent higher labor costs from limiting investment opportunities and thereby limiting production and employment. Higher prices are needed to protect profits in the face of higher labor costs and to preserve, more or less, the original distribution of income in the community.

(3) If labor costs rise, an increase in prices is needed to limit the encroach-

ment of rising labor costs upon savings. To the extent that prices rise to offset the increase in labor costs, the original propensity of the economy to save remains unchanged. Likewise, the rise in prices prevents an unfavorable shift in the investment function. The net result is that both the investment function and the saving function of the economy are virtually the same at the new cost-price level as they were at the previous cost-price level. If this is so, the rate of saving has not been adversely affected by the rise in costs and prices.

(4) Creeping inflation is not likely to break into a gallop. The argument that it will break into a gallop assumes that speculators and others buy in anticipation of an increase in prices, that prices will be bid up, and that as they are bid up the tendency to buy in anticipation of higher prices will be strengthened. This theory runs into the inconvenient fact that prices do not behave as the theory says they do. Among sixteen industrial countries in Europe and North America the rise in the consumer price index between 1953 and 1957 was less than the rise between 1948 and 1953 in all cases except two. The two exceptions were Belgium and Switzerland, where the rise in the consumer price index in both periods was small. In the United States the rise in the consumer price level in the second period was less than half the rise in the first period. Even in countries such as Austria, France, Norway, Sweden, and Great Britain, where the rise between 1948 and 1953 was very rapid, the rate of increase dropped in the subsequent five years. The following table compares the rise in the consumer price index in sixteen industrial countries in Europe and North America in two recent periods:

	1948–53	*1953–57*
Austria	100.0	12.0
Belgium	5.3	7.0
Canada	19.0	6.0
Denmark	23.5	16.0
Finland	56.3	20.0
France	66.7	6.0
Great Britain	29.9	16.0
Ireland	26.6	12.0
Italy	16.3	10.0
Netherlands	28.2	8.0
Norway	35.1	12.0
Spain	26.6	23.0
Sweden	29.9	13.0
Switzerland	4.2	5.0
United States	11.1	5.0
West Germany	7.5	6.0

Various reasons enter into the tendency for the rate of increase in prices to drop, but the most important is the simple and obvious fact that it takes money to buy goods. If people wish to buy in anticipation of higher prices, either they must curtail their purchases of many things (which is deflationary as far as those particular things are concerned) or they must draw on their credit. Their ability to draw upon their credit depends upon their credit worthiness and partly upon the reserve position of the banks. Consequently, whether or not creeping inflation becomes a gallop rests in the last analysis with the monetary authorities. Unless they see fit to provide the necessary reserves to finance galloping inflation, inflation will never become a gallop.

(5) Creeping inflation will not cause the United States to be priced out of world markets. No one can be sure what the future will bring, but, as I have pointed out, prices in most other industrial countries have risen considerably faster than in the United States. Since the principal industrial countries are more or less subject to the same influences (such as powerful trade unions and an insistent popular demand for social services that precludes much reduction in taxes), all of the industrial countries are likely to experience about the same movement of the price level. Unfortunately, foreign countries are hampered in competing with the United States by various special circumstances. In Britain, the largest manufacturer outside the United States in the free world, taxes are exceedingly burdensome and efficiency in much of industry is held down by wasteful union rules and, in the metal trades, by an unruly shop stewards' movement which in many plants has prevented management from exercising proper control of operations.

But American business must expect foreign competition to become stiffer. This will be a good thing for the United States—a useful spur to efficiency and, at least, a modest check on increases in prices. The need for more foreign competition in American markets is shown by the howls of anguish which arise whenever a few imports enter the country. Our exports of iron and steel products in 1958 were more than twice as large as our imports; our exports of machinery were seven times as large as our imports; our exports of cotton manufactures were nearly twice as large as our imports. Nevertheless, all of these industries have expressed alarm over the influx of imports—as if they had the right to pick the pockets of American consumers unchecked by foreign competition.

(6) Creeping inflation is not likely to cause a flight from the dollar. The people who predict a flight from the dollar do not say where the money is to go or what the money is to be looking for. If owners of funds are searching

for a stable price level, they will have difficulty in doing better than keeping their money right here in the United States. If the owners of funds are looking for productive investment opportunities, they can find such opportunities in limited quantities outside the United States, especially in Canada and some parts of Western Europe. In some parts of the world investors had better be prepared to recover their original investment rather promptly because it is likely to be confiscated. The attraction of the United States for funds at the present time is abnormally low because of the unwillingness of the government to pursue expansionist policies. But regardless of which party wins in 1960, a change in the direction of more expansionist policies is to be expected. Such a change will strengthen the dollar by attracting investment-seeking funds.[4]

VII

To sum up: the problem of inflation is less important than many people would have us believe and is diminishing in importance. The dire results predicted for creeping inflation have not happened and are not likely to happen.

I expect that the rate of increase in prices will continue to drop, as it has been doing for twenty years, but I do not expect to see it completely cease in the foreseeable future. I am pessimistic about our chances of completely halting creeping inflation because I am optimistic about the future of the economy. The kind of inflation that we shall get is the kind which often accompanies a vigorous and healthy economy. The features that stand out in the economy of the immediate future are: (1) thriving and increasingly successful technological research; (2) the assumption of larger responsibilities and the provision of more and better services by government; (3) a powerful and dynamic trade-union movement.

Each of these features of the economy is good in itself. Together the three features make for a vigorous and progressive economy. But these features also tend to produce inflation—not galloping inflation, but the slow upward creep in the price level that results from a strong demand for goods and a slow climb in labor costs.

Action against inflation will be tardy and spotty. It will be difficult to get the government to take such an elementary step as paying sufficient in-

[4] Note that the Canadian dollar has been strong in spite of the fact that the Canadian price level has risen more rapidly than the price level here. The reasons are (1) the abundance of attractive investment opportunities in Canada, and (2) the expansionist policies of the Canadian government.

terest to build up a nonbank market for long-term government bonds. Progress in making a critical review of the multitude of subsidies in the budget and in getting rid of the unjustifiable ones will be slow—in fact, it may never occur. Public hostility to inflationary wage settlements may slowly force unions to moderate their wage demands, but their demands may still be inflationary. The need of unions for an idealistic principle to arouse the devotion of their members and to win the approval of the public may lead unions to embrace wage-payment systems that lead all the men in the plant to cooperate in reducing labor costs. The elimination of duties and quotas, though badly needed, will probably make only slow progress, but American industry will have the good fortune to meet increasingly effective competition from abroad.

The fact that inflation is of diminishing importance means that inflation is less important than other economic problems. Certainly at the present time inflation is far less important than the problem of 4.4 million unemployed. Likewise, it is less important than the huge waste of resources caused by the misdirection of production in the farm program. It is less important than the wastes that follow from the lack of adequate facilities to train skilled craftsmen and technicians. And certainly it is less important than the waste and the injustice caused by color bars that exclude Negroes from a multitude of occupations. As the public realizes that the bad results of inflation have been greatly exaggerated and that some of these results will not happen at all, it will give attention to other problems—particularly the problems of unemployment and of achieving an adequate rate of growth. The greatest harm and waste caused by inflation and the fear of inflation is that they have made both government and industry afraid of expansionist policies and have deprived the country of billions of dollars of production and millions of manyears of employment which the country could have had if it had not made a fetish of a stable price level.

13

Current Trends, Problems, and Prospects in the American Economy

The Commercial and Financial Chronicle, February 19, 1959. These comments on economic conditions in the United States were prepared for publication in Japanese by the Nihon Keizai Shimbun of Tokyo.

I. SUMMARY

PRODUCTION continues to expand, and construction is at an all-time high. In January important parts of the economy began producing faster than the rate of consumption.

The employment drop in January was less than seasonal. The principal reason for the limited response of employment to recovery has been the increase in the weekly hours of work which, in turn, is due to the caution of employers who preferred to increase hours rather than to enlarge their forces.

Retail sales in January were slightly below December after seasonal adjustments and were the second highest on record. Sales of durables were the largest on record.

New orders of manufacturers have been increasing and in December were the largest since May 1957. Unfilled orders are also growing, and inventories, which are low relative to sales, have begun to rise.

Prices show no significant changes; wages continue to creep upward; and the moderately tight credit policy of the Federal Reserve is beginning to cause trouble for the Treasury.

The alleged balance in the 1960 budget is a phony balance and is achieved, in the main, by adding important proposed new expenditures to the 1959 budget instead of to the 1960 budget.

The new economic competition from Russia promises to benefit the United States by compelling the country to re-evaluate its economic policies and to pay more attention to economic growth and less attention to a stable price level.

II. PRODUCTION

Steel production in the week beginning February 2 reached 2,288,000 tons, the highest since mid-April 1957. Still higher production at 2,363,000 tons was scheduled for the week beginning Febuary 9. During the last month there has been a sudden upsurge in orders for steel, largely for the purpose of building inventories in anticipation of a possible steel strike. As a result, both production of steel and backlogs of unfilled orders are growing rapidly.

Passenger-car production in January was 545,547 cars in comparison with 593,770 in December and 497,166 in January 1958. The gaining favor of smaller cars, especially in the cities, is shown by the fact that production of Ramblers was more than double the output of January 1958. In February, production of most cars is being scheduled at slightly less per operating day than in January.

Construction is going on at a high rate, especially public construction and residential building. Construction put in place in January, after correction for seasonal factors, was the largest for any month on record and was 12.1 per cent above January of last year.

III. EMPLOYMENT

The drop of 1,267,000 in civilian employment between December and January was less than the usual seasonal drop. It was much less than the drop of 2,148,000 between December and January a year ago. The increase in unemployment of 616,000 to 4,724,000 was considerably less than the increase of 1,120,000 between December and January a year ago. The seasonally adjusted figures of nonagricultural wage and salary employment showed a fairly substantial gain and were the highest since January 1958. The seasonally adjusted unemployment rate was 6.0 per cent in comparison with 6.1 per cent in December. When the February employment report becomes available, it will probably show unemployment somewhat less than that in February 1958.

Some business commentators have called attention to the fact that employment has improved less rapidly in the current recession than in the two previous recessions. Care must be taken in selecting the employment figures to be used because the Bureau of Labor Statistics and the Department of Commerce do not agree on the amount of the gain in employment. Between February 1958 and December 1958, the Bureau of Labor Statistics estimates that nonfarm wage and salary employment outside of households increased by 2,048,000; the Department of Commerce puts the increase at 1,692,000. I have used the Department of Commerce estimates because they are based upon a more comprehensive survey than those of the Bureau of Labor Statistics.

It is true that the gain in total civilian employment (farm and nonfarm) in the first three quarters of the present recovery is slightly less than in the first three quarters of the recovery in 1954–55 and no greater than in the recovery of 1949–50. The great difference in the three recoveries, however, has been in the hours worked. Average weekly hours of all civilian employees dropped in the first three quarters of the recoveries of 1949–50 and 1954–55, but increased in the first three quarters of the 1958 recovery. When total numbers of hours worked are compared, employment gains in the current recovery have been considerably greater than in the two preceding ones. The rise in output per manhour (when output is expressed in dollars of constant purchasing power) for the entire labor force has not been exceptionally high in the present recovery—on the contrary, it has been less than in the two previous recoveries. Table 1 compares the three recoveries with respect to output, employment, and weekly hours worked. In computing percentage changes in employment seasonally adjusted figures were used.

Table 1

	Increase in gross national product (constant dollars)	*Change in total civilian employment (Dept. of Commerce estimates)*	*Change in private wage and salary employment outside of households and agricul.*	*Change in av. wkly hours of work—all nonfarm civilian employees*	*Change in av. wkly hours of work—factory production workers*	*Increase in output per manhour—all nonfarm civilian employees*
Recovery of 1949–50 (second quarter of 1949 to first quarter of 1950)	4.8%	+0.5%	−0.8%	−1.4%	+2.8%	5.8%
Recovery of 1954–55 (second quarter of 1954 to first quarter of 1955)	6.0	+1.0	+1.4	−0.2	+2.9	5.2
Recovery of 1958 (first quarter of 1958 to fourth quarter of 1958)	5.8	+0.5	+0.1	+1.4	+2.2	3.8

This analysis of employment in the last three recessions shows the error in some of the prevalent explanations of the slow response of employment in the 1958 recovery. The explanation is not in automation or other gains in efficiency. The gain in output per manhour has been large, as it always is in the first stages of recovery, but it has been less rapid in the present recovery than in the two preceding ones. The main explanation of the slow response of employment to recovery has been the fact that weekly working hours have increased, whereas in previous recoveries they dropped. The spirit of caution or timidity that has dominated the business world is responsible for the increase in weekly hours. The timidity is also reflected in inventory policy. Until the end of 1958, manufacturers continued to reduce inventories. Timidity caused employers to increase working time rather than add to their forces because they were not sure that the recovery would last.

IV. PERSONAL INCOME

Wage and salary income in December made an all-time high. Total personal income, after adjustment for seasonal factors, dropped slightly in December to an annual rate of $359.3 billion—the second highest month on record. The small drop in personal income was due to smaller-than-usual year-end dividend payments and a small drop in transfer payments as the unemployed exhausted their rights to benefits. It was the fourth straight month of drop in transfer payments. Nevertheless, transfer payments in December 1958 were 8.0 per cent larger than the average for the first quarter of 1958—the bottom of the recession. The rise of transfer payments above the bottom of the recession has been mainly due to the secular increase in pension payments.

V. CONSUMPTION, RETAIL SALES, AND CONSUMER CREDIT

Expansion of the economy was assisted in the fourth quarter of 1958 by a sharp drop in the rate of personal saving from an annual rate of $22.5 billion, or 7.2 per cent, to $19.0 billion, or 6.0 per cent. There was a good increase in the buying of durable consumer goods from an annual rate of $36.1 billion in the third quarter to $38.6 billion in the fourth quarter. But the rate of purchases of durable consumer goods in the fourth quarter was still below the fourth quarter of 1957 and, expressed in dollars of constant purchasing power, below the average annual rate in 1955, 1956, or 1957.

Preliminary figures on retail sales for January, after correction for seasonal factors, show a slight drop of 0.3 per cent from the revised December figures, making January the second highest month on record in retail sales. Between December and January the seasonally adjusted figures show a rise of 0.4 per cent in sales of durables and a drop of 0.6 per cent in the sales of nondurables. Sales of durables in January made a new all-time record, slightly surpassing the previous record of July 1957. Sales of nondurables were higher than in any month except December 1958.

Automobile sales in January of 428,000 cars were 12.6 per cent greater than the sales of 380,000 in January 1958, but sales per day were 12.7 per cent less than in January 1957. In December sales were 3.2 per cent above December 1957. Ford Division of Ford Motor Co. reported that January sales were 35 per cent above January 1958. Rambler sales in January were more than double sales in January 1958, indicating the strong favor that the small car is meeting.

Consumer credit expanded rapidly in December, due to the rise in sales of consumer durable goods generally, but especially the rise in the sales of automobiles. The increase of $1.601 billion in consumer credit in December 1958 was the largest for any month on record, and the year ended with the outstanding volume of consumer credit reaching an all-time high of $45.065 billion. But as a ratio of personal income, consumer credit was still slightly below the figure of December 1957, when the ratio was 12.8 per cent. In December 1958, it was 12.3 per cent. New expansions of automobile credit in December, after adjustment for seasonal factors, were the largest on record.

VI. NEW ORDERS, CONTRACT AWARDS, AND INVENTORIES

Construction contract awards in December were 15.1 per cent above December 1957. Residential building continued to make an excellent showing with contract awards 29.3 per cent above December of last year. On a seasonally adjusted basis, construction contract awards were more than twenty per cent below November and the lowest since December 1957. The seasonal adjustment for December, however, seems regularly to give abnormally low results. Hence, the large drop in the seasonally adjusted figure for December is not significant.

Heavy-engineering construction contract awards in the five weeks ending February 2 were 24.9 per cent above the corresponding period of last year.

In the four weeks ending December 29 they were 19.5 per cent above last year, and in November they were 12.4 per cent above November 1957.

New orders of manufacturers, after adjustment for seasonal factors, increased to $28.1 billion, the largest volume of new orders since May 1957. The increase in new orders was entirely in nondurables, which at $14.6 billion were almost equal to the previous all-time high of April 1957, when new orders for nondurables (seasonally adjusted) reached $14.7 billion. New orders for durables on the other hand, at $13.5 billion, were well below the highest months of 1956 and 1957.

The figures on unfilled orders, which increased in November for the first time since December 1956, rose again in December to $46.8 billion and were larger than in any month since March 1958.

The book value of trade and manufacturing inventories, after seasonal adjustment, increased by about $200 million during December—the second successive month of increase. As in November, the increase in inventories was concentrated in retail automotive inventories, reflecting the stocking of dealers with new 1959 cars. The book value of manufacturing inventories continued to drop during December and was lower than in any month since April 1956.

The National Association of Purchasing Agents reports a sharp rise in the proportion of firms receiving an increase in new orders in January, but little change in the inventories of manufacturers.

The ratio of inventories to monthly deliveries continued to drop, and in most parts of the economy was well below the ratio of December 1956, as Table 2 shows. The ratio of inventories of manufacturers to new orders is low as is reflected in Table 3.

Table 2

	Dec. 1956	*Aug. 1957*	*Dec. 1957*	*Jan. 1958*	*Mar. 1958*	*June 1958*	*Nov. 1958*	*Dec. 1958*
All manufacturing and trade	1.56	1.60	1.66	1.67	1.72	1.62	1.51	1.48
All manufacturing	1.82	1.90	2.00	2.00	2.09	1.95	1.79	1.76
Durable goods	2.12	2.22	2.37	2.43	2.56	2.36	2.10	2.04
Nondurable goods	1.51	1.57	1.65	1.63	1.66	1.58	1.51	1.49
All wholesale trade	1.10	1.12	1.17	1.18	1.20	1.11	1.04	1.03
Durable goods	1.50	1.60	1.74	1.74	1.78	1.63	1.47	1.47
Nondurable goods	0.86	0.85	0.86	0.88	0.88	0.84	0.78	0.76
All retail trade	1.47	1.43	1.45	1.47	1.50	1.45	1.39	1.36
Durable goods	1.84	1.93	2.04	2.05	2.20	2.12	1.91	1.86
Nondurable goods	1.25	1.17	1.15	1.17	1.18	1.17	1.15	1.11

Table 3

	Dec. 1956	Aug. 1957	Dec. 1957	Jan. 1958	Mar. 1958	June 1958	Nov. 1958	Dec. 1958
All manufacturing	1.80	1.99	2.13	2.18	2.10	1.95	1.77	1.75
Durable goods	2.12	2.40	2.73	2.86	2.60	2.32	2.05	2.06
Nondurable goods	1.49	1.49	1.64	1.66	1.66	1.61	1.50	1.47

VII. PRICES

The index of sensitive prices, which was moving downward in December, continued to drop in January, though at a much slower rate. It was 85.3 on January 2, and 84.5 on February 6. Prices of industrial raw materials and metals were virtually unchanged, but the index of the prices of raw foodstuffs dropped from 79.9 on January 2 to 77.9 on February 6. There has been a marked divergence in price trends among the components of the index during the last year. The index of raw food prices fell from 87.0 on January 30, 1958, to 78.5 on January 30, 1959; but in the same period the index of prices of industrial raw materials rose from 83.3 to 88.8 and metals from 85.5 to 97.3. These divergent trends show that inflationary influences are strong outside of the field of agriculture.

The index of wholesale prices continues to show no significant changes (Table 4).

Table 4

	Week ending			*Month of*		
	Feb. 3 1959	*Jan. 27 1959*	*Jan. 13 1959*	*Dec. 1958*	*March 1958*	*Dec. 1957*
All commodities	119.2	119.5	119.4	119.2	119.7	118.5
Farm products	90.7	91.9	91.5	90.7	100.5	92.6
Processed foods	108.5	109.0	109.0	108.8	110.7	107.4
Commodities other than farm products and foods	127.3	127.4	127.3	127.2	125.7	126.1

The consumer price index dropped in December from 123.9 to 123.7. For the last six months the index has been virtually unchanged. It was the same in December as in June. In December there was a particularly large drop in the prices of foods, but it is noteworthy that five out of the eight principal categories in the consumer price index fell between November and December.

VIII. WAGES AND THE PROSPECTS OF STRIKES

The most important development in the labor field during the last month has been the series of 5 per cent wage increases granted in the oil industry and generally accepted by the unions. During this year of recovery, output per manhour will rise at more than the normal rate and the increase in productivity may exceed 5 per cent. In that event this increase will not be inflationary. The increase will have considerable effect upon other settlements, especially those in rubber and iron and steel.

The predominant view in the business world is that there will be a steel strike this year. This belief is well grounded. It is based upon two assumptions. In the first place, the union leaders have announced that they expect to insist on large concessions. The political unrest in the union makes it likely that the union will insist on stiff demands. In the second place, the companies will not wish to incur public ill will by granting stiff demands without first putting up a fight. The union will win the strike and will get most of what it went after, but the companies will gain credit for having tried to protect the public from large increases in wages. The economic effects of the strike, if it occurs, will be limited because most users of steel will have stocked up well in anticipation of a strike.

IX. CAPITAL MARKETS

In spite of an unemployment rate of 6.0 per cent, the Federal Reserve is keeping the member banks almost constantly in debt to the Reserve banks. In four out of the last five weeks borrowing exceeded excess reserves. In the week ending February 4 the excess was $62 million.

The rate for ninety-one-day bills has changed little since the end of September. It averaged 2.793 per cent in October; 2.756 in November; 2.814 in December; and was 2.810 per cent on February 9. The bond market has been firm and quiet during the last month, both for new issues and for seasoned bonds. The Dow-Jones index of forty bonds, which was 86.45 on January 5, was 86.31 on February 9. Of considerable interest is the drop in the backlog of new issues of corporate bonds and preferred stocks awaiting marketing, which dropped from $1.172 billion on January 8 to $891 million on February 5. A year ago the backlog was twice the present level, or nearly $1.800 billion. Why should business recovery be accompanied by a drop in this backlog? There are several reasons: (1) at present interest rates there is no longer a large volume of refunding; (2) corporations as yet have made only modest expansion of their investment spending plans; (3) rising profits are enabling most enterprises to finance their immediate needs from internal funds. But an increase in the demand for long-term external funds is ahead.

The most important development in the money market during the last month was the high rate of attrition in the Treasury's refunding of $9.8 billion in one-year certificates and $5.1 billion in three-year notes early in February. Of these securities, $9.2 billion were in the hands of the public. The holders were offered a choice of a one-year certificate bearing 3¾ per cent interest or a three-year note paying 4 per cent. Nevertheless, holders of $2.1 billion of the maturing securities rejected the exchange offer and demanded cash, forcing the Treasury to raise $1.5 billion through an emergency borrowing operation.

Some financial analysts have viewed this experience with considerable alarm, interpreting it as the effect of inflationary fears upon the willingness of the public to buy fixed income securities. Expectations of inflation are bound, of course, to affect interest rates, and the government must expect to pay market prices. If the government expects to sell long-term securities, it will soon have to raise the ceiling of 4.25 per cent now set by law on federal securities.

The high recent attrition in the government's refunding, however, is explained as the market's natural reaction to Federal Reserve policy rather than by inflationary fears. Thus far the government deficit has been financed by sales of securities to business concerns rather than to banks. In recent weeks, however, the Federal Reserve has been keeping the member banks in debt to the Reserve system. With money already fairly tight and likely to become tighter, business concerns see no point in tying up their funds for a year or more in government securities. Under the circumstances, it is surprising that the attrition in the government's refunding was not greater than it was. A high attrition must be expected when the large volume of short-term securities now held by business enterprises comes due. The bright side to all of this is the prospect that the needs of the Treasury will force the Federal Reserve to ease somewhat its policy of tight money in the face of substantial unemployment.

X. A MISLEADING BUDGET

The budget recommended by Mr. Eisenhower for fiscal 1960 has many commendable features. For example, it seeks to get rid of some of the many subsidies in the budget (such as providing postal service below cost, and the loans at 2 per cent made by the Rural Electrification Administration), and it proposes a healthy increase in expenditures on research and development from $4.841 billion in 1959 to $5.484 billion in 1960. These expenditures may be expected to yield large returns. In fiscal year 1957 outlays of the federal government on research and development were $3.498 billion.

Unfortunately, there are included in the budget large and unjustifiable subsidies, such as free hospital service to veterans for nonservice-connected disabilities and support for prices of farm products. Furthermore, some important growing needs of the country receive small recognition. A small example is the proposed cut in expenditures for recreational resources from $97 million in 1959 to $83 million in 1960. With population growing and the practice of taking vacations rapidly spreading, the country needs an expanding program for recreational facilities.

The most serious criticism of the proposed 1960 budget is that the alleged balance is phony. Three principal devices have been used to create an alleged balance in the budget for 1960. The first device is to add to the budget for 1959 every conceivable expenditure that can be put there, apparently on the ground that since a huge deficit for fiscal 1959 is inevitable anyway, there would be no harm in adding to it. The budget estimates for fiscal 1959 released in January showed expected receipts from the public of $1 billion greater than the estimates released in September. But the deficit predicted in January 1959 was about as large as the deficit predicted in September 1958. The principal reason is that there was added to the supposedly closed budget of 1959 a large new item—the proposed contribution of $1.375 billion to the International Monetary Fund. A more normal procedure would have been to have included this amount in the 1960 budget. If Congress approves the recommendation, the subscription will not be made in the fiscal year 1959, but at some indefinite time in the future. But to have put the item in the 1960 budget would have destroyed the alleged balance, so it was added to the closed budget of 1959.

The second device (a small one) used to create the fictitious balance has been to transfer to the administrative budget some revenues from the cash budget. Such a transfer does not increase the government's cash income, and it does not improve the cash budget which is the one that really determines the impact of government finances on the economy. The principal change is the transfer to the administrative budget of revenues from aviation gasoline taxes.

The third device used to create a fictitious balance has been the underestimating of important expenditures. The principal case is the cost of stabilizing farm prices and farm incomes which the President estimates will be $896 million less in 1960 than in 1959. This estimate is merely an optimistic guess. The cost of price-support operations depends upon the size of crops which depends partly upon the weather and also upon the initiative and enterprise that farmers show in taking advantage of the government's price-support program. The guesses of the President have not been accurate. In January 1958, for example, he estimated that the amount required for stabilization of farm price support and related programs in fiscal 1959 would be $3.253 billion, but in January 1959, halfway through the fiscal year, this estimate had been increased by about two thirds to $5.386 billion. The budget estimates for the fiscal year 1960 are based on the assumption that yields per acre in 1959 will be less than the record yields of 1958. But with the termination of the soil-bank scheme, there will be a substantial increase in acreage devoted to crops. Furthermore, the technological revolution in agriculture is still going on. Finally, the farmers are steadily learning to take advantage of the government's price-support program. Unless price supports are substantially diminished, the President's estimates of the cost of the program will be too low.

Certainly the program of supporting the prices of farm products is one of the most ridiculous ventures ever undertaken by any government anywhere—truly Alice-in-Wonderland economics. The federal government is undertaking to prevent the great technological revolution in agriculture from depressing the relative prices of a few favored crops—and the American people are docilely permitting themselves to be taxed to support this madness. No one has ever explained why wheat growers, cotton growers, tobacco growers, corn growers, or peanut growers are entitled to have the country taxed to buy their output. It makes no more sense than would an undertaking by the government to buy up other surpluses, such as the empty seats in railroad trains, street cars, or moving-picture houses, or to buy the surplus output of buggies, harnesses, old-fashioned coal furnaces, moustache cups, and a vast variety of goods that the public no longer wants except in very limited quantities. President Eisenhower has sent a message to Congress on the subject of agriculture in which he advocates (1) lower price supports, and (2) a larger program for selling surplus crops outside the United States below world prices or giving them away—even though this means unfairly disturbing other economies. President Eisenhower lacks the courage to make a fight for the abolition of this totally unjustifiable government expense.

The budget is full of subsidies of various sorts that have crept in by a piecemeal process as the politicians have sought to buy the votes of this group or that. A comprehensive survey is needed of the many subsidies and their cost so that the people of the country can see their total cost and decide which of these subsidies are worth keeping.

XI. THE GROWING ECONOMIC COMPETITION OF RUSSIA

Khrushchev's speech to the Twenty-First Congress of the Communist Party of the Soviet Union made it plain that the Russians, having attained military equality with the West, if not military superiority, feel able to begin economic competition with the West. Mr. Khrushchev expresses great confidence that the economic balance of power will soon shift from the West to the communist world.

Russia has without question been the most dynamic influence in the world during the last generation. Russian military competition has enormously stimulated the development of science and technology in the United States and has led the government to support research on a scale that the people would not otherwise have tolerated. The great question posed by the new Russian economic competition is whether or not the American economy will respond with sufficient vigor and success to prevent the Russian economic drive from persuading large parts of the world to adopt the institutions of communism.

In an economy such as ours, in which nine tenths of the output is produced by private industry, the rate of growth is largely determined by the decisions of private industry. In recent years industry has done some of the things most necessary for rapid growth. It has rapidly expanded specialized technological research to unprecedented levels, increasing the expenditures of its own money on research from $2.3 billion in 1953 to $3.3 billion in 1956 and still more in 1957 and 1958. And industry has invested huge amounts in industrial plant and equipment.

But in spite of the rapid growth of research and the large volume of investment, output has grown only slowly. The gross national product of the country, measured in dollars of constant purchasing power, increased less than 10 per cent in the four years from 1953 to 1957, and it dropped in 1958. The slow rate of growth is attributable to two principal influences—one private and the other public. The private influence was the failure of business concerns, especially the makers of durable consumer goods, to make sufficient improvements in their goods to stimulate a strong demand. The public influence was the tight credit policy of the Federal Reserve which began in

1956. The marked slowdown in production began with the year 1956 when the increase of output, expressed in constant prices, was only 2.4 per cent above the previous year. In 1957 the gain in output was only 1 per cent. For the year 1956, the average borrowings of member banks of the Federal Reserve system exceeded excess reserves by about one third. In 1957, credit was even tighter. As a result of tight credit policies, total demand deposits and currency outside of banks increased by only 6.2 per cent in the four-year period 1953 to 1957—less than half the normal rate. Between 1955 and 1957 there was virtually no change in the total amount of demand deposits and currency outside of banks.

The way to accelerate the growth of the economy is to stimulate the demand for goods. When demand presses hard upon productive capacity, that capacity is used and industry takes steps to increase it. Pressure of demand upon capacity tends to produce creeping inflation, but this pressure is necessary to attain the maximum rate of growth. Thus creeping inflation is part of the price that we must pay to achieve maximum growth.

The new economic competition of Russia requires that the United States reconsider and re-evaluate its fundamental economic policies, that it make the central objective of these policies the achievement of our full growth potential rather than the stabilization of the price level. If Mr. Khrushchev forces us to make maximum growth the primary objective of our economic policy, he will have done this country a great service.

Part III

INDUSTRIAL RELATIONS

INTRODUCTION

SUMNER SLICHTER was a careful student of industrial relations throughout his full career. It is the area of his unrivaled professional distinction and perhaps his most enduring contribution. The eight selections in Part III span almost forty years, starting in 1920 with the fresh and rewarding analysis of the principal causes of the low state of industrial morale. These selections provide a chronological view of the dramatic transformations in labor, management, and government over the ensuing eventful years, and at the same time show the evolution of Slichter's ideas and policy judgments with the changing times.

Slichter started his university career with penetrating insights into the factory work place, the reactions of industrial workers, and the relations between workers and their supervisors (see Chapter 14). He was no doubt significantly influenced by his own period of factory employment at manual work. This early paper shows him even then to have been a discerning observer with an insatiable curiosity; these qualities were to characterize his work in industrial relations throughout his career and to shape significantly the classics, *Union Policies and Industrial Management* (1941) and *The Impact of Collective Bargaining on Management* (1960). This early paper also reflects his challenging way of making his points: "Workers cannot be expected to be more interested in promoting the prosperity of industry than industry is in promoting the prosperity of workmen. . . . If it is legitimate to get all that is possible and to give as little as is necessary in selling commodities, is it not also legitimate for the laborer to give as little output as he must?"

The 1920 paper on industrial morale explicitly raises the question of the form of industrial organization at the work place, the structure of the relationship between industrial workers and managers: "a change in the organization of industry must be regarded as among the prerequisites to the solution of the problem of industrial morale." In 1929 Slichter was concerned (Chapter 15) with the adverse effects of managerial paternalism on the relationships and performance at the work place. A decade later the policies of the Wagner Act were seen as having arisen from the failure of attempts to induce employers voluntarily to recognize labor organizations (Chapter 16). A decade later Slichter was concerned with the power of some labor organizations to discriminate against certain workers and to inhibit adjustment to technological change. In 1958, in defining "New Goals for the Unions" (Chapter 21), he saw "the need to reform the present organization of production in American industry" and hence a new role for the unions. "The next formal step in industrial relations will be to replace the present contests between managements and employees with organized cooperation"—as illustrated in the Scanlon Plan under which workers are encouraged to make contributions to technological progress.

The growth of labor unions in the 1930s and the public policies represented by the Wagner Act (1935) early led Slichter to advocate the view that the government could not encourage labor organization and collective bargaining without being concerned with the relations of union members to their organizations, with the interference by some unions with the rights of workers which the government sought to assure, and the effects of industrial conflict in some sensitive sectors. His views in advance of the Taft-Hartley law are set forth in "Trade Unions and a Free Society" (Chapter 17).

Chapter 20 constitutes a more general view of the major features of the American industrial-relations system. Slichter here compares our labor-management-state relationships with those of some other countries. He concludes that "the United States should consider itself lucky. It possesses a system of industrial relations that, in its basic characteristics, fits conditions here remarkably well. The system was developed without being planned. . . . Hence, we seem justified in being grateful that we have been favored by fortune and perhaps also in taking modest pride that we have pursued opportunistic policies with considerable flexibility and good sense."

14

Industrial Morale

Quarterly Journal of Economics, November 1920.

I

THOUGH industrial morale is closely related to the state of contentment or unrest of the working force, the two are not to be confused. Industrial morale refers to the degree of cooperation extended by the employees of an enterprise to the management in the course of their work, the interest they manifest in their work and in the enterprise by which they are employed, and their willingness to assume a share of the responsibility that their work is properly and expeditiously done. The test of industrial morale is the degree of cooperation extended by the men to the management in the operation of the plant.[1]

Industrial morale has acquired recognition as a matter of prime importance largely as a result of the shift in economic power from capital to labor which has accompanied the war and which has resulted in the passage in great measure of the control of production from the hands of capital into the hands of labor. Before the war, capital's economic superiority was sufficient in most industries to give it what was regarded as a fairly satisfactory control over the output of its men. By holding over labor the fear of discharge, capital was able in considerable degree to control the speed of work, and to compel labor to produce what the management regarded as a fairly adequate day's work. Because of the control over output which capital's economic superiority placed in their hands, managers, although aware of labor's lack of interest in production, and even of the deliberate efforts of workmen to limit it, did not regard the unsatisfactory state of industrial morale as an urgent and pressing problem. On the contrary, they tended to accept labor's lack of interest in production as more or less inherent in the very nature of

[1] This is not intended to be a comprehensive definition of "industrial morale." In other connections it may prove desirable to give the term a considerably broader meaning. The above statement is intended to give a definite meaning, broad enough for the purpose of the present discussion.

things, and hence were inclined to regard attempts to develop labor's cooperation as not only unnecessary but useless.

As a matter of fact, the control over production which capital's superiority in prewar days gave to management was by no means as complete as managers themselves supposed it to be. Despite their economic inferiority and despite the pressure applied, the men frequently were able to withhold output on a substantial scale, and the efforts of managements to exact more output merely stimulated more concerted efforts among the men to withhold it. In the period immediately preceding the war, managers were awakening to the incompleteness of their control over production and as a result were beginning to realize the importance of industrial morale and the need of developing a more cooperative attitude on the part of their men. The great majority of managers, however, still remained satisfied with the degree of control over production afforded by their dominant position, and for this reason industrial morale failed in the prewar period to obtain general recognition as one of the outstanding industrial problems of the day.

The tendency toward a transfer of control over production from the hands of capital to the hands of labor has given industrial morale a new importance.[2] As long as production could be satisfactorily sustained by economic pressure in the form of discharge or threats of discharge, it could well be a matter of secondary importance whether or not labor was interested in output. But with output dependent primarily upon labor's willingness to produce rather than upon capital's ability to compel production, labor's willingness to produce becomes of supreme consequence. Managers no longer can afford to regard labor's lack of interest as more or less inevitable, to be expected and made the best of. If output depends primarily on labor's willingness to produce, then labor *must* be interested in production. The new conditions have created what may safely be termed the paramount managerial problem of the day—the problem of getting a satisfactory output when the control of production is largely in the hands of labor, of developing in labor, which is too strong to be coerced, an interest in output and a willingness to cooperate in order to obtain it.

Nor is this problem a temporary one, likely to vanish permanently with the first touch of industrial depression or the resumption of immigration. Although, with the resumption of immigration or the coming of depres-

[2] Acquisition by labor of a substantial control over its rate of work does not necessarily involve an equally extensive gain in its control over wages or conditions of employment for less economic power appears to be required to enable labor substantially to reduce its pace than to enable it to exact higher wages or more favorable working conditions.

sion, capital may be expected to regain much of its lost economic power, and in consequence much of its control over output, the permanent trend is likely to be a gradual growth in labor's economic strength and with it an ever-increasing ability on the part of labor to resist driving and to make output dependent on its own willingness to produce. Hence industry must face the fact that the permanent problem will be how to function efficiently with economically powerful labor, how to maintain satisfactory output despite impaired economic control over workmen by management. Though this problem temporarily may become less serious, it is likely in the long run to become steadily more acute.

The fundamental nature of this problem is apparent. The attainment of a high general wage level, with all that it implies from the standpoint of human welfare, requires, according to accepted economic theory, that labor be relatively scarce. But if, as the scarcity and economic power of labor increase, its efficiency decreases, labor's gain in wages will tend to be relative only, not absolute and substantial. The attainment of maximum real wages depends upon the ability to check the tendency for labor's efficiency to decrease as its scarcity increases.

In noting the significance of changes in labor's economic power attention should be directed to the effect of these changes upon managerial methods. Too often in discussions of systems and philosophies of management an absolutist point of view has been adopted and specific systems of management have been recommended as the only true "scientific" systems of management. As a matter of fact the desirability of managerial policies depends largely upon economic conditions. The drive system of management was fairly effective as long as labor was economically weak. But when capital lost its economic dominance, the drive system broke down and managers sought new methods of handling labor. Already with the passing of labor scarcity a return to the old drive methods is occurring. The same dependence of managerial methods upon the relative economic strength of managed and managers is observable in the handling of different classes of labor.

This paper will not attempt to discuss the constructive aspects of the problem of industrial morale, to analyze ways and means by which labor's cooperation in production may be developed. It will be primarily confined to the more fundamental aspects of the problem—to an analysis of the principal causes of the prevailing low state of industrial morale. Analysis of the causes for the existing low industrial morale may suggest constructive measures, but no attempt will be made to outline a definite program.

II

Of the numerous causes which combine to create low industrial morale several of great importance may be passed over with little or no discussion. Fatigue, ill health, and nervous strain are well known to cause low morale but analysis of the extent to which modern industrial conditions and processes produce these physical and nervous causes must be left to the physiologist and the psychologist. No explanation is needed of the effect upon morale of the belief, widespread among workmen and far from wholly unjustified, that if they work too hard they will work themselves out of their jobs. Dissatisfaction of the workers with their treatment by the management is to be counted among the most important causes of low morale, for it is common knowledge that men tend to hold back and to do as little as possible for those against whom they feel a grievance. Another important, though self-evident, cause of low morale is the widely prevalent belief among workmen that there is gross unfairness in the distribution of burdens and benefits in society, that the wage earners, who perform the heaviest, dirtiest, least interesting, and most disagreeable tasks, receive unreasonably small shares in the good things of life. Workmen who feel this keenly do not respond readily to attempts to interest them in more production. They feel that they already are doing more than their share of the onerous work that is to be done and incline to seek compensation for the unattractiveness of their jobs and the meagerness of their pay by doing less rather than more whenever the opportunity occurs. Mitigating the severity or disagreeableness of their jobs by "taking it easy" is the only means at their disposal for partially equalizing what they conceive to be the unjust distribution of benefits and burdens, and they use this means without compunction. Finally, and perhaps most important and self-evident among all the causes of low morale, is the use of drive methods by managements to sustain and increase output. A more effective means of creating low morale could scarcely be conceived, because the drive system renders conflict instead of cooperation between the men and management inevitable. The drive system recognizes no standard day's work. On the contrary, the aim is constantly to force up the speed of work. The men naturally resist these efforts. In consequence the working pace becomes the subject of a constant struggle between the men and the management. But men do not cooperate with those against whom they are struggling. Instead of affording a basis and inducement for cooperation, the drive system compels the men to concentrate their attention and ingenuity upon limiting output, and upon frustrating the efforts of the management to push up the pace.

Low industrial morale is a natural effect of the adoption by workmen of the prevailing business philosophy of the time. This philosophy is one of "getting" rather than "giving," of profit making rather than service rendering. Businessmen frankly admit that they are in business not primarily to render service, but to make money. Anything less is not business, but philanthropy. Business, as the businessman sees it, is a bargaining process in which each party is justified in getting as much and in giving as little as possible. It is not the duty of either party to a bargain to see that the other receives an equivalent for what he gives; on the contrary, the ability to drive an advantageous bargain, to obtain a large return for a small payment, is esteemed as a desirable and important element in business capacity.

Although the prevailing philosophy of business for profit rather than for service may perhaps be justified on the ground that no other arrangement provides sufficient incentive to sustain vigorous business activity, the acquisitive philosophy, when adopted by the workmen, has the serious drawback that it is fatal to morale and efficiency because it justifies workmen in rendering as little service as they dare give for as high pay as they are able to exact. The adherence to this philosophy by businessmen renders inevitable its adoption by workmen. When workmen observe the business world in general to be interested in getting but not giving, in returns rather than service, especially when they observe that their own employers endeavor to get the largest possible output while holding remuneration as low as possible—is it to be expected that the workmen will be guided by a philosophy of service? If it is legitimate to get all that is possible and to give as little as is necessary in selling commodities, is it not also legitimate for the laborer to give as little output as he must? If bargaining power governs wages should it not also govern output? If ability to drive an advantageous bargain, to obtain a large return for a small payment, is a praiseworthy quality in businessmen, is it not also to be esteemed by workmen? When the laborer complains of wages, hours, or conditions in the plant, he customarily has been told, "If you don't like things here, why don't you get out?" May not labor with equal justification (or lack of it) reply to employers' complaints about the quantity or character of the work, "If you don't like the way we work, why do you employ us?" In vain may business leaders denounce the practice of an acquisitive philosophy by labor as long as workmen observe that business enterprises practice the same philosophy.

Not only does the pursuit of business for profit by employers encourage workmen to practice the same philosophy, but the knowledge of workmen that they are employed by organizations which are primarily seeking profit rather than rendering service lessens their interest in work and their willingness to do their best. Realizing that their employers keep for themselves, insofar as they are able, the benefits of the workmen's skill and exertion, and that an increase in their efficiency means first of all larger profits for the employers and only incidentally and indirectly benefits for the public, the men tend to feel themselves instruments for creating private profit rather than for rendering useful service.[3] But they cannot feel inclined to exert themselves greatly in the interest of someone's private gain. On the contrary, the belief that the principal and immediate effect of improvement in their efficiency will be greater gains for their employers, and that by doing more or better work they will more than ever be playing the part of mere profit-making machines, renders them indifferent to how much they do and how well they do it, unwilling to attempt more or better work. Much has been written recently of the creative impulse and of the conditions in modern industry which hinder its development. Important among these conditions are the belief of the men that the principal result of more or better work is the enhancement of private profits and their aversion to playing the part of profit-creating instruments.

Low industrial morale results from fear and resentment inspired among the workers by certain managerial policies. MacKenzie King has emphasized the importance of fear as a complicator of industrial relations.[4] It is not generally appreciated, however, to what extent fear of the management by the workmen has been deliberately and consciously fostered. The steady pursuit of a policy designed to arouse fear of the management among the workers was a natural accompaniment of the so-called drive system of management, the success of which depended upon the men's willingness to submit to being driven. In order to create a docile and subservient attitude on the part of the men and cause them to submit readily to being driven, managements deliberately sought to foster fear of themselves among the men. To this end they maintained as a matter of policy a brusque, more or less harsh, distant, and stern attitude toward their men. They resorted to discharge on fairly slight

[3] The attitude of the workmen is illustrated by a remark of an old lathe hand who ran a machine next to that of the writer in a Chicago factory seven years ago. Speaking of his feeling at the close of the day's work he said, "You don't feel as if you'd accomplished anything. And you haven't. You've just made a horse of yourself so someone else can take things easy. You ought to be put in a stable and fed just like a horse."

[4] *Industry and Humanity: A Study in the Principles Underlying Industrial Reconstruction* (Boston, 1918), pp. 115–117, 233–263, 332–334.

provocation. They discouraged the airing of grievances. The man with a complaint was told, "If you don't like things here, you can quit." To be lenient or friendly or considerate, to give ear to complaints or to grant redress would cause the men to feel that the management was "easy," that it could be "bluffed" or "worked" and that it need not be feared or carefully obeyed. It would destroy the docile, submissive attitude which was essential if the men were to yield readily to drive methods. Above all, it was felt that the men must be made to feel that the management was strong and powerful, determined to have its way and not to be trifled with.

This process of inspiring fear among the workmen was admirably adapted also to inspiring hatred. In proportion as the management succeeded in arousing fear among the men it succeeded also in arousing antagonism. The effect upon morale is obvious. Men endeavor to render good service to those toward whom they bear good will but withhold their cooperation from those toward whom they bear ill will. The drive system stimulated the workers to withhold production merely as an expression of antagonism to the management. With the changed economic position of labor during the last five years, the drive system has had to be severely tempered or abandoned. The old fear of the management has largely gone and labor's habit of docility has at least temporarily been broken. The resentment and antagonism aroused in prewar days by the drive methods still remain, however, and continue to cause a deliberate withholding of output.

III

Among the things which induce men to feel responsibility for the character of their work is the conviction that the job is important, that it makes a difference how it is done, and that in doing it the workman is making himself of some importance. Take away this feeling and the work tends to become drudgery, which the men then seek to lighten by doing as little as possible. Modern industry contains a number of influences which tend to diminish the importance of their work in the eyes of the workmen and consequently their disposition to feel a keen responsibility for the character of their workmanship. The acquisitive philosophy which actuates business enterprises is to be reckoned such an influence because it leads workmen to think of their work as something done for someone's profit rather than for someone's service. The mere vastness of modern industrial establishments is another influence. In the case of certain "key men," vital to the operation of the establishment, large size has the contrary effect; for the larger the establishment dependent upon them, the more important, naturally, the key men feel themselves and their work to be. The ordinary workman, however, tends to think himself and what he does of little consequence, simply because he is one among so many and his work such a small part of the whole.

The feeling of unimportance which is fostered among workmen by their submergence in the vastness of industrial establishments is accentuated by the character of the work. For years managers in their pursuit of economy have been endeavoring, by the subdivision of labor and the development of jigs, fixtures, and semiautomatic machines, to make each job as simple, mechanical, automatic, and fool-proof as possible, to eliminate from it as far as possible all the exacting elements, to relieve the workman of the necessity of exercising dexterity, initiative, ingenuity, judgment, and to reduce his responsibility to the minimum.[5] The results from the standpoint of economy have been admirable, but from the standpoint of morale pernicious. The typical factory job has been reduced to something that "anyone can do" after a few days' or weeks' experience. The workmen have this emphatically impressed upon them by observing new men, often of nationalities which they regard as inferior, being brought into the shop and taught the work in a short time. They realize the unexacting character of their work, how little skill or judgment it requires, and, instead of feeling pride and satisfaction in doing it, look with contempt upon it and feel more or less humiliated because compelled to do it.

To feel the importance of his work and responsibility for the manner in which he does it, the workman must know what he is doing, what purpose the part he is working upon serves in the finished product, and how the service rendered by the finished product will be affected by faulty performance of his operation. Many workmen, however, are ignorant of these matters. The parts they work on are to them merely pieces of wood or metal upon which they perform given operations in given ways, without definite vision of what would happen when the finished product is used should their

[5] The elimination of the exacting elements from the great mass of the jobs is often accompanied by the concentration of these exacting operations in a few "key positions." Thus in machine shops the exacting elements in the work of the machine hand who formerly ground his own tools, set his own machine, and perhaps repaired his own belts have been transferred respectively to tool grinders, machine setters or set-up men, and beltmen. The importance of these "key" positions, the more exacting character of the work attaching to them, the responsibility which they involve, and the pride which the holders are able to feel in their work naturally tend to raise the morale of their holders. It is to be noted as a qualifying circumstance, however, that the exacting elements removed from a single job, instead of being concentrated in a single position, are often, as in the above illustration, distributed among several positions, the importance of which, of course, is thereby limited, to the detriment of morale.

operation be improperly done. It is only recently that enterprises have undertaken to teach men the significance of their jobs.

The practice of working to standards of accuracy tends to prevent the men from feeling themselves and their work of importance because of ability to do exceptionally accurate work. Custom has caused them to regard skill principally as ability to do exacting and difficult work rather than ability to do much work. They tend to feel more pride in ability to do good work than in ability to work fast. The system of working to predetermined standards of accuracy limits the worker's opportunity to distinguish himself by doing work of exceptional quality, for to pass inspection a part need only be of standard accuracy. Parts which are better than the standard are treated no differently from parts which barely pass. The only distinction is between parts which are up to standard and those which are not. A workman, though able to do work substantially superior to that required, will receive no credit for such exceptionally accurate work.

Finally, the policy pursued by many managements of endeavoring to build up in the men the feeling that they are of little importance, their services of little value, and they themselves easily to be dispensed with now prevents the men from appreciating the importance of their work. This policy is similar to the one previously discussed, of endeavoring to create fear of the management and, like it, has been pursued as a part of the drive system and for the purpose of rendering the workmen more submissive to drive methods. Managements have believed that if the men learned to regard their work and consequently themselves as important, they would lose their docility, become self-assertive and difficult to control. To render them docile and easily handled, it is desirable that they regard themselves and their services as of little importance to the enterprise. Hence by such means as criticizing freely but commending sparingly, a hair-trigger readiness to discharge, telling those with grievances to get jobs elsewhere if dissatisfied, and by the general attitude maintained toward the men, managements have endeavored to build up among them a feeling that they are of little consequence.

This policy has had a twofold effect. In the first place, in causing the men to feel themselves of little importance it has inevitably led them to consider their work of little importance. Hence it has tended to lessen the men's feeling of responsibility toward their work. In the second place, the policy has conflicted with the recognition of merit and, as a result, has fostered the feeling among the men that the management did not appreciate merit and was unwilling to recognize it. In order to cause the workers to feel themselves of little importance it was desirable that merit be not freely recognized. Too-generous recognition of merit, it was felt, would encourage the workers to feel themselves of value to the enterprise, develop a feeling of self-confidence and independence among them, and lessen their willingness to submit to drive methods. The effect of lack of appreciation of merit upon morale is discussed more in detail below.

IV

Adequate recognition of merit and good service is an important prerequisite to high industrial morale. Failure of managements to recognize merit and good service adequately means much more than a mere lack of material rewards to stimulate the men to do their best. In the first place, it is important as an indication of the attitude and temper of the management. The lack of material rewards for merit naturally leads the workmen to feel that the management does not appreciate good service. No exertion is more repugnant to workers, however, than that which they believe will not be appreciated. The feeling that good service is not appreciated is nearly as potent as the lack of rewards for good service in deterring the men from exerting themselves to render service of exceptional merit. In the second place, failure to recognize merit tends to deprive the men of definite hopes for better things in the future. Men can endure disagreeable and discouraging conditions for a considerable period without serious lowering of morale, provided they have reasonable expectations of better things. But the hope of better things tomorrow is needed to take their minds off the difficulties of today. To men deprived of reasonably definite expectations for the future the difficulties of today seem doubly onerous. Because the work in modern industry involves much that is disagreeable, it is important, in order to sustain high morale, that workmen see something better ahead. Without such visions they become easily discouraged, disgusted with their jobs, inclined to develop the "don't give a damn" spirit and to seek relief from the disagreeable and discouraging features of their work by doing no more than is necessary.

Modern industry has conspicuously failed to meet the problem of the recognition of merit. This failure manifests itself in a number of ways. Perhaps the most striking has been the practice of arbitrary piece-rate cutting, which has penalized workers of exceptional proficiency instead of rewarding them. When the large earnings which lead to the cutting of the rate are due to the rate being set too high rather than to the exceptional speed of the worker, penalization of merit does not necessarily occur when the rate is cut, but the psychological effect upon the worker is the same. Moreover in practice sufficient discrimination has not been shown between cases where earnings have been high because the rate has been too high and those where they have been high because the workmen have been exceptionally proficient. A less striking but fully as important instance of failure to reward merit has been the traditional wage policy. Instead of carefully observing the performance of each worker, of maintaining individual efficiency records and promptly raising each man when his work showed clear improvement, managements have pursued the policy of paying the minimum wage necessary. The attitude of managements has been, "If the men are willing to work for a given wage, why should we pay more?" The effect of this policy has been that advances in pay, instead of being promptly awarded when deserved, have been delayed as long as possible, being granted only when regarded as necessary either to prevent the men from leaving or to allay discontent. Since old employees often become more or less attached to their jobs and not only less likely to leave but also less likely to complain, the policy of paying no more than necessary has resulted frequently in old and experienced employees receiving less than younger men of less skill and experience but more difficult to hold. It has also resulted in the taking on of new men at higher rates than those received by men already employed, the management being compelled to pay the market rate to obtain new men, but finding itself able, temporarily at least, to hold men already employed at a rate slightly below the market.[6] In short, the tendency of the traditional wage policy has been to cause wage increases to go not necessarily to the most deserving but to those who were regarded as most likely to quit or to make trouble and to those who were good at talking to the foreman and who were not afraid to risk their jobs by asking for more money.[7]

[6] Within the last year the writer was hired by a large factory at five cents an hour more than the rate received by the man who showed him how to run his machine. All new men for the given class of work were given the same rate received by the writer, which was uniformly higher than that received by those already in the employ of the enterprise and doing this particular grade of work.

[7] The traditional wage policy has resulted inevitably in flagrant injustices. For example, an employee in a Midwestern factory received thirty-five cents an hour although other men doing the same work received fifty-five cents. The manager stated that to obtain new men to do the work, he would be compelled to pay fifty-five cents. He also stated that the thirty-five-cent man was as competent as any of the others and worth as much as any of them. He received less, the manager said, because he was an old employee who had been with the firm for some twenty years and had become so attached to his job that it was felt that there was no likelihood of his leaving, especially since his age would handicap him in obtaining a desirable job elsewhere. Hence it had been considered unnecessary to raise him when the others had been raised.

In an Eastern automobile factory one of a gang received ten cents an hour less than the others doing the same work. Asked whether this worker was less competent than the others, the manager replied that he was not but on the contrary was one of the best in the gang. He received less, the manager said, because he was a cripple and hence would have difficulty in obtaining paying work elsewhere. The manager also stated that the workman was somewhat timid and had not asked for an increase or expressed dissatisfaction with his wage. Hence no necessity of raising him had been felt.

Finally, among industry's manifestations of failure to reward merit should be mentioned absence of systematic promotion based on efficiency. Some enterprises, it is true, have attempted to practice a policy of promotion, relying on the foreman's more or less indefinite impression as to who is entitled to advancement. The two essentials to a satisfactory system of promotion in accordance with merit—namely, definite lines of advancement which enable the men to see clearly what they are in line for and individual efficiency records which give the men assurance that selections for promotion will not be a matter of guess work—are to be found only in a small minority of establishments. In fact foremen not infrequently are opposed to promoting exceptionally proficient men on the ground that when a man is exceptionally good at a given operation, it is best to keep him at it rather than advance him to another job at which he may be a failure or merely an indifferent success.

Among the steps taken to combat the numerous causes which combine to create low industrial morale, greatest progress has probably been made in eliminating failure to recognize merit. Although most enterprises still lack a policy of carefully rewarding merit, a rapidly increasing number now pursue such a policy. Systematic promotion on this basis is fast being introduced; wage policies are being altered so that individual rates of pay are raised on the initiative of the management whenever a worker shows himself entitled to more; and the practice of arbitrary piece-rate cutting is being gradually abandoned. (Progress in the abandonment of arbitrary piece-rate cutting has been least satisfactory, for often the abandonment of this policy is more nominal than real. Considerable arbitrary rate cutting is done by slightly changing a job, putting a new rate on it, and calling it a new job.)

The development of the highest degree of interest in the job and the keenest sense of responsibility for the character of its performance presupposes a belief that the job or at least the workman's connection with his employer is more or less permanent. Hence the transitory and precarious nature of much of the employment in modern industry is to be accounted a source of low industrial morale. Herein appears the significance, from the standpoint of morale, of the absence of machinery for the adjustment of grievances, and of the failure either to protect workmen against arbitrary discharge by provision for truly judicial inquiry into alleged cases of incompetency or misconduct, or to protect workers against layoff by regularization of production or by reduction of the working period instead of the force in slack times. Realizing that, in absence of machinery for the adjustment of grievances, to leave is their only recourse in event of dissatisfaction with conditions of employment (barring appeal to the management, which too often has been futile), and realizing also that they may at any time lose their jobs by discharge or layoff, workmen are discouraged from regarding their employment in a given establishment as permanent, from looking forward to an extended career in the establishment, and from cherishing hope of advancing by meritorious service to more responsible, more exacting, and better-paying work. They inevitably feel the slighter degree of interest in their jobs and the less keen sense of responsibility for their workmanship which arise out of the feeling that the work is likely to be but temporary.

V

Most important of all in creating the prevailing low state of industrial morale is the workmen's conception of the relationship between themselves and industry—the feeling on the part of wage earners that, instead of industry's being conducted for their benefit as well as for the benefit of the stockholders, it is devoted almost exclusively to advancing the interests of the stockholders, and that instead of being considered a part of industry and insiders in it, they are outsiders whom industry is not interested in serving but from whom it is interested in getting all that it can.

So contradictory to the non-wage earner's conception of industry is the workman's that it is difficult for non-wage earners to appreciate the workman's point of view. To those outside the wage-earning class, industry is a servant—a tremendously powerful and beneficent servant, which makes possible our relatively high standard of living. The non-wage earner compares the comforts and conveniences of the present day with those of a century ago and realizes that it is modern industry with its machines and technical experts which makes possible the difference. The fact that industry makes possible the existing ways of living is to him its distinguishing feature, the thing which determines his conception of it and molds his attitude toward it. To the non-wage earner, industry before everything else is a *servant*—the efficient servant which enables him to live as well as he does.

To the wage earner with his radically different contact, industry is far from being a willing and efficient servant to which he should be grateful for making possible his present standard of living and for helping him to raise it. The workman is aware of the constant endeavor of industry to make itself more efficient. He knows of the elaborate staff of operating and technical experts which industry maintains to improve machines and processes, to discover new short cuts, and to speed up the men—all for the sake of "more production" and "lower costs." The workman realizes to some extent the zeal and persistency with which these experts apply themselves to the task of increasing the efficiency of industry and the ingenuity and skill which they display. But the workman is also well aware that the object of this pursuit of efficiency is not to benefit him. He knows that industry does not seek efficiency in order to pay higher wages or to grant shorter hours, or to put itself in a position to mitigate the severity of the wage earner's task. He knows that it seeks to serve one interest and one interest only. It seeks to be more efficient in order that it may pay higher dividends. Hence the wage earner, unlike the non-wage earner, is unable to regard industry as his servant. To him it is only the servant of the stockholders.

The workman, however, does not merely observe that industry makes no positive endeavor to advance his interests (except such incidental and unimportant assistance as it extends in the form of "welfare work"). He observes that in the case of each of the three principal prerequisites to the attainment of a richer and more enjoyable life, more money, more leisure, and relief from fatigue, industry positively *opposes* rather than aids him. If the workman desires higher wages he usually encounters opposition. If he desires a shorter working period he likewise finds opposition. Industry has sought to maintain the ten-hour and even the twelve-hour day and in some instances the seven-day week. It has shown little interest in the relief of fatigue and, instead of seeking to lessen the severity of work, has sought constantly to increase speed. The indirect effects of efficiency upon the standard of life, which the economist is fond of stressing, the workman does not see. What he does see is the deliberate and conscious effort of industry to keep wages low and hours long, and to increase the speed of work. Hence he learns to see in industry not a servant seeking to help him to live better but a master seeking to dominate him, to hold him down rather than to help him advance, an obstacle rather than an aid in his struggle for a better life. To the question, "What does industry do for you?" the non-wage earner promptly answers, "Makes possible my high standard of living"; but the wage earner answers, "Works me as hard as it can, pays me as little as it must, and fires me if I kick."

Consider the effect of the workman's conception of industry and of its relation to him upon industrial morale. What could be better calculated to destroy his sense of obligation toward the enterprise by which he is employed, and his willingness to cooperate to make it successful and to promote its prosperity, than the feeling that it is seeking to dominate and use him rather than to serve him, that it is working against him rather than for him, that it is seeking to pay him as little as it finds necessary, to prevent his wages from going any higher than it can help, to keep his working day at as many hours as possible, and to get more and more out of him by pushing up the speed of the work? If one party to an arrangement seeks to give as little and to get as much as possible, is it not natural for the other party to do likewise? No one would expect a workman who feels that his employer pays the bare minimum which economic conditions compel him to pay to reciprocate by doing his best to promote the interests of his employer. Workers cannot be expected to be more interested in promoting the prosperity of industry than industry is in promoting the prosperity of workmen. When industry seeks to keep wages low and hours long, when it consistently resists the workmen's efforts to raise their standard of life, workmen cannot be expected to be interested in helping to make profits large. The workman fails to see why he should help the businessman make money when the businessman is not helping him to make money. An active effort on the part of the workmen to promote the prosperity of industry can scarcely be expected until the workmen feel that industry is a friendly rather than a hostile force; until they believe it is devoted to the promotion of their interests rather than the exploitation of their weakness; until they believe it is interested in making wages higher, in making hours shorter, and in mitigating the severity of the work; until they believe they will promptly and directly share in any increase in the prosperity of industry. Wages and conditions of labor must be determined by the same principle by which dividends are determined—by the *ability* of industry to pay more or to improve conditions not by the *necessity* of so doing.

This appears to touch the crux of the problem of industrial morale. Workmen cannot be expected to feel the maximum interest in the affairs of industry and the greatest willingness to cooperate in order to promote its prosperity unless they are able to identify themselves with industry, to feel themselves to be a part of it, insiders in it, and to feel also a sense of ownership in it. The feeling of belonging to a thing appears commonly to induce a feeling of ownership toward it. They cannot feel themselves to be a part of industry or industry to be in part theirs unless industry is devoted in a substantial measure to the promotion of their interests, unless managements strive just as energetically to raise wages as they do to raise dividends. The thing which now creates a gulf between the men and industry, which causes them to feel that they are not a part of the enterprises for which they work and that the enterprises are not in part theirs, is the fact that industrial enterprises are devoted primarily or exclusively to the service of the stockholders, often at the expense of the interests of the men. When the men observe how completely outside the purposes of business enterprises is the promotion of their interests, they cannot escape feeling themselves to be merely outsiders.

Suppose, however, that the elaborate organizations which the workmen now see devoted so exclusively to the interests of the stockholders were conducted equally for the benefit of both workmen and stockholders, that the object of the ceaseless striving after efficiency and lower costs were just as much the paying of higher wages as the paying of higher dividends, and that every increase in profits meant just as much an increase in wages as it did an increase in dividends. Instead of feeling themselves mere tools employed for the profit of the stockholders the men would be able to feel that industry existed as much for them as for anyone else, that industrial enterprises instead of being their masters, attempting to get as much *out* of them as possible, were attempting to produce as much *for* them as possible. Knowing that industry was being conducted as much for their benefit as for the benefit of the stockholders, the workmen would be able to feel that industry in part belonged to them and that they were a part of it. They would feel themselves to be insiders and would feel the interest in the affairs of industry and the responsibility for its prosperity which an insider, as contrasted with an outsider, feels.

VI

From the foregoing discussion it appears that if cooperation is to be obtained in industry it must be mutual, that labor cannot be expected to give its best effort to industry until industry, instead of being the servant of capital and the master of labor, is the joint servant of them both, devoted equally to the advancement of the interests of each. But the question may be asked, does not this imply the necessity of a fundamental change in industrial organization? If industry is to be made as much the servant of labor as of capital, and if labor is to share just as directly in the increased prosperity or efficiency of industry as does capital, must not labor share equally with capital in the control of industry? The answers to these questions must probably be in the affirmative. Industry cannot be expected to be administered as much in the interest of labor as of capital unless labor participates on a somewhat equal basis with capital in the administration of industry.

Hence the problem of industrial morale appears to be in a substantial degree a problem of industrial organization. The present form of industrial organization, which leaves labor on the outside as regards share in control and direct participation in prosperity, renders it inevitable that, barring the employees of a few altruistic employers, the workmen shall feel that they are simply outsiders used for the benefit of industry. Hence the present form of industrial organization must itself be counted among the causes of low industrial morale; and a change in the organization of industry must be regarded as among the prerequisites to the solution of the problem of industrial morale.

It is impossible in this paper to discuss the complicated problem of industrial organization. It is enough to emphasize the intimate relationship between the problem of industrial morale and the problem of industrial organization. Industry cannot afford to have such an important factor as labor on the outside. The better organized, the more powerful and self-conscious labor becomes, the less can industry afford it. As the importance of labor's cooperation becomes more apparent, the more apparent will become the desirability of making labor an insider in industry with a corresponding voice in its direction. The admission of labor to a full share in the administration of industry is not likely to come except by a slow evolutionary process, but the need of labor's cooperation may be expected to be one of the principal forces impelling changes in industrial organization and shaping its future form.

15

The Current Labor Policies of American Industries

Quarterly Journal of Economics, May 1929.

I

To THE abundance of cheap immigrant labor are primarily attributable the two outstanding features of American labor policy before the war—the tendency to adapt jobs to men rather than men to jobs, and the policy of obtaining output by driving the workers rather than by developing their good will and cooperation.[1] The immigrants, being largely peasants or agricultural laborers, were available only for the least skilled industrial tasks.[2] The extraordinarily wide differential which thus came about between the wages of skilled and of unskilled labor gave managers a strong incentive to develop methods which demanded little skill and experience. This incentive was all the greater because training immigrants was extremely difficult when many supervisors could not speak the language of their men. Consequently managers displayed amazing ingenuity in adapting work to unskilled laborers, but manifested almost no interest in developing the men themselves.

There are several reasons why immigration encouraged the practice of driving workers rather than of developing their cooperation and good will.[3] Differences in language and outlook between immigrants and their supervisors prevented even employers of good intentions from gaining the confidence of most of the workers, and hence their cooperation. On the other hand, the immigrants were easily driven because they came largely from

[1] In 1910, 48 per cent of all persons engaged in mining, 31.9 per cent of those engaged in manufacturing and mechanical pursuits, and 26.3 per cent of those engaged in transportation were foreign born. H. Jerome, *Migration and Business Cycles* (New York, 1926), p. 46.

[2] During the period of July 1, 1907, to June 30, 1923, 26.4 per cent of the immigrants declared their occupation as "laborers" and 25.1 per cent as "farm laborers" (Jerome, p. 48). Nevertheless it is true that immigration played an extremely important role in supplying men for the skilled handicrafts—so much so that the decrease in immigration since 1915 has caused the problem of apprentice training to become acute.

[3] There were, of course, other reasons for the drive system.

oppressed classes or races among which a tradition of docility was well established and because their lack of industrial experience and their ignorance of English made many of them reluctant to leave one job and look for another. And employers were able to prevent concerted resistance to drive methods by mixing workers of different, and often antagonistic, nationalities.

With labor policies so crude and simple, industrial relations were not believed to require the attention of highly paid experts. The handling of men was largely left to the department foremen, who were free to hire, fire, and promote as they saw fit, who set piece rates, and who often possessed considerable discretion in fixing hourly rates of pay.

The European war caused net immigration to drop from 815,000 in 1913 to 50,000 in 1915 and 19,000 in 1916. It also created an intense demand for labor. The labor shortage was accentuated by the rapid spread of the eight-hour day,[4] and later by the entrance of several million men into military service. Labor turnover roughly doubled;[5] strikes increased from 1,420 in 1915 to 3,517 in 1916[6] and 4,450 in 1917;[7] and union membership grew from 2,716,900 in 1914 to 3,508,400 in 1918 and 5,110,800 in 1920.[8] Under these conditions the old drive policies no longer worked—they simply drove men to quit or to strike. Consequently employers suddenly became interested in gaining labor's good will. By the end of 1919, seventy-one enterprises voluntarily established shop committees through which employees could take up grievances with the management.[9] Many firms began to provide their men with life insurance and, in some cases, with disability and sickness insurance. Sales of group insurance increased from $45,474,000 in 1914 to $178,336,-000 in 1917 and $425,574,000 in 1919.[10] The number of concerns which offered

[4] From 1914 to 1919, the percentage of employees in manufacturing who regularly worked no more than 48 hours a week increased from 11.8 to 48.7. United States Bureau of Census, *Census of Manufacturers*, 1923.

[5] For the period 1913–14, the United States Bureau of Labor Statistics found a separation rate of 95 per cent and for the year ending June 30, 1918, of 183 per cent. P. F. Brissenden and E. Frankel, *Labor Turnover in Industry* (New York, 1922), p. 88–89.

[6] *Monthly Labor Review* (April 1916), pp. 13–18.

[7] United States Bureau of Labor Statistics, *Handbook of Labor Statistics* (1924–26), p. 570.

[8] Leo Wolman, *The Growth of American Trades Unions, 1880–1923* (New York, 1924), p. 33.

[9] National Industrial Conference Board, *The Growth of Works Councils in the United States* (New York, 1925), p. 10. Forty-nine of these committee plans were initiated in either 1918 or 1919. In addition, eighty firms had established shop committees at the order of the government.

[10] New York Trust Company, *The Index* (May 1927), p. 7. Group insurance is a plan by which a group of employees is insured. A master policy covering the entire group is issued to the employer, and individual policies are issued to the insured employees. The expense may be borne entirely by the employer or jointly by the employer and employees. The most usual type of group insurance is life insurance, but accident or sickness insurance is sometimes provided.

old-age pensions to their employees increased from 1914 to 1919. Prior to 1914, one hundred and forty-five old-age pension plans had been established in American industry. During the five years ending in 1919, ninety additional plans were instituted.[11] Most important of all, the control over labor in many enterprises was transferred from the foremen to a newly created executive, the director or manager of personnel.

The severe depression of 1920–21 suddenly changed the labor market from a sellers' to a buyers' market. Except for a few months in 1923, the market has remained continuously favorable to employers. The net immigration, it is true, has been less than before the war, but this has been more than counteracted by the enlarged flow of labor from farm to city; labor turnover has been low except for a short time in 1923; and, from 1920 to 1926, the total union membership in the United States dropped about 30 per cent. *In short, every aspect of the postwar labor situation might be expected to cause employers to abandon their newly acquired interest in labor's good will and to revert to prewar labor policies.*

And yet, except in a few cases, this has not happened. On the contrary, the efforts to gain labor's good will have steadily grown. Shop-committee plans increased from 145 in 1919 to 385 in 1922 and 432 in 1926.[12] Most of the group insurance now in effect has been sold since 1921.[13] During the last five years, over three hundred companies have instituted some form of stock purchase for their employees. Of the 370 private industrial pension plans now in existence, 72 were established between 1921 and 1925.[14] Two thirds of 1,058 enterprises which give vacations with pay to manual laborers began the policy since the beginning of 1920.[15] During the last ten years, industrial good will has been rapidly acquiring an importance in American business comparable to that which consumers' good will has long possessed; employers have been developing the same keen interest in the good will of their workers, the same willingness to make large expenditures in order to obtain it, that they have manifested toward the good will of their customers. The outstanding task of one who essays to account for the present labor

[11] Pennsylvania Old Age Pension Commission, A. Epstein, *The Problem of Old Age Pensions in Industry* (Harrisburg, 1926), p. 21.

[12] "An Advance Report of an Investigation of the National Industrial Conference Board on the Growth of Employee Representation in the United States," *Law and Labor,* IX (March 1927), 61.

[13] Prior to the depression of 1920–21, the largest sales of group insurance occurred in 1919, when $425,574,000 was sold. In 1924, however, the sales were $597,765,000; in 1925, $998-784,000; and in 1926, $1,050,605,000. New York Trust Company, *The Index* (May 1927), p. 7.

[14] Epstein, *The Problem of Old Age Pensions,* pp. 115–126.

[15] *Law and Labor,* X (May 1928), 113.

policies of American industry is to explain why this interest in industrial good will has continued to grow, despite the shift of power in favor of employers; why, in other words, the passing of abnormal war conditions has not produced a reversion to prewar labor policies.

II

The failure of the change in the labor market to end the interest of businessmen in labor's good will appears to have been due to three principal reasons: (1) the dread of labor trouble; (2) the inability or the unwillingness of employers to reduce wages in proportion to the drop in wholesale prices; and (3) a better appreciation by managers of the relation between morale and the efficiency of labor. It is desirable to point out that ever since 1910 a foundation for better industrial relations was slowly being built up by the growing use of time and motion studies in setting piece rates. The intimate connection between time and motion study and labor policies has been inadequately appreciated. It is easy, however, to see why inaccurate methods of timing operations prevented satisfactory industrial relations. When a rate was based on too liberal a time allowance, a cut in the rate was, sooner or later, inevitable. Such cuts, of course, excited intense ill will. But they did more than this—they led workmen to restrict output, and this in turn led the management to use drive methods. Time study has tended to diminish driving by making rate cuts unnecessary.

The employers' dread of labor trouble reached its apex in 1920. During the preceding six years, the labor movement had threatened the power of American employers more seriously than ever before. Trade-union membership, as was stated above, nearly doubled between 1914 and 1920. Unionism even established itself temporarily in such open-shop strongholds as the Chicago packing plants, the mills of the United States Steel Corporation, and the shops of the Pennsylvania Railroad. The employers' alarm was accentuated by the belief that American labor was in danger of becoming radical—a fear that was fostered by the general strikes in Seattle and Winnipeg during 1919, the Boston policemen's strike, the great coal strike of 1920, and the support of the Plumb plan by the heretofore staid and conservative railroad brotherhoods. The dread of radicalism was encouraged by interested groups, such as the National Civic Federation and the National Security League, and even by Mr. Gompers and his lieutenants, who skillfully fostered the country's fears in order to present conservative unionism as a bulwark against irresponsible and dangerous groups.

Businessmen did not suddenly lose their fear of labor troubles when the collapse of prosperity filled the streets with job seekers late in 1920. Even at the end of 1921, union membership was a million more than in 1914, and strikes, though fewer than in the immediately preceding years, were still numerous. Furthermore, the precipitous drop of prices made wage reductions imperative, and every cut in wages increased the danger of trouble. At this particular time, however, many concerns were peculiarly unable to risk a strike because, during the boom period, they had speculated heavily in raw materials. When prices fell, these enterprises were left with a large floating indebtedness which they were under the necessity of liquidating as soon as possible. Consequently they were in no position to face the loss of production and the heavy expenses which a strike would entail. The double necessity of reducing wages and of avoiding strikes stimulated the interest of many employers in gaining labor's good will.

In some plants, especially those in which the workers were organized, wage reductions led to strikes, and, in many cases, the unions lost and were destroyed. It is extremely interesting to note the effect of these victories over unions upon the personnel policies of the enterprises. The management was usually determined never again to be troubled by labor organizations. Accordingly, after driving out unions, many concerns immediately embarked upon carefully planned attempts to gain the good will of their employees. Some enterprises followed the destruction of unions with the creation of shop committees to represent the employees. The General Electric Company, the International Paper Company, and many of the railroads are examples. Especially noteworthy is the great interest which many railroads developed in the welfare of their shopmen following the great strike of 1922. Roads which had done little to cultivate the good will of their shopmen as long as the workers were organized suddenly became greatly concerned about good industrial relations when their men returned to work as nonunionists.

Another outstanding determinant of American postwar labor policy has been the inability or the unwillingness of employers to reduce wages in proportion to the fall in nonagricultural wholesale prices. Between 1920 and 1921, nonagricultural wholesale prices decreased about 31 per cent, and between 1920 and 1922 about 30 per cent.[16] Had employers been more willing

[16] *Handbook of Labor Statistics* (1924–26), p. 517. In addition, the physical volume of manufacturing dropped about 23 per cent between 1920 and 1921 (*Federal Reserve Bulletin*, XIII [February 1927], 100). By 1922, the physical volume of manufacturing had recovered to the 1920 level.

to risk labor trouble, they undoubtedly could have reduced wages in proportion to wholesale prices. (The willingness of employers to risk labor trouble in order to reduce wages should be carefully distinguished from their willingness to risk it in order to get rid of unions. The very fear of unions and radicalism which made businessmen overreluctant to reduce wages made them overeager to destroy labor organizations. Consequently, some enterprises recklessly courted costly shutdowns in order to drive out unions, and others timidly refrained from making urgently needed wage reductions.) But the fear of strikes, which has already been explained, checked the reduction in wages. The best measure of wage *rates* is hourly earnings. Between 1920 and 1921, the hourly earnings of factory workers decreased about 14 per cent, and between 1920 and 1922 about 19 per cent.[17] Wage rates undoubtedly dropped somewhat more—possibly from 20 to 25 per cent between 1920 and 1922.

Having failed to reduce wages in proportion to the fall in prices, employers were compelled to make their men more efficient. This might have been done by reverting to prewar methods; but the same dread of strikes which prevented more drastic wage reductions made many managements unwilling to try driving. One course remained—to increase efficiency by developing a stable force and by winning the good will and cooperation of the men. This alternative was widely adopted.

Possibly the most important determinant of postwar labor policies, at least during the last four or five years, has been the growing realization by managers of the close relationship between industrial morale and efficiency. When the severe drop in prices and in sales during 1920 and 1921 caused managers to search meticulously for methods of cutting costs and of increasing sales, many ways were found in which the workers could help *if they would.* Spurred by financial necessity, managers sought the aid of their employees to an unprecedented extent in saving material, reducing the wear and tear on equipment, diminishing the amount of spoiled product, improving the quality of workmanship, and even in soliciting additional business. Some concerns, such as the Bethlehem Steel Corporation and the International Harvester Company, have used their shop committees to reduce costs. The committees have suggested ways of saving labor and materials; they have made improvements in the location of tool rooms and in the methods of issuing tools; they have helped increase the value of scrap by segregating ma-

[17] National Industrial Conference Board, *Wages in the United States, 1914–1927* (New York, 1928), p. 29.

terials of varying composition; and they have assisted in raising the quality of workmanship.[18] Bethlehem Steel has attempted to interest its employees in saving supplies by calling attention through its committees to the expense of certain things which are often wasted.[19] Following the success of the union-management cooperative plan on the Baltimore and Ohio, the Canadian National, and other railway systems, several roads have sought to develop a cooperative plan in conjunction with their "company unions." The Atchison, Topeka and Santa Fe and the Union Pacific are examples. Public-utility companies have endeavored to interest their employees in the more accurate reading of meters and computation of monthly bills. The People's Gas Light and Coke Company of Chicago is an example. Although ten operations are necessary to prepare the bill for each reading, the company reports that in 1926 the errors in meter reading and billing were only about .007 per cent.[20] The Chicago Motor Coach Company and the Boston Elevated Railways have conducted fuel-saving campaigns among their employees. Possibly the most notable attempts to gain the help of employees have been made by the railroads. Almost all roads have instituted fuel-saving campaigns among the engineers and firemen. Many have sought to reduce damage to equipment and freight by appealing to the train crews for smoother handling of cars and to the freight-house employees for more careful handling of less-than-carload shipments. Between 1920 and 1927 payments on loss and damage per carload of revenue freight decreased from $2.66 to $0.72. To a small extent this was due to the drop in the price level. A number of companies have sought the aid of the shopmen in increasing the locomotive mileage per engine failure. Some roads now post the mileage per engine failure in the roundhouses, and the Rock Island publishes the figures by divisions in its monthly magazine. Efforts have also been made to interest the shopmen in reducing the number of locomotives found defective by the federal inspectors,[21] and to gain the cooperation of all employees in improving the "on-time" performance of both passenger and freight trains. The Erie, the Missouri Pacific, the St. Louis and San Francisco, the Southern, and the Chi-

[18] *Bethlehem Review* (April 22, 1925), p. 3.

[19] For example, the company calls attention to the fact that in 1925 its expenditures for soap were $8,161; paper towels, $14,780; brooms, $17,255; window glass, $25,855; shovels, $30,000; electric light bulbs, $200,000. *Bethlehem Review* (April 24, 1924), p. 4.

[20] People's Gas Light and Coke Company, *Year Book* (1927), p. 15.

[21] Some indication of the improved morale and increased efficiency in the railroad shops is given by the decreasing proportion of locomotives found defective by the federal inspectors. In the year ending June 30, 1923, when the percentage was affected by the shopmen's strike in the summer of 1922, 65 per cent of the locomotives inspected were found defective and over 10 per cent were ordered out of service. In the next year, the percentage of defective locomotives dropped to 53 per cent; in the year ending June 30, 1925, to 46; in the year ending

cago and Great Western now announce in their monthly magazines the percentage of passenger trains arriving on time; the Rock Island publishes the on-time performance of both passenger and freight trains and also a list of the trains which have maintained perfect records; and the New York Central publishes the percentage of less-than-carload shipments which arrive on time.

Of course, the efforts of managements to reduce costs and to increase sales by persuading wage earners to go out of their way to help would not have persisted had the results not been satisfactory. But the workers responded to appeals for their help with almost startling generosity. And naturally this response has profoundly affected the labor policies of employers. The more plainly the workers have demonstrated the value of their cooperation, the greater has become the interest of managers in labor's good will. During the war, and to a great extent during the postwar depression, managers sought labor's good will largely in order to avoid labor trouble. As the fear of strikes has diminished and as labor has demonstrated its willingness to cooperate, the desire for labor's help has become the most important single influence molding the labor policies of American employers.

III

The methods by which industrial enterprises have attempted to make their workers more efficient and more contented fall into six principal groups: (1) helping their employees acquire property; (2) helping them acquire a "stake" in the enterprise by which they are employed; (3) protecting them against arbitrary treatment; (4) rewarding continuity of service; (5) giving them opportunities to advance to more responsible positions; (6) giving them security.

The rise of about 11 per cent in the real hourly earnings of factory workers between 1920 and 1925 led to a great increase in saving among wage earners.[22] It was natural that the growing tendency of employees to save

---

June 30, 1926, to 40; and finally, in the year ending June 30, 1927, to 31 per cent. The percentage of locomotives ordered out of service dropped from 8.8 in 1923–1924 and 5.0 in 1924–1925 to 3.6 in 1925–1926, and 2.6 in 1926–1927. The Interstate Commerce Commission, *Sixteenth Annual Report of the Chief Inspector, Bureau of Locomotive Inspection* (1927), p. 1.

[22] From 1921 to 1926, saving deposits in banks and trust companies in the United States increased from over $16.5 billion to nearly $24.7 billion; and between 1921 and 1925 the assets of building and loan associations increased from $2.89 billion to $5.509 billion (*Statistical Abstract of the United States* [1926], pp. 263 and 267). It is impossible to say what proportion of the increase was in the savings of wage earners, but these savings probably increased as rapidly as deposits in savings banks.

should be encouraged by businessmen. The disposition of employers to foster saving was stimulated by their fear of radicalism and by a somewhat naive faith in the power of even small amounts of property to alter the fundamental economic views of its owners.[23] But even though small amounts of property may influence the economic philosophy of wage earners less than most employers believe, the stimulation of saving is undoubtedly good personnel policy because a man who is setting aside a small part of his earnings each week cannot escape feeling that he is getting ahead, even if slowly. This may not make him satisfied with his compensation, but it is likely to take the edge off his dissatisfaction.[24]

The most usual method of encouraging saving is for the employer to obtain an authorization from the employee to deposit to the employee's credit in a savings bank a stipulated deduction from his pay. The employee escapes the temptation to spend his money before he has made a deposit of part of it, and he even avoids the trouble of going to the bank. This plan is followed by the Crompton and Knowles Loom Works. After five years, 80 per cent of its 2,500 employees were participating in the arrangement.[25] Some enterprises offer to hold the savings of their employees. In such cases, the company usually pays the same rate of interest that it would pay a commercial bank for a loan—usually 1 or 2 per cent more than the rate paid by savings banks on time deposits. This is the practice of the Commonwealth Edison Company of Chicago, which has an Employees' Saving Fund, to which, at the end of 1926, 5,165 of its 9,900 employees were subscribers.[26] An exceptionally high rate of interest is paid by the General Electric Securities Corporation which sells its bonds to the employees of the General Electric Company. The bonds pay 6 per cent, to which is added 2 per cent as long as the owner is in the employ of the General Electric Company. Thirty-two thousand employees, or nearly half the force, have purchased these bonds.[27]

[23] For example, John F. Tinsley, Vice-President of the Crompton and Knowles Loom Works, says: "Through a savings plan the employers make more capitalists among the wage earners and I think all must feel that this is a desirable end. The more the wealth of the country is distributed, the less socialistic will be the tendencies among the masses of our people" (*New Phases of Industrial Management* [privately printed, Worcester, Mass., 1926], p. 194). C. J. Hicks, Executive Assistant to the President of the Standard Oil Company of New Jersey, writes: "The employee who is saving his money becomes a capitalist and is no longer hostile to capitalism" (*Harvard Business Review*, II [January 1924], 200).

[24] It is true also that the desire to save is likely to increase the efficiency of piece and bonus workers, who constitute about half of the employees engaged in manufacturing. (See the result of an investigation which I made of this point, and which was published in the *American Economic Review*, XV, Supplement [March 1925], 94–95.) But strange to say, I have been unable to discover a single case in which it is acknowledged that saving is encouraged because of the expected effect upon the efficiency of piece workers.

[25] Tinsley, *New Phases of Industrial Management*, p. 176.

[26] Commonwealth Edison Company, *Annual Report* (1926).

[27] General Electric Company, *Thirty-fifth Annual Report*, p. 21.

Many workers wish not merely to save, but to save in order to acquire homes. From the standpoint of the employer, it is more desirable that an employee have a house which is partly paid for than that he have several hundred dollars in the bank. A man who owns a house near his place of work is more or less tied to his job, unless there are other plants nearby at which he could pursue his occupation. And, more important, a worker who is buying a home is careful to avoid discharge, unlikely to resign (unless he is confident of promptly obtaining another job) or to strike, and more eager to increase his earnings and hence his efficiency. Since the payments on a house usually extend over years, the encouragement of home ownership is an effective way of diminishing the independence of the workers.

Home ownership is encouraged by selling houses or land to employees at low prices, by assisting employees to finance the acquisition of property, by giving free legal and architectural help, and by establishing building and loan associations among employees. The Eastman Kodak Company has built houses in small groups and has sold them at prices which gave the workers the benefit of the economical multiple construction.[28] The Commonwealth Steel Company appraises the land and examines the title without charge, and lends money at 5 per cent, repayable in monthly installments.[29] The Oneida Community sells land at a low rate, provides the services of an architect, assists the employee to borrow from a bank on a first mortgage, and itself lends him money on a second mortgage. On completion of the house, the company gives the worker a bonus of $200. To receive assistance, the worker must have saved 10 per cent of the cost of the house.[30] The Bethlehem Steel Corporation guarantees or purchases the second mortgage on the property, and gives the employee free architectural, engineering, financial, and legal advice.[31] The Milwaukee Electric Railway and Light Company has established a mutual-savings, building, and loan association for its employees. The assets of the association exceed $8 million and more than four fifths of the married male employees own their own homes.[32]

[28] *Law and Labor*, IX (May 1927), 133.

[29] *The Commonwealther*, XIII (June 1927), 3.

[30] Esther Lowenthal, "The Labor Policy of the Oneida Community, Ltd.," *Journal of Political Economy*, XXXV, 122.

[31] Presidential Address of C. M. Schwab before the American Society of Mechanical Engineers, December 1927, *Law and Labor*, X (January 1928), 18.

[32] The Milwaukee Electric Railway and Light Company, *Year Book* (1926), p. 41. It seems clear, however, that in some cases the employees who have been assisted to acquire houses have almost exclusively been minor officials of the company or higher-paid, skilled employees. For example, by the end of 1926, the General Electric Company had assisted 1,125 of its 75,000 employees to purchase homes (General Electric Company, *Thirty-fifth Annual Report*, p. 21). Furthermore, the average value of the houses which the employees were assisted to purchase was $8,000—distinctly more than most wage earners could afford. So far as the

From encouraging employees to save it is a short step to encouraging them to invest their savings in stock of the enterprise which employs them. Some businessmen and personnel experts have acquired amazing faith in the power of a few shares of stock to make workmen interested in efficiency and unwilling to join trade unions or to strike. Glen A. Bowers of the Industrial Relations Counselors, Inc., has stated that employee stock ownership "makes the worker a capitalist in viewpoint and this renders him a conservative and immune from radical ideas"; [33] F. H. Sisson, Vice-President of the Guaranty Trust Company, has said that diffusion in the ownership of industry "will decrease class-conscious antagonism by bringing about a partial identification of interests as between laborers and capitalists," and "will discourage the propagation of dangerous and violent social theories"; [34] and T. E. Mitten of the Philadelphia Rapid Transit Company has stated that "if the principle were applied to all industry, America would within a year become a strike-proof nation." [35] During the last seven years nearly all of the largest enterprises in the country have made special efforts to sell stock to their employees. In order to induce the employees to invest, the shares are often offered at substantially less than the market price. The Union Oil Company of California sold stock to its employees at 5 per cent below the market; the Electric Storage Battery Company at about 20 per cent below. The American Telephone and Telegraph offered stock to its employees in 1925 at $125 a share. The range of the market price for that year was from $130 to $145. Early in 1926, the Pullman Company sold stock at $140. The low for the year on the New York Exchange was $145½ and the high was $199½. Several of the Standard Oil companies gave the employee a share for every two that he purchased. This, of course, amounted to selling the stock at one third below the nominal price. In still other cases, employee stockholders are paid a special bonus, in addition to regular dividends. General Motors Corporation and the International Harvester Company pay a bonus of $2 a share for five years after the employee has paid for his stock; E. I. du Pont de Nemours and Company pays $3; the Bucyrus Company pays a bonus of $5 a share for five years, regardless of whether or not the stock has been paid for.

No recent development of personnel practice has attracted wider atten-

---

effect on labor turnover is concerned, it is probable that the workers who have purchased houses are those who are most inclined to be stable, and who in many cases would probably purchase homes without aid from their employers.

[33] *New Tactics in Social Conflict*, p. 4.

[34] *General Electric News, Lynn Works*, IX (December 2, 1927), 9.

[35] Philadelphia Rapid Transit Company, *Service Talks*, VII (September 28, 1926), no. 21.

tion than employee stock ownership. And yet it is among the least significant of the new labor policies. When a large proportion of employees owns stock, the ground is undoubtedly prepared for the management to insist upon better workmanship or more output, and, in consequence, the task of improving the efficiency of the force may be somewhat easier.[36] But unless the management demands greater efficiency, stock ownership alone is not likely to produce it. Nor is there any real evidence that a few shares in a huge corporation affect the fundamental economic views of the worker, cause him to "feel himself a partner rather than a servant," render him a "capitalist in viewpoint" and "immune from radical ideals," or make him less willing to join a trade union or to strike for higher wages.[37] As a matter of fact, it would be surprising if these results occurred. During 1927 the average factory worker in the United States earned $1,299. In order, therefore, to possess an interest as a stockholder which approximates his interest as a wage earner, the typical factory worker would need about $20,000 of stock. The National Industrial Conference Board has found that the average subscription in three hundred and fifteen corporations is only $1,300.[38] It is scarcely conceivable that the ownership of twelve or thirteen shares would materially alter the attitudes of employees toward wages, hours, or working conditions. Suppose that a man earns $1,200 a year and that he has purchased thirteen shares of $100 each. Dividends at the rate of 7 per cent yield him

[36] In a large number of cases, the proportion of employees owning stock is very large: for example, Bethlehem Steel Corporation, over 60 per cent (*Bethlehem Review* [February 1, 1926], p. 3); the Commonwealth Edison Company, 43 per cent; the Standard Oil Company of California, 86 per cent of 14,200 eligible employees; the Standard Oil Company of Indiana, 71 per cent of 22,000 eligible employees. (Foerster and Dietel, *Employee Stock Ownership in the United States* [Princeton, 1926], pp. 115, 138, 160, 161.)

[37] The defeat of a carpenters' strike in Reading, Pennsylvania, is said to have been aided by the refusal of some carpenters to participate because they owned small blocks of stock and considered themselves "members of the firm" (*Labor Age*, XIV [July 1927], 24). But it is obvious that the carpenters may have given this reason to justify a refusal which rested upon other grounds—probably upon a conviction that the strike would fail. In any event, the effect of a share in a *small* enterprise sheds little light on the probable effect of a share in a large concern. For example, the fact that the photoengravers' union has found it desirable to prohibit its members from buying shares in the small shops which are typical of the photoengraving industry, or that the International Ladies Garment Workers' Union has experienced difficulty in controlling the small shops manned by working partners and known as "social shops," is scarcely indicative of how a worker will be affected by a $1,000 interest in a billion-dollar enterprise such as United States Steel or General Motors.

[38] The New York Trust Company, *The Index* (October 1928), p. 8. Many enterprises limit the number of shares which will be sold to an employee under the stock-purchase plans. The Great Atlantic and Pacific Tea Company restricts subscriptions to one tenth of the employee's annual earnings; E. I. du Pont de Nemours and Company to one fifth; and General Motors to one third. The American Telephone and Telegraph Company permits each worker to purchase one share for each $300 of his annual earnings; the Bethlehem Steel Corporation, one for each $400; and the Electric Storage Battery Company and the Pullman Company, one for each $500.

$91 a year. Assume that the men seek a 10 per cent advance in wages. The company replies that such an increase would necessitate cutting dividends in half, a loss to the employee-stockholder of $45.50 a year. But a 10 per cent advance in wages would give him $120 a year. Is it likely that the title to thirteen shares of stock would diminish his interest in higher wages or prevent him from joining a union or from striking in order to get them?

The traditional drive system of management naturally gave rise to many methods of handling labor which created ill will and resentment. In order that enterprises should gain the good will of their men, it was necessary for them to effect substantial improvements in the practices of foremen and other minor executives in dealing with labor. Three principal methods have been used: (1) centralization of control over discharges; (2) foreman training; (3) shop committees. These efforts to improve the handling of men are among the most important developments in American personnel practice.

Of the three methods, that used most extensively has been the transfer of authority to discharge from the foreman to the head of the labor department. In some cases the foreman is permitted to dismiss men from his own department but not from the service of the firm; in others, the approval of the labor manager is necessary even to remove a worker from a department. Some companies, including several of the Standard Oil companies and the Boston Rubber Shoe Company, forbid discharge for the first offense except in the case of a few serious acts which are listed in the book of rules. Restricting the freedom of the foreman to discharge has profoundly affected his methods of handling men because it has deprived him of his chief disciplinary device. This has compelled him to rely less upon threats for obtaining results and to make greater efforts to get along amicably with his men. The consequence naturally has been a drop in the number of petty grievances.[39]

[39] As a matter of fact, labor managers almost invariably approve the discharges which the foremen recommend. Nevertheless, the centralization of authority over discharges has a profound effect because the foremen interpret it to mean that discharges are not desired. The restrictions upon the freedom of foremen to discharge might be expected to reduce the number of discharges, and to some extent this result seems to have occurred. For example, during the period 1910 to 1915, the United States Bureau of Labor Statistics found a discharge rate of 17.5 per cent among 153 establishments (Brissenden and Frankel, *Labor Turnover in Industry*, pp. 80–81). Among 78 plants, I found a discharge rate of 12.5 per cent during the period 1910 to 1913 (*The Turnover of Factory Labor*, p. 94). The Metropolitan Life Insurance Company, however, found a discharge rate of only 6.5 per cent among 300 plants for 1926, and of 5.5 per cent for 1927 (*Handbook of Labor Statistics* [1924–26], p. 585, and *Monthly Labor Review*, XXVII [July 1928], 27).

But discharge rates based upon the average number of workers employed are somewhat misleading. Discharges vary with hirings as well as with the size of the force, because it is the newly hired men who are most likely to be discharged. The principal cause for the decrease

The eagerness of managers to improve the handling of men has led hundreds of enterprises during the last seven or eight years to establish classes in foremanship. Swift and Company, for example, has put 4,600 of its foremen through a training course. The United States Chamber of Commerce has a record of 324 foremanship courses (exclusive of correspondence courses) conducted during the year ending in June 1926 and of 933 in the year ending June 1927.[40] So rapid has been the spread of foreman training that concerns have been created to conduct classes on a commercial basis, and some trade associations, such as the National Metal Trades Association, have prepared courses for their members.[41] Of less importance than classes on foremanship, but significant of the trend of the times, are the special handbooks for foremen, such as the Bethlehem Steel Corporation's *Hints to Foremen,* the Scoville Manufacturing Company's *Foremen's Manual,* and, most elaborate of all, the Lehigh Coal and Navigation Company's *Mine Management Policies,* running in the revised edition to one hundred and seventeen pages.

These policies with regard to foremen—depriving them of authority to discharge and training them in better methods of handling men—do not entirely eliminate grievances. The steady increase in the number of shop committees since 1921 indicates that many managers recognize the undesirability of permitting grievances to smolder unadjusted. The disposition of the cases handled by these committees is significant. Mere statistics, of course, cannot prove that employees are obtaining justice, but the many decisions in favor of the men suggest that managers consider it wise to be fair in at least a substantial proportion of the cases. The Bethlehem Steel Corporation reports that, out of 2,316 cases, 1,682, or over two thirds, were settled in favor of the employee.[42] Of more than 1,800 matters considered by the plant assemblies of

---

in the discharge rate has been the decrease in the number of hirings. Compared with the number of hirings, however, discharges are not clearly less numerous now than before the war. For the period 1910 to 1915, the Bureau of Labor Statistics found one discharge for every 5.5 men hired; but, for the period 1910 to 1913, I found one discharge for every 8.3 men hired. For 1926, the Metropolitan Life Insurance Company found one discharge for every 8.4 hirings and, for 1927, one discharge for every 7.3 hirings.

[40] U. S. Chamber of Commerce, *Growth of Foremanship Courses in the United States, June, 1926, to June, 1927,* p. 11.

[41] The current methods of training foremen leave much room for improvement. The situation has been well described by L. A. Hartley: "It is well to observe here that many of the foremen training activities conducted at present throughout the country are open to considerable question as permanent methods. The success of the short, intensive foreman training conferences is due very largely to the fact that the present methods of foremanship have been so generally poor that almost any kind of a discussion of present problems is helpful (U. S. Chamber of Commerce, *Employee Training,* p. 17.)

[42] John Calder, "Five Years' Representation Under the Bethlehem Plan," *Iron Age,* CXI, 1,694.

Swift and Company prior to 1925, about 70 per cent were settled in favor of the employee.[43] At the Lynn works of the General Electric Company, 274 cases were settled by the shop committee in the first two years: 76 were decided in favor of the employee, 99 in favor of the management, 7 were compromised, 21 were withdrawn, 14 were not considered, and 52 were submitted to other authorities for decision.[44] Out of the 45,930 cases considered by the employee committees of the Pennsylvania Railroad during the four years ending 1924, 21,904, or 47.7 per cent, were adjusted or compromised in favor of the employee; 13,320, or 29 per cent, were withdrawn or decided against the employee, and 10,693, or 23.3 per cent, were appealed to the next higher officer.[45]

The acute scarcity of labor during the war caused employers to discover the importance and the cost of labor turnover. The postwar drop in prices, which compelled managers to hunt for every possible way of cutting costs, accentuated the interest of managers in reducing labor turnover. One of the outstanding features of recent American personnel policy, therefore, has been the endeavor to increase the efficiency of labor by encouraging continuity of service.

Many of the recent developments in personnel practice—such as group insurance, old-age pensions, promotion of home ownership, protection of employees against arbitrary treatment, and vacations with pay—have the encouragement of continuous service as *one* of their purposes. Except possibly in the case of the encouragement of home ownership, the predominant purpose is not to encourage continuous service. A principal object of insurance and pensions is to provide a regular way of dealing with situations which have often subjected employers and their men to appeals for charity and which have been injurious to morale. Of special importance, however, are specific rewards for continuous service. Many enterprises now advance the wages of workers at given intervals of employment. The Oneida Community, Ltd., adds 1 per cent to the worker's wage at the end of the month. This rises by gradual increments to 5 per cent in twelve months, 7 per cent in two years, and 10 per cent in five years.[46] The Eastman Kodak Company pays a wage dividend which is affected by the employee's length of service. For every dollar in excess of the first dollar paid in dividends on

[43] Swift and Company, *Year Book* (1925), p. 51.

[44] E. H. Morell, *The Lynn Plan of Representation*, chart 3. But the most significant thing about these figures is the small number of cases which arose during a period of two years in a large force. The conclusion appears to be inevitable that the shop committees failed to command the confidence of the employees, or that there were other more satisfactory ways of having grievances adjusted.

[45] Pennsylvania Railroad Company, *Employee Representation*, p. 47.

[46] Esther Lowenthal in *Journal of Political Economy*, p. 118.

common stock the company pays a wage dividend of $5 on every $1,000 earned by the worker in the preceding five-year period. The company is now paying $8 on its common stock. This makes the wage dividend $35 for every $1,000 earned by each employee during the last five years of service.[47] The Studebaker Corporation pays a bonus of 5 per cent of the worker's last year's earnings on each anniversary of his service, and the Crocker-McElwain Company a differential for each year of service up to five, when the worker becomes eligible to apply for a written agreement guaranteeing him full employment.[48]

One of the most effective ways of encouraging continuous service is to transfer men, after a given period of employment, from the hourly to the monthly payroll, thus giving them the privileges enjoyed by the regular salaried staff. This is done by the Commonwealth Edison Company of Chicago at the end of a year's service. An employee on the hourly payroll who is absent a day or so for some reason other than sickness is not compensated, but the man on the monthly payroll receives full pay. A worker on the monthly payroll who becomes ill or is injured receives *full* pay for seven working days. Thereafter, until he returns to work, he is paid a *portion* of his salary. The hourly man is given half of his normal wages for the first seven days of his incapacitation, but after this receives nothing.[49] Most important of all is the fact that the worker who is on the monthly payroll feels that he has a permanent job because reductions in staff are made by first laying off the hourly men. The Standard Oil Company of California also places all employees, regardless of their work, on a monthly salary after a year's service. Every salaried employee, whether common laborer or manager, receives the same privileges—an annual vacation of two weeks with full pay, a pension after a number of years of service, and compensation during sickness and recovery from accident for a certain period depending upon the length of employment, but regardless of whether or not the sickness or accident was incurred in line of duty.[50] Most effective of all rewards for continuous service is a definite guaranty of steady employment to workers who have served a given time. The Crocker-McElwain Company, for example, guarantees full-time work to each man who has been in its employ five years or more.[51]

A highly significant recent development in American personnel policy

[47] *Law and Labor,* IX (May 1927), 132. An official of the company says: "We believe that the payment of these wage dividends has resulted in greatly reduced labor turnover and increased loyalty and efficiency of employees."

[48] "Stabilizing Employment Plans," *Law and Labor,* VIII (May 1926), 140.

[49] Letter from the company to the writer.

[50] W. J. Held, *Forbes Magazine* (June 1, 1925), pp. 261–262.

[51] *Law and Labor,* VIII (May 1926), 139.

has been the creation of definite sequences of promotion and the filling of vacancies in accordance with merit. The mere transfer of the control of hiring and firing from the foreman to the labor manager has tended to bring about advancement on the basis of merit. As long as each foreman hired and promoted his own men, many vacancies were filled not by promotions but by hiring new men. In fact, many foremen preferred not to promote their best men. The better a man performed an operation, the more anxious the foreman was to keep him at it because it meant one less job to worry about. Some foremen deliberately gave the best places to friends. This was done partly out of friendship, but partly also because a group of friends sprinkled throughout the force made the department easier to manage. Occasionally the foreman used his control of jobs to create a personal machine which rendered him more or less independent of his superiors. The firm could not discharge him without causing a large part of the department to quit.

The labor manager, on the other hand, has no reason to refuse to promote a worker simply because the man is especially good at a certain job, nor is he seriously tempted to promote on the basis of friendship because, as a rule, he is intimately acquainted with relatively few wage earners in the plant. In addition, the spread of the policy of promotion by merit has been stimulated by two special causes—the desire to keep down labor turnover and the necessity of adjusting labor costs to the postwar level. Studies of labor turnover revealed that many enterprises were losing good men because workers could obtain better jobs more easily by changing employers than by winning advancement. In order to encourage continuity of service, many labor managers have adopted the policy of hiring outsiders only for the least desirable jobs and of filling the best jobs by promotion. This policy was still further stimulated by the drop of prices in 1920. In order to reduce labor costs in proportion to the fall in prices, it was necessary to provide every possible incentive for workers to be more efficient, and one incentive offered them has been the opportunity to win better jobs by merit.

Not only has advancement in accordance with merit spread rapidly, but many enterprises have established classes in which employees can prepare themselves for promotion. The Boston Elevated Company offers courses in business English, interdepartmental accounts, and automotive maintenance; the General Electric Company has a vast variety of courses of different grades, including machine design, blueprint reading, shop mathematics, armature winding, mechanical drawing, switchboard testing, and courses for clerical employees. The Milwaukee Electric Railway and Light Company has classes in car wiring, boiler-room practice, and the company accounting system.[52] Swift and Company reports that on November 1, 1924, over 6,200 of its 50,000 employees were pursuing educational work offered by the company.[53] This included physics, salesmanship, business English, and a general course —in which were enrolled 500 of the most promising young men in the production departments of thirteen plants—covering the policies and methods of the company.[54] The Crompton and Knowles Loom Works, in the year 1923–24, had about 600 of its 2,500 workers enrolled in its evening courses on loom construction, mechanical drawing, blueprint reading, machine-tool operation, pattern making, molding, forging, welding, weaving, and the properties of iron and steel.[55]

Promotion in accordance with merit is of great importance, because the employee feels that he has more than a job,—that he has the opportunity for a career, a chance to advance into jobs which he had dreamed of holding but which he could never see a way of reaching. And the workers who best appreciate the chance to win promotion by merit are likely to be the ablest and most ambitious in the force, precisely those who, if given no opportunity to advance, would be most active in organizing and leading trade unions. Unionism in the United States has always suffered because of the relative ease with which able wage earners could rise out of their class. Employers are now making advancement for superior workmen more attainable than ever before. In a generation or two, the effect upon the labor movement may be substantial.

Of the most recent developments in personnel practice by far the most important is the endeavor of employers to make the jobs of their men more secure. Why have managers suddenly acquired such a deep and genuine interest in the stability of employment? The severe unemployment of 1921 is not a satisfactory explanation; the grave depressions of 1893, 1908, and 1914 aroused no similar interest. Four principal circumstances appear to explain the present concern of businessmen with the regularity of employment. Possibly the most important has been the desire of managers to reduce labor turnover—a desire which was created, as we have seen, largely by the war boom. It is apparent that whatever is done to make jobs attractive can have little effect if the workers regard their positions as only temporary. Nor is there much point in encouraging continuity of service if, at frequent intervals, one fifth to one third of the force is laid off. A second reason for the

[52] The Milwaukee Electric Railway and Light Company, *Year Book* (1926) p. 38.

[53] Swift and Company, *Year Book* (1925), p. 52.

[54] *Year Book* (1923), p. 49.

[55] Tinsley, *New Phases of Industrial Management*, pp. 103–105.

interest of managers in stability of employment has been the urgent necessity of increasing the efficiency of labor. The extreme inefficiency of labor during the war and the great drop in prices during 1920 led managers to examine more carefully than ever before the causes of inefficiency. As a result, managers were profoundly impressed by the fact that many workers deliberately withhold production and use great ingenuity to conceal how little they are doing because they fear that more output would mean less work. It was apparent to employers that this conscious restriction of output could be removed only by giving the men reasonable assurance of steady work. Finally, the interest of businessmen in security of employment was stimulated by their fear of radicalism and their desire for the good will of their men. Managers readily appreciated that nothing is more likely to make a workman radical than uncertainty of employment, and nothing is more likely to keep him conservative than the prospect of steady work. And as businessmen studied the problems of creating industrial good will, they perceived that most wage earners are not contented unless they have steady jobs and that all efforts to gain labor's good will must rest upon a foundation of regular employment.

The methods by which business enterprises have endeavored to stabilize employment are too numerous to describe here.[56] There is abundant evidence, however, that substantial results have been achieved. Thus, Procter and Gamble now guarantees its men forty-eight weeks of work in the calendar year. In consequence, labor turnover has dropped to the almost unheard-of rate of less than 1 per cent a month in a force of 6,500 men.[57] The Delaware and Hudson Railroad, by using a flexible working day and working week, has avoided laying off a single skilled worker since the plan was put into effect in 1923.[58] During the anthracite coal strike, the entire shop force was kept engaged by working five days a week and by making repairs in advance of the need for them. The best evidence of the general progress in stabilizing employment is the decrease in the layoff rate. The United States Bureau of Labor Statistics, collecting data for the period 1910–19 and for the year ending June 30, 1918, found an average layoff rate of 13 per cent in a group of 261 plants employing the equivalent of 691,681 full-time workers.[59] For the period 1911–15, I found an average layoff of 35 per cent among 78 plants employing 154,933 workers.[60] On the other hand, in 1926, the median layoff rate among

[56] For an excellent description of them, see Professor H. Feldman's book, *The Regularization of Employment* (New York, 1925).

[57] "Stabilizing Employment Plans," *Law and Labor*, VIII (May 1926), 139.

[58] "Stabilizing Employment Plans," *Law and Labor*, VIII (May 1926), 142.

[59] Brissenden and Frankel, *Labor Turnover in Industry*, pp. 80–81.

[60] S. H. Slichter, *The Turnover of Factory Labor*, pp. 86 and 92.

the enterprises reporting to the Metropolitan Life Insurance Company was 6 per cent [61] and, during 1927, 6.5 per cent.

The methods which have been discussed are the most important ways in which businessmen are endeavoring to make their men more efficient and more contented, but they are not the only ways. In concluding this description of personnel practices, it is desirable to indicate briefly a few of the many other methods by which enterprises are seeking to build up good will and efficiency. The Hammermill Paper Company provides garage facilities at a nominal figure and sells gasoline to employees at one cent below the public filling-station price; the Spicer Manufacturing Corporation sells its men coal, gasoline, and oil; [62] L. Bamberger and Company employs a lawyer to advise employees, without charge, on legal matters; [63] and the Hammermill Paper Company provides free notary service and aid in filling income-tax returns. A number of enterprises maintain dental dispensaries, which give free examination, advice, and temporary treatment, and, in some instances, as in the case of Bausch and Lomb Optical Company, do permanent dental work at low rates.[64] Bausch and Lomb maintains an eye clinic, which gives examinations, and supplies frames and lenses far below cost; [65] L. Bamberger and Company has a chiropodist, who visits the store hospital two days a week and does work at a nominal charge.[66] The Standard Oil Company of California has arranged for employees to obtain loans for restricted purposes at 5 per cent interest, using their stock in the company as collateral.[67] *The Employees' Handbook* of the Public Service Company of Northern Illinois says: "It is recognized that there are times when an employee may need temporary financial assistance, on which occasions the company stands ready to extend such assistance" (p. 22). Some personnel departments offer to advise employees in regard to personal problems. *The Book of Information and Instruction for Employees* issued by the Boston Rubber Shoe Company says: "The Industrial Relations Department will gladly help any employee who has a personal matter on which he wishes counsel, such as sickness in the family, financial problems, the purchase of or renting of a home, and so forth. . . . You should feel free to go to the office (with your foreman's permission, if during working hours), with the assurance that your best interest will be served by so doing" (pp. 6–7). *The Employees' Manual* of

[61] United States Bureau of Labor Statistics, *Handbook of Labor Statistics* (1924–26), p. 585.
[62] *Rules and Regulations* (April 21, 1924), p. 24.
[63] *Employees' Information Booklet*, pp. 10–11.
[64] *Instructions for Employees* (June, 1924), p. 7.
[65] *Ibid.*, p. 7.
[66] *Employees' Information Booklet*, p. 9.
[67] Standard Oil Company (California), *Bulletin* (March, 1927), p. 5.

the Scoville Manufacturing Company states that "it is the aim of the Industrial Service Department to render personal assistance to all employees in solving their personal problems. There are many instances when a situation can be faced more bravely and effectively if a friend is at hand to consult; the Employment Office undertakes to be such a friend."[68] *The Employees' Information Booklet* of L. Bamberger of Newark says: "If you need help or advice in finding a place to live, to board, to spend a vacation, or if you are worried about anything, consult with the Social Service Secretary, or see one of the Employment managers, or a member of the education department" (p. 10). Describing the personnel methods of the Commonwealth Steel Company, A. G. Morey says: "The men voluntarily bring many of their human problems to us, and a word of counsel, the use of our legal facilities, or other influences, have enabled us to be of service and advice to the men in many of their personal problems."[69] Among the cases recently handled by the employees' service division of the People's Gas Light and Coke Company of Chicago were the following numbers of requests for several kinds of help: advice in investing money, 32; intercession for reduction of physicians' bills, 15; adjustment of difficulties with installment houses, 18; consultation on business affairs, 91; financial assistance in emergencies, 52; arrangement for hospital, surgical, or medical care, 190; advice in obtaining specialist for dental work, 22; advice in obtaining eye, nose, ear, or throat specialists, 43; assistance in drawing up wills, 33.[70]

IV

One of the best ways of appraising the significance of the new personnel methods is to ask in what degree they are responsible for the present labor situation in the United States. The situation is characterized by four outstanding features: (1) a spectacular increase during the last seven years in the physical production per wage earner; (2) a substantial drop in union membership; (3) a large decrease in the number of strikes; (4) a low rate of labor turnover. The new labor policies have played an important part in producing these results, but it seems reasonably clear that a far more important part has been played by general economic conditions.

Between 1919 and 1925, the per capita production of workers engaged in manufacturing increased about 37 per cent. In other lines of industry the

[68] Edition of February 1, 1927, p. 25.
[69] *The Commonwealther,* XIII (June 1927), 4.
[70] *People's Gas Club News,* XVI (November 15, 1928), 7.

increase was almost as great. To some extent this great increase is attributable to the new labor policies. The practice of promoting in accordance with merit has undoubtedly stimulated many workers to produce more; and the interest which employers have aroused in saving and home ownership has probably increased the efficiency of many piece and bonus workers. Of special importance has been the greater security of employment, for which the new labor policies are partly responsible. The job has ceased to be merely a temporary position which the worker is bound to lose soon and has become a valuable piece of property which he can probably keep for the rest of his life, *provided he meets the management's standards of efficiency.* The fact that he now has something worth keeping has produced a radical change in his willingness to do his best. Stabilized employment means that enterprises are hiring fewer men for temporary jobs. The result is that a man who loses his job finds employment more difficult to obtain and unemployment becomes a more serious matter. Thus stabilization of employment tends to discourage resignations and to increase the workers' fear of discharge or layoff. Finally, the creation of industrial good will has undoubtedly tended to make men more efficient. Its effect, however, has probably been primarily indirect. Employees who are well disposed toward their superiors are not, because of that fact, necessarily more industrious or more painstaking. But good will does render workmen more responsive to demands made upon them by the management, and thus it enables alert and aggressive executives to obtain better results from their men.

The most important causes for the increased production per worker, however, have not been personnel policies. Undoubtedly the greatest cause of all has been the elimination of inefficiencies which grew up during the war and postwar boom, when speed was all-important and when less than usual attention was paid to costs. A second important cause for the greater output per worker has been the movement of prices, especially the downward trend of nonagricultural wholesale prices in general and of interest rates in particular, and the tendency of wages to fall less than other prices and, during the last five years, not to fall at all. The great fall of prices in 1920 and 1921 created an imperative necessity that enterprises quickly and drastically reduce costs. This led managers to search as they had never searched before for ways of obtaining more output from fewer men. Falling prices have also hastened the normal tendency for production to be concentrated into the newest plants. These, as a rule, are precisely those which are best equipped and in which labor is most effective. The pronounced downward trend of long-time interest rates since 1921, the rise in wages between 1922 and 1924, and the stability of wages since 1923 have made it profitable for employers to replace methods of production which require less waiting and more labor with methods which require more waiting and less labor. Such changes, of course, increase physical output per laborer. Finally, production per worker has been increased by the abundance of labor. This in turn is a result of the concentration of output in plants where labor is most effective, of the spread of labor-saving methods of production, of the depression in agriculture (which has accelerated the movement of men from farm to city), and of the failure of wages to fall with the decrease of wholesale prices. Despite the restrictions on immigration, therefore, the supply of labor has been large in relation to the demand. At certain times and in some places there have been serious labor shortages in the building trades. There was also a more or less general shortage for a few months late in 1922 and early in 1923. Naturally, only the best workers have been hired and there has developed a serious unemployment problem among the older and the less efficient men. And because wage earners have found jobs none too easy to obtain, they have hesitated to resign and have improved their efficiency in order to avoid discharge.[71]

The second outstanding feature of the labor situation is the drop in union membership. Since 1920, the membership of the American Federation of Labor has decreased about 30 per cent. This figure, however, is somewhat misleading because the building boom has enabled the building-trades unions to grow. Between 1920 and 1923 the membership of thirty-three organizations which draw their adherents primarily from manufacturing dropped from 1,220,100 to 648,000, or nearly half. Between 1923 and 1928, despite the stability of the business situation, the membership of the same unions decreased nearly 18 per cent, from 648,000 to 532,000.

The precipitous fall in union membership between 1920 and 1923 was due principally to the withdrawals which normally accompany severe unemployment and to the break-up of unions after unsuccessful strikes. The failure of the strike was, of course, due to the severe unemployment which prevailed throughout 1921 and most of 1922. About half of the drop in membership between 1923 and 1928 occurred in the International Ladies Garment Workers' Union, an organization which has been badly disrupted by the communists rather than by the employers. The remainder of the shrinkage

[71] The evidence does not appear to bear out the oft-repeated assertion that the increase in output per worker since 1919 is primarily due to the use of more machinery or of more power per worker. I have analyzed the evidence briefly in my article, "The Secret of High Wages," *The New Republic* (March 28, 1928), 183–185. To some extent the efficiency of labor has probably been affected by installment buying because the desire to keep up monthly payments on cars, houses, and radios and at the same time to maintain customary standards of living has undoubtedly stimulated piece and bonus workers to increase their output.

after 1923 was caused primarily by the decrease of about 5 to 6 per cent in the number of workers engaged in manufacturing. Among the skilled craftsmen—who constitute the bulk of the union membership—the decrease was probably more than 5 or 6 per cent.

But have not the new personnel policies at least prevented the spread of unionism and thus are they not *indirectly* responsible for the fall in union membership? To this question the answer must be that the effectiveness of the new labor policies in checking the spread of unionism has not been tested because in few cases has a determined effort been made to organize plants in which the new policies are found. The first real test of the new personnel practices is likely to come in the railroad shops. During the war, the railroad shop workers were strongly organized, but the unions were driven out of about half the shops in the bitter strike of 1922. Many roads which destroyed the unions have adopted the new personnel methods—"company" unions, group insurance, employee stock ownership, and security of employment. It is certain that the shop-craft unions will soon endeavor to re-establish themselves on the unorganized roads. Because the tradition of unionism still remains among these workers and because the men are largely skilled craftsmen, the efforts to reorganize the shops should furnish a real test of whether the new personnel policies make workers satisfied to remain unorganized. Thus far the effort to organize the employees of the Interborough Rapid Transit Company in New York City is the most notable attempt to spread unionism among the employees of a company which practices the new methods of handling men. It is undeniable that during recent years the interest of wage earners in unionism has been weak, but this is most plausibly explained by the advance of about 11 per cent in the real earnings of factory workers between 1920 and 1926, and by the fact that, during most of the time since 1921, jobs (outside of the building trades) have not been easy to obtain.

The third outstanding feature of the American labor situation is the drop in the number of industrial disputes from 3,630 in 1919 to 1,035 in 1926.[72] The number of employees involved fell from 4,160,000 to 330,000.[73] Undoubtedly the new personnel policies have tended to diminish strikes. But they are not responsible for this great decrease. Over four fifths of the strikes in the United States are called by labor unions. The new methods of handling labor, however, have made greatest progress in nonunion shops. Industrial disputes

[72] *The Handbook of Labor Statistics* (1924–26), p. 572. In 1917 there were 4,540 disputes, but the total number of employees involved was less than one third the total of 1919.

[73] *The Handbook of Labor Statistics* (1924–26), p. 570. In the case of many of the smaller disputes, the number of employees involved was not reported. The figures given above include 2,665 disputes in 1919 and 783 disputes in 1926.

appear to be primarily products of price fluctuations. They are most numerous when changes in the cost of living or in wholesale prices cause workers or employers to seek changes in the customary wage rates. The remarkable fewness of disputes since 1922 is primarily attributable to two facts: the stability of the cost of living and the failure of the rather substantial drop in non-agricultural wholesale prices since 1923 to produce a movement to reduce wages. For the latter fact, however, as will be pointed out presently, the new labor policies are in some degree responsible. Important also in reducing the number of disputes have been the increase in the real earnings of factory workers and the weakening of many unions by the depression of 1921, so that they have been unable to undertake aggressive organizing campaigns. The reduction in the number of strikes since the abnormal war period has been world-wide and has been quite as great in other countries as in the United States. The National Industrial Conference Board has estimated the number of workers involved in strikes and lockouts per 1,000 of population as follows:

	1920	*1927*
United States	40 (in 1919)	3
Germany	135	6
Great Britain	63 (in 1919)	2
Belgium	40	5
France	35	2
Netherlands	10	2
Canada	16 (in 1919)	2

Only in Australia has there been an increase. There the persons engaged in industrial disputes were 19 per 1,000 of population in 1919–20 and 25 in 1927.

The fourth outstanding feature of the labor situation is the low rate of labor turnover. Before the war, turnover rates in manufacturing averaged in good years not far from 100 per cent. In 1926, a fairly active year, the Metropolitan Life Insurance Company reports a median turnover rate of 47 per cent among several hundred factories.[74] In 1927, a less active year, the median rate was 41.4 per cent.

The protection of workers against arbitrary treatment, rewards for continuous service, and stability of employment have all, of course, tended to diminish turnover. Stabilization of employment has been doubly important. It has reduced turnover directly by decreasing the number of lay-offs, and indirectly by diminishing the necessity of hiring new men, among whom

[74] *The Handbook of Labor Statistics* (1924–26), p. 585.

resignations and discharges are greatest. The decrease in turnover tends to be cumulative, because as resignations and discharges decrease, hirings also decrease; consequently new jobs become more difficult to obtain and men become more reluctant to resign. But the outstanding causes for lower turnover rates have not been personnel policies. The most important single influence has probably been the condition of the labor market—the relative abundance of men and scarcity of jobs which have existed (outside the building trades) almost continuously since 1920. This is indicated by the fact that for several months early in 1923, when there was a shortage of men, resignations underwent a spectacular increase.[75] A second important influence has been the increasing efficiency of wage earners. Labor turnover is largely a function of hirings. It is greatest when forces are being expanded. The rising output per worker has made possible a gradual decrease in the number of men employed in manufacturing.[76] This has greatly diminished the number of hirings and consequently the turnover rate. A third reason for the small turnover has been the relative stability of wages since 1923. Resignations increase during periods of rising wages because men leave the plants which are slow in advancing wages to seek positions in plants which have increased their scales. This is well illustrated by the sudden jump in the resignation rate during the late winter and the early spring of 1923. In this time occurred nearly half of the entire increase in hourly earnings which marked the business recovery of 1922–23.[77] During February, March, and April of 1923, the turnover rate (adjusted for seasonal variation) was higher than at any time between the middle of 1920 and the end of 1927.[78] Since the end of 1923, however, factory wages have been stable and labor turnover has been low.

V

But the fact that the new personnel policies have thus far produced only limited effects upon the labor situation in the United States should not lead us to underestimate their significance. In at least two respects they are likely to produce results of substantial importance.

In the first place, the new policies have materially strengthened the bargaining position of labor. The effect may not be sufficient to compel employers

[75] See *Handbook of Labor Statistics* (1924–26), p. 585.

[76] The number of factory wage earners decreased from 8,768,491 in 1923 to 8,351,257 in 1927 (*Statistical Abstract of the United States*, 1926, p. 745, and *New York Times*, February 28, 1929, p. 12).

[77] National Industrial Conference Board, *Wages in the United States, 1914–1926*, p. 27.

[78] *Handbook of Labor Statistics* (1924–26), p. 586.

to increase wages more promptly in times of rising prices, but it is sufficient to retard or to prevent decreases in wages during times of slowly falling prices, such as the period 1923 to 1928. The new personnel policies have increased the bargaining power of labor because they have made the efficiency of labor depend more than ever before upon the willingness of men to do their best. As a result, enterprises find themselves compelled to retain labor's good will in order to avoid a loss in output. Consequently, when a fall in prices reduces the marginal worth of labor, it is not necessarily advantageous to reduce money wages—to do so might still further diminish the worth of labor by provoking a withholding of efficiency. The most economical (or the least unprofitable) course may be to incur some expense in order to increase the efficiency of labor. There is abundant evidence that the reluctance of managers to reduce wages in the face of declining prices since 1923 has been partly due to the fear that wage cuts would destroy the good will which has been built up at considerable trouble and expense.[79]

In the second place, although the new personnel policies are not responsible for the recent decrease in union membership, it is probable that they will at least retard the spread of unionism. Modern technology has tended to create class cleavage by making the wage earner believe that he is destined always to remain a wage earner. Convinced that he has slight prospect of getting ahead as an individual, and that his welfare depends upon the welfare of his class, he becomes interested in organizing to improve the condition of his class. In the United States, with its rapidly expanding industries, the tendency of workmen to rely upon collective action rather than upon individual effort has been less pronounced than in Europe, but even here there has been a substantial growth of unionism, especially since 1897. Modern personnel methods are one of the most ambitious social experiments of the age because they aim, among other things, to counteract the effect of modern technique upon the mind of the worker, to prevent him from becoming class-conscious and from organizing trade unions. To the ablest, the most ambitious, and the most energetic workers, the very men who would resent most keenly the lack of an opportunity to rise and who would be most likely to become leaders of unions, modern personnel practice offers the chance of a career—promotion by merit through carefully graded steps and along carefully planned roads, and classes in which to prepare for more responsible

[79] Between 1923 and 1926, nonagricultural wholesale prices decreased over 9 per cent and, between 1926 and 1927, over 5 per cent. Hourly earnings of factory workers, according to the National Industrial Conference Board, remained practically stationary between 1923 and 1926. The slight movement was upward. Between 1926 and 1927, the hourly earnings of factory workers increased from 56.2 cents to 56.9 cents (*Wages in the United States, 1914–1927*, p. 29).

positions. To the best men promotion thus becomes a more certain and often an easier way of gaining higher wages than is trade-union action. To the average and subaverage man, the wage earner who cannot expect to advance by unusual skill, knowledge, or exertion, and who is most likely to be interested in group action, modern personnel management offers security—steady work, protection against arbitrary discharge, a pension in old age, and, in some cases, insurance against sickness. (The adequacy of the security is not here in question. Apparently it is sufficient in a period of stable prices to take the edge off the discontent of the wage earners, and that possibly is all that it is intended to do.) In addition, it encourages him to form the habit of relying not upon himself but upon the employer for help in the ordinary problems and even in some of the great crises of life. If the worker has a toothache, the company dentist will cure it; if he has a headache or a cold, he can get treatment from the company doctor (the Standard Oil Company of Louisiana even announces that it is prepared to administer cold vaccine to any employees who desire it); if he or a member of his household needs an operation, the company doctor will help him find a competent surgeon; in some cases, the company optometrist will measure him for glasses, and the company chiropodist will treat his corns. If he has legal difficulties, he can obtain free advice from the company's lawyer; if his wife or children are sick, a nurse from the company will visit his home to render such assistance as she can; if he wishes to save money, the company will act as agent for a bank, deduct the money from his pay check, deposit it in the bank, and do the bookkeeping for him; if he needs to borrow money, the company will lend it to him at a low rate of interest; if he wishes to own his house, the company will build one for him and sell it to him on easy terms, or help him to borrow the money to build it himself.

The efforts of personnel management to check the growth of unionism suggest what is probably the most serious criticism of current labor policies. The criticism is essentially the same as that which John Stuart Mill made of paternalistic government. Mill said:

A people among whom there is no habit of spontaneous action for a collective interest—who look habitually to their government to command or prompt them in all matters of joint concern—who expect to have everything done for them, except what can be made an affair of mere habit and routine—have their faculties only half developed; their education is defective in one of its most important branches. . . . There cannot be a combination of circumstances more dangerous to human welfare than that in which intelligence and talent are maintained at a high standard within a governing corporation, but starved and discouraged outside the pale. . . . The only security against political slavery is the check maintained over governors, by the diffusion of intelligence, activity, and public spirit among the governed. . . . It is therefore of supreme importance that all classes of the community, down to the lowest, should have much to do for themselves; that as great a demand should be made upon their intelligence and virtue as it is in any respect equal to; that the government should not only leave as far as possible to their own faculties the conduct of whatever concerns themselves alone, but should suffer them, or rather encourage them, to manage as many as possible of their joint concerns by voluntary cooperation.[80]

Substitute "employers" for "government" and the words of Mill become peculiarly applicable to industry today. Clearly, modern personnel management does not encourage wage earners "to manage as many as possible of their joint concerns by voluntary cooperation." Plainly, it does seek to prevent the development of any "habit of spontaneous action for a collective interest."

The case against paternalism is probably weaker today than when Mill wrote. Only through some kind of paternalism, apparently, can the wage earner be protected against many of the hazards of modern life or can he obtain the benefits of many scientific discoveries and the services of many professional experts. It is clear that employers, at little or no extra cost, can often give help which the worker could obtain for himself only at considerable trouble and expense. But is there not need among wage earners for more initiative and enterprise, for more mental independence, and for more disposition to rely upon cooperative self-help than modern personnel practice is disposed to encourage? Is it not, in general, desirable that men be encouraged to manage their own affairs rather than that they be deliberately and skillfully discouraged from making the attempt? And if much paternalism is inevitable, would it not be more satisfactory, from the standpoint of the community, that it be paternalism of the government rather than paternalism of employers?

[80] J. S. Mill, *Principles of Political Economy*, bk. V, chap. 11, sec. 6.

16

The Changing Character of American Industrial Relations

American Economic Review, Supplement, March 1939.

I

THREE times since the turn of the century a major effort has been made to induce American employers voluntarily to base their labor policy upon the recognition of trade unions and the acceptance of collective bargaining, and three times the attempt has failed.[1] The result has been the Wagner Act which not only prohibits employers from interfering with the organization of their workers but also imposes on employers the obligation to bargain with representatives of a proper bargaining unit. Thus the determination of the fundamental labor policy of American industry has been taken from employers and has been made a matter of public instead of private decision.[2] Although the Wagner Act may be amended in superficial respects, there are no signs that the country in the foreseeable future is likely to change the fundamental policy of the Act.

Underlying the change in public policy is the change in the composition of the working force of American industry. Immigration has virtually ceased. At the same time the number of high-school graduates has increased twenty-fivefold since 1890. Indeed, slightly more than half of the children in this country now complete a high-school education and almost all of them

[1] The first effort was made about 1898 to 1902 under the leadership of the National Civic Federation, Mark Hanna, and other business leaders. The second effort was made by President Wilson in the fall of 1919. His Industrial Conference endeavored to develop into a form acceptable to business and labor alike the principles of employer-employee relations temporarily accepted during the war. It failed because the representatives of business insisted upon the right of employers to start company unions. The third effort was represented by Section 7a of the National Recovery Act which sought to pledge employers to the principle of noninterference with the organization of their workers. Note that in 1926 the employers and unions in the railroad industry did succeed in agreeing upon the terms of a fundamental labor policy for the industry. The result was the Railway Labor Act of 1926.

[2] Small wonder that this attempt to change by act of Congress some of the most firmly established mores of American industry has been difficult to administer. The Wagner Act, however, has been enforced with surprising effectiveness.

have two or three years in high school. Such workers may or may not desire to form unions, but they are quite insistent that they may be permitted to have unions in case they wish them. It outrages their sense of justice when the employer discharges someone because he tries to form a union. Evidence of the change in community sentiment on this point is found in the statements of policy of many employers asserting that the management will not discriminate against any employee for joining a union. Such statements are found in many employee-representation plans adopted in the period 1918–1920. It was the failure of business in general, however, to perceive the change in public opinion and its persistent effort to enforce a labor policy of which the public disapproved that eventually led the government to take the determination of the fundamental labor policy of American industry out of the hands of employers and to make it a matter of public policy.

The new public policy may be expected to have profound effects upon the labor movement, the operation of industry, the functioning of our economy, and even upon our political institutions. It may, for example, compel the labor movement to abandon its traditional policy of awarding exclusive jurisdiction over particular groups of workers to a given union and to adopt the policy of the British Trades Union Congress that no union has the exclusive right to organize any class of workers. Depending upon the nature of the working rules adopted, it may enhance or diminish the ability of industry to adapt itself to changes in conditions. Depending upon whether a good or bad job is done in setting the price of labor, it may either diminish or increase the volume of unemployment and, therefore, raise or lower the standard of living. Finally, it may be either a bulwark or a threat to democratic institutions. By spreading democratic habits of thought into industry it may broaden the acceptance of the democratic way of life. On the other hand, by retarding the expansion of industry it may impair the very foundations upon which political democracy rests.

It is not my purpose, however, to explore the probable consequences of collective bargaining, because these will depend upon the policies that are pursued by each side. The immediate problem that confronts us is one of making collective bargaining work. Collective bargaining has two principal aspects. First, it is a method of introducing civil rights into industry; that is, of requiring that management be conducted by rule rather than by arbitrary decision. Second, it is a method of price fixing—fixing the price of labor. The problem of making it work, therefore, may be defined as the problem (1) of introducing civil rights into industry, and (2) of fixing the price of labor in such a manner as to increase the national income—or at least so as not to retard its increase. That is the problem to which I invite your attention.

II

The introduction of civil rights into industry raises two major problems: (1) the preservation of a proper balance between the employer's freedom to manage his plant and the protection of workers from arbitrary management; (2) the avoidance of rules which become obsolete. If the management is given too much freedom, hostile employers may take advantage of it to destroy the union. If the management is too severely restricted in rewarding efficiency or in discarding old methods of production, collective bargaining becomes a method of protecting the old against the new, of retarding technological change, and of protecting vested interests in obsolete methods. Thus it becomes a method of keeping down the standard of living. The railroads are a conspicuous illustration of an industry in which changes in the location of plant, type of equipment, and methods of operation have been substantially restricted by the terms of trade agreements and union-sponsored statutes. Many of these restrictions are easily defended, but let anyone who doubts the seriousness of some of them note the obstacles (some imposed by statute and some by trade agreement) which confront railroads which wish to combine terminals, to pool traffic, or to meet truck competition by running shorter, faster, or lighter trains, or by having road crews perform yard service. The history of collective bargaining in this country is full of instances of unions, such as the old window-glass workers, the cigarmakers, or the upholstery weavers, which destroyed themselves or made themselves weak by imposing excessive restrictions upon employers.

There are several reasons why trade agreements in American industry have tended to develop into long and complicated documents which, in the course of time, were bound to contain many obsolete rules. The most important one has been the fear of the men that the employer would destroy their unions by discriminating against the most active members—a natural result of the great organizing difficulties experienced by unions in this country. Consequently, unions have felt it necessary to restrict the employer's discretion at every point where he might discriminate. A second reason for complicated agreements has been the lack of effective managerial control of department heads, with the result that favoritism rather than efficiency has determined many promotions and layoffs. A third reason has been the tendency of some employers to keep unions weak by making it difficult for them to get prompt and satisfactory adjustment of grievances. In some instances, this failure has led employers to deny redress where the agreement contained no specific rule governing the issue. A fourth reason for detailed and complicated agreements has been the attempt of unions to meet technological and market changes by sponsoring make-work rules rather than pursuing a policy of adjustment. The primary effect of a policy of restriction is to promote the security of the group, but the secondary effect is to undermine the security of the group. Hence, in a rapidly changing world real security is achieved only by pursuing a policy of adjustment. Nevertheless, it is natural that some unions (particularly inexperienced ones) should base their policies upon the immediate rather than the long-run interests of their members.

There is danger that instead of profiting from the mistakes of the past we shall repeat these mistakes on a larger scale. Most of the new unions are deeply concerned over their existence and must fight hard for restrictions upon discrimination by employers. Furthermore, the new agreements are being developed so rapidly and usually with so little understanding by either side that in settling specific issues they are unwittingly settling matters of basic policy. Indeed, many new agreements are more complicated and elaborate than agreements (such as those in the glass-bottle or the flint-glass industry) which have been in existence for fifty years. The tendency toward elaborate agreements is well illustrated by the recent development of seniority rules. Among 387 predepression agreements, seniority rules were found in only 117; but among 300 agreements made since 1933, seniority rules were found in 171. Let me assure you that it is not an accident that strong unions, such as the United Mine Workers, the flint-glass workers, the molders, the glass-bottle blowers, the potters, the women's-garment workers, or the men's-clothing workers, have made little or no use of seniority.[3] It is not an exaggeration, however, to say that at the present time virtually no one either inside the labor movement or out of it knows very much about seniority, particularly when applied to factory industries. The only safe procedure is to develop policies by the case method. Most employers, for example, at present are strongly in favor of departmental seniority rules. The day will come when these employers will wish that they had never restricted the flexibility of their operations by surrounding each department with a seniority wall. Many unions, which think that they are protecting their existence by seniority rules, have adopted these

[3] In these samples, agreements from the building trades were excluded because it was known that they almost never contained regulations of layoff procedure.

rules in such unqualified form as to threaten the life of the union. Observe that where frequent violent fluctuations of employment occur, as in the highly seasonal garment industries, seniority has the effect of dividing the workers into two groups—those which bear the full burden of unemployment and those which have steady work at the expense of the others. This is one reason why unions in seasonal industries have found it necessary to avoid seniority rules except in a severely restricted form—as when dealing with the problem of overcrowded sections or considering permanent layoffs for other reasons.

A few unions, such as the Amalgamated Clothing Workers, the hosiery workers, and the Steel Workers' Organizing Committee, have made the maintenance of short, simple, and flexible agreements a matter of definite union policy. The leaders of these organizations understand that they can protect the security of their members in a rapidly changing world only by pursuing a policy of adjustment and that elaborate and detailed agreements hinder the pursuit of a policy of adjustment. Curiously enough, however, thinking on this matter seems to be much farther advanced among unions than among employers. Indeed, few employers seem to have made the promotion of simplicity and flexibility in trade agreements a definite objective.

What policies are indicated if trade agreements are to be kept short, simple, and flexible, and if workers are to be protected against arbitrary management by the administrative method of settling individual cases as they arise in the light of particular facts rather than by the legislative method of spelling out rules in advance? First, let the employer eliminate the issue of union status, either by encouraging membership in the trade union or by granting the closed shop. To most American employers the "closed shop" is a symbol for union domination. As a matter of fact, the employer is likely to have more freedom in a closed shop or its equivalent than in one where the union is uncertain of its status. (In the latter, the union must view with extreme suspicion every decision which favors a nonmember as against a member. When all employees are members, the union's interest in the employer's decisions becomes of substantially less importance.) Instructive on this point is an analysis of the restrictions on layoffs in 300 agreements of which 173 provided for a closed shop and 127 for the open shop. Among the open-shop agreements 109, or 85.8 per cent, restricted the employer's freedom to make layoffs, but only 93, or 53.7 per cent, of the closed-shop agreements contained similar restrictions. Second, let the management develop effective control over the decisions of secondary executives for the purpose of assuring that these decisions are either based upon objective facts or, where judgment is unavoidable, upon carefully reviewed judgment. This will require substantially better records of individual employee performance than have been customary under nonunion conditions. Third, let managements plan technological changes well in advance and introduce them gradually. Fourth, let both sides do a good job of setting the price of labor. One source of make-work and restrictive rules has been the attempt of unions to provide work for men who have lost their jobs because their labor has been improperly priced. Fifth, let both sides develop union-management cooperation for the purpose of keeping costs in union plants from becoming too high in relation to costs in nonunion plants. Excessive costs in union plants which produce unemployment among union members are another source of make-work and restrictive rules. Finally, let managements take particular care that unions are satisfied that the administrative method gives them an adequate opportunity to get their cases heard and to protect the interests of their members. Arrangements for adjusting differences are more important than the specific rules in trade agreements, and agreements cannot be kept simple unless the machinery for adjusting cases works smoothly. Notice the bearing that all of this has upon the proposal, frequently made by employers' associations, that trade agreements be made enforcible by law. The step has already been taken in this country with respect to agreements on the railroads. It is, I believe, a backward step. It takes away from the parties the right to interpret their own agreement and places this responsibility in a court of law. Thus the parties are hampered in adjusting the interpretation of their agreements to changes in industrial conditions.

III

Collective bargaining is a form of price fixing—a way of fixing the price of labor. It introduces a revolutionary change in the relationship between employment and the price of labor. Employment must adjust itself to the price of labor rather than the price of labor to employment. With five or six million men in trade unions, collective bargaining represents price fixing on a scale large enough to have important repercussions upon our economy. By skillful pricing of labor we can add to employment and production; by unskillful pricing we can subtract from employment and production. It is probable that the pressure of unions for higher wages will accelerate technological change. It is probably inevitable that collective bargaining will produce some maldistribution of resources. It is probable, but not certain, that collective bargaining will limit investment opportunities. Whether collective bargaining at the end of a given period has raised or lowered the standard of living will depend upon whether its tendency to accelerate technological change has offset (1) its tendency to produce some maldistribution of resources, and (2) its possible tendency to limit the volume of investment. The subsequent discussion will deal with these two topics.

I have said that collective bargaining may be expected to produce some maldistribution of resources, but examination of the marketing policies of trade unions suggests that this maldistribution has been greater than it need be. There are three principal reasons for this belief: (1) the tendency of many trade unions to underestimate the elasticity in the demand for labor; (2) their failure to determine carefully the effect of wage differentials in union and nonunion plants upon the demand for union labor; and (3) the failure of some unions to adjust wages to changes in markets and technology.

Most unions assume that they can raise wages by moderate amounts with little or no effect upon employment. They are probably right, provided a short enough time is taken into consideration. There are several reasons, however, for concluding that the plant demand for labor is quite elastic when periods of several years are involved.[4] One is competition between the old and the new—the most pervasive form of competition in our economy and the one most completely neglected in economic treatises. The competition between the old and the new is not confined to industrial equipment or other durable goods. The NRA discovered that old hair cuts were in competition with new hair cuts and that if the price was put above fifty cents, people let their hair grow longer. The NRA also discovered that a dirty suit competed with a clean suit and that if the price of cleaning were substantially raised, suits are cleaned much less frequently. Old cars compete with new cars, old furniture with new furniture, old houses with new houses, and an old coat of paint on a house with a new coat. If one is particular about the appearance of his house, he may have it painted every four years, but sufficient protection is usually achieved if it is painted about every six—a great difference in the demand for painting.

A second reason is the ever growing pervasiveness of product competi-

[4] As a matter of fact, there is undoubtedly a marked difference in the elasticity in the demand for most products with the lapse of relatively short periods of time. This fact has not been adequately recognized by business enterprises and, consequently, has not affected selling policies as much as it should.

tion. Paper containers compete with wood, cotton, burlap, glass; aluminum competes with steel and copper; wood competes with concrete, brick, stone, and other materials; plaster competes with plywood and wallboard; letterpress printing competes with other types of printing, some of which are making heavy inroads upon it; coal competes with oil; trucks and buses with railroads. Numerous durable consumers goods compete with each other for the eight to twelve billion dollars a year that consumers spend on durable goods. A third is the rise of large buyers among both retailers and manufacturers who purchase to their own specifications from the lowest bidder (often doing the development work on the product themselves). In competition for the business of such buyers, small differences in costs are of decisive importance. A fourth is the rapid spread of organized industrial research with its tendency to increase the elasticity of substitution both between products and between factors of production.[5] As the technical schools turn out an increasing number of better-trained men, the elasticity of substitution will continue to increase.

When trade unions underestimate the elasticity in the demand for labor, the handicap imposed on union employers and hence the unemployment among union members are greater than they otherwise would be.[6] Ultimately the unemployment of men attached to union plants will cause some of them to drift into the nonunion part of the industry and unemployment will take the form of capital unemployment in union plants rather than labor unemployment. At any rate, the ultimate result of the union's mistake in judging the elasticity of the demand for labor will be to aggravate the tendency for collective bargaining to produce maldistribution of resources.

A special case of the general tendency of unions to underestimate the elasticity of the demand for labor is the failure of many unions to determine carefully the effect of wage differentials between union and nonunion plants upon the volume of employment in union plants. Two situations may be distinguished in the relation of union to nonunion wage scales. One is the case where the union scale governs the nonunion scale rather completely. The other is the case, and it has been the usual one, in which the union is so remote or so weak that nonunion wages are relatively independent of

[5] Elasticity of substitution is usually defined in terms of constant technology and refers simply to the changes in the proportions with which factors of production are combined when their relative prices change. I am using the expression above in a very different sense to mean the capacity of industry to change the proportions in which products or factors are used by making technological changes in response to changes in price relationships.

[6] This raises the question of whose income collective bargaining is expected to maximize—the income of the entire union (or group of unions) or only the income of the working majority of the bargaining group.

union ones. The differentials in terms of labor cost are usually not as large as differentials in wages because the high union wage scales tend to attract superior workmen and union employers cannot afford to retain inferior men. Because the withdrawal of capital from an industry involves cost, one must distinguish between the rate that will attract new capital and the rate that will cause the indefinite maintenance and replacement of capital already invested. Most unions have failed to determine the critical differential in labor costs beyond which capital leaves the union part of the industry.

For example, between 1915 and 1920, the tapestry carpet weavers in Philadelphia acquired control of that market and pushed up their wages by about 165 per cent. At the height of its prosperity in 1920, the union had about 1,800 members. It was believed that the union mills could stand a differential of 10 or 15 per cent above the nonunion, but the differential grew until it became about 50 per cent. By 1926, the union had only 800 members working in Philadelphia and more than half the union mills had ceased operating. In 1920, the union part of the bituminous coal industry produced nearly 60 per cent of the bituminous output. The union endeavored to maintain a basic wage of $7.50 a day. Nonunion mines were paying from 30 to 50 per cent less. By 1927, the union mines were producing only 40 per cent of the output. In 1922, the hosiery workers' union controlled 90 per cent of the market. Union wages during the twenties rose to roughly double nonunion. By 1929, union control had shrunk to 30 per cent. Thanks to the NRA, the Wagner Act, and skillful organizing campaigns, the union control is now back to 70 per cent. During the last several years it has been threatened by the rapid growth of the industry in the South where wages have been about 30 per cent lower and where three fourths of the new machines installed during the last seven or eight years have gone. The union has recently taken steps to meet Southern competition by accepting wage reductions in return for an agreement by the employers to purchase up-to-date machinery.

Some large differentials between union and nonunion plants are the result not of union policy but of the efforts of employers to defeat union organizing campaigns. As a general rule, however, they are a result of the fact that the bargaining power of most unions is greater than their organizing power.[7] Many large differentials are the result of temporary bulges in demand. The union takes advantage of the bulge to push up its rates substantially. After the demand has subsided or after production facilities have

[7] Note that excessive differentials are almost inevitable in case the union underestimates the elasticity of the demand for the labor of its members.

caught up with the demand, the union is reluctant to cut its rates and the drop in nonunion rates creates a dangerously large differential. Some of the differentials which proved so disastrous to unions during the twenties were the result of high rates bargained during the war which the unions were unwilling to adjust to the lower level of prices and wages that followed the drop in war demand. The differentials between the union and nonunion parts of the bituminous coal industry are an example. The large differentials in the hosiery industry were the result of style changes which almost overnight produced an enormous jump in the demand for full-fashioned hose. Excessive differentials may be the result of failure to adjust union piece rates to increases in productivity. If rates in nonunion plants are cut, the difference may become dangerously large. Examples of this kind of differential are found in the flint-glass industry, shoe industry, and hosiery industry. In the hosiery industry most of the rates which had been rendered out of line by changes in conditions have been eliminated.

The first remedy for excessive differentials always proposed by the unions is organization of the nonunion plants in the industry. When the plant demand schedule for labor is elastic, the differential may enable workers in nonunion plants to earn more than workers in union plants and thus may be a serious obstacle to union organization. The lamp-chimney department of the flint-glass workers union experienced this difficulty in acute form. The first remedy for excessive differentials which employers suggest is wage reductions in union plants. This procedure often fails because nonunion plants counter with offsetting cuts. The nonunion employer may use the fact that the union workers had consented to a cut as a reason why the nonunion workers must accept a corresponding cut. There are techniques, however, particularly in piece-working industries, by which union rates can be reduced without provoking counter-reductions in nonunion plants. Differences in wages do not inevitably mean differences in labor costs. A few unions have attempted to reduce the disadvantages of union plants by helping management improve efficiency. The hosiery workers have employed this method in the seamless-hosiery industry; the Amalgamated Clothing Workers have used it extensively; and now the Steel Workers' Organizing Committee is using it. In fact, the Steel Workers' Organizing Committee is helping some employers reduce costs who got themselves into competitive difficulties by raising wages in an attempt to keep out the union!

Once unions achieve a given wage rate, they have a strong tendency to cling to it however much markets and technology may change. The anthracite miners have maintained their 1923 scale while the sales of anthracite have dropped almost in half. The railroad unions have actually raised wage scales while railroad traffic was falling in half. Perhaps these unions were pursuing a sensible marketing policy from the standpoint of their members. Their officers might argue in each instance that the price of the product and *pro tanto* the price of labor had little to do with the decline of sales. These extreme cases of price rigidity in the face of violent market changes, however, raise two principal questions. (1) Are the union members being guided by future as well as present considerations—in other words, are they underestimating the long-run elasticity in the demand for labor? (2) Whose income is the union intended to maximize—the income of all members regarded as an entity or simply the incomes of a majority? Many cases of rigid wages simply reflect the fact that union members do not know that their long-run interests conflict with their short-run. Hence they do not attempt to determine whether wage cuts today might substantially retard the decline in employment. Of particular interest is the question of whose income the union is trying to maximize. If the union is attempting to maximize the income of all its members, then wage reductions in the face of technological and market changes would often be indicated because men with specialized skill will earn more at reduced rates at their customary occupations than in new jobs. If, on the other hand, unions simply undertake to maximize the income of a controlling majority of their members, they become organizations by which some workers exploit other workers.

IV

Most momentous of all is the question of the effect of collective bargaining upon the demand for investment funds. I shall discuss this question under the heads of the effect of collective bargaining upon (1) technological change; (2) the propensity to consume; (3) the relations between costs and selling prices; (4) the relation between the prices of capital goods and other goods; and (5) the adjustment of the price of labor to cyclical changes in business. The discussion will necessarily be suggestive rather than exhaustive.

The great pressure which collective bargaining puts on wages will tend to accelerate technological change so long as collective bargaining does not extend to research workers and does not, therefore, tend to raise the cost of discovery. It is reasonable also to assume that pressure for higher wages will encourage labor-saving rather than capital-saving inventions and thus will facilitate the absorption of savings by industry.[8] About 57 per cent of the employment and half of the payrolls in American industry outside of railroads and agriculture are in approximately 1.7 million concerns employing less than four hundred workers. Nearly all of these enterprises are too small to perform their own research, and outside facilities for giving them research service are far from adequate. Since the pressure which collective bargaining is bound to create for higher wages makes industrial research more imperative than ever, perhaps the state universities can make research available to the small concerns by offering it at cost.

Efforts to raise the propensity to consume by increasing the price of labor and encroaching upon profits seem to reduce the propensity to invest even more than the propensity to save. This is inevitable because otherwise the previous situation would not have been one of equilibrium. The best opportunity to raise the propensity to consume in such a manner as to increase the propensity to invest is by keeping the prices of personal services and of durable consumer goods relatively low.[9] The demand for these goods seems to be elastic and they are purchased in large measure with funds that would otherwise be saved. About 30 per cent of the saving in the commu-

[8] Observe, however, that several special influences, such as the rapid rate of technological change itself and certain changes in markets (particularly the rise of large buyers who may switch large orders from one producer to another), are encouraging capital-saving inventions. The possibility of losing the account of a mail-order house or automobile company in a year or two compels producers to show a lively interest in ways of keeping down the capital required to produce a given article.

[9] Keynes seems to think about reducing the propensity to consume simply in terms of taxing the very rich (*The General Theory of Employment, Interest, and Money*, pp. 372–74). He does not visualize the important competition between durable consumer goods and savings. Unless the taxes on very large incomes are carefully devised, they have repercussions which Keynes has overlooked. Investment opportunities are created by pioneering—by men who put funds into new products and new processes and demonstrate their profitability. This actual demonstration that new products can be made at a profit or that new processes are practical is necessary to attract more timid capital. Hence, the pioneering type of investment may be regarded as opening up investment opportunities. It is obviously of particular importance to encourage rather than discourage the pioneering type of investment. The persons who are best able to undertake the riskiest type of investment are the persons with very large incomes, and it is from such incomes in the past that a large part of pioneering investment funds have come. Heavy taxes, however, on high incomes are likely to cause the very persons who are best able to take risks to shift from risky to safe ventures. Thus the heavy taxes which Keynes advocates are likely to reduce not merely the volume of savings but, even more, the opportunities to invest. The oversight is a natural one for Keynes to make because his entire analysis is worked out in a framework that visualizes static technology—a convenient simplification, but, after all, a shocking limitation in a work that purports to offer a general theory of employment. When very high tax rates are imposed on incomes in the higher brackets, a differential should be made between income from interest and income from dividends with substantially lower tax rates upon income from dividends. Furthermore, pioneering capital should be encouraged by liberal loss carry-over provisions in the income-tax law. A new venture is likely to be in the "red" for from two to five years after its beginning.

nity is done by persons with incomes of less than $10,000 a year and nearly half by persons with incomes of less than $25,000 a year.[10] It is impossible to predict whether collective bargaining will be conducted so as to keep the prices of personal services and of durable consumer goods relatively low. In an economy in which collective bargaining was quite prevalent, wages might be expected to vary with the bargaining power of the several groups of employers and the several groups of wage earners. Bargaining power may be defined as the cost to one party of imposing a loss on the other. Cost to the group of wage earners would include to a rather indefinite extent the unemployment that might follow an increase in wages. Hence, when the product is elastic in demand (as in the case of durable consumer goods), the union might be restrained by the fear of unemployment from pushing up the price of labor very far. As I have indicated above, however, two difficulties stand in the way of accepting this conclusion. One is that trade unions seem to underestimate the elasticity of the demand for the services of their members—just as most employers under conditions of monopolistic competition put the price of their products too high. A second is that the majority of the union may not care whether a minority is unemployed, provided the minority is not dangerously large.

Will collective bargaining raise operating costs so high as to restrict the utilization of present equipment and to narrow the outlook for profits and restrict the demand for investment funds? So long as collective bargaining is far from covering all of industry and is growing slowly, union wage policy may open up large and attractive investment opportunities in the nonunion parts of industry. At the cost of considerable duplication of plant, therefore, collective bargaining may substantially increase investment and employment. Let us assume, however, that collective bargaining becomes so prevalent that union wage policy determines the general wage level. The productivity of a large proportion of the working population of the United States is substantially less than the present union wage scales in the several occupations. Indeed, precisely here we have a large part of the explanation of the somewhat surprising success of union plants in holding their own against nonunion plants—union plants, as pointed out above, can attract superior workmen and cannot afford to keep inferior men. Hence, unions tend to become devices by which superior workers enforce differentials for their efficiency.[11] Because of this very condition, however,

[10] See the estimates of M. Ezekiel, *Review of Economic Statistics* (November 1937), pp. 178–191.

[11] As a matter of fact, if the evidence of existing wage scales and profit statements mean anything, a surprisingly large proportion of the workers do not produce as much as fifty cents

an attempt to apply present union wages scales to a very large proportion of industry would have disastrous results.[12]

Mr. Keynes and his followers would disagree with this statement. They argue that *MV* may be depended upon to translate changes in the price of labor into changes in the prices of finished goods and to keep the volume of output unchanged subject only to the effect of changes in *MV* upon the rate of interest. I have tried without success to persuade myself to accept this comfortable conclusion. Suppose that there is a general increase in the price of labor. There is no reason to expect an instantaneous change in *MV* sufficient to translate the higher price of labor into correspondingly higher prices of finished goods, because businessmen feel higher costs before they experience a higher demand for goods. Hence it is reasonable to expect businessmen to curtail production pending at least a test of the higher prices made necessary by higher costs. The businessman is not acting irrationally when he adopts a "wait-and-see" attitude because he knows that consumer resistance to higher prices even in the face of rising consumer incomes is a reality. Witness the experience of the United States in the latter part of 1936 and the early part of 1937. Between May 1936 and April 1937 the cost of living rose about 5.4 per cent, and nonagricultural labor income rose about 15 per cent. Despite the fact that labor incomes were outrunning the increase in prices, definite consumer resistance to the higher prices developed about the end of 1936. The New York Federal Reserve Bank's index of physical distribution to consumers reached its peak in December 1936 and January 1937. Thereafter, the index dropped. The event proved that any businessmen who may have accepted the Keynesian assumption that higher expenses are equivalent to a proportionate increase in demand were wrong.

The Keynesians may argue, however, that an ultimate increase in *MV* will occur because at any volume of output less than the original one the community will attempt to invest more than it saves. If this were not so, the original position would not be one of equilibrium. It is true that if businessmen curtail production in response to the increase in the price of labor, incomes and, hence, the propensity to save would be reduced. But it does not

---

worth of goods per hour. This, of course, is not necessarily the fault of the employees. It represents in part the scarcity of managerial ability and in part the fact that the amount of capital per worker in American industry is still quite small—not much above $4,000 per worker in industry as a whole. The fact, nevertheless, remains that a very large part of the workers have a productivity of less than fifty cents an hour and many of them a productivity of considerably less.

[12] The case of piece-work scales is somewhat different, provided these scales do not include a time rate guarantee.

follow (as the Keynesians assume) that investment opportunities would be reduced less than the propensity to save. Investment opportunities are partly determined by physical volume of production, and this has been reduced. They are also determined by the relationship between cost schedules and income. Cost schedules have been raised, but incomes have been little changed.[13] Hence it is quite possible that investment opportunities may be reduced even more than the propensity to save and that still further contraction of production is necessary before equilibrium is reached. This is not inconsistent with the fact that the economy may have been in equilibrium before a general increase in wages occurred because that equilibrium was predicated upon the (then) existing cost schedules, and labor cost schedules were raised by the general increase in the price of labor.

More important than these logical difficulties is the appeal to experience because, after all, in discussing *MV*, we are dealing not merely with a quantity in an equation but with the behavior of human beings. Between 1929 and 1937, wage rates in the United States increased about 21 per cent in manufacturing and about 10 or 15 per cent in other branches of industry. In the same period the price level of finished goods dropped 10 per cent. The real change in the price of labor is uncertain because the change in labor efficiency is not known. That it was not sufficient to offset the changes in wages and prices is indicated by the state of profits. Even as late as 1936 scarcely two out of five of the 478,000 active corporations in the United States made any money. Indeed, corporate profits in 1936 were substantially less than in 1924, a year of mild depression when the index of industrial production was 10 per cent below 1936. They were even lower than in 1922, another year of depression when the index of industrial production was 20 per cent below 1936.

Will collective bargaining seriously narrow the opportunities for investment by raising the prices of investment goods and thus reducing the marginal efficiency of capital? The danger of this does not appear serious in the case of industrial equipment. The demand for equipment seems to depend upon the businessman's judgment of the total business situation. Changes in his expectations cause violent shifts in his demand curve for capital goods, but the curve at all times is pretty inelastic. Quite different, however, appears to be the case of residential building. There is a certain minimum demand for housing that is little affected by the prices of housing. After this minimum, the demand becomes increasingly sensitive to prices, and it is,

[13] They may be slightly increased or even slightly decreased because a smaller volume of production is occurring at a higher price level.

of course, the elasticity of demand at the margin which counts. The building-trades unions have seriously misjudged their market and are pursuing a price policy that is not only injuring their members but is substantially reducing the ability of private industry to absorb the savings of the community. Residential building is now at half the level of the twenties. The prices of building materials are 11 per cent below the levels of 1926, but union wage scales in the industry are nearly 5 per cent above 1926, the peak of the boom. In the face of this situation, union wage agreements in the building trades were raised 6 per cent in 1937, the largest annual increase since 1923. High labor costs have been only one of several obstacles to building, but the very existence of other obstacles is a reason why there should not be added to them the burden of a wage scale substantially above boom levels. In the spring of 1937 the increases in union wage scales seem to have affected the wages actually paid residential building even though the union scale was often not paid. At the present time most of the building-trades unions in most cities have priced themselves out of the private residential building market. In small housing operations, it is difficult for the employer-employee system to compete with the working contractor system. In 1937, residential building costs (according to the Boeckh index) were practically the same as in 1926. The prices of many durable goods, such as automobiles, refrigerators, and radios, were from 25 to 50 per cent below 1926. As a result, in 1926 the housing industry got about one out of every three dollars spent by consumers for durable goods and, in 1937, only one out of every seven dollars. Most important of all, however, the community was deprived of a major outlet for its savings.

Highly controversial is the question of the cyclical wage movements which will best maintain investment and employment. All economists probably would agree, however, that business stability is not prompted by a continued rise in wages after business has turned down. In the past, negotiators on both sides have often failed to take account promptly of the cyclical movements of business. In 1930 union scales in the building industry rose 4.2 per cent above 1929. There was even a slight increase in building wages during 1931 over 1930! The experience in earlier depressions was similar. In 1908, for example, union wage scales in the building industry rose nearly 6 per cent above 1907. Union scales in book and job printing rose 12 per cent between 1920 and 1921. In the last depression they continued to rise until 1932, when they were 3.3 per cent above 1929. Union wage scales in general continued to rise well after the downturns of both 1920 and 1929. By June 1937, the movement of raw-material prices, demand deposits, and bond prices all indicated that a recession in business was at least probable. Wages, both union and nonunion, continued to rise throughout the summer and even well into the fall.

As a general rule, it may be assumed that unions discourage wage cuts in time of depression. The question of whether wage cuts aggravate or mitigate the severity of depressions breaks up into more parts than economists have been accustomed to assume. To the makers of trade-union policy the question of whether wage cuts aggravate or mitigate the severity of depressions may be of only academic interest. Only by accepting substantial wage cuts during the Great Depression was the Amalgamated Clothing Workers able to keep its employers in business and to obtain moderate employment for its members. Had the hosiery workers not accepted a 40 per cent wage cut in the fall of 1931, it is doubtful whether enough of the union would have survived to make the remarkable comeback that it achieved several years later. At certain points where the demand for labor is instantaneously elastic, wage reductions are needed in times of depression in order to increase labor income and raise the propensity to consume. I have pointed out above that most forms of durable consumer goods seem to be elastic in demand and so also are many of the services which consumers are buying in rapidly growing quantities. The expenditures of consumers on durable goods regularly run somewhat higher than the expenditures of all forms of industry on capital goods. Consumers' purchases of services are even larger. Expenditures on durable consumer goods and services together amount to more than 40 per cent of the total outlay by consumers. Expenditures for both durable consumer goods and services are, of course, competitive with savings. Here is a broad field, therefore, in which there is an opportunity to encroach upon savings and stabilize consumers' expenditures by making reductions in prices. Wage cuts to facilitate such price reductions would raise the propensity to consume and thus mitigate the severity of the depression. The case in favor of wage cuts may be broader than I have just indicated. Once a depression gets well started, the mere drop in incomes leads consumers to expect lower prices and to postpone buying until prices reach what the public regards as a proper level.[14] Under these circumstances, general cuts in wages may raise the propensity to consume.

When wage reductions are being made more or less simultaneously in a large number of plants, there is danger that they will produce a reaction

[14] Note in this connection that inventory liquidation under pressure from maturing bank loans may have driven prices below reproduction costs but the public may strongly resist paying a higher price.

somewhat different from isolated cuts—that they will arouse an expectation of still further cuts and thus induce postponement of commitments. The effect of wage cuts upon the postponement of commitments depends upon how the cuts are made. Certainly there is more danger of a general postponement of commitments when sweeping cuts are announced by large corporations. Over two thirds of the employment in American business, exclusive of railroading and agriculture, is in small concerns with less than a thousand employees and more than half of it in concerns with less than four hundred employees. Most of these enterprises can make cuts without producing general market effects. The timing of wage cuts is important. In seasonal industries it is possible to avoid a postponement of commitments by timing cuts to correspond with the seasonal upturns. Particularly important is the avoidance of general and sweeping wage changes. The system of payment by the piece lends itself to gradual but steady rate adjustments. Piece prices which are out of line may be changed, and new lines and new operations may be priced on a somewhat lower level than the old, all with the result of appreciable reductions in labor costs without definite or sweeping decreases in rates. Finally, collective bargaining itself offers a way of making wage reductions without arousing expectations of an uncontrolled downward spiral.

Up to the present there has been relatively little experimentation under collective bargaining with techniques for facilitating the adjustment of wages to changing conditions. Scattered efforts have been made to link wages to the cost of living or to the price of a commodity, but none of these schemes, however satisfactory under the particular conditions of its operation, promises general usefulness. In 1921 a profit-sharing scheme was embodied in the collective agreement in the British bituminous coal industry. Though hailed by unions and employers alike as an epoch-making achievement, one of its principal effects has been to breed friction as to the dividing line between profits and expenses. The growth of collective bargaining, however, is bound to compel the development of devices for introducing some element of contingency into wages and relating them to the ability of employers to pay. This might be achieved by making most wage changes take the form of temporary advances to or deductions from base rates. The addition or deduction would have a termination date before which continuation of the addition or deduction would be subject to negotiation. This procedure was followed in 1932 when temporary reductions were negotiated from base rates in the railroad industry. Certainly there is no reason in nondeclining industries why the temporary necessity for lower labor costs should lead to changes in the base rates themselves. And since the average annual increase in per capita productivity is about 2 per cent, there is no reason why a temporary improvement in business should produce more than very small increases in base rates. Certainly there was no economic justification for permitting the temporary improvement in 1936 and 1937 to produce permanent increases of 10 to 15 per cent in the price of labor in many industries—increases which seem to have intensified the depression and impeded recovery.

V

What is the use of discussing the effect of collective bargaining upon the volume of employment? Are unions politically capable of considering the effect of their policies upon employment? Since they are democratic organizations, are they not bound to be devices by which the majority advances its interests quite regardless of the effect upon the minority and, above all, quite regardless of the effect upon the general economic situation?

I venture the opinion that considerable practical good may come of the exploration of the relationship of union policies to employment. In the first place, the fact that a given policy causes a minority to suffer does not necessarily mean that a majority is benefiting. The policy may reflect not the exploitation of a minority by a majority but simply the failure of the union leaders to formulate wise policies. Consider, for example, the efforts of some unions to protect their members against technological change by pursuing a policy of restriction rather than adjustment. When protection takes the form of permanent make-work rules, the ability of union employers to hold their own in competition with nonunion employers is impaired and a minority of the union members are thrown out of work without a corresponding gain to the majority. Indeed, in the long run the majority itself is better protected by a policy of adjustment than by a policy of restriction. In the second place, whether the union is divided between a majority that is indifferent to the effects of union policies upon employment and a minority that bears the burden of unemployment depends upon how unemployment is distributed among the members. If it is concentrated by seniority rule among the junior members, the union may have little interest in employment problems. This goes far to explain the marketing policies of the railroad brotherhoods. On the other hand, if unemployment is spread thin among all members by limited equal-division-of-work, the union may be politically capable of interest in even a moderate degree of unemployment. In the third place, when the union members are keenly aware of their long-run as well as their short-run interests, the conflict between a majority not interested in unemployment and an exploited minority tends to disappear because in the long run the majority must consider the effect of union policies upon employment.

All in all, one finds about the same differences in the marketing policies of trade unions as one does among corporations. At one extreme one finds the men's-clothing workers and the hosiery workers with their sensitiveness to changes in markets and their willingness to adjust the price of labor to changes in demand. At the other extreme one finds the building trades and the railroad brotherhoods with little disposition to adjust the price of labor to conditions in the market—in fact with a tendency to buck the market and to put up the price of labor quite irrespective of demand. No one would assert that the first two unions do a poorer job of representing their members than the second group. In fact, most persons would probably agree that they do a better job. The difference simply is that the marketing policies of the first are more realistic and that in consequence they do a better job of selling labor. As trade unions gain more experience in selling labor, I venture the prediction that the successful marketing policies of the men's-clothing workers and the hosiery workers will receive wider acceptance.

My discussion of our changing industrial relations has related solely to economic issues. In concluding, let me remind you that far more than economic issues are at stake. It is frequently said that political democracy cannot exist without industrial democracy. There is truth in the statement. It also is true that industrial democracy, if unwisely operated, may threaten the existence of political democracy. The basis for free institutions is economic opportunity because it is opportunity that keeps social conflict mild, and only when social conflict is mild are men willing to settle their differences by voting, by negotiating, or by arbitrating rather than by fighting. The basis for opportunity is expansion. In the happy days of the nineteenth century one could rely upon the rapid expansion of industry to correct the mistakes of policy. Now we must rely upon wisdom in policy to encourage expansion. Whether the spread of collective bargaining helps or hinders the preservation of democratic institutions will depend fundamentally upon whether it is so conducted as to encourage the expansion of industry.

17

Trade Unions in a Free Society

Revision of a paper prepared for a Bicentennial Conference on the Evolution of Social Institutions at Princeton University, October 8, 1946; Cambridge, Harvard University Press, 1947.

MODERN technology has built a new type of community—a community composed almost entirely of free employees. Such communities have existed only within the last several generations. In the United States about three out of four workers are employees. This change in the nature of the community is bringing about a revolutionary shift in power from business to labor. Many kinds of employees are organizing themselves into trade unions, and these unions are the most powerful economic organizations of the time. Indeed, none of the great "captains of industry" of previous generations—the Rockefellers, the Morgans, the Carnegies, the Hills, or the Harrimans—possessed as great a power over the industries of the country as that held by the coal miners' union, the steel workers', or some of the unions in transportation. A laboristic society is succeeding a capitalistic one.

How will the rapid rise of trade unions affect the operation of free institutions? The best way to answer this question is to see how unions affect the three basic problems which confront a free society: (1) the problem of developing the kind of attitudes, thinking, and institutions which enable men of different beliefs and interests to preserve good will and to handle their affairs with a maximum of cooperation and a minimum of conflict; (2) the problem of assuring a fair distribution of freedom and opportunity and preventing the abuse of power; and (3) the problem of working out a satisfactory balance between the pursuit of individual interests or group interests, on the one hand, and the pursuit of interests which all or nearly all members of the community have in common, on the other hand.

The first of these problems arises because the institutions of a free society are designed to serve individuals, not to regiment or dominate them. Hence the members of a free society are bound to have widely differing preferences, objectives, and philosophies. It is a distinctive and important part of the philosophy of freedom that uniformity of preferences and objectives is not necessary to friendly relations and that men of widely different preferences and objectives can live together harmoniously and cooperate effectively in meeting common problems. The second problem arises because it is an essential characteristic of a free society that all members shall have a fair share of freedom and an opportunity to live satisfying and fruitful lives. This means that individuals and organizations must have restrictions placed upon their freedom and that great concentrations of economic power must be prevented or controlled. The third basic problem arises because the pursuit of individual interests cannot be relied upon to promote the interests which all or nearly all members of the community have in common. During the nineteenth century the philosophy of freedom was largely laissez faire—and extraordinarily optimistic. It held that if people were in the main let alone, save for some restrictions on monopolistic combinations, and if contracts were enforced, both individual and common interests would be realized. In fact the pursuit of individual interests was regarded as a way of achieving common interests. Twentieth-century thinking is far less optimistic. It recognizes many serious conflicts between individual or group interests, on the one hand, and common interests, on the other. Men must decide how much importance shall be attached to individual and group interests and how much to common interests. Furthermore, they must develop arrangements which will permit individual and group interests to be pursued without undue harm to common interests and which will permit common interests to be pursued without undue harm to individual or group interests.

Let us address ourselves, therefore, to the following three principal questions:

1. How do unions affect the amount of conflict and cooperation in the community and the capacity of the community to settle issues by cooperation instead of fighting?

2. How do unions affect individual rights and the distribution of freedom and power?

3. How do unions affect the relative importance which people attach to their special interests and their common interests, and the capacity of the community to solve common problems and to pursue common interests?

I

The effect of trade unions upon the ability of men and groups with divergent interests to live in harmony, to keep differences to a minimum, and to settle disagreements with a minimum of conflict will depend largely upon what sort of process collective bargaining turns out to be. One extreme possibility is collective bargaining conducted on the basis of power, with each side endeavoring to get the best terms that can be had without a fight. If each side knows accurately the other's willingness to fight, no strike or lockout will ever occur. Each controversy will be settled on terms which equate the union's and the employer's willingness to fight. Collective bargaining conducted in this way may produce peace, but it will not produce good industrial relations. Indeed, a certain amount of militancy will be needed for bargaining purposes on each side. At the other extreme is collective bargaining based upon a keen desire on each side to develop and maintain good relations. If good relations are valued highly enough, changes in conditions will not be forced by threats—they will occur only after the other party has been convinced that a change is reasonable and fair. This kind of bargaining presupposes confidence by each party in the reasonableness of the other, in the willingness of the other to face facts honestly, and in its desire to be fair.

Collective bargaining in practice is a mixture of these two extremes. The more closely collective bargaining approximates the second extreme, however, the greater will be the contribution of trade unions to building a community in which men and groups with diverse interests live in harmony. The character of collective bargaining depends upon a multitude of conditions which will vary from plant to plant and union to union. Let us examine briefly some of the principal conditions which determine the way in which collective bargaining works.

(1) *The number and importance of interests which the union and the employer have in common.* Common interests limit the willingness of each side to press for conditions in the labor contract which are favorable to it and unfavorable to the other side. Interests, of course, are determined in large measure by scales of value. For example, the higher the valuation placed by workers upon the long-run effects of union policies, the greater is the likelihood of a community of interests between themselves and employers.

The number and importance of common interests also depend upon the market structure within which bargaining occurs. Let us assume that a craft union negotiates with an employer over the wages of a small fraction of his employees. The union will ordinarily be little interested in the effect of the wages of its members upon either the employer's costs or his price policies. If the employees in the enterprise are represented by a number of small craft unions, wage costs and the total size of the wage bill may have little effect upon the positions taken by the several unions. On the other hand, a truly industrial union may well be greatly concerned with the effect of its wage policy upon the employer's costs.

(2) *The relation of the cost of strikes and lockouts to the gains of victory.* The higher the cost of strikes or lockouts relative to the probable gains, the farther union representatives and employer representatives will be willing to go in making compromises. Of course, the cost of strikes has an effect only to the extent that men and management are aware of it. A year and two thirds of steady work, for example, is required to make up the loss of pay from a strike of one month (twenty-two working days) if the wages offered by the employer are only 5 per cent below those demanded by the union. The active rank and file of unions are likely to underestimate the cost of strikes—at least until they have been through a prolonged strike.

(3) *The kind of men who become heads of unions and of enterprises.* Widely divergent qualities help men rise to the top in business organizations and unions. Some get ahead because they are tough and ruthless seekers of power; others because they are able to make friends easily and to build effective teamwork. Some leaders of unions and business enterprises are men of social vision and high responsibility; some are shallow demagogues. Any of these qualities may help a man to win and hold union office, or to rise in the business world. Industrial relations are bound to reflect the innumerable combinations of character and temperament in the leaders of the two sides.

(4) *Political conditions inside unions.* Union officers who are fearful of losing their jobs are likely to be messenger boys rather than negotiators. They dare not be influenced by facts or arguments; they are little interested in understanding the employer's problems; and, above all, they are unwilling to carry back to the rank and file information about the employer's problems or recommendations that the union make concessions or accept compromises. Hence the weaker the political position of union representatives within the union, the more conflict and the less cooperation there will be between the union and the employer.

(5) *The ambitions of union leaders.* Some leaders are content with their positions in their own unions and other leaders are in a hurry to get ahead

in the labor movement and to win greater influence and prestige outside their unions. The desire to achieve a quick rise in the labor movement is likely to place a premium upon toughness and upon winning immediate concessions from employers to the neglect of the long-run effects of a given settlement.

(6) *Rivalries among unions.* Most of the 190-odd national unions in the United States live together in peace and harmony, but among some of them competition for members is keen and bitter. Furthermore, competition among unions is growing rapidly in extent and bitterness. So long as nearly all unions in the country were affiliated with the American Federation of Labor, relations among unions were governed by the principle of exclusive jurisdiction. According to this principle the union which men join is primarily the concern of the labor movement rather than of the men, and each union affiliated with the Federation has the exclusive right to organize the workers in given occupations or industries. The principle goes back to the origin of the Federation, and it worked quite well for many years. Technological changes and the development of new industries, however, gradually made obsolete the pattern of jurisdictional lines established over fifty years ago. Eventually there was a revolt and the formation of the CIO. Old boundaries between unions are now held in low esteem, and much organizing effort is devoted to persuading men to leave one union and join another—even when both unions are within the same federation.

Rivalries among unions are a major obstacle to realism in negotiations and to good relations between unions and employers. These rivalries tend to prevent leaders from presenting unpleasant facts or unwelcome proposals to the members, from challenging the prejudices or illusions of the members, and from urging the members to consider their long-run interests as well as their short-run interests. Negotiators who dare not face facts frankly and who are unwilling to pay attention to the long-run as well as the short-run interests of the workers cannot be expected to build good relations between employers and unions.

II

How do trade unions affect the distribution of rights, opportunities, and power in the community? Do they help achieve a more satisfactory and better-balanced distribution of rights, or do they create the need for a new distribution?

Through trade agreements with employers, unions have provided (1) a framework of rules which are binding upon managements and within which managerial discretion must be exercised, and (2) ways by which the exercise of managerial discretion may be reviewed and injustices corrected. These rules and procedures introduce into industry the equivalent of civil rights, and they greatly enlarge the range of human activities which are governed by rule or law rather than by whim or caprice. All of this represents a major contribution toward building a better civilization—probably the greatest achievement of trade unions.

The rise of trade unions raises many problems concerning the relations of individual union members to the unions themselves. Whenever powerful organizations grow up, too much emphasis is likely to be placed upon the interests of the organization as such or upon the interests of its officers and too little upon the interests of the people whom the organization is intended to serve. Unions may prevent the fair distribution of opportunity and freedom by:

(1) control over jobs (by means of the union shop or closed shop) without keeping membership in the union open on reasonable terms to all men qualified to do the work covered by the agreement;

(2) depriving union members of employment or otherwise subjecting them to severe discipline without appeal to a neutral;

(3) depriving local unions or districts of self-government for inadequate reasons or for unreasonable periods of time;

(4) discouraging broad participation by the membership in policy making, and unduly concentrating policy making in the hands of professionals;

(5) using organizing methods which deprive individuals of a fair opportunity to select the union which they prefer.

No one can dispute the general principle that all occupations and industries must be open to all employment-seekers regardless of race, creed, or sex, and regardless of ability to pay more than a nominal admission fee to a union. Unions started out as small private clubs, and a few of them took pride in being exclusive, but the rise of large unions and the widespread use of the union shop and the closed shop have made the "exclusive club" idea of unions obsolete. Wherever a union imposes a union shop or a closed shop, its admission requirements become affected with a public interest and the union becomes a quasi-public organization. Quite rightly the Supreme Court of California recently held that unions which impose closed shops must maintain open doors.

The widespread requirement that workers maintain good standing in the union in order to hold their jobs (represented by most maintenance-of-membership clauses, the union shop, and the closed shop) causes the administration of discipline by unions to be affected with a public interest. Indeed, it is estimated that about eleven million employees work under arrangements which require them to maintain good standing in unions in order to hold their jobs. Professor Taft, in examining the constitutions of eighty-one unions, found that twenty-nine permit members to be disciplined for such vague offenses as "slandering an officer," fifteen for "creating dissension," twenty for "undermining the union or working against its interest," twenty-five for "action which is dishonorable or which might injure the labor movement," twenty-one for "circulating written material dealing with trade union business without permission of the general executive board."[1] Unions have the problem of protecting themselves against members who are agents of employers or of outside political groups or who are irresponsible cranks, but arrangements which permit unions to deprive members of their jobs for "slandering an officer," "creating dissension," "undermining the union," and for similar undefined or indefinable actions are a potential threat to a healthy political life and can easily be used by dictatorial administrations to suppress revolts. The importance of the problem is not measured by the number of cases which have arisen because provisions which authorize discipline for vague offenses may discourage the kind of activity which would produce cases.

Of late years there has been a growing tendency for the national officers of unions to place local unions in national custody—that is, to appoint national representatives to take over and handle the affairs of the local. Authority to do this is needed because local officers may abscond with funds, sell out to employers, or refuse to execute national policies. Nevertheless, locals may be seized in order to stamp out incipient rebellion against the national officers and to avoid the trouble of operating a democratic organization. Mr. Lewis has for many years appointed the officers of almost half the districts of the United Mine Workers on the ground that the districts are too new to be ready for self-government.

The organizing methods of unions frequently show scant respect for the rights of individuals and the rights of other unions. As rivalry among unions has grown and respect for traditional jurisdictional lines has declined, unions have made freer and freer use of economic coercion to compel men to join a certain union or to abandon one union and shift to another. For example, a union may compel men to join it by refusing to handle the

[1] Philip Taft, "Judicial Procedure in Labor Unions," *Quarterly Journal of Economics* (May 1945), pp. 370–385.

products which they make, or it may throw a picket line around the plant and arrange for the teamsters to make no deliveries to the plant unless the men join the union. The teamsters' union is in the process of forcing a large proportion of the members of the brewery workers' union to shift to the teamsters'. They do this by the simple process of refusing to give service to breweries where the men in dispute persist in remaining in the brewery workers' union.[2]

Many people have expected trade unions to make a major contribution to controlling large concentrations of economic power. Certainly the trade agreements negotiated by unions have, as I have explained above, imposed useful checks upon the discretion of managements. But trade unions are themselves great aggregations of economic power. Their power rests upon an extraordinary privilege which has been granted to employees but denied to the rest of the community—namely, the right to combine for the purpose of raising the price of the product which they sell. A group of employers who combined for the purpose of raising the price of steel or coal or meat would quickly find themselves in trouble under the antitrust laws, but the employees in these and other industries are permitted to shut down either individual enterprises or whole industries in order to force an increase in the price of labor. The power of the employees is counterbalanced to a substantial extent by arrangements which facilitate the combination of capitalists into corporations and by the privilege given to employers to combine for the purpose of keeping down the price of labor—at least when they are negotiating the terms of employment with unions.

The interdependence which modern technology has introduced into the community enables a relatively few men by stopping work in concert to throw many thousands of others out of work and to imperil the public health, the public safety, and the general welfare. Unions are able to cut off large cities from gas or electricity and, therefore, not only from light but also, for many people, from heat and refrigeration. They can stop the trucks which

[2] Other recent examples of the efforts of unions to force changes in the affiliation of workers or to punish workers for joining the "wrong" union are provided by the Lakeshore Electric Manufacturing Company of Cleveland and the Neon Products Inc. of Lima, Ohio. In October 1945 the employees of the Lakeshore Electric Manufacturing Company voted for the United Electrical, Radio and Machine Workers (CIO) as their bargaining agent. The International Brotherhood of Electrical Workers, which lost the election, refused to handle the switchboards and power panels made by the CIO workers. So the company closed its electrical contractors' department. The Neon Products Inc. made an agreement with the United Electrical Workers (CIO) in 1939. Soon customers began to report that AFL employees, members of the International Brotherhood of Electrical Workers, were refusing to erect their signs. The company has laid off one third of its workers. *Newsweek*, June 14, 1946, p. 78.

deliver milk and food; they can cut hundreds of industries off from the flow of steel or coal; they can limit the output of steel for many months by stopping the flow of iron ore; they can deprive the country of railroad transportation or of telephone service. A few unions are in a position to cripple or halt the operation of government departments.

Some unions in strategic positions (policemen, firemen, and some government employees) have provisions in their constitutions prohibiting their members from striking. For many years, the railroad unions observed a sort of unwritten law that nation-wide railroad strikes would not be called, and a similar restraint seems to have existed in the electric light and power industry and the gas industry. During the last year, however, unions in key positions have shown a reckless willingness to inflict calamitous losses upon the community in order to get preferred treatment for their members, in order to win trivial gains, or in order to compel the government to make changes in public policy. The elevator operators in New York tied up elevator service and threw a million people out of work in order to force a larger wage increase than the National War Labor Board had awarded them. Last spring the subway employees of New York City threatened to strike if the city carried out a plan to sell a power plant to a private buyer. The plan was abandoned. Two transportation unions stopped the nation's railroads because an emergency board appointed by the President awarded them no more than a board of arbitration gave eighteen other railroad unions. Four hundred thousand coal miners, after rejecting a wage increase of 18.5 cents an hour, threw millions of nonminers out of work in order to win gains for themselves beyond those achieved by other unions. The employees of the Duquesne Light Company rejected arbitration, crippled light and power service in Pittsburgh for a month, and for part of the period threw more than one hundred thousand people out of work. The strike occurred six months after the employees had received a wage increase of 18 cents an hour. This fall the coal miners cut off the country's supply of coal for a second time, in an attempt to compel the government to accept Mr. Lewis' interpretation of their contract with the government—although the only binding interpretation of the contract could be made by the courts. The reckless and irresponsible use of the strike which has occurred so frequently in essential industries during the last year calls for well-planned and vigorous action to defend the public interest. The rise of unions confronts the country with a new form of the old problem of controlling the use of great concentrations of economic power.

III

How do trade unions affect the scales of value in the community and the relative importance attached by people to their special interests and to their common interests? So long as competition in selling labor was prevalent, the relative weight attached by individuals to their special interests and their common interests was not important. Will the growth of unions mean that workers are taught to think narrowly of their interests as carpenters, miners, and steel workers, and to be little concerned with their interests as members of the community?

The importance of these questions can scarcely be exaggerated. More vigorous pursuit of special interests by 190-odd national unions cannot be expected to increase the total income to be divided. Indeed, the great interdependence which modern technology has introduced into the community makes the level of the national income depend upon the willingness of many diverse groups to exercise restraint in pursuing special interests and to cooperate in advancing their common interest in a larger national income. The capacity of groups to cooperate, however, depends upon their preferences or scales of value. They may prefer to put more time and effort into fighting over the division of a small income and less time and effort into cooperating to increase income.

Certainly the possibility is great that the growth of trade unions will substantially strengthen the forces of particularism. Unions are intended to be organizations which advance special interests of their members, and no union is large enough to be greatly concerned with the effect of its policies upon the community as a whole. The problem may be illustrated by the possible "second round" of wage increases which seems now about to begin. There is great doubt whether a second round of wage increases would tend to promote or to hinder high and stable production. Some people think that new wage increases would be inflationary; others think that they would be deflationary. The crucial point, however, is that the unions which determine whether or not there will be a second round of wage increases are not interested in the general effects of their decision upon the community. If the decisions of the unions happen to promote higher and more stable production, that will simply be a happy accident. It is plain that the community needs to face the possibility that the rise of unions (and other special-interest groups) will cause policy decisions to be dominated by narrow and parochial considerations and that it will reduce the capacity of the people of the country to deal with common problems.

IV

What can the community do to cope with the problems created by trade unions and to make unions better instruments for helping a free society realize its ideals more completely? Let us again consider the three basic problems of a free society: (1) the problem of achieving and maintaining good will and harmonious relations among men and groups with divergent preferences and interests; (2) the problem of distributing rights and opportunities fairly and of controlling the use of great concentrations of power; and (3) the problem of striking a reasonable balance between special interests and common interests and of building effective cooperation among divergent groups in the pursuit of common interests.

What can be done to make collective bargaining a more effective instrument for enabling men and groups with divergent interests to live together harmoniously? Widespread knowledge of the results possible through bargaining would help because it would introduce much-needed realism into negotiations. It would also prevent workers from expecting too much from bargaining and would keep them from becoming bitter and disillusioned when bargaining failed to justify their hopes. For example, employees can expect to gain little by appropriating income at the expense of property because only about one fifth of the national income goes to property. Small reductions in the rate of return on property might raise the disposition of many people to save. Even this gain, which would be an uncertain one, would be offset in part at least by the greater disposition of some people to hoard rather than to invest. Finally, labor as a whole cannot expect technological progress to raise wages more than about 3 per cent a year—unless industrial research achieves results far faster in the future than in the past. Any group which seeks to push up wages by more than about 3 per cent a year is simply seeking to raise its income at the expense of other groups.

The analysis in section I indicates that relations between unions and employers would be improved by arrangements which increase the security of union officers and which restrict the keen competition between unions. The possibility of achieving these two results will be discussed in the next section. In large measure, the problem of making collective bargaining operate with good will must be solved plant by plant, by methods of administration which are more under the control of managements than of unions. For one thing, unless employers inform local and national officials of unions about the problems of business which are also the problems of workers, how are the union representatives to learn about them? Although some businessmen have excellent contacts with local and national union leaders, most managers still have little to do with union representatives. The great shift of power from business to unions makes the traditional aloofness of managers an anachronism. Furthermore, managements make most of the decisions around shops. The nature of these decisions, the way in which they are made, the way in which workers and union representatives are treated when they find fault with management's decisions, seek information, or offer advice determine in large measure the attitude of union members and leaders toward management. Once good will exists, both sides like to preserve it and will make sacrifices to keep it.

If collective bargaining is to produce good will and mutual understanding, the parties must not be able too readily to shift to the government the responsibility of bringing about a settlement of disputes. It must not be easy for them to get the government to extricate them from difficult or extreme positions. They must not be helped to be unrealistic, extreme, and uncompromising by the willingness of the government to save their faces and to bail them out. Conciliation has its place and the government should be prepared to offer it; but it should be used sparingly. Especially during the last year, conciliation by the government has been greatly overdone. Indeed, knowledge that the government would intervene has impeded real bargaining. Cool indifference by the government to the difficulties of the parties will often have a wholesome effect upon bargaining. Furthermore, nothing is likely to be so effective in bringing about realism and frank facing of facts in future bargaining as for both parties to go through a long and tough struggle. The actual experience of a strike may be necessary in order to make both men and management realize vividly the cost of a strike. Hence, strikes are often a necessary step in laying the foundation for industrial peace.

V

What can be done to protect individual workmen or union members against arbitrary treatment by unions and to protect the community against the abuse of the great economic power of unions? Employers, if they would, could do much to protect the rights of individual workers and of union members within the organization. For example, they might refuse to grant the union shop or closed shop unless the union agrees to maintain an "open door." Furthermore, employers might insist that employees who are disciplined by the union shall have the right to appeal to the same arbitrator who passes on discipline by the employer. Keeping all trades and industries open to all employment seekers on fair terms and protecting workers against arbitrarily being deprived of union membership and hence of the right to hold a job, however, are not matters which should be left to the accidents of bargaining. The government cannot escape the responsibility of requiring that unions which impose the closed shop also maintain open doors and that maintenance-of-membership clauses, union shops, or closed shops do not expose workers to the danger of being deprived of employment without reasonable cause and without appeal to a neutral.

Unions which permit members to be disciplined for vague and essentially political offenses such as "creating dissension" or "slandering officers" should not be eligible for certification as bargaining agents in any plants where they are not now certified. Members of unions who work in union shops or closed shops or under maintenance-of-membership clauses should be given the right by the government to appeal discipline by the union involving suspension, expulsion, or fines of over a certain amount (say, fifty dollars) to the same arbitrator who passes on discipline by the employer or, in case arbitration is not provided by the agreement between the union and the employer, to the National Labor Relations Board. This Board, which now handles cases in which the employer is charged with dismissing men for union activity, is well qualified to review discipline by unions. Assuring members a real review of discipline imposed by the union is of central importance. Otherwise, either the union shop or the closed shop becomes a threat to democracy within unions.

Abuse of the custody of local unions by national unions can be prevented by authorizing the National Labor Relations Board, on complaint of members of a local, to require a national union to show cause why the national should not be ordered to restore self-government in the local. This proceeding is appropriate because it is the purpose of the National Labor Relations Act to assure that employees are represented by agents of their own choosing. Refusal of a national union to permit self-government in a local union may deprive workers of the right to be represented by their own bargaining agents.[3]

Democracy is not a way of life which can be imposed on the members of a union or any organization from without. All that the government can do is to give the members of unions a fair opportunity to develop demo-

[3] The authority of the National Labor Relations Board should be made broad enough so that the Board might require the restoration of the local union's charter in cases where the local was clearly deprived of its charter simply to prevent it from being represented by persons of its own choice.

cratic habits. The members must do the rest. The problem of democracy in American trade unions is made difficult by the fact that paid officers are given the responsibility of *both* making policies and executing them. Hence disagreements on policy between the national officers, on the one hand, and the rank and file and local officers, on the other, may jeopardize the jobs of the national officers. The officers are tempted to protect themselves by building strong political organizations and by suppressing opposition. The tradition that policies shall be made by professional labor leaders is so strongly established in American trade unions that new arrangements will not easily be brought into existence. Security for the officers and a better opportunity for a vigorous democratic life within the union could be achieved, however, by adopting the British practice of making the salaried officers of the union executors of policies and advisers on policy decisions but giving the responsibility for making policies to nonsalaried executive boards. Under this arrangement conflicts over policy do not involve the full-time officers of the union, criticisms of policies are not criticisms of these officers, and officers need not be changed in order to change policies.

Particularly formidable is the problem of protecting the rights of individuals, unions, employers, and consumers in the keen competition of unions for members. This competition, as I pointed out in section I, is growing by leaps and bounds, and is being carried on with ruthless disregard of whom it hurts. In some communities, such as Seattle, the use of strikes and boycotts to control the affiliation of workers is a well-established practice. The building trades have already gone far in controlling the union affiliations of the men who make building materials. It would be a logical step for the United Automobile Workers some day to dictate the union affiliations of the men who make automobile parts. If the use of economic coercion by unions to control the affiliation of nonmembers were developed to its logical extreme, the economy would eventually be split up into two parts, one an AFL part, consisting of firms employing AFL workers and buying and selling only from other firms employing AFL workers, and the other a CIO part, consisting of firms employing CIO workers and buying and selling only from other firms employing CIO workers. The presence of such privately constructed trade barriers within the country is plainly intolerable.

The problem of interunion competition is beyond the capacity of either the labor movement or employers to solve. Only intervention by the government will protect employees, employers, and consumers from the growing anarchy in the labor movement. Both the government and the community, however, should be clear concerning the implications of a policy of intervention. An attempt by the government to prevent the use of economic coercion for the purpose of controlling the affiliation of workers would produce a head-on collision between the government and powerful union leaders who are determined to expand their unions and hence increase their own prestige and power regardless of the preferences of individual workmen or the rights of other unions. It is a grievous mistake for the government to take a position which it is not prepared to enforce with vigor and determination, and then yield to strikes against the government.

Strikes for the purpose of compelling workers to shift from one union to another or for the purpose of punishing men for joining the "wrong" union should be declared illegal. This means that the strikers will be regarded as having terminated their employment and that, if the employer rehires them, they come back with only the vacation rights, seniority rights, and pension rights of new employees. In order to prevent the strikers from bargaining with the employer over the restoration of their status as employees, it should be made an unfair labor practice for the employer to rehire them except as new employees. Picketing, payment of strike benefits, and other activities in support of the illegal strikes should be prohibited and penalized. The attempt to force workers to change their union or to punish them for joining the "wrong" union may take several forms—refusal to handle materials made by members of the "wrong" union; refusal to service establishments where members of the "wrong" union work; or establishment of picket lines around stores which sell goods made by members of the "wrong" union. Employers should be authorized to discharge men for refusing to handle materials made by members of the "wrong" union. Furthermore, all of the above forms of boycott should be declared to be outside the legitimate purposes of trade unions and should subject union officers and union members to the penalties of the Sherman Act, just as would a combination of employers which boycotted an enterprise because it purchased raw materials from a concern of which the combination did not approve.

Most important of all, and most difficult, is protection of the community as a whole against the abuse of the great economic power of unions. A variety of problems are involved, but I direct attention to only some of them, namely three types of strikes and boycotts: strikes (and boycotts) to compel employers to violate the law (for example, to violate the Wagner Act by dealing with an agent other than the authorized one); strikes to force changes in public policy; and strikes which imperil the public health, public safety, or general welfare.

When the problem of strikes is mentioned, the suggestion is almost invariably made that the Conciliation Service be strengthened in various ways. Effective conciliation can be exceedingly useful, but in some cases conciliation is inappropriate and in other cases it is not enough. For example, if men propose a strike to compel employers to violate a law or to coerce the government, conciliation is inappropriate—at least, conciliation from government agencies. Fellow trade-union leaders may plead with the union and its leaders to do nothing reckless, but no representative of government should stoop to pleading or to suggesting compromises when a strike to compel violation of law or to coerce the government is in question. When a strike would imperil the public health, public safety, or general welfare, the government should be armed with something better than an excellent conciliation service. Centuries of experience with the effect of great power upon human beings in all walks of life show that moral suasion has never been able to prevent the abuse of power. It cannot be expected to deter powerful unions in strategic situations from insisting on their terms.

What should be done? Strikes to compel violations of law or to coerce the government present no problem. They must obviously be outlawed. They are a threat to free institutions, and calling them or participating in them is a serious violation of democratic principles. Men who participate in them should lose their status as employees, and employers should be forbidden to rehire these men except as new employees with the seniority, pension, and vacation rights of new employees. Support of such strikes by picketing or payment of strike benefits should be penalized.

What about strikes in certain key industries such as gas, electric light and power, or railroads? No one would contend that a large city could go for weeks without light and power or that the country would tolerate a nation-wide railroad strike while the two parties test which is able and willing to stand the longer shutdown. And yet thus far the public has not seen fit to take away the right to strike from any group of men on the ground that they supply goods or services which the community must have without interruption. Does this mean that the community has decided that in *all* industries and occupations the freedom of unions and employers to fight each other is more important than the need of the community for continuous service? Probably not. The man in the street knows perfectly well that long strikes in hospitals, in electric light and power plants, in railroads, or even in the coal industry or the steel industry cannot be tolerated. A more realistic description of the community's policy would be "trusting to luck." The community has not wished to deprive workers of the right to strike. Consequently the public has hoped that the men in essential industries would not use the right to strike and thus force the public to restrict it or to take it away from them. The experience of this last year, however, shows that this policy of "trusting to luck" is obviously inadequate. What should be put in its place?

Two principal policies are possible. One is to give public officials authority to deal on an *ad hoc* basis with strikes (or lockouts) which imperil the general welfare. The other is to provide a special status for employees who perform jobs on which continuous service is necessary. This special status should provide special duties and special privileges for these employees. Let us analyze these two policies.

The *ad hoc* policy should be based upon a declaration of the rights of the community—a public bill of rights. This declaration should assert the right of the community to an adequate supply of essential services and commodities. It should place upon the President (or in the case of state legislation, the governor) the duty to declare that a public emergency exists when a threatened or an actual strike or lockout so seriously limits or threatens to limit the output of essential goods and services as to imperil the public health, the public safety, or the general welfare. The declaration of an emergency should require the union to rescind any strike instructions and to order back to work any members who may have struck. Union officers who failed to perform these duties or who failed in good faith to make a reasonable effort to induce men to return to work might be required to show cause before the National Labor Relations Board as to why they should not be found unfit to hold office in any union subject to the Wagner Act. Such a finding would make it an unfair labor practice for any such union to keep them in its employ. Likewise a union which failed to discipline members who disobeyed its back-to-work orders might be required to show cause before the National Labor Relations Board as to why it should not be deprived of bargaining rights in the plants affected. Men who declined to return to work should be held to have terminated their employment, and it should be an unfair labor practice for employers to rehire them except as new employees.

Picketing in the support of strikes which have been found to imperil the public safety, public health, or general welfare should be forbidden, and likewise payment of strike benefits and other activities designed to promote the illegal shutdown. The parties should be given the option of settling the dispute by (1) continuing negotiations in their own way, (2) submitting the unresolved issues to arbitrators selected by themselves, or (3) submitting the dispute to arbitrators selected by the head of the Conciliation Service from a permanent panel maintained by the Service. The findings of the Board should be retroactive to the expiration of the date of the previous contract and should be binding upon both parties for six months. This period is long enough to enable the two parties to negotiate a lasting settlement which may be more to their liking than the findings of the Board.

The proposed policy has the advantage of being based upon a declaration of the rights of the public which no one in the labor movement or outside can successfully challenge. It limits as little as possible the right to strike—imposing restrictions only in cases where the general welfare is imperiled. It is flexible. It gives public officials an opportunity to use their judgment about declaring an emergency. If an official believes that the public in a given situation is too indifferent to its interests to give proper support to him, he is not required to act. Finally, the policy works through the unions and gives them an opportunity for becoming instruments to protect the community against disastrous interruptions of service.

The principal criticism of the *ad hoc* policy is that it does not squarely face realities. The reality is that there are a few industries or occupations—such as electric light and power, gas, hospitals, railroads, possibly telephones, and, in many cities, elevators—in which the public cannot permit the parties to see which can stand the longer shutdown. Why, therefore, *pretend* that the men in these industries have the right to strike? They have the right only on condition that they do not use it—except on a very limited scale. Rights are given to be used. The public is not justified, however, in giving men rights which it cannot afford to permit them to use. Certainly the public is not justified in finding fault with men for using the rights which the public has given them. The present ambiguous and contradictory situation in which the public pretends that the men have rights which it will not tolerate their effectively using is not fair either to labor or to the community.

The honest and fair way to solve the problem is for the community to make up its mind concerning where it wishes to draw the line between the occupations and industries in which the freedom of the parties to fight each other is more important than the need of the public for a continuous service and those in which the need of the public for continuous operation is more important than the freedom of the parties to fight. The holders of jobs on which continuous service is necessary should enjoy a special status. In accepting employment on these jobs, workers should undertake not to engage in strikes, and no union should be eligible to bargain for workers in these jobs which does not make strikes of members in these categories a violation of its constitution. In order to make strikes uncalled for, the workers on designated jobs should be assured that their wages will be reviewed once a year and increased in proportion to the rise in the general wage level. In addition, the "special-status" workers should be entitled to pensions of a given percentage (say 15 per cent) above the pensions provided in the Social Security Act. Railroad employees, of course, already have far more liberal pensions than those provided by the Social Security Act. "Special-status" employees should receive more liberal vacation privileges than employees in general. Violations of the obligation not to engage in strikes should be penalized by appropriate sanctions, such as the loss of status of an employee and the necessity of being rehired, if at all, as a new worker with consequent loss of accumulated seniority, vacation, and pension rights. The aim, however, should be to make the special-status jobs sufficiently attractive so that they would be eagerly sought and so that the holders of them would consider themselves fortunate and would not think of risking the loss of such good jobs by going on strike.

VI

Should the scales of value produced by the rise of organized labor be accepted without question, or should an effort be made to prevent the growth of unionism from increasing the importance attached by various occupational and industrial groups to their special interests at the expense of the importance attached to common interests? Can the various national unions, representing in each case only a small fraction of the work force, be expected to be concerned with the broad interests of labor as a whole? What can be done to develop an organization of labor which will effectively represent the interests of labor as a whole as well as the interests of particular groups of workers?

Whatever reduces competition among unions, increases the security of union leadership, or improves relations between unions and employers will tend to induce union leaders and union members to attach more importance to the interests which all groups of workers have in common and which employees as a whole have in common with business owners and with the self-employed. The gradual spread of knowledge will also help improve the balance between the importance attached to special interests and the importance attached to common interests. This is true because common interests as a whole are less obvious and less easily seen than special interests. The negotiation of trade agreements, as I have indicated in section I, affords opportunities for business managers to learn about the problems of labor and for union leaders to learn about the problems of business. Union leaders are playing broader roles in community affairs by participating actively in the work of community chests, Red Cross, school boards, and other civic enterprises. All of these contacts give them insight into problems of other groups and at the same time help other groups learn about the problems of labor.

Gradual processes of education, fundamental and necessary as they may be, are not enough. The processes of competition, which are fairly effective in regulating the activities of individual enterprises and of individuals, have little effect upon the policies of the great organized groups in the fields of labor, business, and agriculture. Hence the rise of organized groups makes the problem of giving adequate attention to common interests the most pressing economic problem of the age. It cannot be left to solve itself. The scale of values which emerges as a result of the rise of powerful organizations in various occupations and industries cannot be expected to produce a satisfactory balance between the importance attached to special interests and the importance attached to common interests.

There is urgent need for stronger and more influential machinery to represent the interests of labor as a whole. This means that the executive councils of the two federations need to exercise more initiative in policy making and need to have more influence over the constituent unions. In order that the executive councils may effectively assume greater responsibilities, they need to be well staffed with economists of ability and independence of judgment. It is true that experience in corporations and in government shows that staff employees will rarely assume the risks of offering unpalatable advice, especially upon major matters. Nevertheless, an alert and able staff will suggest many issues for consideration and will recommend many important policy decisions for approval. In the last analysis, however, the influence of the executive councils in the labor movement must depend upon their own conception of their responsibilities and upon how their policies stand the test of being put into practice. There is no use in building up a record of giving false warnings, sponsoring ill-founded optimism, dodging tough issues, or engaging in wishful thinking. Hence, the councils must win influence for themselves with the labor movement and the community by the breadth of vision, the wisdom, and the courage of the men who compose them.

Changing the orientation of the labor movement from extreme particularism to a deeper concern for the interests of labor as a whole will not be easily or quickly accomplished. The strongly established traditions of autonomy and independence among the several unions will be a difficult impediment. Nevertheless, one should not be too pessimistic. The University of Hard Knocks, which all of us attend constantly, is an excellent teacher. The experience of labor organizations in attempting to raise wages during the year 1946 has led a few of the unions, at least, to re-examine the effect of union wage policies upon real wages. President Green and other leaders of the American Federation of Labor have observed that large increases in money wages have had the principal effect of raising prices rather than raising the standard of living of workers. This has led Green to call for more output per manhour in order that increases in money wages will also produce advances in real wages. The tremendous economic power of trade unions is likely to compel them sooner or later to consider the stake which they have in the supply and vigor of enterprise in the community. The number of jobs depends in part upon the amount of enterprise in the community —upon the number of men who attempt to derive at least part of their incomes from business ownership and upon the willingness of managements to be venturesome in adding new products, in improving old ones, and in seeking to expand. All unions, therefore, have a common interest in the amount of enterprise. As unions become aware of this, the trade-union movement may well become the most powerful instrument by which a nation of employees encourages enterprise and thus increases the demand for labor.

Can the community master the many problems which have been so suddenly thrust upon it by the shift of power from business to labor? Can it prevent the shift from plunging the community into frequent costly conflicts? Can it prevent trade unions from becoming tightly run oligarchies or dictatorships which have little regard for the rights of members and which tolerate little democratic activity? Can it prevent the shift from producing great aggregations of economic power which defy control by the community, or from making men narrow and parochial with little concern for their common interests and little capacity to cooperate in the pursuit of common interests?

Only time will give the answers to these questions. The difficulties in solving the problems created by the shift of power from business to labor are enormous. Solution of these problems, as I have explained, requires radical changes in the philosophy, the policies, and even the structure of the labor movement, and equally radical changes in public policies toward unions. The most formidable obstacles to these changes arise from the necessity of recognizing new facts and problems and dropping many ancient preconceptions and traditional points of view. So rapid and recent has been the shift of power that many employers and workers do not yet realize what has happened. They still regard trade unions as underdogs. They do not realize that the rise of trade unions confronts the community with the old problem of controlling great concentrations of economic power and of seeing that this power is used with due regard to the public interest. So long as out-of-date preconceptions are widely held, the new problems created by the rise of trade unions cannot be effectively attacked.

Although the difficulties are formidable, the stakes are immense. The success or lack of success of the community in bringing about appropriate internal changes in the labor movement and in developing appropriate public policies toward trade unions will determine whether unions become powerful instruments for realizing the philosophy of freedom or whether they become a new and formidable threat to freedom. There are enough examples of ruthless dictators among unions heads, enough strikes for the purpose of coercing the government, enough instances of aggressive pursuit of narrow special interests by unions to show that trade unions cannot necessarily be counted upon to be instruments of freedom. Friends of freedom, both inside the labor movement and outside, have no time to lose in bringing about a development of both union practices and public policies to take account of the new power and responsibilities of trade unions.

18

Are We Becoming a "Laboristic" State?

New York Times Magazine, May 16, 1948.

FEW major transformations in the American community have occurred more rapidly than the rise of trade unions during the last fifteen years. The growth of unions means far more than the substitution of collective bargaining for individual bargaining. It means that the United States is gradually shifting from a capitalistic community to a laboristic one—that is, to a community in which employees rather than businessmen are the strongest single influence. A community in which employees are the principal influence will have its own ways of looking at things, its own scale of values, its own ideas on public policies, and, to some extent, its own jurisprudence. It will also have new and distinctive problems and its own ways of dealing with them. Hence, the rise of trade unions means that the United States stands on the threshold of major changes in its economic and political institutions.

I

Many people will deny that the United States is becoming a laboristic community. Trade-union leaders in particular are inclined to question it. They are used to thinking of the country as the stronghold of capitalism and they point out that many persons who make policy today are not sympathetic to the aims of labor. It is true that on many matters of public policy employees have not developed a common and distinctive point of view. Perhaps on many matters they never will, because there are great differences in viewpoint among various groups of employees. There is no doubt, however, that on many issues employees are the most influential group in the community and that they are growing stronger. Today, the United States is virtually a nation of employees because three out of four persons who work for a living are on someone else's payroll. Employees outnumber stockholders about five to one.

The growing influence of employees is best shown by the steadily expanding labor legislation of the community. Some of this legislation, such as laws prescribing rules and standards to protect the safety and health of workers and workmen's compensation laws, has of course been in existence for over a generation.

With the rapid rise in union membership during the last fifteen years, the influence of employees has been increasing by leaps and bounds. It is manifested in the Social Security Act, in the Fair Labor Standards Act, and, most conspicuously of all, in laws encouraging employees to organize to bargain over the price of labor. Any other sellers who combine to raise the price of their product commit a crime and are liable to fine or imprisonment.

The Taft-Hartley Act was in some respects a setback for labor, but there is much evidence that on many points covered by this law the official position of unions did not represent the preferences of employees. At any rate, the act did not disturb the basic policy of encouraging employees to combine for the purpose of raising the price of their labor.

A recent development of great importance is the rise of community leaders from the ranks of labor. In the past the labor movement has produced only a few real community leaders—that is, men who have had influence far beyond the ranks of labor and whose ideas have pertained to matters other than questions of labor policy. Samuel Gompers, John Mitchell, and Sidney Hillman are examples. Today, the participation of trade-union officers in community affairs is spreading rapidly. In scores of places, labor leaders are helping to direct Red Cross campaigns, community chest drives, government savings-bond drives. A few colleges and universities now have union officers among their regents or trustees. Some public corporations have directors who come from the labor movement.

Union leaders are contributing to the thinking of the community on a wide range of topics outside the field of trade unionism. In increasing numbers, for example, union speakers are found presenting papers on questions of business administration or public policy before meetings of businessmen, engineers, and professional managers. Several colleges this spring will confer honorary degrees on trade-union leaders—a new recognition of their services to the country.

The emergence of community leaders from the ranks of labor means that the country is better prepared to deal with its problems and to adjust itself to changing conditions. New problems are seen sooner and more clearly, and policies, both in public affairs and business, are based upon more complete information and better understanding of conditions.

II

The shift of power from business to labor confronts the community with many new problems of great importance and difficulty. Five of these problems are of particular importance.

(1) *The right of individuals to belong to trade unions*—that is, the right to join a union and the right to remain in one. So long as trade unions included only a small part of the labor force, everyone conceded them the right to admit or exclude anyone that they saw fit. Today the livelihood of many workers depends upon their opportunity to belong to a union.

Most unions maintain an open door, but a few discriminate against certain racial groups and some charge high initiation fees. The constitutions of some unions permit members to be suspended or expelled for such vague offenses as "slandering an officer," "creating dissension," "undermining the union or working against its interests," or for "action which might injure the labor movement."

New York and Massachusetts have pioneered in protecting the right to belong to a union. Each state forbids unions from denying membership on the ground of race, color, or creed. The Taft-Hartley Act attempts indirectly to deal with the problem by forbidding employers from discriminating in hiring against workers to whom membership in the union is not available. It also requires that unions which enter into union-shop contracts shall not charge "excessive" initiation fees.

Little has been done to protect workers in their right to remain in a union, though the Taft-Hartley Act forbids employers from discharging workers who lose membership for any reason other than refusal to pay regular union dues and assessments. Massachusetts has attempted to deal with the problem (a) by prohibiting unions from requiring the discharge of men who are appealing their cases through the regular machinery within the union, and (b) by giving workers the right to appeal from the highest tribunal within the union to the State Labor Relations Board. If the worker wins his appeal before the Board, the union may still expel him from its ranks, but it may not require the employer to discharge him.

(2) *The nature of the bargaining process.* Is collective bargaining to be a mere appeal to power in which the stronger party gets the better of the

deal, or is it to be an appeal to principle and reason, an attempt to settle differences on the basis of what is fair? Merely settling wages on the basis of bargaining power would cause jobs requiring similar degrees of skill and responsibility and done under similar working conditions to be compensated at widely differing rates. Furthermore, if collective bargaining is merely an attempt to settle wages and other conditions on the basis of power, it can hardly produce good relations between employees and management, and it can hardly command the respect and support of the community.

How can collective bargaining be made an appeal to principles and evidence? Obviously only by the development of a body of thought concerning how the fairness of wages shall be tested. This does not mean that solutions in particular cases can be reached by a mechanical procedure or that there will not be room for argument over principles as well as over facts in each case. It does mean, however, that collective bargaining must be guided by a well-developed body of thought about the economic consequences of different types of wage adjustment—a body of thought which carries weight with both sides and with the public and which, therefore, affects the outcome of negotiations and arbitrations.

(3) *The possibility of developing cooperation between managements and unions to deal with common interests.* Many union leaders and managers realize that it would be a calamity if unions were to do little more than represent workers in conflicts of interest between themselves and management. Formal cooperation between unions and management, however, is not easily accomplished.

Managers fear that it may become the beginning of interference by unions with routine administrative decisions; union leaders sometimes fear that cooperation with management will be interpreted by the rank and file as evidence that the officers are not vigilant in representing the members. Nevertheless, arrangements for cooperation between union representatives and management are slowly being developed. In the course of time, they promise greatly to improve the administration of business concerns and to make managers better aware of problems of employees and employees better aware of problems of management.

(4) *The protection of the community against interruptions of production which jeopardize the public health, safety, and economic welfare.* Several times during recent years strikes have deprived the community of essential services. This happened once in the case of railroads, once in the case of steel, and several times in the case of coal. Indeed, never in the history of Western civilization have relatively small groups of men, such as coal miners, rail-

road workers, or steel workers, been in a position to shut down the entire economic life of the country. It is plain that the community cannot tolerate extended stoppages or even threats of strikes or lockouts in vital industries. But it is not plain what the country should do about it.

The most sensible arrangement for dealing with disputes in vital industries would probably be one similar to the agreement between the unions and the employers in Great Britain to meet the emergency caused by the fall of France in 1940, but still in effect. Under this agreement, the unions and the employers refer to the Minister of Labor disputes which cannot be settled by collective bargaining or other processes. The Minister may refer the dispute to a national arbitration tribunal which makes a binding award. This does not mean universal compulsory arbitration, but it does mean that the unions and employers have given the government an opportunity to protect the community against all stoppages which might create a national emergency.

It is not necessary, of course, that deadlocks be submitted to an arbitration tribunal through the government—the parties might submit them directly. An arrangement by which the parties agree in advance to submit deadlocks to arbitration means that the unions, by agreeing not to use the right to strike, relieve the government from the necessity of restricting this right.

(5) *The effect of collective bargaining upon the price level.* This is a matter of great importance which has been much neglected. During the last hundred years, technological progress has had the principal effect of raising wages rather than reducing prices. At any rate, hourly earnings rose about eightfold between 1840 and 1940, but the price level changed little. Output per manhour rose about 2 per cent a year. In view of the rapid rise of expenditures on industrial research, output per manhour is likely to rise more rapidly in the future than in the past—perhaps as much as 3 per cent or 4 per cent a year. The unions, however, are likely to force up wages faster than the engineers and managers can raise output per manhour.

If output rises by 3 per cent a year and money wages by 5 per cent, prices will need to rise by about 2 per cent a year. Otherwise there will be a creeping increase in unemployment. If prices do not rise of their own accord, the government will be compelled either to check the rise in money wages or to encourage a rise in prices. Of these two policies, the government, it is safe to say, will adopt the latter because helping a rise in somebody's price is usually more popular (or less unpopular) than attempting to hold down a price.

The prospect that universal collective bargaining will lead to a slow rise in the price level raises questions of profound importance. Pensions or life insurance, which men started to buy on entering the labor force at about the age of twenty or twenty-five, would have lost more than half their purchasing power by the time the workers had reached the age of sixty-five or seventy. With prices rising 2 or 3 per cent a year, who would wish to own a savings account, government bonds, or other securities paying 2 or 3 per cent a year?

All fixed-income securities would have to sell at yields which discounted the expected drop in the purchasing power of the principal. After ten or fifteen years millions of people would have noticed that collective bargaining was gradually reducing the purchasing power of their pensions, savings accounts, life insurance, and bonds, and they would demand that something be done about it. Hence the government might be faced with the widespread demand that it require wage settlements made by collective bargaining to conform to a national wage policy.

As a matter of fact, this question has already become important in other countries where collective bargaining has become fairly universal and where there has been danger that the wage policies of unions might conflict with the efforts of the government to control prices. In Norway the wage policies of the unions have been subordinated to the interests of the community in stable prices. In England the reconciliation of national interests and the policies of the several unions has been more difficult because the traditions of the labor movement give much autonomy to the unions. The Labor Government, however, has discouraged unions from pressing wage demands. On February 4, 1948, the government issued a White Paper entitled "Statement on Personal Incomes, Costs and Prices," in which it stated: "It is essential . . . that there should be no further general increase in the level of personal incomes without at least a corresponding increase in the volume of production."

The United States is not yet prepared to recognize that there are likely to be important conflicts between the national interest in stable prices and free collective bargaining. Sooner or later, however, the community is bound to become aware of these conflicts. What changes in policies and institutions will follow is anyone's guess. If the decision is to accept rising prices in order to avoid interfering with collective bargaining, pensions and life insurance will have to be adapted to this fact, and the government and corporations will have to issue bonds payable in purchasing power rather than a fixed number of dollars. If the policy is to stabilize prices, the government will have to develop ways and means of formulating a national wage policy to guide the operation of collective bargaining.

III

Many people view the shift of power from business to employees with much misgiving. Naturally one wonders what employees will do with their power and how the policies which they support will affect the operation of American industry. The American economy is the most productive and the most dynamic in the world. With about 6 per cent of the world's population, it produces between one third and two fifths of the world's goods.

Two outstanding characteristics explain the great productivity of the American economy. One is the large number of business enterprises—about 3.5 million outside of agriculture. This means that there are millions of places where a new idea may be born and where experiment may be authorized. Regimented economies with few centers of initiative can scarcely be expected to compete in dynamic drive with an economy which has millions of centers of initiative. The other characteristic which explains the high productivity of American industry is the opportunity to obtain immense rewards by pioneering. These rewards have supplied both incentives and capital for enterprises to grow from small beginnings to huge concerns within a generation.

Employees have fared exceedingly well under the American economy. Although the amount of capital per worker has been rapidly rising, the share of the national income going to property in the form of profits, personal rents, and interest has not been increasing. In 1940 capital per worker was about three times as large (in dollars of constant purchasing power) as in 1880. In each year, however, the share of the national income going to property was only about one fourth. In 1947, only about one sixth of the national income went to property owners. Most of the gains of technological progress have gone to people in their capacity as employees rather than in their capacity as consumers. For example, between 1840 and 1940 there was little change in the general price level, but hourly earnings of nonagricultural workers, as I have pointed out, increased about eightfold. It remains to be seen whether a nation of employees will feel a sufficient stake in industrial progress to keep essentially unimpaired the conditions which have made American industry highly dynamic, or whether they will follow some European countries in attempting to introduce great centralization of decision making with more or less drastic control over the rewards of enterprise.

My guess is that the help which unions are likely to give the community in solving its problems will be more important than the new problems which unions create. The most important fact about the world today is the conflict between the philosophy of life represented by Russia and the philosophy which Western Europe and the United States have inherited from the Greeks and the Anglo-Saxons. The Russian philosophy asserts that the community has interests which are independent of and superior to those of its members. Indeed, it recognizes no rights of the individual against the government. The philosophy of Western Europe asserts that the supreme values are found in the interests of individuals and that institutions exist in order to serve individuals.

In this great conflict between two philosophies the trade unions are an important ally of the West. In the first place, they are an effective champion of the idea of the dignity of the individual. They have introduced the equivalent of civil rights into industry and have given workers protection against arbitrary treatment by management. Thus they have made a major contribution toward implementing the philosophy of the West.

In the second place, the rise of trade unions and the gradual development of a laboristic community opens up to employees great opportunities to participate in policy making both in the plant and in the community. Russia is gradually creating a community in which individuals are vassals of the state—a new form of serfdom. Such an economy has little chance of holding its own in competition with a laboristic economy in which responsibility for decisions is widely dispersed and in which millions of employees have a chance to feel that they have a stake in the community.

19

Labor's New Victory: Threat or Promise?

The Atlantic Monthly, September 1955.

I

No settlement in union-employer negotiations since the dramatic agreement of 1937 between John L. Lewis and the United States Steel Corporation has aroused so much comment from editors, economists, and business leaders as the recent agreements between the United Automobile Workers and Ford and General Motors. Although the provision for the payment of supplementary unemployment compensation represents only one third of the cost of the companies' concessions, it is this feature of the agreements that is entirely responsible for the widespread comment.

The president of the National Association of Manufacturers charged that agreements to pay men for not working "could have seriously damaging effects on the American economy, perhaps leading to a socialistic state and a controlled economy," and the NAM called an emergency conference to discuss the danger. Many papers and some economists questioned whether small employers would be able to do what Ford and General Motors are doing and suggested that small companies would be squeezed out of existence and the concentration of industry accentuated. Still others asserted that the higher labor costs represented by supplementary unemployment compensation would start an inflationary spiral of costs and prices.

A few commentators forecast that such payments would accelerate "automation"—taking it for granted that this would be bad. Many businessmen expressed the fear that employees would be discouraged from working. A frequently expressed fear was the possibility that supplementary unemployment compensation would lead managers to plan less boldly for expansion—that, in the words of the *Baltimore Sun,* the characteristic adventurousness of American industry would fade away.

Supporters of the Ford and General Motors agreements are as numerous as the critics. The agreements have been hailed as evidence of the ability of American employers and unions to defy tradition, to work out their own arrangements for dealing with problems by bargaining—a method superior to the European practice of relying upon social legislation. A thoughtful article in the *Christian Science Monitor* described the Ford agreement as proving "that labor and industry are working out a new social system in the United States." Supporters of the new agreements stress their influence in encouraging managements to work out more stable year-round production schedules, and they argue that additional unemployment compensation, by helping to maintain the demand for goods in periods of business recession, will strengthen the resistance of the economy to contraction.

Both the critics and the supporters of the Ford-General Motors agreements assume that provision for supplementary unemployment benefits will be added to many union-employer contracts during the next few years—just as supplementary pension schemes spread rapidly after the precedent-setting agreements in the steel industry in 1949. This assumption is correct, subject to the important qualification that these unemployment benefits will meet far more resistance from employers than supplementary pensions and thus will spread more slowly. But if there is a considerable spread of supplementary unemployment compensation, what will be the results to business and the economy, and who will turn out to be right—the critics or the supporters of the Ford-General Motors agreements? Before attempting to answer these questions, let us see briefly what the agreements provide.

The agreements are long and detailed because they cover many technical points. In essence, however, both Ford and General Motors have agreed to contribute five cents for each hour worked by hourly rated employees to a trust fund from which supplementary unemployment compensation shall be paid. No matter how small the amount in the trust funds, the obligation of the companies to make contributions shall not exceed five cents an hour. Furthermore, when the funds exceed a certain size in relation to the number of employees, the contributions of the employer are to cease.

The payments will not begin until June 1, 1956. After that date employees with at least one year's senority who are laid off will be paid supplementary benefits sufficient, when added to state unemployment compensation, to give them 65 per cent of their weekly aftertax straight-time wage for the first four weeks of unemployment, usually after a one-week waiting period, and 60 per cent for the next twenty-two weeks, but in no event more than $25 a week. After twenty-six weeks the employees shall cease to draw supplementary unemployment benefits. Since the average benefits under state unemployment compensation schemes have been only about 35 per cent of average straight-time earnings after taxes, the Ford and General Motors schemes nearly double the unemployment compensation received by the employees of those companies.

II

Are the Ford and General Motors agreements a radical innovation in industrial relations embodying an important new principle: namely, that employers have an obligation for the welfare of workmen whom they lay off? I think not. The very fact that the Ford and General Motors agreements provide only for *supplementary* unemployment benefits shows that they were not setting up a new principle. The new principle that employers have the duty to provide income for laid-off employees was established first by the state of Wisconsin in 1932 when it set up a state scheme of employer-financed unemployment compensation, and later by the federal government in 1935 when Congress, through a special payroll tax, virtually forced the states to set up unemployment-compensation schemes. The Ford and General Motors agreements simply attempt to make up for the inadequacy of benefits under the state laws—an inadequacy that was pointed out by President Eisenhower in his economic reports for 1953 and 1954.

Will the spread of agreements of the Ford and General Motors type squeeze the small and less successful employers out of business? No criticism of the Ford and General Motors agreements has been made more frequently than this one. The charge naively assumes that large concerns are better able to keep down layoffs than small concerns. The spread of the Ford–General Motors type of agreement would obviously help those companies which are best at keeping the number of layoffs low in relation to the number of workers on the payroll. This means that the Ford–General Motors type of agreement, if widely adopted, would confer advantages (1) on those companies which are growing rapidly, and (2) on those which are good at limiting the seasonal and cyclical fluctuations in their output. The agreements would add to the difficulties of the enterprises which for any reason are not able to keep layoffs low—firms in declining industries or high-cost and inefficient companies.

In short, the spread of unemployment-compensation agreements would help the most efficient companies (large or small) and all enterprises in expanding industries, and would hurt the less efficient concerns and all firms in contracting industries. In some industries success in keeping down layoffs may be associated with largeness, in other industries with smallness, and in still other industries it may be quite independent of size. Hence, it is wrong to suggest as a broad generalization that the widespread adoption of unemployment pay will tend to squeeze out the "little fellow."

The extent to which the spread of supplementary unemployment compensation tends to concentrate production and employment in the hands of those firms (large or small) that are best at keeping down layoffs will depend upon the bargaining policy of unions. Unions must decide whether to insist on different rates of contribution to the trust funds by different employers in order to make possible the same scale and duration of supplementary benefits regardless of the employer's layoff rate, or whether to accept differences in the scale and duration of unemployment pay in order to keep uniform the contribution rates of different employers.

Long experience has taught unions that they get into trouble both with employers and with their own members if they go very far in imposing more onerous terms on some concerns among a group of competitors than on other enterprises in the group. Hence, one is reasonably safe in predicting that unions will not vary the rate of contributions made by various competing employers. It follows that the spread of the Ford–General Motors type of agreement would have only a moderate tendency to concentrate production in the hands of firms that are best at keeping down layoffs. Some advantage, however, would still accrue to the firms with low layoff rates because contributions are made by the employer to the trust fund only when the fund is less than a specified ratio to payrolls. The lower the layoff rate, the smaller the proportion of the time that the employer would be contributing.

The tendency for the spread of the Ford–General Motors type of agreement to concentrate production in the firms with the lowest layoff rates will be limited by the fact that unions will not be able to negotiate such agreements with the very weakest firms and in the declining industries where the shrinkage of employment has been greatest. Thus the failure of supplementary unemployment compensation to extend to some of the weakest and least efficient firms will help these firms to survive.

Will the spread of the Ford–General Motors type of agreement encourage the use of machines to run machines—so-called automation? The answer to this question is "yes." Hand methods have the advantage over machine methods, from the standpoint of employers, that they entail fewer fixed costs. When business falls off, the employer who uses hand methods can get rid of a considerable part of his payroll by dropping men, but most machine costs (interest on the investment, depreciation, obsolescence, insurance) go on whether or not the machine is running. Unemployment pay makes hand-method costs more like machine-method costs because it lessens the savings that employers achieve in slack times by making layoffs. To that extent, supplementary unemployment compensation will encourage the shift to machine methods.

But so strong are the present incentives for employers to shift to machine methods that the practical effect of the spread of supplementary unemployment compensation will be small. Cutting tools in recent years have become so efficient that slow and cumbersome hand methods of loading and unloading machines greatly limit machine capacity and keep machines idle a large part of the time. Hence, enormous gains are to be made from the development of (1) machines for loading and unloading other machines, and (2) machines that perform several operations on a part without being reloaded. Unemployment pay would add only a small amount to the gains from automation.

III

Will the spread of the Ford–General Motors type of agreement add substantially to the stability of the economy by increasing the incomes of unemployed workers during recessions? A moderate gain in stability may be expected. Obviously, the laid-off workers who receive supplementary unemployment compensation will be greatly helped in maintaining their demand for goods since, as I have pointed out, their unemployment benefits will be almost doubled. But the effect of the supplementary unemployment compensation will be limited by the fact that, even after it has spread to the fullest practicable extent, it will reach only a small fraction of all employees. It will not extend to any important degree beyond union members, of whom there are about 16 million in private industry. But many union members are in industries in which for one reason or another it is either not necessary or not feasible to negotiate supplementary unemployment benefits. Hence, unless union membership grows quite rapidly in the next few years, supplementary unemployment compensation is not likely to cover more than about 10 million workers, less than one fourth of the nonagricultural employees in American industry and only about one fourth the number covered by the various government unemployment-compensation schemes.

On the other hand, supplementary unemployment-compensation agreements are likely to be concentrated in manufacturing, mining, transportation, and construction—the industries in which the cyclical ups and downs of employment are greatest. Hence, even if supplementary unemployment compensation covers less than one fourth of the nonfarm employees, it will raise the incomes of a much higher proportion of the unemployed.

What substance is there to the charges that unemployment pay will make men unwilling to work and that it will be an important inflationary influence in the economy? Paying men unemployment benefits of 60 per cent or 65 per cent (or even 75 per cent) of their straight-time earnings after taxes is not likely to deter many men from working. In the first place, wives do not care to have idle husbands around the house when jobs are available, and the influence of the wives is not to be overlooked.

In the second place, consumption in the United States is rather competitive, and the family with only 65 per cent of its usual income after taxes cannot live in the way that it has been accustomed to live and in the way that the neighbors are living. A drop of 35 per cent in income means postponing the buying of many things that the family would like to have, cutting down on recreation and trips, and perhaps changing plans for the education of children. People who fear that American workers will be content with $50 or $60 a week unemployment benefits when jobs are to be had paying $20 or $30 a week more are not aware of the enormous unfilled wants of most families.

To the extent that unemployment pay sustains incomes in periods of recession and thus limits the drop in the demand for goods that accompanies recessions, it will be an inflationary influence. In fact, *any* arrangement that limits the severity of recessions is inflationary because such arrangements tend to prevent prices from falling sufficiently during recessions to offset the rise in prices that accompanies most booms. But supplementary unemployment compensation will not be a *major* influence determining the long-run movement of the price level in the United States.

Since various antirecession measures (of which supplementary unemployment compensation is only one) will prevent much of a drop in the price level during recessions, the long-run movement of prices will depend upon how much prices rise during booms. The principal determinants of the movement of prices during booms will be (1) the strength of trade unions, (2) the willingness and ability of employers to resist the demands of unions, and (3) the rate of technological change. These three conditions will determine the movement of labor costs to which the price level must adjust itself.

A widely expressed fear is that unemployment pay will weaken the spirit of adventure that has always characterized American industry. If adding new employees to the payroll imposes heavy obligations on the employer, will not enterprises be reluctant to expand?

This argument is without merit. Employers who have orders or who expect orders are going to hire enough employees to fill them. Failure to receive good service would cause customers to take their business elsewhere. It would take a very high rate of unemployment benefits to make employers prefer to lose customers rather than to add workers who may be needed only temporarily.

In two ways the spread of more liberal unemployment pay will encourage industry to expand. In the first place, as I have pointed out, the broad adoption of the scheme will confer advantages on the firms that through expansion and other means are able to keep down the rate of layoffs. In the second place, to the extent that supplementary unemployment benefits limit the severity of recessions they reduce the risks of expansion. On the whole, one must conclude that the widespread adoption of supplementary unemployment compensation would strengthen rather than weaken the dynamic influences in the American economy.

Up to this point the survey of the pros and cons yields a verdict in favor of agreements of the Ford–General Motors type. Such agreements, if widely adopted, would tend to concentrate production and employment a little more in the enterprises (large or small) which are most efficient, would stimulate in small measure the spread of automation (surely a desirable result), would add modestly to the resistance of the economy against recessions, and would stimulate moderately the expansion of industry. The fears that generous unemployment benefits would undermine men's willingness to work do not seem to be well founded. To a small extent supplementary unemployment compensation would be an inflationary influence, but this criticism can be made of any arrangement or policy which mitigates the severity of recessions.

But I have yet to present the most important criticism of supplementary unemployment pay. It is a criticism which, despite its importance, is rarely made either by employers or by union leaders. The criticism is that supplementary unemployment compensation, even if widely adopted, is not a satisfactory substitute for adequate normal unemployment benefits. In other words, it does not give the country what it needs—an adequate system of unemployment compensation.

I have pointed out that, at the best, supplementary unemployment-compensation agreements could be expected to reach only about one out of four of the workers now covered by government unemployment-compensation schemes. Furthermore, in the very spots where unemployment is most serious, in declining industries and among weak firms, unions will have the greatest difficulty in negotiating agreements of the Ford–General Motors type.

There is no doubt that the unemployment benefits provided by the present state unemployment-compensation laws are inadequate. President Eisenhower in his last economic report pointed out that the ratio of benefits to the average weekly wages of covered employees is only 34 per cent—in some states below 30 per cent. Back in 1938 the ratio was 43 per cent. President Eisenhower recommended that benefits be raised so that the great majority of covered workers will be eligible for payments that are at least half their regular earnings. He also recommended broadening the coverage of these laws.

President Eisenhower's recommendations received far less publicity than the Ford–General Motors agreements; yet their adoption would do far more to give the country an adequate system of unemployment compensation than can be expected from the spread of supplementary unemployment compensation. Undoubtedly, the provisions in the Ford–General Motors agreements calling for total unemployment benefits (regular and supplementary) equal to 65 per cent of wages after taxes for the first four weeks will help the state legislatures raise their conception of what are "adequate" benefits. Surely President Eisenhower's recommendation of half of "regular earnings" is too low—though not far below 60 per cent of straight-time earnings after taxes as provided in the Ford–General Motors agreements between the fifth and the twenty-sixth weeks of benefits.

An important characteristic of an adequate scheme of unemployment compensation is that it costs less than nothing—it is an asset to the community, not a burden. The test of whether any economic or political arrangement is a burden or an asset is whether it tends to add to or to subtract from production—whether it makes for a higher or a lower standard of consumption. Adequate unemployment compensation, if properly managed, does not subtract from production and consumption in times of boom, and it does help check the drop in production and employment in times of recession. Hence, over the entire business cycle it tends to increase production and consumption.

An adequate system of unemployment compensation would not only add to the security of workers—it would also add to the security of business enterprises and would enhance the value of the investment in American industry and the value of every farm. It is amazing that the businessmen and farmers have not sought to stabilize their markets by insisting that the government provide an adequate system of unemployment compensation.

20

The American System of Industrial Relations: Some Contrasts with Foreign Systems

Arbitration Today, Proceedings of the Eighth Annual Meeting, National Academy of Arbitrators, Boston, Massachusetts, January 27 and 28, 1955.

THE year 1954 saw important developments in the field of industrial jurisprudence. A New York arbitrator held that it is not permissible to fire a waiter because he is writing a book about the customers and the owner of the restaurant. The New Jersey Supreme Court held that a bartender, hit by flying beer steins, may collect workmen's compensation. An Australian tribunal held that compensation was proper in the case of a dislocated jaw suffered while yawning at work. There were also important new laws and administrative orders. Boxers appearing in professional bouts in Indiana were required to take non-Communist oaths. The town of Waterloo, Nebraska, forbade barbers to eat onions between 7 A.M. and 7 P.M.

Before an audience such as this it might seem appropriate for me to discuss these and other important recent developments in industrial jurisprudence. But your president knows that I am not competent to do this, and he wisely suggested that I refrain from talking about the kind of problems that you are so expert at handling. Something broad and general that might give you what he called "background" and that would not too painfully reveal my ignorance of arbitration was what he suggested. The broadest topic that I can think of in the labor field is comparisons between the systems of industrial relations of different countries. Consequently, I am going to discuss a few aspects of the American system of industrial relations and contrast them with corresponding parts of some foreign systems of industrial relations. But I intend to do this mainly in the words of foreign visitors to the United States, because an understanding of how our industrial relations impress foreigners is in itself worth having.

I

Perhaps it is wrong to designate as a "system" a group of arrangements that has grown up without being planned as a whole. I do not care to argue that point, which seems to me to be unimportant. Our arrangements in the field of industrial relations may be regarded as a system in the sense that each of them more or less intimately affects each of the others so that they constitute a group of arrangements for dealing with certain matters and are collectively responsible for certain results.

The American system of industrial relations, like nearly all other systems, has three principal groups of components. One group represents the arrangements provided by the government; the second group consists of arrangements coming from the trade unions and their relations with employers; the third group represents those coming from management. I do not intend to say much about differences in the role of the government in systems of industrial relations—important as these differences are. As you all know, the activities of the government in this field in the United States have increased enormously in the last twenty years. Even today, however, the role of the government in industrial relations in the United States is of less importance than the role of the government in most other countries. Certainly, the government here has less to do with the immediate setting of compensation and many conditions of employment than the governments of most other industrial countries. Perhaps it would be desirable if our government were to do considerably more than it now does in determining the incomes going to retired persons, unemployed persons, sick and disabled persons. On the other hand, when one looks at the activities of some other governments, such as those in France and Italy, one is inclined to ask whether it would not be desirable to shift some of the decisions in those countries from the government to collective bargaining.

The two most interesting aspects of the American system of industrial relations are the roles of trade unions and employers. I wish to discuss briefly some of the activities of trade unions and employers. Let me begin with the unions.

Three characteristics of American industrial relations stand out no matter what country is compared with the United States:

(1) The relatively high development of local unions including the considerable degree of local autonomy.

(2) The prevalence of local or company bargaining rather than industry-wide bargaining.

(3) The considerable degree to which the rights of workers are defined by terms of agreements between unions and employers.

These differences are particularly marked if one compares industrial relations in the United States with industrial relations in Continental countries where the development of local unions has not gone very far. These points of differences, however, also impressed union visitors from Great Britain, where unions are much more like American unions than are the unions of the Continent. A team of ten union officers was sent to the United States by the General Council of the British Trades Union Congress in 1949. Of local unions in the United States the British team said: "The essential difference between American locals and British trade union branches is the degree of autonomy exercised by the former. They often have their own officers and full-time clerical staffs, do their own administration, handle disputes and grievances insofar as they are able, and frequently conduct negotiations with 'their' companies. In many cases locals determine much of their own policy."[1]

Americans, familiar with the various ways in which national unions influence and limit the policies of local unions, would probably not describe the locals as having a considerable measure of autonomy, but everything is relative, and to British unions our locals possess a considerable degree of autonomy. Although American local unions usually act subject to a veto by the national or subject to national rules, the locals are allowed considerable initiative and are given considerable discretion. Furthermore, when one recalls the difficulties of some national unions in preventing abuses in welfare funds negotiated by their locals, one reaches the conclusion that the British were right in being impressed with the large amount of autonomy still left to local unions in this country.

The British related the autonomy of local unions in the United States to the American practice of negotiating local agreements. In the words of the British team: "Much of the autonomy exercised by Locals is directly associated with the practice of collective bargaining on a plant or company basis, as distinct from an industry-wide basis as in Britain" (p. 17).

I suspect that the British team was not aware of the extent to which the final stage of negotiations between local unions and employers is taken over by national vice-presidents and representatives or of the control which national unions from time to time impose on the terms that locals may accept. But even when the local negotiators give way to a representative sent out by the national office, a local or company agreement, affecting the local union and its employer or employers, is at stake.

[1] British Trades Union Congress, *Trade Unions and Productivity*, p. 17.

The British visitors were impressed too by the extent to which agreements negotiated by American unions contain many specific rules to protect the rights of union members. The British on the whole seem to pay somewhat less attention to these matters, though, as is well known, they have from time to time stubbornly challenged the right of the employer to dilute skilled labor. Questions which in the United States would involve interpretations of the trade agreement and which, if unsettled, would often go to an umpire are taken in Britain to joint district or joint national committees which are not bound by specific rules but which make a decision on the basis of a rule of reason.[2] The British team described American practices in the following words: "To a large extent matters dealt with by joint consultative committees in Britain are in the U. S. A. written into union-company agreements. . . . Problems on the whole can be dealt with immediately and there is no need to report to anyone outside the plant unless a problem becomes so big that the international union representative has to be called in" (p. 57).

The British trade unionists were impressed by the fact that in many American plants shop chairmen spend all or virtually all of their time looking after the interests of employees and processing their grievances. You will be surprised, I think, at the way in which the British team described the practice in some large plants of management's paying for the time of a specified number of shop chairmen. To the Britishers the employer was *hiring* the shop chairmen to look after grievances. I am sure that most managements would find this a new and surprising way of looking at the practice. Here is what the British unionists say about the matter:

> We were greatly impressed with the practice in many plants of companies engaging union officials or shop stewards on a full-time basis, looking after the affairs of the union with particular regard to day-to-day production matters inside the plant. Any suggestion that such officials in dealing with management lose the confidence of union members is cancelled out by the fact that the officials are elected annually and that their continued stewardship depends on retaining the trust and confidence of the members (p. 57).

[2] I called attention to the difference between British and American procedures some years ago in an article entitled "The Contents of Collective Agreements—The Wisdom of Hindsight," *Journal of the Society for the Advancement of Management*, vol. III, no. 1 (1938), 16. In this article I pointed out some of the advantages of the British procedures. It seems clear, however, that they require some kind of a national agreement, at least one relating to the processing of cases. The British procedures could not now be introduced without undermining the important seniority rights which have been built up in American plants. But ways are needed to introduce some flexibility into these rights and to prevent their creating a sort of industrial serfdom.

At another point in its report the British team added the following comment on the same matter: "Companies obviously find it worth while to employ union officials in this manner" (p. 11).

The fact that the British team was a bit confused as to the relationship between shop chairmen and employers should not obscure the important point that the British unionists were struck by the vigilance and initiative with which unions in the United States look after the day-to-day interests of the individual worker.

II

Let us now look briefly at some of the distinctive characteristics of American management that have great significance for industrial relations. Again it is useful to look at American practices through foreign eyes. Of particular usefulness is the productivity report of the British team of industrial engineers which visited the United States in 1953 under the auspices of the Anglo-American Council on Productivity.[3] The members of the British team saw many features of American management which they considered more or less unique. It is true that most of the differences between American and European managements are differences in degree rather than differences in kind, but the differences in degree are so great as to amount to differences in kind.

The British specialist team on industrial engineering was particularly impressed by the interest of American managements in expansion. The team stressed the fact that American enterprises do not merely attempt "to fill a market" but that they were engaged in "finding and in fact creating a market" for manufactures (p. 2).

Other features of American management which impressed the British team were the relatively high development here of preparatory planning, "the aggressive cost consciousness" of American managements "at all levels" which the British team described as "much more" than in the United Kingdom, and "emphasis of costing as a tool of management" and the use of cost analyses in advance planning to estimate risks (pp. 17, 19, 20, 22). In the words of the British team, "the risks American business men are willing to take are calculated and based on complete cost information, which is

[3] The title of the report of the team is *Productivity Report on Industrial Engineering* and copies may be obtained through the Office of Technical Services, Department of Commerce, Washington. For a good description of European managements as seen by American observers see the article by F. H. Harbison and E. W. Burgess, "Modern Management in Western Europe" in the *American Journal of Sociology* (July 1954), pp. 15–23.

analyzed before any project is started. Whereas in the United Kingdom the cost accountant very often is brought into a project only after it has begun, in the U. S. he is almost invariably brought in at the time of the first discussions, and when plans are settled, checks that the expenditure does not exceed the limits set" (p. 22). The British team was of the opinion that the development of the planning of new projects in the United States substantially affected the willingness of American enterprises to take the risks of starting new projects.

The most outstanding thing about American management, particularly the management of large concerns, is the success of top managers in avoiding becoming overwhelmed by routine and detail, and their success in reserving a considerable part of their time for planning innovations and expansion. I suspect that fundamentally the scale and structure of management is an effect of the interest of managers in expansion that grew up in the early days of the country. But there is an interaction between cause and effect. Today the fact that managers have provided themselves with an abundance of personnel and have kept themselves free to think and to engage in long-range planning undoubtedly helps to sustain and increase their interest in expansion.

In Europe the situation seems to be quite different. American observers are impressed with the small number of managerial positions in most European firms, the limited delegation of authority, the absence of staff, the absorption of top managers in routine detail, all with the result that the small and overworked top managements have little time or energy to devote to innovations and expansion. European observers in this country, on the other hand, are impressed with the lavish use of staff to help line management, and the considerable amount of time and effort devoted to planning change and development. It is of interest, however, to note that the great use of staff to assist line management in the United States has been a development of the last fifty years. There were almost no staff positions in American industry before 1900. Even large banks did not have credit departments fifty years ago.

Although top American managements as a group have realized far better than administrators, public or private, in any other part of the world the importance of having time to think and to make long-range plans, American managers as a class have not succeeded in protecting themselves against overwork and excessive worry. The incidence of ulcers and other symptoms of overwork and worry is high. But the American managers have succeeded on the whole in not becoming submerged by routine. If managers quite frequently suffer from ulcers, at least these ulcers have been largely acquired as the result of efforts to make innovations and to plan expansion.

III

What are the consequences of the characteristics of the American system of industrial relations which I have selected for discussion? It would be tempting to attempt to explain differences in the movements of productivity and real wages between the United States and Great Britain or between the United States and other countries in terms of differences in the system of industrial relations. Between 1900 and 1950, for example, output per capita in the United States rose about three times as rapidly as in Great Britain—though from 1948 to 1954 the increase in output per capita in Great Britain has been slightly greater than in the United States. Real hourly earnings in the United States have been rising faster in the United States than in Britain. They increased about 18.5 per cent here between 1947 and April 1954, or almost twice as rapidly as in Great Britain where the rise between April 1947 and April 1954 was 9.8 per cent.[4] Comparisons of this sort, however, would be meaningless and, indeed, misleading. Changes in productivity and wages are the result of a multitude of influences of which the system of industrial relations is only one. Furthermore, one of the activities of the British system of industrial relations of the postwar period was to impose on the country a conscious policy of wage restraint, a policy not found in the United States, except briefly during the Korean War.

But although one cannot isolate and measure the effects of the systems of industrial relations, one's common sense tells one that there must be effects. Hence, one is justified in asking what consequences one might reasonably expect to follow from the systems of industrial relations. It is particularly illuminating to note what results foreign observers attribute to conditions here which they pick out as being quite different from conditions in their own countries.

Two important effects are ascribed by foreign observers to the distinctive characteristics of American industrial relations—greater pressure on management to increase the productivity of labor and greater interest by the employees of each enterprise in the prosperity of the concern.

[4] The rise in hourly earnings in the United States is based upon the weighted average of hourly earnings in manufacturing, bituminous coal mining, building construction, class I railroads, the telephone industry, wholesale trade, retail trade, laundries, and agriculture, weighted by employment in April 1954. The average hourly earnings in Great Britain are derived from the *Ministry of Labor Gazette* (September 1954), p. 301.

The analysis by the British trade unionists of the impact of American industrial relations upon productivity is particularly interesting. The British unionists reached the paradoxical conclusions (1) that the interest of American unions in production is weak, but (2) that their influence upon the increase in productivity is considerable. "We found," said the British union team, "most American union officials and members, in spite of their engineering departments and activities, less concerned about the need to increase productivity than trade unionists in Britain because in the main they can rely on management to be sufficiently progressive."[5]

The practice of bargaining company by company, in the view of the British unionists, explains the strong influence of American unions on productivity. The British unionists state the case thus:

> Unions recognize that some companies will always be ahead of others and will continually improve their efficiency to increase profits. They [the unions] contend that if they bargained on an industry-wide basis, they would have to accept the wage rates and working conditions obtainable in the worst, or at most, average companies. This would enable efficient companies to make unreasonably high profits, remove part of the pressure on them to continue to improve their efficiency. . . .
>
> Under union-company bargaining wage rates and piece rates vary between companies in similar industries. Theoretically, a union is always striving toward similar rates throughout its industry in that having secured good rates with the most profitable company it tries to lift wage rates in others to that level. Meanwhile, the efficient companies have again increased their output per manhour and profitability, and the unions then start the rounds again (p. 53).

The British exaggerate the willingness of American unions to make different settlements with similarly situated employers, but they are correct that unions begin negotiations with the company that is most likely to yield and that this practice raises the pressure on managements to improve technology. Experience under industry-wide bargaining in the bituminous coal industry seems to be an exception to the above generalization. As a matter of fact, however, the special position of the captive mines has enabled the union to whipsaw the employers, and the ambitions of Mr. Lewis have limited the effect of economic considerations upon union wage policies.

A second consequence of American collective-bargaining practices, particularly company-union agreements, is to stimulate the interest of employees in the prosperity of the company. On this point the British industrial engineering team said: "Local negotiation of wages and conditions adds to

[5] British Trades Union Congress, *Trade Unions and Productivity*, pp. 10–11.

the interest taken by employees in the activities of their own company, since their trade union's success in wage negotiation is closely related to the success of the company."[6]

The British industrial engineers also added the belief that American unions accept the view "that higher benefits for their members can only be obtained if they support management in measures which will increase the efficiency of production and strengthen the position of the company" (p. 47).

The British industrial engineers noted, however, the absence in the United States of formal arrangements for participation by unions in promoting efficiency: "We found that joint production committees as understood in Britain are not popular. The attitude of unions is that managerial problems should be settled by management alone and that the unions' function is to investigate their [the managements'] plans only where they affect workers' interests" (p. 45).

To the British trade unionists the lack of formal arrangements for promoting efficiency was a matter of surprise. The British unionists said:

> A fact we found surprising therefore was the unions' lack of interest in formal joint consultative machinery, especially as many of them seem well qualified to make a contribution to plant efficiency through such machinery. The truth is that most unions do not expect or, we suspect, want to be consulted about the running of the plant. . . . There is nothing restrictive in this attitude, even if it is not cooperative. The job of managing is left to management (p. 57).

The British trade unionists added the following interesting comment: "The absence of joint consultative machinery does not mean that union-management relations are necessarily 'distant.' In fact, we got the impression that relations generally are better than in many British factories" (p. 57).

Interest of workers in the success of the company is, of course, stimulated by the practice of promoting from the ranks. The industrial engineering team mentioned "the undoubted greater opportunities compared with Britain to rise from the shop floor to senior managerial positions" (p. 6). The team was also impressed by the fact that managements "recognize and encourage an ambitious attitude on the part of the worker" (p. 46). This team thought that the general relationship of workers to management in United States industries is "often significantly different from that found in factories in Britain." The team attributed the difference in part to "the lack of class barriers in American industrial life" (p. 46).

If unions count on gaining benefits for their members from the success

[6] *Productivity Report on Industrial Engineering*, p. 73.

of the company, one would expect them to be aggressive in their demands. The British industrial engineering team was of the opinion that American unions are more aggressive than British unions in pushing demands. The British team stated that British managers working in the United States "argued that the main difference between British and American unions is the aggressive American attitude" (p. 72).

Foreign observers have not commented on how industrial relations have been affected by the large amount of attention given by top managements in the United States to plans for innovation and expansion. Sometimes innovations have created conflict between groups of workers and managements. These conflicts, however, have on the whole been of superficial importance. The fundamental effects of innovation and expansion have been better industrial relations. Many opportunities have been created for men to move into better jobs. The growth of opportunity is reflected in the fact that skilled and professional workers have been becoming a larger proportion of the labor force. The attention of managements to innovation has been fundamentally responsible for the rapid growth in output per manhour. The increase in output per manhour has meant (1) there has been quite a bit to bargain over and (2) that managements have not been disposed to resist too strongly even stiff demands from trade unions. Hence, the attention of managements to innovations has increased the importance of collective bargaining and has tended to make collective bargaining work more or less satisfactorily to both sides, but particularly to the employees.

IV

Does the American system of industrial relations lead to more or less interruption in production than systems where bargaining is usually on an industry-wide basis rather than on a local or company basis? A truly scientific answer to the question cannot be given because the scale of interruptions in production is affected by many conditions other than the methods of bargaining. Our figures on strikes and lockouts are shockingly poor and admit of little classification. Until Congress provides funds for much more elaborate figures than are now compiled, one cannot get very far in isolating the effect of various conditions in producing strikes and lockouts.

One would expect the kind of bargaining that one finds in the United States to produce a higher rate of stoppages than would be produced by the industry-wide bargaining of Britain or Sweden. I grant that under industry-wide bargaining employers will usually be more inclined to resist union demands than when bargaining is by companies or even by localities. Although industry-wide bargaining reduces the cost of concessions by employers, it greatly reduces the cost of resistance because it prevents one competitor from taking away the customers of other firms. On the other hand, unions under company bargaining and to a less extent under locality bargaining are likely to make stiff demands because they will not be held back by those of their members who work for high-cost employers. The stiff demands increase the likelihood of conflict. When is the risk of conflict greatest—when the pattern of settlement is being negotiated or when the union is attempting to spread it to high-cost plants which cannot afford to pay it? I think that the recent history of strikes in the steel and automobile industries shows that stoppages are most likely to arise over the terms of the pattern settlement, but I would like to see a statistical study of this point.

But the principal reason why one would expect a higher stoppage rate under the American system of bargaining than under the British or Swedish is that shutting down a company or the companies in a locality is not particularly serious to the economy as a whole, whereas shutting down an industry or a group of industries may be too serious to be tolerated. Deadlocks frequently occur in industry-wide bargaining in Britain, but, if the industry is an important one, the result is not usually a stoppage but government intervention, a court of inquiry, further bargaining on the basis of the court's recommendations, and usually further concessions. In spite of the prevalence of industry-wide bargaining in Britain and Sweden, the average number of workers per strike or lockout in those countries is usually less than in the United States—for the period 1927 to 1953 inclusive it was 239 in Sweden, 448 in Britain, and 507 in the United States. Of course, these figures simply reflect the fact that industry-wide strikes rarely occur in Britain or Sweden.

The record of the last year in Britain is illuminating on this point, particularly the experience in the engineering industry and the railroad industry. Incidentally, an important change seems to be occurring in the operation of the British arrangements for handling major disputes and the British are confronted with the question of how seriously the operation of boards of inquiry will be undermined by the growing disposition of the unions to reject the awards of the boards. One is reminded of the change that occurred in the operation of the railway labor act in this country before and after about 1941.

Whatever may be the reasons, the result is what one would expect—the rate of industrial conflict in the United States is considerably greater than in

Britain or Sweden. Of the various available measures of the rate of industrial conflict, I think that by far the most meaningful is working days lost as a multiple of union membership. This measure allows for the fact that strikes among unorganized workers are few and short. Hence, the measure is a fairly satisfactory indication of the propensity of union members to strike and of the success of collective bargaining in producing agreements. (It would be desirable to use only the working days lost among union members in stoppages called by unions.) Ross and Irwin's interesting comparison of strike experience in five countries found that the time lost per union member during the period 1927–1947 was far greater in the United States than in either Britain or Sweden—3.2 working days per member per year in the United States, 2.2 days in Sweden and 0.5 days in Britain.[7] I have had the Ross-Irwin table extended through 1952. For the entire period 1927 to 1952 inclusive the working days lost as a multiple of union membership were 3.1 in the United States, 1.8 in Sweden, and 0.4 in Britain.

I do not suggest that the prevalence of local or single-firm bargaining here in contrast with industry-wide bargaining in Britain or Sweden solely explains the difference in time lost per union member from stoppages. Other important differences, such as the strong rivalry between unions in the United States, the vigorous efforts of American unions to extend their membership in contrast with the more passive policies of British and Swedish unions, the absence here of legal restraints on strikes (such as existed in Britain from 1940 to 1952), the longer use of an official policy of wage restraint in Sweden and Britain, all help to account for the differences in the time-lost rates between the United States, Sweden, and Britain.[8]

The case of Canada deserves brief comment. Although the system of bargaining in Canada is virtually the same as in the United States and although the Canadian system of industrial relations in most respects is quite similar to that of the United States, working days lost from stoppages per union

[7] A. M. Ross and Donald Irwin, "Strike Experience in Five Countries, 1927–1947—An Interpretation," *Industrial and Labor Relations Review* (April 1951) p. 332. The figure Ross and Irwin give for the United States is 3.0 days per member per year, but they use unsatisfactory figures for membership. They accept the estimates of the Bureau of Labor Statistics for 1945, 1946, and 1947 which are based on badly inflated estimates of the CIO membership and they fail to subtract the Canadian membership of unions with headquarters in the United States. When corrections are made for these errors, the figure comes out 3.2 instead of 3.0.

The Ross-Irwin article also contains an error in the Swedish figures which seems to be due to a misprint. The figure for the year 1928 should be 10.3, not 0.3. This error seems to have affected the computations. Ross and Irwin get 1.7 working days lost per union member for the period 1927–1947. The figure should be 2.2.

[8] Ross and Irwin, p. 338. Incidentally, Ross and Irwin express the belief that "unions are less aggressive where bargaining on a multi-employer basis," thus agreeing with the British industrial engineering team that American unions are more aggressive than British ones.

member in Canada for the period 1927 to 1952 was only about one third that of the United States and considerably below that of Sweden. It was slightly more than three times as high as the extraordinarily low British rate. For the period 1927 to 1952 working days lost in stoppages per union member in Canada were 1.3. How is the very low Canadian rate to be explained? Does it not cast serious doubt on the view that the low rates in Britain and Sweden are the result of the prevalence of industry-wide bargaining?

My belief is that the principal explanation of the low Canadian strike rate is that most Canadian unions and employers are content to follow employers in the United States in making wage changes. In other words, the low strike rate in Canada reflects the fact that Canada is a pattern follower rather than a pattern maker, and it brings out one of the advantages of being a pattern follower. If one measures the propensity to strike by the workers involved in strikes as a percentage of union membership (rather than by days lost per union member), Canada is only second to the United States—well above Britain and Sweden. For the period 1927–1952 workers involved in strikes as a percentage of union membership were 18.3 in the United States, 11.7 in Canada, 5.9 in Britain, and 2.9 in Sweden.[9] All of this means that, though strikes in Canada are quite frequent, they are also quite short—as one would expect in a pattern-following country. They average only slightly half as long as in the United States, only little more than one fourth as long as in Sweden, but they are longer on the average than the extremely short strikes in Britain.

Working days lost as a multiple of workers involved in strikes in the period 1927 to 1952 inclusive were 18.4 in the United States, 11.9 in Canada, 46.7 in Sweden, and 6.9 in Britain. In recent years virtually all strikes in Britain have been so-called "unofficial" strikes—not sanctioned by a union.

The fifth country included by Ross and Irwin in their article was Australia. Lack of time prevents my discussing the difference between Australia and the United States. Working days lost per union member in Australia has been low—from 1927 to 1947, slightly less than in Canada but considerably less than in Sweden. The figure has changed little and since 1948 has been well below Canada (0.9 per year in Australia) but, of course, far above the very low postwar rates of Sweden. On the whole, the arbitration machinery of Australia seems to do a pretty good job of producing a low time-lost rate. But workers involved in strikes as percentage of union membership in Australia are high—almost as high as in the United States and well above Can-

[9] For the period 1927–1947 I have used the figures in Ross and Irwin's excellent article, making appropriate corrections in their figures on trade-union membership in the United States.

ada, and, of course, far above Sweden or Britain. For the entire period 1927 to 1952, the percentage was 16.7; for the period 1927 to 1947, 15.0; and for the period 1948–1952, 24.2. But the high propensity to strike in Australia is coupled with very short strikes. Australian strikes are about as short as the British and seem to be getting shorter. For the period 1927–1947, the average Australian striker lost 8.8 working days; for the period 1948–1952, 3.9 days. The extremely short strikes in Australia keep down the time-lost rate in spite of the high propensity to strike.

V

Let me close these remarks with a few words of appraisal. The fact that time lost from strikes and lockouts per union member in the United States is far higher than in Sweden or Britain might be regarded as a reflection on our system of industrial relations. But systems of industrial relations should not be judged solely by their success in maintaining peace.

One must admire the success of Britain and Sweden in maintaining an exceptionally low rate of time lost from industrial disputes in recent years. The competitive positions of their economies in world markets, of course, have made the avoidance of stoppages of considerable importance. The trade unions in both Britain and Sweden have developed a willingness to accept central direction which enables them to go far in cooperating with governments to safeguard the economic interest of the entire community. Qualifying collective bargaining by considerations of national interest to the extent that the British and Swedish unions have done (and also unions in other countries, including Denmark and the Netherlands) would be out of question in the United States. The federations here lack the influence over national unions possessed by the federations in Britain and Sweden, and the national unions here usually see no particular reason for being concerned with interests of the country as a whole. All of this is a way of saying that the differences in the economic situations of the United States, Britain, and Sweden have given the unions in the several countries somewhat different objectives. The unions in the United States are much more concerned with raising wages than the unions in Britain and Sweden, and the unions here are frequently not concerned at all with either the general level of employment or the competitive position of the country.

The methods of bargaining that exist in the United States have great advantages under our conditions. No one would pretend that our methods would work elsewhere. There are great advantages in having employers under strong pressure to increase efficiency, as they are when under individual-enterprise bargaining or even local bargaining, but less so under industry-wide bargaining. (The conditions which make bituminous coal mining an exception to the above generalization should be kept in mind.) There are great advantages also in having the bargaining unit small enough so that the bargainers can give proper attention to the many issues and conditions that ought to be considered. When a bargain applies to a whole industry comprising many plants, the bargainers can discuss only a small proportion of the many matters that ought to be considered. The British have attempted to deal with this problem, as I have previously indicated, by joint district or national boards which have broad authority to decide cases by rule of reason. There is much to be said for this method of protecting the interests of individual workers under industry-wide agreements, but it does not seem to be as effective as the kind of agreements which can be negotiated under single-enterprise or local bargaining. Even in single-enterprise bargaining the bargaining unit may be so large that the negotiators cannot easily deal with all matters that should perhaps receive consideration. Some single-enterprise bargains in the United States (those of General Motors or United States Steel) cover more workers or plants than are found in any industry in Sweden.

Just as industry-wide bargaining carries with it certain problems, so also does the industrial-relations system of the United States. The considerable degree of autonomy permitted local unions sometimes becomes a source of abuse and opens the opportunity for the invasion of the labor movement by racketeers. This problem is serious in several cities at the present time. Furthermore, conditions are so favorable for collective bargaining in the United States that this instrument is used for dealing with matters which, in my judgment at least, might be more appropriately handled by legislation. For example, the great development of supplementary pension plans in recent years seems to me to have been badly overdone and is probably impeding much-needed improvements in the national pension plan.

By and large, however, I think that the United States should consider itself lucky. It possesses a system of industrial relations that, in its basic characteristics, fits conditions here reasonably well. The system has been developed without being planned. Perhaps that is why it represents a pretty good adaptation to conditions—it is simply the sum total of various efforts to solve problems rather than the expression of a plan which might faithfully reflect certain principles but which, because of that very fact, might not very well fit conditions. Our system of industrial relations would probably not work anywhere else, but it gives the American worker better protection of his day-to-day interests than is received by workers anywhere else; it puts American employers under greater pressure than the employers of any other country to raise productivity; and, though it gives unions a wonderful opportunity to whipsaw employers, it gives employers a freedom to bargain which they like and for which they seem willing to pay a big price. Hence, we seem justified in being grateful that we have been favored by fortune and perhaps also in taking modest pride that we have pursued opportunist policies with considerable flexibility and good sense.

21

New Goals for the Unions

The Atlantic Monthly, December 1958.

I

Trade unions have been one of the great instruments of progress and reform in American society. They have introduced the equivalent of civil rights into a large part of industry, replacing personal management with management based upon agreed rules and procedures, and they have established in much of industry the practice of determining wages by negotiation instead of by the employer's unilateral appraisal of the market, thereby giving employees a chance to bargain over the gains of technological progress. Most important of all, trade unions have broadened the decision-making processes in the American economy by adding a third power center to the two previously existing centers, business and government. This three-way division of power and influence gives the American economy an admirable diversity of viewpoint and promotes moderation and stability in economic policies by compelling important decisions to be reached by compromise and agreement.

Helped by government policies designed to encourage collective bargaining and by the war, trade-union membership has increased more than sixfold in the last twenty-five years. Trade unions have nearly eighteen million members, or about 34 per cent of the nonprofessional and nonsupervisory employees of American industry. Unions have been particularly successful in organizing the production workers in large plants. The largest groups of nonunion workers are the employees in small plants, the white-collar workers, and government employees. Almost half of the twenty-one million "blue-collar" workers (craftsmen, operatives, repairmen, and laborers) are union members.

But today, in spite of their brilliant success (indeed, in large measure *because* of it), trade unions are suffering a great loss of prestige and moral influence. This loss of standing is manifested in various ways: by the mounting volume of critical editorial comment on unions; by the considerable number of states that have passed "right to work" laws, which are a sort of symbol of community hostility to unions; and, most of all, by the reluctance of workers to join unions and by the virtual cessation of the growth of union membership.

The conspicuous economic success of unions has not led workers to organize unions on their own initiative, as they did on a large scale in the thirties. Members must be gained in large measure through high-pressure organizing campaigns in which organizational picketing and other forms of economic pressure are often used to force men to join. Unions still win a comfortable majority of the elections conducted by the National Labor Relations Board, but the proportion of elections lost by unions has risen from 25.5 per cent in 1949–1950 to 39.2 per cent in 1957–1958, and the proportion of nonunion votes cast in all elections has more than doubled since 1950 to an all-time high of 39.2 per cent in the fiscal year which ended June 30, 1958.

Unfair labor practice charges brought by individuals against unions have been skyrocketing. They more than doubled to 2,000 in the last fiscal year. In the four years ending June 30, 1953, they averaged only 584 a year. There is no record of the proportion of cases in which the complainant won his point, but the back-pay awards against unions in unfair labor practice cases increased from $128,950 in the four years ending June 30, 1953, to $283,959 in the four years ending June 30, 1957. These figures are not large relative to the nearly eighteen million union members, but the trend is significant.

The loss of prestige and moral influence by the trade unions is only partly explained by the exposure of corruption and racketeering in the labor movement—though the corruption has been far more widespread than anyone had suspected. No less than ten international unions have been shown to have been headed by corrupt officials at some time during the last twenty-five years, and there has been considerable corruption at the local level. The disillusionment of the public with trade unions springs mainly from two causes: first, unions have turned out to be much stronger than the public expected them to be and, second, they have turned out to be much less democratic than they were represented as being.

The policy of encouraging union membership was urged on the community on the ground that unions were needed to balance the economic power of big business. Unions have done much more than equalize the power of business and labor. When eighteen million workers are organized, a union of a given size becomes considerably more powerful than when only three million or four million men are organized. The union's capacity to influence the wages paid by nonunion firms is greater, and this means that its capacity to get concessions from union employers is greater. As a result in large measure of the great power of trade unions, the hourly compensation of nonagricultural workers in the last ten years has risen more than twice as fast as the increase in output per manhour.

The influence of unions has been particularly apparent during the period of credit restraint in 1956 and 1957 and during the recession, when the demand for labor was shrinking. Twenty years ago, unions were champions of the underdogs and were fighting for very elementary rights, such as recognition, a contract, machinery for handling grievances, and the like. Today, unions are fighting to get more pay for the very workers who already enjoy the best wages and conditions in industry. Twenty years ago the public wondered whether unions could hold their own against powerful employers; today the public wonders whether unions can be prevented from forcing creeping inflation on the community.

Strangely enough, the conspicuous success of unions is now hindering their growth. Many workers, especially those in prosperous companies, are not interested in joining because their employers, out of fear of unions, give union rates of pay and other union conditions. Still other workers, especially those in small and weak concerns, do not wish to be organized because they are afraid that a union would put their employers out of business.

The public has also become disillusioned with unions because unions have not turned out to be the instruments of industrial democracy that their early leaders, friends, and well-wishers said they would be. The more or less standard description of a union was that it was an organization through which the individual employees participated in determining the conditions under which they work. But the average worker has a very limited desire to participate in determining the conditions under which he works. He wishes a union to bargain for him, but he demonstrates his unwillingness to participate in determining his conditions of work by his refusal to attend union meetings, in spite of the efforts of officers to encourage attendance. He assumes that the union officers know roughly what he wants, and he is content to let them handle dealings with the employer.

The officers of unions know in a general way the wishes of the rank and file and try to gratify these wishes. But the officers have a better idea than most members concerning what is possible and practicable. Hence, the officers may discourage certain types of demands, such as proposals to fight technological change. As a rule, the officers are more conservative than the small part of the rank and file that takes an active interest in the union. Subject to this qualification, the officers usually do a pretty good job of representing the rank and file. Only in this limited and indirect fashion do workers "participate" in determining the conditions under which they work.

Although union officers, on the whole, do a good job of representing the members, they do not take kindly to criticism of their policies from the members—particularly from members who are suspected of aspiring for office in the union—and, especially at the national level, union officers are exceedingly hostile toward efforts to displace them. The result is that, while there is a fair amount of competition for local union offices, competition at the national level is unusual. Professor Philip Taft found that among seven national unions which held 764 elections for national office in the thirty-one-year period of 1910 to 1941, there were contests in only 130 cases. In three unions (the teamsters, the bricklayers, and the street railway workers) there were no contests for national office in the thirty-one years.

In a few unions control of districts or locals by national officers has been greatly overdone, usually as the result of internal political differences. Parts of the pressmen's union, of the operating engineers' union, and of the musicians' union that challenged national officers were deprived of self-government and kept under appointed officers for years. In the United Mine Workers, the officers of most of the districts are "provisional" officers who for many years have been appointed by John L. Lewis. Every convention of the union sees many resolutions from the districts asking that they be allowed to elect their own officers. At the 1952 convention a delegate said: "Give us opportunity; give the young men opportunity to aspire to something in the organization. Give them something to plan for and look forward to, to study the movement and know something about it. This way we don't have any initiative. You don't allow us that right—the members have become apathetic, for somebody higher up is going to do everything for us . . . they don't bother to attend meetings." But Mr. Lewis still appoints the officers of most of the districts.

The upshot of all of this is that, though unions are democratic in the sense that they strive for what the members want, they do not fulfill the ideal of giving workers a chance to participate in determining working conditions or even to run the unions, especially beyond the local level. The indifference of most members toward union affairs and the hostility of officers toward competition for their jobs mean that unions are run by the officers, not the members. Particularly at the national level most unions are oligarchies, not democracies.

The great power and influence of the officers in unions create important problems and dangers. Certainly they increase the difficulty of keeping out corruption, since freedom from corruption must depend upon high personal standards among officers rather than checks from the rank and file. Furthermore, they hinder unions in gaining members, since many workers do not care to put themselves under the direction of men about whose judgment and purposes they know little. Finally, they produce disillusionment and lack of sympathy for unions on the part of the public, since unions fall far short of meeting the democratic ideals that the public has been taught to look for in them. But in spite of these disadvantages, trade unions are bound to remain oligarchies. This is what a majority of the members desire, and they are not likely to change their minds.

In regard to the excessive economic power of trade unions and their tendency to raise money wages far faster than is justified by the growth of output per manhour, public policy can do little, though employers and public opinion could do much. Amending the Taft-Hartley Act to limit the right of unions to conscript neutrals in industrial disputes through secondary boycotts would end injustices but would have little effect on the economic power of most unions. Attempts to equalize the bargaining power of unions and employers by using monetary policy to create unemployment would inflict as much injustice as they would prevent and would obviously be wasteful. Recent experience indicates that a fairly high rate of unemployment would be needed. In the recent recession, with unemployment running from 5 per cent to 7 per cent, hourly earnings in manufacturing rose by about 2.9 per cent in the twelve months from September 1957 to September 1958.

Equally impracticable is the proposal that national unions be broken up so that they would be unable to shut down whole industries or to whipsaw employers by selecting one competitor to shut down while rivals take away his customers. Breaking up unions would not necessarily prevent concerted action among the parts. Furthermore, this remedy is too drastic to command popular support, and it is a remedy that is worse than the disease. Hence, the tendency of wages to outrun productivity must be dealt with by other methods.

Employers can do much to limit the tendency of hourly earnings to outrun production per manhour. The great need is to raise output by methods which do not at the same time tend to raise wages by increasing the demand for labor. Perhaps the most commonly thought-of way of raising productivity is through the use of labor-saving equipment. But labor-saving equipment must be made by labor. Hence this method of increasing productivity has the immediate effect of increasing the demand for labor, and thus it tends to raise wages as much as it raises productivity. But there are other methods of increasing productivity which economize equipment and which, therefore, do not increase the demand for labor. Examples of these equipment-economizing methods are better selection and training of workers, better scheduling of production, better maintenance of equipment, better control of raw materials, redesign of products to simplify their fabrication and assembly, better setting of production standards, and better supervision in general. All of these output-increasing methods are used in industry today, but industry in general needs to improve greatly its capacity to economize in the use of equipment.

Can public opinion, over the course of time, affect the outcome of bargaining between unions and employers? Union members naturally expect their leaders to get the best terms that can be obtained without precipitating a strike or lockout, and most members do not particularly care whether or not the public likes the bargains that their organizations drive. But, except for a few very strong unions, the members do not like to incur strong public indignation. Hence, if the public shows that it is outraged by wage settlements that exceed the average rise in output per manhour, union leaders will become less insistent upon inflationary wage increases. But until the public shows strong and definite hostility toward inflationary wage settlements, we must expect rising labor costs to push the price level slowly upward. Public apathy is the ally of inflation.

II

What can be done about the internal government of trade unions, and who can do it and how? It is important to remember that there is no broad demand from trade-union members for democracy in unions. Since union members are quite commonly not sufficiently interested in the affairs of their unions even to attend meetings, it is unrealistic to attempt to force democracy on them. The objective should be a modest one: to protect the members from the abuses of oligarchy rather than to convert unions into democracies.

In the main, the problems must be solved by government action, in spite of the fact that a large majority of union leaders are sincerely interested in fair and honest union government. In fact, standards of honesty are higher in most trade unions than in many city and state governments, where the politicians have discovered many legal but dishonest ways of plundering the taxpayers. But trade-union leaders with high standards of honesty can do little outside their own unions. They are fatally handicapped in dealing with problems of union government by their lack of authority to interfere in the affairs of other unions. Thus, the AFL-CIO has no authority to compel testimony or reports or to prevent the destruction of records, and it has no effective sanctions to enforce any recommendations or orders which it may attempt to apply to constituent unions.

Five principal steps by the government are needed:

1. Prohibit the holding of union office by persons convicted of felony. Since union members are often perfectly willing to keep crooks in office, this prohibition is needed to protect employers and to discourage the invasion of the trade-union movement by professional criminals.

2. Require honest and reasonably frequent union elections. If this requirement is to mean anything, simple means must be provided for union members to challenge elections and to get new elections under government auspices in cases where investigation reveals fraud.

3. Require unions and union officers to file certain financial reports, with penalties for omissions and misrepresentation. Most unions now make fairly elaborate financial reports to their members, but so long as the officers can determine the classification of expenditures, these reports may be meaningless. And officers do not disclose income that they or members of their families may receive from dealing with the union or with employers whose employees are represented by the union.

4. Restrict the right of national unions to deprive local unions and districts of self-government. There are frequently good reasons for the national union to appoint "trustees" to run local unions; but the trustees should be required to report regularly, and the trusteeships should be limited to two or three years, subject to the right of the national to extend the trusteeship if special conditions warrant.

5. Provide an outside and neutral source of appeal for union members who are disciplined by the union officers. This protection is important if union members are to feel free to criticize their officers and the policies of their unions and to run for national offices against incumbents. When the national secretary of the bakery workers' union made charges of corruption against the national president, the national executive board exonerated the president and deprived the secretary of his job. Later the Ethical Practices

Committee of the AFL-CIO sustained the charges of the secretary, but it could not give him back his job.

These proposed regulations would mean considerable paper work for both unions and government, and they would have no great effect upon the operation of most unions. Nevertheless, the proposed regulations would be worthwhile. They would help keep crooks from invading the labor movement; minorities and dissenters would be given considerable protection; union members would have a better chance to change their officers if they desired, and the officers, in turn, would be made somewhat more sensitive to rank-and-file opinion, especially to opinion among radical and dissatisfied minorities. The public should realize that the proposed reforms would tend to make the trade unions more aggressive and more radical. Hence, unions would have a stronger tendency to produce creeping inflation. But a slightly faster creep to inflation would be a small price to pay for increasing the influence of the rank and file in the unions.

III

America needs a trade-union movement that is strong, that commands public confidence, and that is a source of responsible and well-informed criticism of our economic institutions. In order to gain the esteem and confidence of the community, unions will have to do much more than use their power to get more for their own members, who already have so much. They will have to embrace new and broader goals.

Fortunately for unions, they have an opportunity to adopt goals that will please their present members, attract new members, and gain for unions the strong approval of the entire community. This opportunity comes from the need to reform the present organization of production in American industry. The unions, if they desire, will be able to play a major role in raising the productivity of industry, helping both consumers and their own members.

The present organization of production in most plants will not bear rational examination. The production process is in large part a contest between management and workers over how much will be turned out—management trying to get as much as it can, the workers holding back to avoid producing any more than they regard management as entitled to receive. The wastes of this process are appalling, because the workers devote part of their skill not to improving methods but to concealing the fact that they are restricting output. And worse than the wastes are the moral effects upon the workers, who are unable to gain the satisfaction of doing their best to promote worthwhile objectives.

The next forward step in industrial relations will be to replace the present contests between management and employees with organized cooperation—a change that will be as epoch-making as the establishment of civil rights for workers in industry. But what pressures and inducements will bring about this change? The opposition is formidable from both managements and unions. Managements fear that formal cooperation would diminish the authority and prestige of supervisors and enhance the importance of the union; unions fear it would weaken the militancy of local unions and would develop strong loyalties to the company that in turn would weaken the influence of the national union with its members.

But though unions may be slow to help their members gain the chance to raise their wages by using their brains as well as their muscles, the members are bound eventually to insist upon having this opportunity. The strong need for cooperation has already led to considerable experimenting with plans for giving the employees the opportunity and the desire to participate in promoting technological progress. The best-tested and most promising plan is the well-known Scanlon Plan, under which employees earn a bonus by reducing the ratio of plant payroll to income from sales. The plan does not work automatically—it requires enthusiasm and effort—but it does give management and employees a common interest in reducing labor costs.

When rank-and-file workers become eager to raise their pay by cutting labor costs, amazing things begin to happen. The workers display a remarkable capacity to make technical suggestions pertaining to the product and to methods of operation. They improve their interest in the quality of work. Their attitude toward each other and toward management changes. The worker who was previously regarded as smart because he "got by" doing less than a fair day's work is regarded as the antisocial person that he really is. The workers become critical of shortcomings of management, such as failure to do a good job of production scheduling or of controlling quality. No longer are the easy-going supervisors the popular ones; the workers come to desire supervisors who are efficient and technically competent and who are good at keeping down the payroll-sales ratio. Some managements have difficulty in adjusting themselves to the new critical attitude of workers.

The opportunity to help transform the organization of production in American industry is precisely what unions need. It gives them a good chance to serve their members—a must for any labor organization—but it also gives them what they now lack, a goal that can command the approval of the community. No institution can prosper in the long run unless it enjoys the esteem and support of the public, and trade unions can never win the needed esteem and support merely by devoting themselves to getting more and more for the best-paid workers in industry.

Part IV

ECONOMIC ANALYSIS AND POLICY ISSUES

INTRODUCTION

THE seven papers in this part are concerned with the application of economic analysis to particular issues of public policy. This is not meant to imply that the earlier selections did not also involve these features. But the choices for Part IV involve more comprehensive and somewhat more formal economic analysis, and each selection is concerned with a fairly specific range of public-policy issues. Many of these papers are related to determination of wages and the consequences of wage fixing under collective bargaining for the community.

Sumner Slichter brings to these policy problems a resourceful and imaginative application of economic analysis. The presentation involves no elaborate formal models; the assumptions are not always made explicit, and the chains of reasoning are short. The method invites criticism, and opposite conclusions could be supported with different assumptions and more comprehensive models. But Slichter was largely uninterested in formal analysis for its own sake. He sought to illuminate issues for the policy choices of government, management, and labor. He high-lighted relationships which appeared to him to be strategic and fundamental to the problem at hand.

The first selection (Chapter 22) is concerned with technological unemployment. Although written in 1932, the paper is still fresh and stimulating. His policy suggestion today deserves serious consideration for the creation of a federal labor board composed of "six or seven industrialists and labor leaders with possibly the Secretary of Commerce and the Secretary of Labor as *ex officio* members." Slichter saw clearly the need for "an organization capable both of doing research and of creating cooperation." In the decade of the 1960s the community is likely to be confronted as never before with problems of adjustment to technological change and with pressures to increase the rate of change. This paper is to be read today with profit for both its analysis and policy suggestions.

Slichter's long interest in social security is illustrated by the analysis of the impact of this social legislation upon mobility and enterprise (Chapter 23). He was characteristically less concerned with detailed provisions of the law, although he was thoroughly familiar with the statute as a member of the Committee on Economic Security, than with the many facets of the economic consequences of the social-security program.

The third selection (Chapter 24) is Slichter's presidential address to the American Economic Association on December 29, 1941. He was concerned with the public-policy conditions for an expansion in output and employment. He rejected the view that expansion was basically inhibited by the drop in population growth or the disappearance of the geographical frontier. He characteristically laid emphasis on industrial research, which he regarded in its infancy, and saw that the unsatisfactory recovery from the Great Depression was substantially influenced by the permanent shifts in power and changes in public policy arising from the depression. "Nothing can prevent us from realizing the possibilities of modern technology except unwillingness to place a high valuation upon certain common interests—particularly our interests in enterprise, experimentation, innovation. Never have the rewards of a broad view of common interests been more attractive. Never has the folly of narrowly pressing special claims been greater. The economic future of our country and of the world depends upon the clarity with which this is seen."

The next two papers (Chapters 25 and 26) are concerned particularly with wages and the consequences for the community of wage setting under collective bargaining. The final two selections are likely to be particularly controversial and are included because they involved for Slichter a reversal of a position. He argued in 1949, in the debate over the Nathan report (Chapter 27), that higher wage rates cannot halt a contraction and raise money incomes and employment. In the 1959 paper he again considers the mechanism of the impact of wage-rate changes under collective bargaining on money incomes; he concludes that higher wage rates do not merely redistribute income but increase total income and output. The rejected purchasing-power argument reappears in new forms. Labor organizations and collective bargaining, institutions which set the price of labor, are thus affected with even greater public interest.

22

Technological Unemployment—Lines of Action, Adaptation, and Control

American Economic Review, Supplement, March 1932.

A RECENT survey by the Mellon Institute indicates that there are approximately one thousand industrial research laboratories in the United States, and that these laboratories employ over sixteen thousand scientists and possess an annual budget in excess of $100 million a year.[1] This does not include the less formal research performed by the engineering departments in thousands of enterprises. Forty years ago industrial research was almost nonexistent. During the last decade the number of laboratories increased about 60 per cent. It is safe to predict that industrial research will continue to grow by leaps and bounds because business enterprises are perpetually striving to outdo each other in achieving economies and in improving their products.

Plainly ours is a society committed to rapid industrial change—one might almost say dedicated to it. Not only is change an important method of making profits, but the government has added to its effectiveness by the patent system which gives innovators monopoly rights in their inventions. Unfortunately competition affords no method by which the benefits of innovations can be balanced against the costs, because both the benefits and the costs fall in large degree upon the community at large rather than upon those who decide whether or not changes shall be made. Whether or not change occurs at the most economical rate, rather than too fast or too slow, is sheer accident.[2] Competition may compel enterprises to rush through

[1] E. R. Weidlein, "Industrial Changes Due to Chemistry," *Annals of the American Academy of Political and Social Science* (September 1928), 32.

[2] The inability of the competitive system to effect an accurate balancing of the costs and the benefits of change is perhaps the strongest argument in favor of communism or some form of socialism.

enormously expensive changes which are of relatively little benefit to anyone because, if they do not promptly adopt the new methods, rival firms which do will capture the market. Insofar as the costs of change fall upon the community at large—upon those whose property or occupations are rendered obsolete—rather than upon those who make the innovations, change is being subsidized just as much as if Congress appropriated millions to accelerate it. This enormous subsidy, which is woven into our very institutions, is one of the outstanding economic facts of the age. It means, of course, that the cost of change tends to be excessive and that many changes occur at an uneconomically rapid rate. Inevitably the questions arise: What shall we do about the tremendously powerful dynamic forces which our institutions have released? What steps ought we to take to guide and control them? Is it wise to subsidize change on such a vast scale? How can the cost of change be kept at a minimum and the rate of change prevented from being either uneconomically slow or uneconomically rapid? In a world which is as highly dynamic as ours, can adjustments to changes be trusted to work themselves out or do they need to be guided and assisted? And if they need to be assisted, how can this be done most effectively? In short, we face the basic problem of developing economic institutions which will work reasonably well in a society which is highly dynamic and which is likely to become more so. Obviously the problem has wide ramifications, for it involves the protection of all classes in the community—landowners, owners of industrial equipment, owners of securities, and wage earners—against the consequences of too-rapid change. This paper will discuss only a small segment of this general problem: namely, the protection of wage earners against industrial change.

I

Returns of the unemployment census indicate that less than 6 per cent of the unemployed attribute their idleness to causes which fall under the general heading of "technological unemployment."[3] It would be a mistake, however, to infer that the displacement of labor is not a serious problem, because the occupational statistics for agriculture, manufacturing, mining, and transportation show plainly that changes in technique and markets have produced displacement on a large scale. The results of the unemployment census are explained partly by the fact that many changes in technique and

[3] The title used by the census to cover unemployment caused by labor-saving devices, mergers, and so on, is "industrial policy."

shifts in demand produce idleness, not by increasing the layoff rate, but by decreasing the hiring rate and partly by the fact that many dismissals, which are fundamentally due to labor-saving devices, appear to the workmen to have been produced by seasonal or cyclical causes. Labor-saving methods that are adopted during the busy season or during a business boom may produce no immediate layoffs, but, after the busy season ends or the boom subsides, the force shrinks more than it otherwise would. To the men who are laid off, their dismissal appears to have been due to seasonal or cyclical causes.

Economists have usually regarded the problem created by technological changes simply as one of helping men adjust themselves to changes in the kind and the location of jobs. This conclusion has rested upon the extraordinarily optimistic assumption that each labor-saving device, by reducing the cost of producing goods, releases exactly enough purchasing power to create a new job for every one which it destroys. This idea is sometimes expressed by saying that technological changes do not create permanent unemployment. But why should we assume that the purchasing power released by labor-saving devices creates exactly enough new jobs—no more, no less? It is elementary that each technological change creates a new situation with respect to both the supply of labor and the demand for labor. On the supply side, it may release older men from employment and on the demand side increase the need for younger men. Or perhaps it releases men who are capable of doing heavy and fatiguing work and increases the demand for women workers who have deftness and speed. In any event, the existing wage rates are rendered more or less obsolete, for the rates which formerly brought supply and demand into equilibrium no longer do so. Some rates may be too high; others, too low. More than this, however, the wage structure as a whole may be either too low or too high. As a matter of economic theory one cannot assert that it will necessarily be one or the other, but it is important for us to see why labor-saving inventions are likely to render the general level of money wages too high. Such inventions often reduce the cost, and hence the price, of capital goods. Inventions of this kind are likely to necessitate a drop in the money wages of many classes of labor. Otherwise it would pay enterprises to use such a large proportion of capital and such a small proportion of labor in production that the number of jobs would increase less rapidly than the number of job seekers. Wages, however, are a sluggish price—slow to rise and as slow to fall. When technological improvement reduces the price of capital goods, money wages are likely to remain about the same and industry's demand for men is likely to fall below the supply. In other words, in a society in which technological progress is causing prices to fall, the sluggishness of money wages may cause real wages to rise too rapidly. Temporarily, while the proportion of capital to labor is being rapidly increased, there may be substantial growth in the demand for labor because men are required to make the capital goods needed to increase the proportion of capital to labor. But the number of jobs is soon likely to become insufficient to absorb both the displaced men and the normal increase in the labor supply because it is possible to increase the proportion of capital to labor by dropping men as well as by adding capital. The decrease (or the slower increase) in the number of jobs occurs in several ways. New plants which attain low costs by using a large proportion of capital and a low proportion of labor threaten the markets of older enterprises which employ a large proportion of labor. Under the pressure of competition some of the older concerns discover many opportunities for getting rid of men. Other concerns are less successful in reducing expenses and lose much of their business to the newer, low-cost enterprises. Still other old concerns cease operation altogether.

What actually happens depends largely upon whether independent monetary conditions are causing the general price level to rise or fall. If prices are rising, the tendency for technological progress to cause real wages to advance too rapidly is counteracted by the tendency for money wages to lag behind other prices. On the other hand, when the price level is falling, the tendency for technological improvements to increase real wages too rapidly is reinforced by the tendency for wages to fall less rapidly than prices in general. Under these conditions, unemployment may be serious and chronic. In fact, displacement may become more or less cumulative because the tendency for falling prices and technological progress to leave money wages too high stimulates managers to search more vigorously than ever for ways of economizing labor. As they succeed and as competition compels them to pass on the savings in lower prices, the disparity between wages and other prices widens and the incentive to discover ways of displacing men grows still more compelling.

Something of this sort appears to have been happening in the United States between 1920 and 1929. During that period, the average price of producers' goods fell by about one third, but money wages in manufacturing, as measured by hourly earnings, slightly increased. (The Bureau of Labor Statistics dropped the classification "producers' goods" in its index of price movements in 1927. The statement that the average price of producers' goods in 1929 was about one third below 1920 is based on the assumption that there was no significant change in the average between 1927 and 1929. The fact that there was practically no change in the averages of raw materials, semimanufactured goods, or finished products between 1927 and 1929 indicates that this assumption is undoubtedly correct.) In other words, a radical change in the relationship between wages and the prices of capital goods gave employers a tremendous incentive to discover ways of economizing labor and led them to reduce the number of factory employees by 500,000. It also drove out of business thousands of small concerns which used a large proportion of capital. Even during the relatively prosperous years of 1923, 1924, 1925, and 1926, the failures among the American manufacturers exceeded those of 1921, a year of severe depression. And although the number of factories had been steadily increasing up until 1919, it dropped over 17,000 in the decade 1919–29.[4]

II

If technological change affects the number as well as the kind and the location of jobs, a program for dealing with it naturally falls into two principal parts: (1) a program for adjusting the labor supply to changes in the kind and the location of jobs; and (2) a program for preventing labor-saving devices from retarding too much the growth in the number of jobs. First let us consider the problem of adjusting the labor supply to changes in the kind and the location of jobs. There are three general ways of dealing with this problem: (1) retarding the rate of displacement; (2) encouraging the transfer of displaced men within plants by employers; (3) providing better facilities in the labor market for transferring the displaced men between plants and localities.

Space does not permit a discussion of the contribution which trade unions might make to solving the problem of technological unemployment. One might expect that union history would reveal many successful attempts to reduce the impact of technological changes and to help union members adjust themselves to new conditions. As a matter of fact, this is precisely what one does not find. A few exceptions stand out, conspicuous because they are exceptions, such as the oft-cited experience of the Typographical Union with the linotype machine. In most cases, the first reaction of unions to technological changes is to attempt to protect their members against displace-

[4] A more detailed discussion of the effect of price movements upon employment is contained in my paper, "Market Shifts, Price Movements, and Employment," *American Economic Review, Supplement* (March 1929), pp. 1–22.

ment by discouraging the introduction of new methods into union shops and to make work for displaced workers by enacting restrictive rules. Unfortunately, after embarking upon a policy of opposition and restriction, unions find great difficulty in shifting to a policy of guidance and control.

During recent years a heavy displacement of labor has been occurring in the railroad industry and it is likely to continue. This is an industry in which unions are more or less strongly entrenched. During the immediate future we should have an opportunity to learn, from the actions of the railroad unions, what strong and well-led organizations can do to ease the burden of technological unemployment. Up to the present, the accomplishments of the railroad unions in dealing with the problem have been limited. Two important things, however, have been achieved. In the first place, some unions have organized the shifting of men from one part of the country to another. Most notable is the employment bureau of the trainmen's union in Chicago through which roads needing new trainmen can draw on furloughed trainmen in other parts of the country. On a smaller scale something of the same sort has been done by the shopmen's unions. In the second place, the seniority rule of the railroad unions has been of great value in concentrating the burden of displacement upon the junior men, who, in most cases, are best able to shift to other occupations. It is safe to say that, in the absence of the seniority rule, much displacement would have occurred among the older men and that this would have brought acute distress, because most of them would have been unable to find steady work in other industries. Grave as is the unemployment problem in railroading, it is infinitely less serious than it would have been were the seniority rule not in existence.

It is clear that the slower the rate of technological change, the greater is the possibility of absorbing a shrinkage in the working force by the normal labor turnover. If, for example, the combined resignation and discharge rate in a certain occupation is 25 per cent a year, new methods which dispense with half the force may be introduced without producing many layoffs, provided the change is spread over two years. If the resignation and discharge rate is 25 per cent, why could not the new methods be introduced without producing any layoffs, provided they were spread over two years? For the simple reason that most resignations and discharges occur among newly hired men. Consequently, a labor-saving change which practically eliminates the hiring of men in a certain occupation also reduces the number of resignations and discharges. Although the annual resignation and discharge rate may have been 25 per cent as long as each resignation or discharge led to a hiring, the rate would drop far below 25 per cent as soon as replacement ceased. It has been pointed out, however, that, under existing economic arrangements, labor-saving devices tend to be introduced too rapidly because the cost of adopting them falls, in large measure, not upon the enterprises which introduce them, but upon the rest of the community. An obvious way to prevent change from occurring too fast is to assess a larger part of the costs against the enterprises which reap the benefits and one way of doing this is to require every concern to pay a dismissal wage to each man whom it permanently lays off.[5] A dismissal wage would be helpful, of course, in assisting workmen to shift to other occupations, but its real importance would consist in the fact that it would correct a serious flaw in our social cost accounting and would encourage managements to reduce layoffs to a minimum. The principle of the dismissal wage has long been accepted by business, for it has been customary to pay several months' salary to important executives who are laid off or discharged. During recent years a handful of enterprises (less than eighty in all) have extended the dismissal wage to a few long-service manual laborers. But the dismissal wage is not likely to be adopted on a wide scale unless it is made compulsory. Unfortunately authority to require the payment of dismissal compensation is divided among the legislatures of forty-eight states. In order to encourage the states to act and also to encourage individual enterprises to act in advance of the states, it would be desirable for the federal government to permit corporations which establish reserves for the payment of a dismissal wage to count a part of their contributions to such reserves as a credit on their federal corporate income-tax payments. The credit should not be given, of course, unless the funds were vested in independent trustees, and, consequently, the reserve funds should be registered with and approved by the Treasury Department. It would be reasonable to give a credit of fifty cents on the corporate income tax for each dollar contributed to an approved reserve fund.[6] Such a credit would cut the cost to the corporation in half.

A second way of preventing the displacement of men by technological

[5] It is not possible to estimate in each individual case the cost of a layoff to the workman. Consequently, it is desirable to pay a standard dismissal wage to all men who are laid off. The amount should vary with the workman's length of service. This would give employers an incentive to retain long-service employees who would probably have most trouble shifting to new occupations or industries. Employees of less than six months' service should receive no dismissal wage. A question of considerable importance, especially from the standpoint of problems of administration, is whether the dismissal wage should be paid to any men who are discharged for cause. Space does not permit a discussion of it here.

[6] It might be advisable to limit the credit to a certain portion of the tax paid by the corporation. Credit should be allowed also on all payments by corporations into reserves against unemployment, provided the reserves are vested in independent trustees and meet other general requirements imposed in the interest of the beneficiaries.

changes is to encourage their transfer to other work in the same plant. Here we encounter another grave flaw in our economic arrangements, for employers at present have no adequate incentive to make transfers. And again the dismissal wage furnishes the needed incentive. Experience has demonstrated that, when a thorough search is made for jobs which men with given qualifications can fill, a surprising number will often be discovered. Especially noteworthy is the success of the Western Electric Company in finding work which various classes of handicapped men can perform as well as nonhandicapped workers. But searching carefully for jobs to which displaced men might be shifted is not enough. A real effort should be made to create opportunities for transfer by adapting either the work to the men or the men to the work. There is no reason, for example, why we should not use our mastery of science to create the kinds of positions which the labor supply requires. Of course, the market itself provides an incentive to adapt technique to the labor supply, because when a class of labor becomes superabundant and cheap, it pays to invent machines which such labor can operate. When thousands of unskilled European peasants flooded this country and waited for work at every factory gate, engineers soon discovered how this cheap labor could be used to make scores of more or less complicated commodities. But surely it is not a satisfactory situation when technique is not altered in response to a surplus of men until that surplus has become conspicuously large and represents a grave problem of unemployment. There is need for a method of making technique adjust itself more promptly and in a more selective manner to the labor supply. Such a method is provided by the dismissal wage. Rather than pay $200 or $300 to men who have been displaced, it would often be more economical for the employer to reorganize some department or to develop jigs, fixtures, and mechanical aids so that these men could be transferred to other work.

More promising than the adjustment of technique to men is the adjustment of men to technique. In a society as dynamic as ours, it is important that workers be reasonably versatile. Unfortunately industry, instead of producing versatile employees, goes out of its way to develop narrow specialists. Furthermore, the wage-payment systems which are in general use, such as piecework and bonus and premium plans, make the men themselves prefer to specialize narrowly and even cause many of them stubbornly to resist efforts to give them a broad training. The establishment of a dismissal wage would give employers a badly needed incentive to develop general-purpose men who can be shifted to other departments or other work when changes occur. It would also encourage employers to retrain men. In order to give the maximum incentive to retrain, it would be desirable to permit enterprises to pay the cost of retraining by drawing on the reserves which are accumulated to provide for dismissal compensation. In other words, these reserves should not be purely dismissal compensation reserves but they should be dismissal compensation and retraining reserves. The amount that might be withdrawn to pay for retraining a given man should be limited, of course, by the dismissal compensation to which he is entitled.

The operation of a dismissal wage raises many important problems, which there is not time to discuss. It has been pointed out that reserves should be accumulated in order to assure that dismissal compensation will be paid. These reserves should be created in such a manner that the employers' incentive to prevent layoffs will not be dulled. In order to encourage enterprises to concentrate layoffs among the younger employees who, as a rule, can adjust themselves most easily, the dismissal wage should increase with the length of service. A problem of great difficulty arises when a worker refuses to accept the management's offer to transfer him to another job. In case this refusal necessitates his dismissal, should he receive dismissal compensation either in whole or in part? Possibly the job which he rejected pays much less than he has been accustomed to earn. In this case his claim for dismissal compensation would seem to be a strong one. But possibly the job pays almost as much as he has ever earned. In this event his claim seems weak. But where and by whom should the line be drawn? A dismissal wage, if improperly designed and administered, will create an incentive for workers to refuse to be transferred. And what is the good of encouraging enterprises to make transfers if, at the same time, we encourage the men to refuse them? The successful operation of a dismissal wage will depend in large degree upon the skill with which this problem is solved.

But although a dismissal wage is an important method of correcting our system of social cost accounting and although it furnishes employers with a much-needed incentive to avoid displacing men, it is not enough. It would not prevent many technological improvements from being adopted at an uneconomically rapid rate. Furthermore, one of the principal ways in which technological changes produce unemployment is by forcing old and obsolete plants to shut down. The whole forces in such plants present a transfer problem. Any society which is highly dynamic and which uses highly specialized labor needs efficient facilities for placing the thousands of men whom industry is constantly throwing on the market. The more dynamic the society and the greater the degree of occupational and territorial specialization, the greater is the need for a well-organized labor market.

But precisely what facilities are needed? Let me say emphatically that efficient public labor exchanges, although of great importance, are far from enough. The problem of keeping the labor supply adjusted to the changing requirements of industry is far more than a matter of sending unemployed men to the vacancies for which they happen to be fitted. In fact, insofar as technological changes displace certain types of men and create a demand for other types, the labor supply will probably not correspond closely to the demands of industry. Consequently, the problem of keeping the labor supply adjusted to the ever-changing demands of industry is partly a problem of showing employers how they can use more of the types of men who happen to be available; it is partly a matter of inducing employers themselves to explore the possibilities of using more of these types; it is partly a matter of discovering the occupations to which the surplus men can most easily be shifted; and it is partly a matter of inducing employers, trade unions, or communities to retrain the displaced workers for new employments.

These are to some extent problems of research and they are to some extent problems of inducing action on the part of industry. They require, therefore, an organization capable both of doing research and of creating cooperation.[7] This need could be met by the establishment of a federal labor board composed of six or seven industrialists and labor leaders with possibly the Secretary of Commerce and the Secretary of Labor as *ex officio* members. The board would be provided with a research staff and connected with industry by a national advisory committee. The federal employment exchanges would be transferred to the control of the board, which would be provided with funds for expanding their services. If the federal government cooperated with the states in providing a joint federal-state employment service, the federal grant-in-aid would be administered by the board. In addition, it would be given an appropriation to subsidize projects in vocational retraining.

How would the board proceed? Every technological or geographical change presents, in large degree, a unique problem. The number and kind of men who are displaced and the alternative employments for which they are best qualified are never the same. As soon as it became evident that a new machine or a geographical shift would displace labor on a substantial scale, the change would be the subject of intensive study by the technical staff of

[7] In the state of Massachusetts, for example, workers are being crowded out of the textile and the shoe industries, but the manufacture of women's garments and, in less degree, men's garments is growing. To what extent, if at all, does there exist the possibility of transferring workers from the textile and the shoe industries into some branch of the clothing industry? Obviously this question can be answered satisfactorily only after special investigation. This means research. After research has supplied the answer, industry must be persuaded to cooperate in assisting the transfer. Possibly the communities and trade unions must be induced to help.

the board. How many men are likely to be displaced and how rapidly? How can the influx of young workers into the shrinking occupation be promptly stopped? How can employers who need men in the occupation obtain them from other enterprises which are laying off men? Into what other pursuits can the displaced men be most advantageously transferred? What training should they receive before being shifted and how and by whom should it be given? The technical staff would prepare a tentative plan which would be submitted by the board to the industry. After receiving criticisms and suggestions, the board would prepare a revised plan which it would ask the industry to accept. The board would, of course, have no power to compel acceptance of its recommendations. Its effectiveness would depend upon the reasonableness of its suggestions and the respect which its members, by virtue of their ability and fairness, would be able to command.

There is, however, one important legal tool with which the board might be equipped. That is power to attach conditions to patent grants for the purpose of protecting men against displacement. No one will question the general policy of encouraging invention by giving patents to inventors, but if the government grants a patent, surely it is fair to require that reasonable steps be taken to avoid unnecessary displacement of labor. Whenever it appears that a new invention is likely to create a serious problem of displacement, it should be the duty of the patent office to refer the matter to the federal labor board and the duty of the board, after investigation, to draw up reasonable rules for the protection of labor. The board should also be authorized to intervene on its own initiative in case an invention appears to threaten serious displacement. The patent should be granted only in the event that the applicant accepts, both for himself and for his licensees, the reasonable requirements of the board. In particular, patents which are likely to produce serious displacement should not be granted unless the applicants agree both to provide a reasonable dismissal wage and to cooperate in providing reasonable facilities for retraining the displaced men.

Permit me to add a word about the problem of vocational retraining and the federal labor board's relation to it. At present, we have practically no experience to guide us in handling this important problem. We do know that the problem involves great difficulties because it is not easy to induce men to prepare themselves for a new occupation unless they feel reasonably sure of getting employment in it, and it is not possible, as a rule, to assure displaced men of jobs. We also know that the problem varies from locality to locality and from industry to industry. In some cases there may be an opportunity to transfer men into an industry where plants are large. In such instances, it may be best to provide the training in the plants which hire the men. But when men are to be transferred into small plants, such as garages or women's-garment factories, training must be given by the community or by a number of cooperating small plants. Several of the most notable retraining experiments have been sponsored by trade unions, and in many instances the cooperation of unions should be exceedingly helpful. In view of the fact that the problem is different in every situation, the best way to promote retraining is to give a central body such as the federal labor board an appropriation to subsidize retraining projects which it approves. A national body, such as the board, would be in a position to take the lead in initiating projects when and where they were needed and to support them as long as the need lasted. It would be able to apply in each place the experience gained in other places and to avoid making the same mistake too many times. It would be in a position to command the cooperation of individual employers, trade associations, trade unions, and the local communities. It would undoubtedly act more promptly, with better judgment, with richer experience, and with more vision than any other body.

III

What can be done to prevent technological improvements from producing unemployment by causing wages to become too high relative to the prices of capital goods? It is possible that the widespread adoption of the legal dismissal wage, by retarding the adoption of labor-saving devices, would reduce the displacement of labor sufficiently to counteract the too-rapid rise in the price of labor relative to the prices of capital goods. But one cannot be certain of this. In the event that the number of jobs fails to increase as rapidly as the labor supply, what can be done?

An obvious suggestion is to reduce wages. But there is no machinery for doing this, and it is difficult to see how such machinery could be constructed. Another alternative would be to stimulate the accumulation of capital. If the proportion in which it is most economical to combine capital and labor has changed from, say, six units of capital for each laborer to seven units of capital for each laborer, it is obvious that an increase of one sixth in the amount of capital is needed in order to prevent unemployment. The more quickly this increase is achieved, the more quickly will unemployment be eliminated. Unfortunately our apparatus for regulating the rate of capital accumulation is even less adequate than our apparatus for controlling wages, and there is small prospect that we shall soon be able to control the annual additions to capital. Still another alternative would be to inflate the general price level slightly. As wages are not highly sensitive to price changes, a small rise in other prices could occur without substantially affecting wages. Thus the proper relationship between wages and the prices of capital goods might be restored. As yet we lack instruments upon which we can rely to inflate prices slightly but not too much; that is, without permitting the inflationary movement to get beyond control and go too far. Possibly within a decade or two we shall possess them. At any rate, the policy of slight inflation has more practical possibilities than either the policy of controlling wages or the policy of accelerating the accumulation of capital. There are reasons why a slow inflation is undesirable as a steady policy. In fact, although slow deflation greatly accentuates the problem of unemployment, it is probably to be preferred on general economic grounds under most circumstances both to an absolutely stable price level and to a slowly rising price level. Rapid deflation is, of course, an entirely different matter.

But is there no prospect of more immediate relief when labor-saving devices prevent the number of jobs from keeping pace with the supply of labor? It is frequently suggested that unemployment be converted into leisure by reducing the hours of work. The trend of working hours has been downward for well over a century, but most cuts in hours have been the result of bargaining. Unfortunately, when working hours are determined in this way, reductions are likely to occur most slowly at precisely the times and the places that labor-saving devices are producing most idleness. Undoubtedly we need the planned creation of leisure in exactly sufficient amounts to prevent technological unemployment, but reducing the hours of labor involves more problems than is ordinarily suspected.

Working time may be cut by reducing either the working days per week or the hours per day. Today the proposals most frequently discussed are the five-day week with an eight-hour day and a six-day week with a six-hour shift. It is usually assumed that a six-hour shift would mean two shifts a day. From the noneconomic point of view, the five-day week with the eight-hour day is preferable to the six-hour shift six days a week, because a week end of two days can be used more advantageously by most workmen than two hours of additional leisure each day. Furthermore, if the six-hour shift means the use of two or more shifts a day, interference with family life may result when one member of a family works on a morning shift and another member on an afternoon shift. From the economic point of view, however, the five-day week has the grave disadvantage that it is likely to decrease rather than increase the number of jobs and hence increase the volume of unemployment. It is generally assumed that the five-day week will be coupled with an increase in hourly wages sufficient to counteract the reduction in working time. Otherwise the shorter week would not be acceptable to the men. But the unemployment which the five-day week is intended to remedy arises because money wages have become too high relative to other prices, particularly the prices of capital goods. If hourly wages are raised to offset the reduction in working time, the disparity between wages and other prices will, for some time at least, be aggravated. Will not this largely, if not wholly, cancel the effect of shorter hours upon the number of jobs? Eventually, of course, the effect of higher wage rates may be translated into higher prices for commodities in general. In the meantime, however, the higher hourly rates will tend to keep down the number of jobs. Whether this effect more than counteracts the gain from the shorter work week depends upon the elasticity of the demand for labor. Since it is probable that the demand for labor is elastic, no one can be surprised if the five-day week with one shift of eight hours and a compensating increase in wage rates aggravates rather than diminishes the problem of unemployment.

Far more promising as a method of converting unemployment into leisure is the six-hour shift, provided that the six-hour shift means the use of two or more shifts each day. This method, it is true, might create a transfer problem of some magnitude in the labor market, because the substitution of two six-hour shifts for one eight-hour shift would enable the more efficient plants to capture a larger share of the business and would compel some of the less efficient plants to shut down. The total number of jobs, however, would probably be increased rather than decreased because the advance in hourly rates necessary to compensate for the reduction in working hours would in most cases be more than offset by the savings in overhead made possible by the use of two six-hour shifts each day. Suppose, for example, that the overhead and the direct labor cost of a plant operating forty-eight hours a week are precisely the same. The plant changes to two six-hour shifts a day and raises wages exactly enough to compensate each employee for the reduction in his hours. If output rises in precise proportion to the increase in the hours, unit cost will fall by one sixth. Of course, in industries where overhead is small, the saving from the use of two shifts might be insufficient to offset the higher wage rates. It seems plain, however, that if labor must be compensated for the reduction in hours, the only way to destroy unemployment by converting it into leisure is through a plan which permits industry simultaneously to achieve substantial savings in overhead.

But how could a movement to reduce hours be initiated and carried out? Who would determine when shorter hours were needed and who would persuade business enterprises to reduce them? Clearly there is little hope of reducing hours by law, for here again the government's authority over most branches of industry is divided among forty-eight state legislatures.[8] Probably the body best able to induce competitors simultaneously to cut hours would be the federal labor board. Its close and constant contact with the problems of technological unemployment would give it intimate knowledge of when and where cuts in hours were needed. The board would require for its guidance far more accurate statistical information than is now available concerning the number and kind of displaced men who had not been absorbed by industry. The board would probably find it wise not to attempt to effect a more or less general shortening of hours in all industries but rather to accelerate reductions in those industries where changes in methods or markets were producing a large displacement of men. These reductions would probably not entirely prevent the displacement of workers, but they might be sufficient to adjust the total number of jobs in all industries to the available labor supply. Furthermore, they would occur, for the most part, where they would do the most good. The board's success in inducing industry to cut hours would depend upon conditions. Undoubtedly its success would be greater in industries where technological progress was enabling enterprises to achieve substantial economies than in industries which were being destroyed or reduced in size by progress in competing industries. And, of course, its success would depend partly upon the strength and the vitality of the labor movement. The moral influence of vigorous trade unions is great even in industries in which union membership is small.

For two centuries now, we have permitted the Juggernaut of industrial revolution to run wild. We have developed institutions which subsidize change on an enormous scale and which cause it to occur far more rapidly than in any previous age. And yet we have failed, for the most part, to recognize that change presents a major social problem; we have made almost

[8] Do legislatures possess the constitutional authority to compel a reduction in the hours of male adult workers for the purpose of reducing unemployment? This question has never been decided by the courts. Some of the more reactionary courts might deny the authority. Nevertheless, the elimination of unemployment would appear to be a legitimate public purpose and there is reason to believe that the more enlightened courts would sustain reasonable legislation for its accomplishment.

no effort to keep down the cost of change or to prevent change from occurring at a wastefully rapid rate. We have done virtually nothing to assist men to adjust themselves to industrial changes. Almost without raising a little finger to prevent it, we have permitted the development of industry to wreck thousands of lives and to produce an enormous human scrap heap. Prominent organizations of employers have resisted all efforts to modernize the labor market as stubbornly and as bitterly as any trade union ever opposed the installation of labor-saving devices. After two centuries of industrial revolution, is it not high time that we recognize that change is bound to occur too rapidly and to produce misery and degradation unless it is controlled and intelligently directed and unless men are assisted to adjust themselves to their new environment? Is it not high time that we recognize that change is now occurring on such a vast scale that we can no longer simply permit it to happen regardless of the consequences which it produces? Surely if we deliberately stimulate change, we should go out of our way to protect those who are injured by it. The suggestions which I have advanced are conservative and would fall far short of adequate protection. But they would be an immense improvement over doing nothing and they are probably sufficient for a first step. Long enough we have accepted the naive and fatalistic philosophy that everything will be all right provided only that we carefully refrain from attempting to make it all right. Let us recognize clearly that few forms of industrial waste bulk larger than the unnecessary costs of progress and that few economic problems are more important or more difficult than this problem of how to control change so that it will occur less wastefully and will inflict less misery.

23

The Impact of Social-Security Legislation upon Mobility and Enterprise

American Economic Review, Supplement, March 1940.

I

By the mobility of labor I mean the willingness and the ability of labor to move from one employer to another, one place to another, or one occupation to another in response to changes in the demand for labor. Mobility must be distinguished from movement because much movement is initiated by the employer through layoffs. Hence increases and decreases in movement do not necessarily mean increases or decreases in willingness or ability to move. Some movement is necessary in order to achieve an optimum distribution of resources, but movement in excess of this amount is wasteful. Movement of both capital and labor is, of course, necessary in amounts determined by the relative costs of moving each. Movement is to some extent necessary in order to develop men. When people wonder about the effects of social-security legislation upon mobility of labor, they are usually fearful that social security will prevent the movement from reaching the optimum amount. The probable effects of the social-security program upon mobility must be analyzed in the light of the amounts and kinds of mobility in the American labor market and of the conditions which determine mobility.

The American labor market is only beginning to be explored. Nevertheless, I feel safe in asserting six propositions concerning the mobility of labor: (1) the majority of the working population are relatively stable and do little moving either between employers or places or probably between occupations; (2) the amount of movement in the labor market is large and, indeed, is much larger than is generally suspected; (3) the amount of movement from employer to employer and from place to place is declining; (4) the character of movement has been changing from a voluntary to a forced movement; (5) the obstacles to movement between employers are increasing; (6) changes in managerial policy and the spread of unionism are tending to increase the proportion of layoffs that are temporary rather than permanent, to reduce the proportion of casual work, and to sharpen the distinction between regular and temporary employers.

Twenty-five years ago, when labor turnover was first studied, most employers thought that it was of negligible importance, despite the fact that it turned out to be about 100 per cent a year. The employers were misled by the concentration of turnover among a small part of the force—usually one fourth or less. Although the number of separations might be as large as the force itself, from two thirds to three fourths of the names on the pay roll at the beginning of the year would be there at the end. Today the nation suffers from the same optical illusion. It still seems to be true that in any given plant from two thirds to three fourths of the employees do not move in the course of a year. The prevalence of geographical stability is suggested by the Michigan study of mobility which indicates that during the fifty-seven-month period from April 1930 to January 1935, 87.1 per cent of the workers did not make the kind of geographical change defined as movement for purposes of the study.[1]

Despite the fact that the great majority of the workers do not move, the amount of movement is large—much larger than most people have supposed. Evidence is found in the figures on business births and deaths, in the labor-turnover figures, in the large movement between agricultural and nonagricultural pursuits, and in the large number of account numbers issued by the social-security administration. Business births and deaths run each about four hundred thousand a year. Many of them represent merely a change in ownership, but special studies indicate that there are about two hundred thousand births of new going concerns each year and almost the same number of deaths. The average number of employees in the two million nonagricultural enterprises is between thirteen and fourteen. It is probable that the infant concerns and also the dying concerns have less than the

[1] *Monthly Labor Review* (April 1939), pp. 789–802. A person was considered to have made a move whenever his work history showed a change between communities under one of the following circumstances: (1) between places of work, when the person was employed both before and after moving, (2) between places of residence, when the person was unemployed both before and after moving, or (3) between place of work and place of residence, when the person was employed at one end of the move and unemployed or not seeking work at the other, provided in this case that the move was longer than between adjoining counties. This restriction was adopted because short-distance moves between employment and unemployment were usually of the "commuting" type which did not involve a definite transfer of workers from one labor market to another.

average number of employees. If we assume that the average dying concern has less than half the average number of employees, say about five, two hundred thousand deaths would produce one million terminations a year. If new concerns on the average have four employees at the end of the first year, they would represent the employment of about eight hundred thousand persons. Concerns which die are likely to have a considerable shrinkage of employment for several years before their death. Likewise, some new enterprises grow rapidly for the first few years. Of course, a very large proportion of concerns have a life of less than a year. The separation rate in manufacturing industries in 1936 was 40.35 per cent; in 1937, 53.11 per cent; and in 1938, 49.22 per cent. As temporary layoffs are not ordinarily included in separations, these figures represent terminations of employment with the enterprise. The movements of labor between agricultural and nonagricultural pursuits are not accurately known but appear to be large. Woytinsky estimates that the number of farmers working in nonagricultural pursuits reaches a peak of about a million and a half at the turn of the year and that the seasonal demand for hired help by farmers rises in July to nearly a million and a half over the level of January and February.[2] The number of account numbers issued by the social security administration is about 60 per cent greater than the number of persons employed in the covered industries. At the end of 1939, 47.5 million account numbers had been issued. The number of persons whose usual employment is in the covered industries was about 27.5 million at the end of 1938 and about 28.5 million at the end of 1939. Allowance must be made for the fact that many account numbers have been issued to unemployed persons, that many holders of account numbers have retired or died, and that a few duplicate account numbers were issued. Nevertheless, Woytinsky estimates that during 1937 and 1938, 9.6 million persons who usually work in employment not covered by the old age pension tax were engaged at least part of the time in covered employments.[3] This does not include the persons who receive temporary or intermittent work entirely within covered employments. Probably one fourth of the country's labor force in any one year works for more than one employer. Many of these workers are employed in more than one industry. Lack of definite information about who these workers are and what is the pattern of their employment is a most serious gap in our information about the labor market.

[2] W. S. Woytinsky, *Seasonal Variations in Employment in the United States* (Washington, 1939), p. 95.

[3] W. S. Woytinsky, *Fluctuations in Employment Covered by the Federal Old-Age Insurance Program* (Washington, 1939).

The amount of movement from employer to employer and probably from place to place is declining. Before the war, separation rates of 100 per cent were normal. In 1920, separations in manufacturing started to decline. By 1929, the rate was less than half the level of 1920.[4] During recent years the changes in the total separation rate have been moderate, but the general drift has been downward with the rate for 1937 definitely below 1930. Evidence of changes in the amount of movement from place to place over time is scanty. There are several types of geographical movement and they may not be changing in the same direction. However, the estimates of the Department of Agriculture show a decline in the farm-city movement from 10.8 million in the five years ending in 1928 to 5.6 million in the five years ending in 1938, and in the city-farm movement from 7.7 million in the first period to 3.9 million in the second. These are movements of persons, not necessarily workers, but the movement of workers may be expected to be roughly proportionate to the movement of persons.

Not only is the amount of movement declining, but its character has changed during the last ten years from predominantly voluntary to predominantly involuntary. This change does not go back beyond 1929, and it remains to be seen whether it is the result of temporary conditions. Until 1929, the turnover reports of the Metropolitan Life Insurance Company showed that over 70 per cent of the separations were resignations. Layoffs constituted about 15 per cent, and discharges about 13 per cent. In 1936, 61.2 per cent of the separations were layoffs; in 1937, 67.3 per cent; in 1938, 82.2 per cent. In 1937 scarcely one out of four of the quits was a resignation, and in 1938 scarcely one out of seven.[5] Layoff rates today appear to be higher than before the war or before the depression. The reason in the main is the drop in the resignation rate which prevents employers from letting resignations produce adjustments in the size of the force.

In some respects movement is easier today than ever before. The automobile and the greatly improved public employment offices facilitate movement both between employers and places. On balance, however, the obstacles to movement seem to be increasing. The greatest change in recent years has been the spread of union rules governing layoffs and to a lesser extent hiring. Equal-division-of-work rules discourage involuntary movement because they limit layoffs: But equal-division-of-work rules also reduce the number of

[4] *Monthly Labor Review* (July 1929), pp. 64–65.

[5] Deaths and retirements (the latter not always entirely voluntary) are included in resignations. The resignation rates in manufacturing are today only one fifth to one tenth of the prewar resignation rates.

hirings, and this discourages resignations. Seniority rules discourage resignations because new employees in a plant must start at the bottom of the seniority list. Furthermore, when the seniority rule provides, as it often does, that workers with seniority status shall be given preference in hiring, it discourages the movement of workers who have been laid off. The depression has greatly stimulated the interest of workers in protecting themselves against layoffs. Among several hundred union agreements negotiated between 1923 and 1929, only about one out of three contained regulations of layoffs. Among another group of several hundred agreements negotiated since 1933, two out of three regulated layoffs.

The experience of union officials confirms these statistics. An international officer in one of the paper unions says: "When we first began to sign agreements with paper manufacturers, seniority was not much of an issue. However, since the depression, this question of seniority seems to loom larger in the workers' minds than anything else. It is very difficult to write a satisfactory seniority clause in a trade agreement. As a matter of fact, if employers would agree to let us write our own seniority clause, I do not believe the union could write a clause that would be satisfactory to all our members." A high official for many years in one of the unions of the glass industry says: "I have been in the glass industry for over a generation and never once had to work under the seniority rule. That came into the trade-union movement after I had given up active work in the glass factory. When getting around the country I find that this is the paramount question in local meetings. It seems to overshadow all other questions before the group."

When a seniority rule provides that the workers laid off shall be rehired, if qualified, before other persons are engaged, it has the effect of converting permanent layoffs into temporary ones. Such a rule may attach a large number of persons to a plant in hope of sometime being rehired. Whenever a union imposes an equal-division-of-work rule it is necessary to define clearly the persons who are entitled to share in the work. This brings about a sharp distinction between temporary and permanent workers. A seniority rule has the same effect because temporary workers are usually denied seniority status, especially with respect to rehiring. Sometimes a closed shop sharpens the distinction between regular and temporary employees because the union may not require that temporary employees be members. The general tendency of trade agreements, therefore, seems to be (1) to reduce the proportion of permanent layoffs, (2) to reduce the amount of work done by temporary workers, and (3) to sharpen the distinction between regular and temporary workers. It is not clear, at this stage of development, that union layoff and hiring policies cause an excessive number of men to be attached to union plants or industries. Probably they do.

II

It is against this general setting that we must appraise the effect of the social-security program upon the mobility of labor. We must consider separately the effects of (1) pensions, (2) unemployment compensation, and (3) relief.

The pension plan will tend to encourage mobility. In the first place, it will lead to retirements at an earlier age, and the vacancies thus created stimulate movement. In a majority of cases this movement is a forced rather than a voluntary one. The employer feels able to retire men earlier because the men are provided for by pensions. This, indeed, has always been one of the principal arguments used by insurance companies in selling pension plans to employers. In the second place, it will permit employees to move from one employer to another without losing pension rights. Practically all of the private pension plans which sprouted so luxuriantly during the twenties and in the early part of the depression were carefully designed to discourage movement. The man who left lost all the employer's contribution and in some instances his own. Private pension plans will continue to supplement the public pension plans for some years to come, and they will tend to discourage movement. Their effect, however, will be limited by the public pension plan.

The brief experience with state unemployment-compensation schemes indicates that their effect upon mobility will be small. Experience rating will cause the conversion of some intermittent or casual employment into regular employment.[6] This will reduce the amount of movement but not the willingness to move. Some of the unemployment-compensation acts give employers an incentive to spread work rather than to make layoffs. This will reduce involuntary movement and indirectly voluntary movement. There are two principal reasons for concluding that unemployment compensation will have little effect upon mobility. One is that most of the men who qualify for benefits are in the stable rather than the mobile group of employees. The provisions concerning qualifications vary. Of the states

[6] This will not be true, however, if the layoff of workers who have not qualified for benefits is not counted in measuring experience.

specifying definite minimum earnings during a specified base period (usually the preceding year), only seven put it below two hundred dollars,[7] and of the states requiring earnings of a given multiple of weekly benefits only fourteen require earnings of less than twenty-four weeks' benefits.[8] A large part of the people who constitute the mobile part of the working force will not qualify for many weeks' benefits. Unfortunately there are no figures available on the number of persons laid off who lack sufficient employment or earnings to qualify for benefits. Indeed, the total number of layoffs in covered employments is not known because there are many layoffs for which claims are not presented. In manufacturing, the layoff rate during the first ten months of 1939 was running at the annual rate of 26.45 per hundred employees, a rate probably 20 per cent higher than in nonmanufacturing industries. If Massachusetts experience is representative, there were about 6.5 million (permanent) layoffs in covered employment during 1939. Temporary layoffs are not included in the turnover figures and are more difficult to estimate. The unemployment census of April 1930 found one temporary layoff to every 3.2 permanent layoffs. This ratio may not be typical as the proportion is likely to vary with conditions in the labor market and even with the season of the year. I suspect that in April 1930 the proportion of permanent layoffs was unusually high. If we assume, however, that the ratio 1 to 3.2 is fairly typical, the total number of layoffs, both temporary and permanent, in covered industries in 1939 was approximately 8.5 million. Returns for three quarters of 1939 indicate that the number of layoffs in which unemployment compensation was paid would be about 5.7 million for the entire year. Apparently, there were about 2.8 million layoffs in covered industries in which no unemployment benefits were paid. In some of these cases the workers had sufficient wage or employment credits, but failed to draw benefits because they obtained employment before the expiration of the waiting period. In other cases the workers failed to obtain benefits because they lacked sufficient wage or employment credits. It is unfortunate that we do not know how many employees fall in each of these two classes. All that we know is that there were a number of claims disallowed because of insufficient wage credits. During the first three quarters of 1939, about

[7] Rhode Island, $100; Delaware, $125; South Dakota, $126; North Carolina, $130; Idaho, $140; and Maine, $144.

[8] Pennsylvania, thirteen; Arizona, fourteen; Iowa, fifteen; and Alabama, Arkansas, Georgia, Kansas, Louisiana, Mississippi, Missouri, Nevada, New Jersey, Oklahoma, Virginia, sixteen. Three jurisdictions require a specified number of weeks of employment: Wisconsin, over four; District of Columbia, thirteen out of the fifty-two ending with the last week of employment; and Ohio, twenty in the base year.

10 per cent of the claims from workers who had wage credits in covered employment were disallowed because of insufficient wage credits. In the first quarter the percentage was 12.2, in the second, 8.7, in the third, 9.4.

Sample studies of the people who are receiving unemployment benefits indicate that they do not ordinarily suffer long periods of unemployment and that few of them have ever been on relief. Many of them have only been temporarily laid off; they have not lost their check numbers; and they have not lost their jobs. They do not expect to move, and they would not move even if they did not receive unemployment benefits because, although they may not have work, they still have jobs. It is this fact rather than the receipt or nonreceipt of unemployment benefits which determines their willingness to move. As indicated above, union policy is increasing the number of persons in this class because unions endeavor to replace permanent layoffs with temporary ones and to give people who have been laid off a right to re-employment before outsiders are engaged.

Another reason why unemployment benefits are not likely to have great effect upon mobility is that they are paid for only a few weeks—fifteen or sixteen in most states. Even if they were paid for twenty-six weeks, the effect on mobility would be small.[9] With the end of his benefits never far away, a worker is not likely to neglect hunting for employment. It is significant that in England only about one out of four vacancies is filled by the public employment offices; most of the men get their own jobs.[10] Undoubtedly, unemployment benefits will cause the unemployed worker to be more particular about the job he accepts and thus may extend somewhat the average period of unemployment. Even in bad years, there is a considerable amount of hiring. In both 1931 and 1932, for example, the number of hirings by manufacturing establishments included in the sample of the Bureau of Labor Statistics, was over three fourths as large as the number of separations. In 1931, the monthly accession rate was 3.05 per 100 employees on the pay roll, and the separation rate, 4.03; in 1932, the monthly accession rate was 3.32 per 100 employees, and the separation rate, 4.33. Unemployment benefits may discourage long-distance movement of workers in search of work. It

[9] In Great Britain, for example, where a twenty-six weeks' benefit is paid, it is the relief program rather than unemployment insurance which affects mobility. M. B. Gilson, *Unemployment Insurance in Great Britain* (New York, 1931), p. 204.

[10] The public offices have been endeavoring for some years to increase the proportion of vacancies which they fill and with moderate success. In 1926, the proportion filled by the public employment offices was about 18 per cent. In 1932, it was 21.2 per cent; in 1933, 26.6 per cent; in 1934, 24.8 per cent; and in 1935, 26.9 per cent. Cornelia M. Anderson, "British Employment Exchanges," *Harvard Business Review*, XVI, 96.

is not likely, however, to discourage the kind of search which a man can now make in his car without failing to report at his local public employment office once a week. Furthermore, it should be observed that in the past there has been much aimless wandering by the unemployed and that this should be discouraged. The transfer of men over great distances should be made by the public employment offices in response to requisitions which cannot be filled in the local market.

The main impact of the social-security program upon the mobility of labor will occur in connection with relief. Persons on relief seem to be more mobile than persons not on relief.[11] This does not mean that relief usually encourages mobility. Indeed, it probably does the opposite, but relief is most likely to affect the workers who do not belong to the regular working force and who do the most moving—not because of preference but because of necessity.[12] Up to the moment, the effect of relief upon the mobility of labor has not been tested. It can be tested only by a substantial increase in the number of jobs. The effect may be expected to vary with the type of labor. Among the 53 or 54 million persons who constitute the would-be gainfully employed, there are great variations in employability. Perhaps 10 or 15 per cent have a very high degree of employability and another 10 to 15 per cent a very low degree of employability. Among the 5 million persons of low employability, the effect of relief upon mobility will undoubtedly be great. Payments of fifty dollars a month for twelve months in the year would give probably most of these persons more than they would earn in industry.

Of course, the persons on relief, particularly work relief, do not necessarily consist of the least efficient 10 per cent of the would-be gainfully employed. The longer the relief program is in operation, however, the more completely its rolls will consist of persons of low employability. Even during the worst of the depression the re-employment rate among persons with a year or less of unemployment seems to have been about 40 per cent among males and even higher among females.[13] Each time someone leaves

[11] The Michigan study of 149,379 workers showed that 13,621, or 10.9 per cent, of 131,532 not on relief made a geographical move during the period under study and that 4,226, or 17.2 per cent, of the 24,589 workers on relief made a move (*Monthly Labor Review*, January 1939, 16–24). The same conclusion was reached by C. E. Lively and C. Taeuber in their study, *Rural Migration in the United States* (Washington, 1939), pp. 116–118.

[12] There are some cases in which relief definitely does encourage mobility, but the kind of mobility it fosters is not necessarily desirable. Relief is likely to encourage movement in the direction of relief opportunity rather than in the direction of employment opportunity.

[13] See the forthcoming study by W. S. Woytinsky on this point. [*Three Aspects of Labor Dynamics*, Washington, Committee on Social Security, Social Science Research Council, 1942, Part II.]

relief there is a chance that he will be replaced by a person of low employability. No one knows what the chance is. At any rate, if separations from the relief rolls frequently mean the addition of a person of low employability, the relief rolls will more and more consist of persons for whose services industry cannot hope to compete with relief. Among the unemployed in Philadelphia, according to the samples collected by the Industrial Research Department of the Wharton School and the Works Progress Administration, the percentages unemployed for three years or more increased as follows:

	Males	*Females*
1931	2.8	1.8
1932	3.3	2.2
1933	7.9	4.9
1935	34.9	19.6
1936	34.4	27.3
1937	37.7	26.1
1938	25.7	17.5

In other words, precisely the reverse process goes on among the unemployed as goes on in industry. Just as employers by constantly sifting the employed gradually build up a better-selected force, so the same process of selection and rejections gradually converts the unemployed more and more completely to a group of low employability. This is how the "hard core" of unemployment is created. A hard core of unemployment is bound to be created in any period of unemployment long enough to permit the segregation of the least employables among the unemployed. When the volume of employment fluctuates at only slightly below the labor supply (in other words when unemployment is low), the persons of low employability are not effectively segregated. Congress has attempted to deal with the problem of the hard core of unemployment insofar as the WPA is concerned by requiring that persons employed continuously on WPA for eighteen months be dropped for at least a month. It is not clear that this is a wise approach to the problem. Possibly the objective of public policy should be not to keep persons of low employability off WPA but to take care of them there. That may be precisely the place for them. Certainly work relief is not a good device for taking care of persons whose employability is high and whose unemployment, therefore, is likely to be very short; it is a more appropriate device for taking care of those whose employability is so low that they have slight chance of getting work again in private industry.

Not only will relief compete effectively with industry for the services of several million of the least employables, but it will hold many thousands of persons in regions where employment opportunities are low, unless operated to encourage movement. The great migrations of human history have been a mixture of pushes and pulls. The strongest push areas in the United States seem to be the Southern Appalachians, the cutover lands, the cotton areas of the Southeast, the dust bowl. There are, however, many cities which are push areas. Relief may be administered to offset the pushes of these unfavorable environments and to cause people to remain where employment opportunities are poorest. Or it may be used to create movement among those best fitted to move and to encourage the growth of a subsistence economy among the persons who are not fitted to move.

Will not the tendency of relief to keep persons of low employability out of industry and to hold present inhabitants in regions of meager employment opportunities be broken by the first pronounced boom in business? A substantial growth of employment would undoubtedly produce an appreciable reduction of even the long-term unemployed. I venture the prediction, however, that the percentage of the population between the ages of sixteen and forty-five actually at work in gainful nonagricultural employment may expand above the level of the 1920s while leaving half or more of the five million least-employable on relief. The actual result will depend partly upon the wage policies of the country. The United States, however, has enormous reserves of labor not only among the unemployed, but also among the nonemployed; that is, women and young people who are not working and not seeking work. In addition, there are at least two million persons attached to agriculture at a low intensity of employment who could easily be drawn into nonagricultural pursuits. Industry will draw heavily upon the nonemployed and upon agricultural workers before rehiring the least employable among the unemployed.

III

Who will bear the cost of the social-security program, and how will the program affect wages, enterprise, and employment? As the cost for some years will be met by the payroll tax, an inquiry into the incidence of the program requires an analysis of the incidence of the payroll tax. The effects in the short run (too short to permit the capital of industry to be adjusted to changes in the prospect for profits) must be distinguished from the long-run effects.

It is assumed that the price of labor is too sticky to be immediately affected by a tax on payrolls. In that event the incidence of the tax in the short run is dispersed in several directions. Since the marginal costs of existing plants in the short run consist of labor and raw materials, an increase in the price of one causes the demand curve of the other to move to the left.[14] Hence, part of the payroll tax in the short run falls on the suppliers of raw materials. The rise in marginal costs produces an advance in the prices of finished goods so that the cost falls partly on consumers. The rise in the price also limits the quantity sold which means that labor bears part of the cost in the form of less employment. The rise in labor costs and the limitation of the quantity sold means that profits are reduced and that capital bears part of the cost.

In the long run the effect of the pension and unemployment-compensation schemes upon enterprise must be judged by the relationship between the benefit disbursements and the collections under the payroll tax, because the noninsurance schemes (such as old-age assistance, aid to dependent children and the blind) must be financed out of the general budget. But since the payroll tax and the relief schemes were made effective by the same act of Congress, it is more realistic to appraise the immediate effects of the act by considering it as a whole. From the beginning of 1937 to the middle of 1939, tax collections and benefit payments under the Social Security Act were as shown in the table below (in millions).

	Collections [a]	*Pension and unemployment benefit payments*	*Other payments* [b]	*Excess of receipts over payments*
1937	$1,184	$ 3	$ 383	$ 798
1938	1,316	404	495	417
1939 (first half)	755	237	273	245
	$3,255	$644	$1,151	$1,460

[a] Includes collections under state unemployment insurance schemes of $586.5 million.
[b] Includes old-age assistance, aid to dependent children, aid to the blind.

During 1937 collections exceeded disbursements by $798 million. Perhaps not more than half of the excess of collections over payments, however,

[14] This point is important also in judging the consequences of wage cuts in times of depression. Even if the demand for labor in the short run is inelastic, wage reductions, by moving the demand curve for raw materials to the right, may cause an increase in disbursements by business enterprises. Since raw materials are largely produced by a group (farmers) who have even a lower income level than industrial workers, wage reductions may increase low-bracket consumer incomes even in those cases where the plant demand for labor is inelastic.

fell upon profits and of this perhaps between $300 and $350 million fell upon corporate profits.[15] This was equivalent to an increase of one third of the federal corporate income tax. As corporate profits in 1937 were $3.9 billion, the effect upon profits was moderate. The payroll taxes had no direct relationship to the downturn in the spring of 1937, but they were an important factor in preventing profits in 1937 from rising above 1936 and so must have materially restrained the vigor of the expansion. Even in 1937, the best year of the recovery, corporate profits were low—42.3 per cent below 1926, when gross corporate income was virtually the same as in 1937. In fact, only two out of five corporations made money in 1937 as against three out of five in 1926. Perhaps it is true that when profits are very low, the influence of any encroachment upon them is magnified. In 1938, the excess of receipts over expenditures was only $417 million, but the effect on enterprise may have been more serious than in 1937. Returns from 167 large companies indicate that profits were less than half the level of 1937. Thus they may have been about $1.8 billion. If half of the excess of collections over receipts fell on profits, the net income of corporations would have been cut by 10 per cent. Such a cut may well have materially affected investment policy and substantially accentuated the depression.

More serious was the effect of social-security taxes upon the railroads because the roads cannot even temporarily pass on higher costs in the form of higher prices. During the year 1937, the net cost of social security to the roads was about $76 million and their net profits were $98 million. In 1937, therefore, social security cut the profits of the roads by nearly 44 per cent. In 1938, the roads had a deficit of $124 million, and the net cost of social security to them was $67 million. In this year social security was responsible for 54 per cent of the deficit.[16] It is evident that social-security taxes add greatly to the difficulties of this grievously depressed industry.

Who will bear the payroll taxes in the long run? Three principal theories have been suggested. One is that the tax will produce higher prices so that all nonrecipients of benefits, in their capacity of consumers, will

[15] This guess may be too low since there was considerable resistance by consumers to higher prices. On this point see my paper, "Corporate Price Policies as a Factor in the Recent Business Recession," *Proceedings of the Academy of Political Science*, January 1939.

[16] The Railway Pension Act of 1937 provided that persons on the pension rolls of the railroads should be transferred to the public pension scheme beginning July 1, 1937. As a result, the roads were relieved of pension payments to about 54,000 employees who had been receiving on the average slightly more than fifty dollars a month. The saving to the roads during the second half of 1937 was slightly more than $16.2 million and during 1938 slightly more than $32.4 million. In estimating the net cost of social security to the roads these amounts must be deducted from the $92.4 million in social-security taxes paid by the roads in 1937 and the $99.5 million paid in 1938.

bear it. A second is that the social-security program, by producing forced saving, will reduce the rate of interest, especially during the next twenty years. To that extent the cost would fall on owners of capital. A third theory is that the tax will move the demand curve for labor to the left so that the burden will fall on labor.

What is the possibility that the tax on payrolls will produce higher prices and thus fall largely upon consumers? Keynes and others have argued that, given proper monetary policies, a rise in marginal costs will raise prices rather than reduce output. Higher prices presuppose either an expansion of demand deposits or a rise in their velocity. The demand for demand deposits and the willingness to spend them depends upon the outlook for profits and the scale of operations that businessmen plan as a result. Until an increase in expenditures occurs to raise prices, the advance in marginal cost must be regarded as reducing the marginal efficiency of capital and causing the demand curve for short-term loans to move to the left. Because the demand for short-term loans is inelastic, it is not practical to reduce their supply price sufficiently to prevent the shift in the demand curve from reducing the volume of demand deposits. It is even more difficult by reducing the supply price of short-term loans to produce an increase in demand deposits sufficient to raise expenditures and prices in proportion to the rise in costs and thus to restore the marginal efficiency of capital to the level prevailing before the increase in costs. There is slight prospect, therefore, that banking policy will cause the payroll tax to produce higher prices with no restriction on production and with the cost falling in the main upon consumers and to some extent upon capitalists. If the banking system were able to control the supply price of venture capital, this conclusion might have to be altered.

Will the payroll taxes increase the amount of saving with the result that (1) the amount of capital per worker is increased; (2) the marginal worth of labor (and hence the price of labor) is raised; and (3) the return on capital is reduced? Were these results to follow, the cost of the social-security program would fall in the main upon property owners in the form of lower interest rates but partly upon consumers in the form of higher prices. It would fall partly upon consumers because there is a connection between long-term and short-term interest rates. Hence the forced saving which reduced long-term interest rates would produce some increase in short-term funds and some increase in demand deposits and prices.

At one time it was estimated that a pension reserve fund of over $40 billion would be accumulated by 1980. No guesses concerning the size of the reserve a few years hence can pretend to be accurate, but changes in the estimates of costs and changes in the law itself now indicate that the reserve will reach a maximum of roughly $7 billion about 1955. The accumulation of such a reserve will increase the volume of investment-seeking funds by less than 5 per cent a year. During prosperous times the unemployment-insurance schemes will run a surplus. The amount will depend upon the terms of the laws, which are still in a state of flux. Perhaps it will be $300 million a year. At any rate, during the next fifteen years the social-insurance schemes may increase the volume of investment-seeking funds by about 8 per cent in good years and perhaps 1 to 2 per cent in bad years. During the next fifteen years the liquidation of the unemployment insurance funds in time of depression will not quite offset the accumulation of the old-age reserve. At most periods of the business cycle the demand for investment funds seems to be inelastic, although the demand for funds for housing at times seems to be elastic. If the demand is inelastic, the burden of the social-security program for the next fifteen years may fall to an appreciable degree upon capital. After that period, the accumulation of the old-age reserve will cease, and the burden on capital from the shift in the supply curve of investment funds to the right will be negligible. The liquidation of the unemployment-insurance funds during periods of depression will provide an outlet for savings and help support the rate of interest at such times. The increase in consumer incomes made possible by the liquidation of the unemployment funds will also improve the general business situation. Consequently, during periods of depression, property owners will gain but not at the expense of other groups in the community.

If the payroll tax does not produce an increase in incomes and prices, the demand curve for labor will shift to the left. At the wage rates prevailing before imposition of the payroll tax, the quantity of labor employed will be reduced. Unemployment will retard the increase in wage rates as technological progress raises the marginal worth of labor. It might be supposed that the retarding of the increase in wage rates would continue until the unemployed displaced by the payroll tax had all been absorbed. This presupposes, however, that the benefits paid have no effect upon the labor-supply curve. Pensions, even though low, will undoubtedly produce a few retirements. Likewise, unemployment benefits will slightly raise the reservation prices of unemployed workers and make them less willing to accept the first job that comes along. May not the payment of benefits reduce the reservation prices of labor? The workers in covered industries receive protection which workers in uncovered employments do not enjoy. Will not workers, therefore, be attracted to the covered industries? As between the covered and the uncovered industries, this is probably true at least to some extent. The fact remains, however, that reservation prices are to considerable extent determined by the amount of resources upon which unemployed workers may draw. Pensions and the unemployment compensation may reduce slightly the reservation prices of workers with respect to employment in the covered industries, but all payments in compensation of unemployment tend to raise the reservation prices of workers as a whole. More important than either unemployment compensation or old-age pensions upon the reservation prices of labor will be relief payments. The social-security program by producing unemployment may cause an expansion of relief payments. To the extent that social-security benefits and relief move the supply curve of labor to the left, they counteract the tendency of the payroll tax to keep down the price of labor.

Even though the social-security program (including relief) raises the reservation prices of labor, it is not likely to affect materially the number of workers available at prevailing wage rates to existing nonagricultural enterprises. In existing concerns the price of labor seems to be set during periods of contraction by the employed rather than the unemployed—by the resistance of the employed to cuts rather than the willingness of the unemployed to accept less than prevailing rates.[17] If the reservation prices created by social security affect the volume of employment, it will be through their effect upon wages in new concerns and, therefore, upon the number of business births. Even in periods of contraction the number of business births is close to two hundred thousand a year for new going concerns. The wage rates paid by new concerns in periods of great unemployment appear to be substantially below prevailing rates. Consequently, the reservation prices established by social security may substantially affect wages in new concerns and thereby reduce the business birth rate.[18] If so, social-security legislation (and wage-hour legislation as well) may affect the resiliency of our economy—its capacity to spring back after a shrinkage in employment. This, however, is still an unexplored field. Little is known about the determinants of the birth rate of new enterprises. Until exploration has occurred, we remain very much in the field of conjecture and we must not be surprised if the unintended consequences of public policies are more important than the intended ones.

[17] In periods of expansion the effect of the unemployed upon wages in old concerns is probably greater than in periods of contraction.

[18] However, the effect of the social-security program upon the wages paid by new enterprises will be substantially less in most industries than the minimums established under the Wage-Hour Act.

IV

Thus far we have discussed the incidence of a payroll tax on the assumption that the price of labor is set by supply and demand. To an increasing extent, however, the price of labor is an administered one, fixed by bargaining between trade unions and employers. To explain the effect of social security in such a world, one must consider how it will affect the bargaining power of unions and employers. Bargaining power may be defined as the cost to A of imposing a loss upon B. Part of the cost to union members of raising wages beyond a given rate is unemployment. To the extent that unemployment is compensated by insurance or relief, unions will be willing to endure larger amounts of it in order to raise the wages of their members. Trade-union wage policy has been influenced by the fear of nonunion competition. To the extent that social security and relief diminish the birth rate of new concerns they will limit the influence of nonunion competition upon union wage policy. Hence we may conclude that in a world of administered prices of labor, social security will tend both to raise the wages of the employed and to increase the number of the unemployed.

Will the increase in the bargaining power of labor be harmful to enterprise? Possibly, but not necessarily. The greater pressure on employers to raise the price of labor will (1) accelerate technological discovery, but (2) reduce the proportion of new ideas which are considered worth exploiting. It is sometimes said that wage increases will not increase the use of labor-saving inventions because (unless labor costs are less important in the capital-goods industries than in other industries) the price of capital goods will be raised in the same proportion as wages.[19] But the expectation of wage increases will produce labor-saving inventions as a method of embodying today's labor costs into tomorrow's production costs. Likewise, the expectation that higher wages will raise the prices of capital goods will stimulate the making of capital-saving inventions. The proportion of labor-saving and capital-saving inventions may not be changed, but the rise in the bargaining power of unions will increase the marginal efficiency of expenditures on discovery and thus will raise the proportion of the community's resources devoted to discovery.

Although the rate of discovery will be raised, it is not certain that the volume of investment will expand. The volume of investment depends upon

[19] See H. G. Hayes, "The Rate of Wages and the Use of Machinery," *American Economic Review*, XIII, 461–465, and P. H. Douglas, "The Effect of Wage Increases Upon Employment," *Proceedings of the American Economic Association*, 1939, pp. 138–157.

the prospects for profits over the long period. If employers expect wages to be promptly bargained upward whenever profits appear, their estimates of the marginal return on capital will be lowered and the proportion of the new discoveries which seem worth developing will be reduced. It is impossible to determine whether the net effect of a faster rate of discovery and a more selective exploitation of discoveries will be a larger or smaller volume of investment.

This analysis must be qualified by the observation that collective bargaining is still in a very rudimentary stage and that the policies of unions are likely to be influenced more by experience with collective bargaining than by the effect of the social-security program upon their bargaining power. For example, experience in selling labor is likely to alter the tendency of unions to underestimate the elasticity of the demand for labor and to overlook the fact that the elasticity over a period of several years is much greater than the elasticity at a given moment. Nor must the present crude and simple wage structures necessarily be regarded as final in a rapidly changing world. Wage systems may develop which greatly increase the interest of the unions in the volume of employment.

V

The following general conclusions stand out from this analysis:

1. About one fifth of the labor supply is mobile and works for more than one employer in the course of the year.

2. Despite the fact that the amount of movement in the labor market is considerably less than in prewar times, it is probably excessive. It is excessive in the main because it is forced and represents organization of work to an uneconomical extent upon a casual basis, but partly because much of it is uninformed.

3. Little is known about the ten million or more persons who supply the demand for temporary workers. Many of them undoubtedly have a principal occupation which dovetails with temporary employment outside of it. Some of them are seeking only part-time employment either for a few months of the year or part-time throughout the year. Some are young workers who have not succeeded in obtaining the status of regular employees. Until more complete and definite information concerning the suppliers of temporary labor becomes available, we shall be in the dark in deciding many important questions of policy.

4. The excessive amount of intermittent employment creates a strong

prima facie case in favor of experience rating. This does not mean that specific experience-rating provisions in existing legislation are well conceived.

5. The old-age provisions of the Social Security Act tend to break down barriers to movement—a desirable result. To some extent their effect will be counteracted by the old-age assistance plans which are based upon residence requirements that should be altered.

6. Definite information is lacking on how many and what kinds of people fail to qualify for unemployment benefits because their earnings or employment is insufficient.

7. Unemployment insurance is not likely to affect the mobility of most of the covered workers because the great majority who qualify for benefits have attachments to particular employers, which discourages them from moving, and because the duration of benefit payments is short. To some extent, however, unemployment benefits may discourage movement by encouraging workers to remain on the chance that more or less indefinite reemployment opportunities may become realities. This is likely to be a good result in a majority of cases.

8. The present trend is to make eligibility requirements for unemployment compensation stricter. Perhaps the trend should be reversed as the present laws seem to give protection to the workers least in need of it and not to reach those workers most in need of protection. The problem of more liberal eligibility requirements is complicated by the fact that many short-term or intermittent workers are not seeking full-time employment. Until more is known concerning the persons who fail because of insufficient earnings or employment to qualify for unemployment compensation, we are not in a position to judge the desirability of changes in eligibility requirements.

9. Relief is likely to affect the mobility of many thousands of persons of low employability. However, the effect of relief upon mobility must not be exaggerated. The rise in hiring standards will probably cause industry to draw on the huge labor reserves among the nonemployed and in agriculture before engaging the persons of low employability on relief. Hence, an expansion of the proportion of the population at work in nonagricultural pursuits to substantially higher figures than prevailed in the twenties will probably not reduce unemployment (over and above seasonal unemployment) to below 2.5 million.

10. Social-security taxes encroached upon profits to a moderate extent in 1937 and limited the expansion of business. The excess of collections over

disbursements was less in 1938, but the proportionate reduction in profits was greater. Although the social-security taxes were not an influence of first importance in intensifying the depression, the encroachment upon profits must have restricted commitments. In both 1937 and 1938, the social-security taxes substantially affected the profits of the railroads.

11. It is unlikely that the incidence of the payroll tax in the long run will be broadly diffused throughout the economy by higher costs which will induce larger income flows and thereby higher prices. For a period of fifteen years interest rates may be moderately affected by the program. After that time its effect upon interest rates will be negligible. In the area of competitive wage determination, the payroll tax will move the demand curve for labor to the left. To a small extent the payment of benefits will also move the supply curve of labor to the left. This will affect new enterprises far more than existing ones. It remains to be seen whether or not the program will materially affect the birth rate of new enterprises and the resiliency of our economy.

12. The social-security program will increase the bargaining power of trade unions and tend to reduce the interest of unions in the effect of their wage policies upon the volume of employment. It will tend to increase the rate of discovery but to reduce the proportion of discoveries that are worth exploiting. Its effect upon the volume of investment, therefore, is uncertain. Trade-union wage policies, however, are likely to be less affected by social security than by longer experience of unions with collective bargaining. But since the social-security program tends to diminish the concern of trade unions with the volume of employment, it creates the need for developing wage structures and forms of wage payment which increase the interest of unions in employment.

24

The Conditions of Expansion

American Economic Review, March 1942; presidential address delivered at the Fifty-fourth Annual Meeting of the American Economic Association, New York City, December 29, 1941.

IN 1940, output per manhour in American nonagricultural industries was roughly double that of 1920. In few periods of history has capacity to produce goods grown more rapidly than in the last twenty years. The industrial research staffs of American business in 1940 were nine times as large as in 1920, and so also were expenditures on research. At no time in the country's history had its capacity to increase production been so great. And yet the community which possessed this unparalleled productive capacity to improve methods and products did not glory in its strength. It was perplexed and baffled. Instead of looking forward confidently to achieving ever-rising standards of living, it dreaded the future. It asked whether investment opportunities were becoming permanently insufficient, whether the rules for achieving prosperity were undergoing fundamental changes, whether new conditions were making its economic institutions no longer workable.

This sense of doubt and inadequacy did not exist, in the United States at least, before 1929. It was created by the depression and by the disappointing recovery. The great national effort required by the war may prove to be precisely what is needed to restore the country's faith in its capacity to master great problems. Nevertheless, the task of winning the peace requires that we face frankly the questions raised by the depression and the disappointing recovery. Is it true that new conditions—the decline in geographical expansion, the drop in population growth, shifts in economic and political power, and changes in public policy—are radically altering the problem of maintaining employment, so that plans for the postwar world must envisage important changes in policies and institutions? The thesis of these remarks is that the answer to this question is a qualified yes.

I

Since the questions under consideration were first raised in this country by the disappointing recovery from the depression, it is convenient to begin our survey by a brief examination of some of the circumstances affecting recovery.

Whatever may be the ultimate effects of the decline in geographical expansion or the drop in the growth of population, neither of these influences appears to explain the depression or the disappointing recovery. Of course, it would have helped had there been another Mississippi Valley to develop. But no sudden change occurred in the state of our natural resources between the twenties and the thirties. Furthermore, older and more developed countries experienced a milder depression and recovered more completely.[1] As for the spectacular drop in the rate of population growth between the twenties and the thirties, evidence is lacking that it produced either an unfavorable shift in the consumption function or an unfavorable change in the slope of the function. Indeed, the number of nonemployed persons per member of the working force has shown no appreciable change in forty years.[2] The possibility that drop in the population growth might have retarded expansion by limiting the opportunity to widen capital is excluded partly by the fact that the increase in the number of families dropped only slightly, and partly by the large and persistent unemployment which characterized the period. As far as the labor supply was concerned, ample opportunity to widen capital existed.

To a considerable extent the depression and the unsatisfactory recovery are explained by conditions which do not reflect permanent changes in the economic environment. Failure of banks was probably the most important single influence in making the depression more severe in the United States than in most other countries. No one would contend, however, that the vulnerability of our banking system to depression was a necessary or permanent condition. The very severity of the depression and the bank failures which accompanied it were themselves major impediments to recovery. Consider

[1] By 1936, when twenty out of twenty-three countries reporting industrial production to the League of Nations had surpassed the output of 1929, industrial production in the United States was still 7 per cent below 1929. This country was in twenty-first place out of twenty-three countries in recovery from 1929. The industrial production in the United Kingdom in 1936 was 15.8 per cent above 1929; in Sweden, 35.0 per cent; in Finland, 39.0 per cent; in Denmark, 30.0 per cent; in Hungary, 18.4 per cent.

[2] The number of nonemployed for every gainfully employed worker has changed as follows: 1900, 2.61; 1910, 2.41; 1920, 2.54; 1930, 2.51; 1940, 2.50.

their effect in diminishing the fortunes of thousands of local capitalists and in making these men reluctant to risk the remainder of their resources. Small local capitalists have always been an important dynamic influence in the economy. Some indirect evidence of the effect of the depression upon local capitalists is provided by the income-tax returns. For example, if one compares the volume of income after taxes in 1931 and 1935, two years in which the national income was about $55 billion, one finds that incomes of $25,000 or more in the former year totaled $1.9 billion, and in the latter, $1.5 billion, or 21.9 per cent less.[3] These figures do not allow for capital gains and losses. Since the year 1931 was one in which capital losses were large, the realized incomes of over $25,000 before capital losses in 1931 were undoubtedly considerably more than $1.9 billion.

An impediment to recovery after 1933 that has been neglected is the scarcity of business savings. The principal source of venture capital always has been the plowed-back earnings of business enterprises. These have always been the spearhead of expansion, the prerequisite for drawing in funds from the outside. Although individual corporations were able to save, corporations as a whole had no savings in the entire period from 1929 to 1939. And between 1935 and 1938, dividend disbursements exceeded earnings by a billion a year.

Corporations failed to save in the main because during the twenties they had established high dividend rates which they were attempting to restore. The disbursements of dividends were encouraged in 1936 and 1937 by the undistributed profits tax. Of course, enterprises had depreciation allowances, but there were severe demands upon them because of the postponed maintenance from the worst years of the depression. Even when allowance is made for funds from depreciation allowances, the amounts available for reinvestment by corporations in 1935 and 1936 were far smaller than in 1923, when the national income was comparable in amount. In 1923, undistributed profits and depreciation of nonfinancial corporations were $5.3 billion. In 1935 and 1936, undistributed profits, depreciation, and depletion were $2.0 billion and $2.7 billion respectively.[4]

An important aspect of plowed-back earnings is that they are venture capital. They increase the equity of the business owners. Plowed-back earnings must be regarded as an even more important dynamic influence than the investments of the well-to-do. In the five years, 1922, to 1927, for example,

[3] Imre de Vegh, "Savings, Investment, and Consumption," *American Economic Review, Supplement*, XXX (February 1941), 238.

[4] T.N.E.C., *Hearings*, part 9, "Savings and Investment," p. 4039, Exhibit 582.

business savings were $13.4 billion.[5] Income of persons receiving more than $25,000 a year (after the payment of federal income taxes) in the same period was $21.9 billion.[6] If we assume that half of the incomes above $25,000 were saved, the investment-seeking funds from this source in the period 1922 to 1927, were not quite $11 billion.

Many economists have regarded business savings as a deflationary influence. In periods of contraction they probably are. The view that they are always a deflationary influence overlooks the fact that expansion begins with the plowing back of earnings. This is a preliminary step to getting outside capital. This is why business savings constitute the spearhead of expansion. In order to judge the full effect of plowing back of earnings, one must allow for its contagious effect. An expansion or improvement by one competitor compels rivals to make investment in an attempt to hold their position. This involves a "multiplier" which is different from the consumption multiplier used by Keynes. The Keynesian multiplier is based upon the amount of additional consumption which will be induced by a given expansion of investment. The investment multiplier indicates the additional investment that will be directly induced by a given expansion of investment.

The bank failures and other special circumstances were also largely responsible for the great amount of distress housing which hung over the market until 1937. This prolonged the depression in residential building long after the rest of the economy had revived. In the absence of this distress housing, building construction in the period 1934 to 1937 would undoubtedly have been two to three times the rate which prevailed. Since housing has always been the most important single outlet for investment-seeking funds, the persistence of the depression in housing was a main deterrent to recovery. Part of the difficulties in housing must be attributed to unsatisfactory financial instruments, particularly short-term second mortgages.

But conditions of a more permanent nature have influenced the recovery. The depression produced, or at least greatly accelerated, shifts in economic and political power which are likely to be permanent, and it enormously stimulated the making of economic policy by the government. These shifts in power and changes in public policy not only affected recovery from the depression, but altered the long-run problem of giving employment. It is important to examine their influence.

[5] Simon Kuznets, *National Income and Capital Formation, 1919–1935* (New York, 1937), p. 24.

[6] Imre de Vegh, p. 238.

II

On the whole, the shift in economic and political power impeded recovery. It did this in three principal ways. In the first place, the very fact that a great shift in power was going on created uncertainty concerning the long-term yield on capital and hence created an abnormal preference for short-term production plans. In this way, uncertainty narrowed investment opportunity and reduced temporarily the marginal return on capital. The extent to which the shifting of economic power and the imposition of new responsibilities upon business caused short-term plans to be preferred to long-term plans is roughly indicated by comparing for the two periods 1922–29 and 1933–39 expenditures on equipment in relation to expenditures on plant. Since expenditures on equipment are in large measure for replacement and expenditures on plant are in the main for the enlargement of capacity, the change in the relation between the two roughly illustrates the change in the importance of expenditures on long-run plans in relation to expenditures on current needs. Between 1922 and 1929, 81.3 cents was spent by business enterprises on plant for every dollar spent on equipment; between 1933 and 1939, only 44.5 cents was spent on plant for every dollar spent on equipment. Between 1922 and 1929, expenditures on plant were $29,774 million and on equipment $36,626 million; between 1933 and 1939, expenditures on plant were $10,850 million and on equipment $24,155 million.

In the second place, the shift in economic power altered in many plants the control of managements over labor costs and increased the difficulty of converting a rise of output into profits. It is instructive to compare the revival of profits after 1934 with the revival after 1921—two years in which national income was about $50 billion. In 1921, nonfinancial corporations had a deficit of $355 million, in contrast with a profit of $884 million in 1934. Between 1921 and 1923, a rise of the national income of $17.2 billion to a level of $70 billion produced a $5.5 billion gain in the profits of nonfinancial corporations. Between 1934 and 1937, a slightly larger rise in the national income ($21.1 billion) to a level of $71.4 billion produced a gain of $3 billion in profits. When profits come hard, the disposition to venture is weak.

The lesser success of enterprises in converting a rise of business into profits after 1933 than after 1921 is explained by a variety of circumstances, but very largely by the movements of labor efficiency and wages. Physical productivity per manhour grew twice as fast after 1921 as after 1933 or 1934, but wage rates went up twice as rapidly in the second period as in the first. These differences were not entirely compensated by price movements. Between 1921 and 1923, manhour productivity in manufacturing increased 3.06 per cent per year as against 2.0 per cent between 1934 and 1937. In mineral industries it increased 7.1 per cent a year in the first period and 5.0 per cent in the second; in railroading, 4.3 per cent in the first period and 3.8 per cent in the second.[7] Hourly earnings in manufacturing increased 3.2 per cent between 1921 and 1923, according to the National Industrial Conference Board. Between 1934 and 1937, hourly earnings in manufacturing increased 15.7 per cent according to the U. S. Bureau of Labor Statistics, and 19.6 per cent according to the National Industrial Conference Board.

In some respects it is more satisfactory to compare the period 1921 to 1926 with the period 1933 to 1937. In the first period manhour productivity in manufacturing increased 4.3 per cent a year as against 1.7 per cent in the second; in the mineral industries, it increased 8.0 per cent a year in the first period and 3.7 per cent in the second; in railroading, it increased 3.3 per cent per year in the first period and 3.0 per cent in the second. Between 1921 and 1926, hourly earnings in manufacturing rose 8.4 per cent; between 1933 and 1937, 40 per cent.

In the case of electric light and power, productivity per manhour apparently increased more rapidly following 1933 than following 1921—6.9 per cent a year between 1933 and 1937, instead of 2.8 per cent a year as between 1921 and 1926. The actual difference was probably considerably less than the figures indicate because there was much more construction in the industry in 1926 than in 1937. Some of the construction is done by outside contractors whose employees are not counted as in the industry. Much of it, however, is done by employees of the utilities. Since the construction is not counted as part of the product of the industry, the use of employees of the industry tends to reduce the output per manhour. The changing proportion of employees working on noncurrent operations (together with the changing proportion engaged on maintenance and repairs as maintenance is now postponed and then accelerated) makes all figures on manhour productivity more or less unreliable. In the case of comparisons between 1921–26, on the one hand, and 1933–37, on the other, the changes in construction and in maintenance policy probably cause the difference in increase in efficiency to appear to be less than it really was.

Finished goods declined relative to raw materials in both recoveries (as is usual) but more so in the second recovery than in the first. The following are the indexes of wholesale prices of raw materials and finished goods:

[7] S. Bell, *Productivity, Wages, and National Income* (Washington, 1940), pp. 269, 271, 274.

Year	*Raw materials*	*Finished goods*
1921	88.3	103.3
1922	96.0	96.5
1923	98.5	99.2
1926	100.0	100.0
1933	56.5	70.5
1934	68.6	78.2
1935	77.1	82.2
1936	79.9	82.0
1937	84.8	87.2

A comparison of 1926 and 1937 is of interest. Output per manhour in manufacturing in 1937 was apparently 33.2 per cent above 1926; hourly earnings 22.4 per cent above 1926. Finished goods were slightly higher relative to raw materials than in 1926. Nevertheless, nonfinancial corporations made profits of only $3.8 billion on sales of $108.4 billion in 1937, as against profits of $5.8 billion on sales of $106.2 billion in 1926—a margin of 3.54 cents per dollar of sales in 1937 and of 5.44 cents in 1926.

During the period when shifts in economic power and public policy substantially reduced the attractiveness of long-range plans, government fiscal policy was developing in ways that greatly reduced the marginal efficiency of capital and especially diminished the attractiveness of ventures involving considerable uncertainty and risk. To begin with, a large deficit in the regular budget persisted undiminished, except for one year, in the face of a substantial rise in the national income and of large increases in taxes. Deficit financing is too new to be well understood. We are still in the stage of trying to find out why the course of events does not correspond to the theoretical models. Nevertheless, it is possible to see why deficit financing at the best is an unreliable device and why it may do little good and may even impede an expansion of privately produced income. Since the saving function is considerably more elastic relative to national income than the investment function, a relatively large deficit is necessary to raise the national income by a small amount. But a deficit may cause the investment function to shift to the left, especially if it arouses the expectation of higher taxes and if the government has manifested a strong propensity to tax profits. In this event, all or nearly all of the stimulus of the deficit may be canceled. Satisfactory information on the saving function is virtually impossible to obtain because the relation of consumption to income payments has been affected in recent years by changes in taxes and other conditions. These changes may or may not be permanent. Further changes appear to be ahead. At any rate, they indicate that attempts to deduce the saving function from time series are likely to have little significance for the future. Such information as is available indicates that in the range between a national income of $60 billion and $80 billion there is an increase of about 40 cents in saving for a one dollar increase in income. Hence, a persistent deficit (or an increase in investment) of $4 billion is necessary to raise the national income by about $10 billion. If the persistence of the deficit were to produce an unfavorable shift in the investment function sufficient to cut private investment from $7 billion to $5.25 billion (or 25 per cent) at a national income of $70 billion, almost half the benefit of the deficit would be lost. A shift of even greater magnitude in the investment function might easily be produced by expectations of higher taxes. During the last decade deficits have been working most of the time against a sharply declining marginal propensity to spend or invest additional income, as the drop in the velocity of bank deposits outside New York from 28.0 in 1933 to 22.6 in 1939 and 21.6 in 1940 plainly indicates. Of course, the drop in the marginal propensity to spend must be attributed to a variety of causes, but one of them seems to have been a conjunction of persistent deficits with a disposition to increase those taxes which must directly limit the marginal efficiency of capital. When neither rising national income nor rising tax rates reduced the deficit, who could avoid concluding that substantially higher taxes were ahead and that, in view of the record, they might fall in substantial measure on profits?

To the influence of the deficit in producing an unfavorable shift in the investment function must be addded tax changes well designed to discourage innovations and experimentation and to reduce the attractiveness of risky ventures. Between 1929 and 1936, the effective rate of the corporate income tax was virtually doubled. The base rate, which was 11 per cent in 1929, was raised to 12 per cent in 1930 and 13.75 per cent in 1932. The consolidated return was abolished for all corporations except railroads in 1934, intercorporate dividends were taxed in 1935, a tax on undistributed profits was added in 1936. Other changes which increased the effective burden, such as abolition of the loss carry-over and restriction on credits for capital losses, are discussed below. The corporate income tax was further increased by substantial additions to the base rates in 1938 and 1939, not to mention the subsequent increases required by the defense program. It is no answer to say that the tax is eventually shifted, because it is passed on only by restricting the volume of investment. And since corporate profits are produced in a large measure by innovation and experimentation, doubling the tax on corporate profits amounted to doubling the tax on innovation and experimentation.

Some changes in tax laws were especially well designed to penalize chance-taking. The loss carry-over provision in the corporate income tax was limited to one year in 1932, abolished in 1933, and not restored until 1938. Capital losses, which had been fully deductible up to 1932, were deductible only to a very restricted degree throughout the entire critical period between 1932 and 1938.

Similar changes on an even more drastic scale were made in individual income-tax rates. Until 1932, the highest surtax rate was 20 per cent, applicable on incomes over $100,000. In 1932 surtaxes were greatly raised. They were raised again in 1934 and 1936. Dividends from corporations were made subject to the normal tax in 1936. By 1938, the normal tax and surtax took 35 per cent of additional income immediately above $50,000; 51 per cent immediately above $74,000; and 62 per cent immediately above $100,000. How drastically tax increases reduced the marginal returns on investments in equities by the persons who did the most saving is illustrated by the fact that by 1938 a man with an income of $50,000 would need a yield of 8 per cent before his tax to obtain a return of 5.4 per cent. At the same time, the capital-loss provisions of the income tax were modified to narrow greatly the opportunity to deduct capital losses.[8] In other words, the government was greatly increasing the difficulty of adding to one's capital by successful ventures and at the same time was severely limiting the possibility of charging unsuccessful ventures against successful ones. Can one imagine a better arrangement for encouraging investors to avoid venturesome commitments?

III

What of the long-range outlook? If to shifts in economic and political power, which have already created difficult problems, is added a narrowed opportunity for extensive investment, does not the problem of providing

[8] Up to 1932 capital losses could be deducted in full for periods up to two years. Above two years the taxpayer had the option of paying 12.5 per cent as a tax or deducting 12.5 per cent as a loss. The act of 1932 greatly restricted the deduction of short-term losses and the act of 1934 restricted the deductions of all capital losses to the amount of capital gains plus $2,000. Alexander Sachs stresses the deterring effects in the act of 1938 of the disconnection between long-term and short-term gains and losses. If a long-term gain and a short-term loss are realized in the same year, the latter cannot be used to offset the former. Furthermore, if the short-term gain is not realized, the enterpriser is exposed to the danger that, in the event of the gain's becoming a loss, it can be credited only to the extent of 15 per cent or 20 per cent.

employment become so formidable as to require great changes in policies and institutions?

One may assert with reasonable confidence, I think, that the consumption function will slowly become more favorable to employment. For more than a generation the propensity to consume has been rising just about fast enough to prevent the increase in per capita incomes from causing a drop in the proportion of the national income currently consumed. It is noteworthy, however, that in the twenties, despite the rapid rise in per capita income, capital formation was relatively less than in the preceding decade—19.6 per cent of gross product as against 22.8 per cent.[9] In the postwar world, the propensity to consume will be higher than in the twenties. Corporations will be hampered, as they have been for nearly a decade, in devoting part of their income to capital formation by pressure from stockholders to maintain dividend rates. It is not generally known that throughout the recovery until 1939 dividend disbursements each year exceeded corporate earnings by a billion dollars or more. Postwar tax collections by the federal government will probably be at least twice prewar. The additional amounts will be collected largely from the middle incomes. Satisfactory data are not available for estimating how much a higher tax burden would reduce savings in the middle incomes. One may roughly estimate, however, that in the case of incomes from $10,000 to $50,000 a year every additional dollar taken in taxes will reduce the volume of saving by 25 to 50 cents. The higher taxes will tend also to affect the slope of the function, making less pronounced the rise in the volume of savings which accompanies a rise in income. It might appear that this change, while making the economy more responsive to any stimulus, would also make it more unstable. This tendency will be largely offset, however, by the spread of unemployment insurance. Much of the saving of recent years has been temporary rather than permanent. This is

[9] Simon Kuznets, "Capital Formation, 1879–1938," *University of Pennsylvania Bicentennial Conference* (1939), p. 70. The real rise in the individual propensity to consume was considerably more than is indicated by the figures of gross capital formation. The change in individual propensities to consume cannot be inferred entirely from the proportion of output devoted to capital formation. In the twenties a considerable increase in public capital formation (roads and bridges) was financed by new taxes such as gasoline taxes. Such capital formation, of course, represents no increased disposition on the part of individuals to save. It may be thought that the proportion of income devoted to consumption was abnormally high in the twenties because of the making of purchases postponed during the war and the liquidation of Liberty Bonds for that purpose. This may have been true for the first several years of the decade. But annual figures on capital formation indicate that the proportion of output devoted to capital formation tended to decline between 1923 and 1929, despite a rise in per capita real income. Capital formation by corporations was facilitated by the fact that managements were not under pressure to restore previously high dividend rates and hence were fairly free to plow back a large proportion of increased earnings.

true of the saving represented by premiums for life insurance, annuities, and pensions which in the main are intended to be consumed rather than to provide permanent sources of income. Benefit payments of life-insurance companies are gradually catching up with their premium receipts and eventually the difference between the two will be little greater than the operating expenses of the companies.[10]

Too much importance, however, must not be attached to prospective changes in the consumption function. If there is a decline in the disposition to take risks in order to increase capital, and a rise in the desire to avoid risks in order to conserve capital, a drop in thriftiness may be accompanied by a rise in unemployment. This is simply one way of saying that a favorable shift in the consumption function may be offset by an unfavorable shift in the schedule of liquidity preference. The desire for security of principal will be satisfied to a considerable extent by holding idle cash in the event that venture capital is not sufficiently abundant to provide a satisfactory cushion for new fixed-income securities. There are several elements in thriftiness and they may change in relative importance. The kind of thriftiness that does most good is that which is based upon an attempt to increase one's capital. It is possible, of course, to have steadily increasing unemployment because of an insufficiency of savings. The annual increments of investment-seeking funds may not be sufficient to provide plant and equipment necessary to enable the increment of workers to earn the prevailing scale of wages.

The large shift in the consumption function in the United Kingdom between the prewar and the postwar decades, as indicated by Colin Clark's estimates, did not prevent the persistence of a large amount of unemployment throughout the twenties.[11] Too much attention has been paid by recent economic theory to mere changes in the amount of thriftiness and too little to changes in the kind of thriftiness and to shifts in the propensity to invest.

[10] Prior to 1929 the premiums of life-insurance companies were increasing far faster than payments to policyholders. Between 1929 and 1940 the payments of life-insurance companies to policyholders increased more than premium payments. Between 1929 and 1940 total premium income of life-insurance companies increased from $3,350 million to $3,944 million, or $594 million. Payments to policyholders increased from $1,962 million to $2,681 million, or $719 million (*The Spectator Life Insurance Yearbook*, 1935, pp. 414–415; and 1941, p. i).

The disposition to save in years immediately after the war will be affected by the extent to which individuals and business enterprises reduce their debts during the war. Reduction of private indebtedness will assist in financing the war, provided creditors put the proceeds into government bonds. Reduction in mortgage indebtedness and installment debts should be encouraged both to finance the war and to create the basis for a high level of consumption in the years after the war. A large rise in the price level during the war may have the net effect of raising the postwar propensity to save because it will probably induce some attempts to restore the purchasing power of savings or of the income from savings.

[11] Colin Clark, *National Income and Outlay* (London, 1937), p. 185.

Liquidity preference appears to be sensitive to changes in investment opportunity. An improvement in the marginal efficiency of capital not only produces more investment under a given state of liquidity preference but also actually changes the state of liquidity preference; that is, produces a shift in the schedule of liquidity preference. Likewise, a drop in the marginal efficiency of capital produces a rise in liquidity preference. Furthermore, a rise in liquidity preference produces a drop in the marginal efficiency of capital and hence a further rise in liquidity preference. Because the marginal efficiency of capital and the schedule of liquidity preference are not independent variables, a change in either one of them is more important in determining the capacity of the economy to expand than changes in the consumption function.

The effect of the drop in the rate of population growth upon investment opportunity might seem to depend in the main upon how rapidly the marginal return on capital falls as capital per worker increases. Except for the investigations of Douglas, little work has been done on this point. The problem, of course, is not how marginal efficiency of investment behaves under static conditions but how it behaves under the rate and kind of technological change and the price movements that may be expected to occur. It is highly probable (though not inevitable) that technological change will increase the amount of capital that each worker can advantageously manage because inventions consist largely of making apparatus more automatic and adding automatic attachments. Douglas estimates that an increase of 270 per cent in fixed capital per worker in manufacturing between 1899 and 1922 was accompanied by a drop of 44 per cent in the marginal physical productivity of capital.[12] This is not a rapid drop, and it occurred when technological research was on a far smaller scale than it is now. It is interesting to observe that the drop in the marginal physical productivity of capital was accompanied by a large rise in interest rates.[13] This contrast between the movement of interest rates and the marginal physical productivity of capital suggests in how great measure the marginal return on capital is determined by price trends and by expectations.[14] Of course, if the United States by any

[12] P. H. Douglas, *The Theory of Wages* (New York, 1934), pp. 121, 125, 130, and 146.

[13] Macaulay's index of the adjusted yield of railroad bonds rose from 3.182 in 1900 to 5.168 in 1920. F. R. Macaulay, *The Movements of Interest Rates, Bond Yields and Stock Prices in the United States Since 1856* (New York, 1938), pp. A 152, A 157.

[14] As men were thrown out of work in the capital-goods industries through failure of the increase in the working force to create opportunities for extensive investment, the unemployed would become available for employment in new plants and on new machines and thus would furnish opportunities for extensive investment. But the idle plant produced by the contraction of employment would limit the return on new investment and thus tend to discourage it. Whether

chance were able to arrange its affairs to permit the exportation of capital on a considerable scale in the postwar world, the problem of opportunities for extensive investment would be a generation or two in the future.

Technological research is growing rapidly, as the ninefold increase in personnel in twenty years indicates, and it will undoubtedly continue to grow rapidly. Indeed it must now be regarded as one of the most important instruments of economic adjustment. But even today there are only about thirty-five hundred industrial research laboratories in the country. Out of over $100 billion of sales by corporations only $300 million goes into industrial research, or less than one third of one per cent. Virtually half of all industrial research is done by four industries—chemicals, petroleum, electrical apparatus, and electrical communications. In 1940, there were about fifteen thousand chemists in industry and about the same number of engineers, but only two thousand physicists.[15] Some people believe that the present war will put the physicists into industry in much the same way that World War I put the chemists into industry. Private enterprise has never yet had to face squarely the question of whether it is able to provide over the long term the amount of employment which the community expects. When it is confronted with this question, the expansion of industrial research may be considerable. Likewise one may expect considerable expansion of "new product" departments charged with the responsibility of discovering opportunities for new products and assisting in their development. Only a few concerns now possess such departments. Little has been attempted by public policy to make industrial research more easily available to small enterprises. All of this points to the conclusion that industrial research is in its infancy and that it offers a way of providing investment opportunities that will be far more important in the future than in the past.

IV

By the end of the war, roughly one third of the payrolls of industry will be directly determined by collective bargaining. Wage rates in many nonunion plants will be sensitive to changes in union scales. The marginal efficiency of capital depends, among other things, upon the control of man-

---

or not unemployment produced extensive investment, therefore, would depend upon the terms on which the unemployed would accept work. They would need to be willing to accept employment at sufficiently below current rates to make new investment opportunities attractive despite the existence of idle plant and machines.

[15] National Resources Planning Board, *Research—A National Resource*, II, *Industrial Research* (Washington, 1941), pp. 176–177.

agement over costs. In the face of large and powerful labor organizations, will American business possess sufficient control over costs to maintain a high marginal efficiency of capital? Or will unions keep investment opportunity limited by promptly converting any increase in demand for labor into higher wages? In other words, will unions prevent any expansion of demand from producing more employment by causing it to produce higher wages?

Many economists believe that bargained changes in costs are bound to be completely translated into higher prices, so that changes in the general wage level produce solely price effects and not output or employment effects. The relationship between bargained changes in costs and prices is undoubtedly the most important issue in the theory of employment. The conclusion that rises in costs are translated into higher prices so that the return on investments is not affected presupposes, among other things, a self-contained economy. But even in a self-contained economy, the assumed relationship between costs and prices requires a theory of liquidity preference which is not convincing. It is assumed that higher wages reduce liquidity preference and that the shift in the schedule of liquidity preference so increases the volume of active deposits that prices rise in proportion to the advance in wages. All of this amounts to assuming that the volume of deposits held idle is a residual and that it is independent of the purchasing power of the idle deposits.[16] These assumptions are far from realistic. If general increases in the wage level cannot be counted on to produce offsetting increases in expenditures and prices, a rise in labor's bargaining power will tend to reduce the marginal efficiency of capital.[17] The resulting unfavorable shift in the

[16] Suppose that the first reaction of managements to a rise in costs were to advance prices in proportion. To sustain the higher price level the public would have to be willing to hold a smaller amount of real purchasing power in cash. It is not clear why a rise in prices should produce this result, except as higher prices reduce the purchasing power of incomes. This might produce some tendency to reduce idle deposits. But the drop in the purchasing power of money would also limit the decrease in idle deposits since the quantity of money which people desire to hold idle is presumably affected by its purchasing power. Equilibrium would eventually be reached at some point below the original volume of output and employment, but with money expenditures somewhat above the original level. In the above analysis, it is assumed that the demand for assets in the form of idle deposits is such that idle deposits drop as the purchasing power of money drops. It is possible, however, that a drop in the purchasing power of money will cause an increase in the number of dollars held idle. In that event an effort to pass on an increase in costs in the form of higher prices would produce an even greater drop in output and employment.

[17] It is conceivable that wages might get so low and that such a large proportion of the national income might go to savings and such a small part to labor that further reductions in wages would cause more than a proportionate drop in total expenditures. As the increase in investment-seeking funds produced a drop in the marginal return on investments, the proportion of money held idle would increase. Eventually it would increase so rapidly as more than to offset the effect of the drop in costs and prices upon the physical volume of transactions. Hence two zones might be distinguished: one in which expenditures change proportionately less than

investment function is not offset within the usual range of national income by the favorable effect of the redistribution upon the savings function.

The problem which confronts the individual investor or the enterprise is not the effect of general increases in wages on prices, but the effect of the spread of union organization upon the probable return from a particular investment. When one examines this matter, it is difficult to avoid the conclusion that large and powerful unions tend to reduce the marginal efficiency of capital. It is true that collective bargaining frequently raises plant efficiency by giving management better information about conditions and by giving representatives of the men an opportunity to point out mistakes of management. Nevertheless, powerful unions increase the likelihood that successful concerns will have to share their prosperity with the employees. Until recently there has been no offsetting protection against losses. The development of the policy of union-management cooperation during the last twenty years has interesting theoretical implications. Most of the cooperative plans have been started in high-cost plants. They have been a way by which the workers in these plants tried to safeguard their jobs. If union-management cooperation were to become widespread in high-cost plants, it would go far to offset reduction in the marginal efficiency of capital produced by the encroachment of unions on the profits of the most successful concerns. For the time being, however, one must conclude that the spread of unionization tends to reduce the marginal return of capital.

Are unions likely to reduce the return so seriously as to limit materially the capacity of the economy to expand? That is a possibility, but not a necessity, as the experience of the United Kingdom and Sweden shows. One may assert with confidence, I think, that even a large and powerful labor movement will be less harmful to expected returns on investments than the shift in power that has been going on since 1933. Such a period of shifting creates great uncertainty over the future of costs. In the face of such uncertainty managers may be more reluctant to make long-term commitments than they would be after unions are better established and stronger but when economic power is no longer shifting. It is to be observed also that the large

changes in wages and in which wage increases are unfavorable to employment; and one in which expenditures change proportionately more than changes in wages and in which wage increases are favorable to employment. In the former zone, the usual one, the effect of wage changes on the investment function would not be offset by their effect upon the savings function; in the latter zone, the effect of wage changes upon the investment function would be offset by their effect on the savings function. The latter zone would appear to be an unstable one because wage increases, by reducing unemployment, would produce more wage increases and because wage cuts, by producing more unemployment, would produce more wage cuts. As a matter of fact, wages in relation to prices apparently never get down into the zone of instability.

wage increases between 1936 and 1937, when the hourly earnings of factory workers increased by 12 per cent, were not in the main directly produced by trade unions. In large measure they represented an unsuccessful effort on the part of employers to stop the spread of labor unions. As a matter of fact, the wage increases seem to have stimulated the growth of unions by convincing the men that there was a lot of easy money around which they might get by organizing. Some employers who gave a wage increase to prevent their men from organizing had to give a second increase after the men had formed a union.

There is nothing fixed or inevitable about the way in which collective bargaining operates and the effects which it produces. I have in mind a case where union policy has reduced output per manhour over 40 per cent in seven years. I have in mind also a steel mill where the president recently said that he would not sell his plan of union-management cooperation for a million dollars. Such are the possible extremes. Management has it within its power to influence greatly the way in which collective bargaining operates. As managers become reconciled to the necessity of dealing with trade unions, they may be expected to be increasingly successful in gaining help on operating problems from unions. The effect of collective bargaining upon the marginal efficiency of capital will also depend upon the willingness of employers to organize. American employers have always been reluctant to organize for the purpose of dealing with labor. Most of their existing bargaining organizations are flimsy affairs with little discipline and meager resources. The success of collective bargaining in Sweden and the United Kingdom is largely attributable to the way in which the return on capital has been protected by large and powerful organizations of employers.

The readiness with which an economy translates the results of technological progress into new investment, the resistance which it shows to depression, and the ease with which it recovers depend in large measure upon the willingness of individual enterprises to increase their expenditures for equipment and for the development of new products more or less regardless of the general business situation—to step out in advance of other concerns and make commitments. In other words, it depends upon the relative attractiveness of venturesome and daring production plans in comparison with cautious production plans. The dynamic influence of venturesome production plans has been underrated in recent economic analysis, largely because the contagious effect of investment by one firm in compelling offsetting investments by rivals has received little attention.

The government, through the way in which it raises its money, has wide discretion in determining the relative attractiveness of different types of production plans. This is especially true when the government takes such a large proportion of individual and corporate incomes as it now does. Taxes in recent years have been remarkably well designed to bear heavily on any enterprise which displays daring, which backs an innovation or an experiment, especially an experiment which is pretty certain to experience losses for several years. The loss carry-over provisions of the corporate income tax could be modified, for example, to facilitate substantially the accumulation of capital by new concerns. In times of poor economic visibility and rapid technological change, much is to be said for a flexible treatment of depreciation allowances. Enterprises should be encouraged to write off half of the cost of new assets during the first three or four years of their life. This would increase the subsequent tax liability of the concern, but it would make uncertain ventures less risky. A large reduction in the tax on that part of corporate profits spent for plant and equipment (the reverse of the undistributed profits tax) would help restore the practice of plowing back earnings—so important if new concerns are to furnish stiff competition for old ones and important in the case of all concerns in stimulating the kind of investment which starts expansion and improves the ability of the enterprise to attract funds from the outside. A similar principle might be applied to the personal income tax. In the case of this tax there is conflict between the community's interest in the principle of ability to pay and its interest in expansion. Stiff surtaxes greatly reduce the marginal efficiency of any investments made by large-income recipients. These surtaxes are in conflict with prevailing theories of liquidity preference. It would not be necessary to repeal the surtaxes. The attractiveness of uncertain ventures to large-income recipients (or even persons in the middle brackets) could be increased by a substantial reduction in the surtax on that part of income invested in nonrefunding equities. The effect of the tax upon production plans depends in substantial measure upon whether enterprises are discounting increases or decreases in taxes. Postwar adjustments will be greatly assisted if enterprises are discounting decreases in taxes. Certainly the prospect of tax reductions was an important stimulus to business during the five years following the First World War. If one may assume postwar federal budgets not in excess of $14 to $15 billion a year, the prospect of reduction in taxes would be good.

The ability of the community to supply itself with enterprise will depend also upon the organization of the capital market. At the present time this is in a state of flux, partly because of recent legislation and partly because changes in the tax system require that machinery be developed for obtaining venture capital from income brackets which have provided little of it. It is important to realize that neither the volume of investment opportunities nor the volume of investment-seeking funds is fixed. Each is the result of discovery and of effort. It takes work and money to find good credit risks which could use funds and to find people who might be persuaded to buy particular types of securities. Many men make their living by doing these things. How dynamic the economy is able to become will depend partly upon how good a job is done in adapting the machinery of the capital market to new conditions.

To a very substantial extent, of course, the opportunities for investment will be affected by the policies which the United States elects to pursue toward the rest of the world after the war. If conditions are reasonably stable, opportunities will exist for large international movements of capital and for extensive investment on a broad scale. Indeed, the potentialities of this are enormous. Here we see perhaps more plainly than ever how dependent investment opportunity is upon policy, for the problem of providing the basis for large international capital movements which will greatly raise the standard of living of the entire world is, in the main, a political one.

V

One may infer from this survey that the outlook for employment during the postwar generation is not necessarily dark. In fact, it may turn out to be distinctly good, especially in the event, by no means improbable, that the country is able to create favorable conditions for large capital exports. Should the defeat of Germany mean domination of Europe by Russia, the economic future of the United States will be determined in great measure by Russian economic and political policy. If American businessmen are sufficiently ingenious to develop a large market here for Russian goods and if Russia does not revive her policy of world revolution, the possibilities of a large and mutually advantageous exchange of goods between Russia and the United States are bright. The prewar experience of Germany, the United Kingdom, and the United States indicates that trade need not be in the main between industrial and agricultural countries.

But my purpose in this analysis has not been to speculate about the future, because anything can happen. Rather my purpose has been to focus your attention upon certain characteristics of our economy. The conclusion to which I invite your attention is that most of the variables which determine the amount of private employment and the rate of expansion are influenced within wide range by policies, public and private. This is true of the relation between costs and prices; of the way in which cost curves shift in response to changes in demand; of the quantity of resources, public and private, devoted to technological discovery; of the disposition to venture, and the relative preference for various types of production plans; of the position and income elasticity of the savings function. No fixed or inevitable values may be assumed for these determinants of expansion. Hence there is no fixed amount of investment opportunity, no fixed willingness to take chances, no fixed demand for goods or for people to make goods. All depend upon conditions, and all may be greatly influenced by policy.

Some of the policies which determine the volume of employment represent a deliberate choice between employment and something else. There may be a clash, for example, between the interest of the community in full employment and its preference concerning the distribution of wealth. Since tax changes which would raise the marginal return on investments by the well-to-do would facilitate the acquisition of large fortunes, the community may accept a limited amount of private employment in order to achieve a more even distribution of wealth. One of the broadest conflicts in the community is the competition between the old and the new. Much intervention on behalf of the government is simply a way of protecting the old from the competition of the new. Of course, the farther the government goes in protecting the old from the new, the more it limits investment opportunity and, to that extent, employment. But most of the community may prefer less private employment to a faster rate of change. The policies which represent a deliberate and informed choice between employment and something else are not our problem. Many of the policies which affect employment, however, are not intended to do so. The groups which produce the policies are too small to consider their consequences for employment, and yet the total effect of the policies of thousands of organizations of businessmen and farmers, thousands of local unions, and many states, counties, and cities upon cost-price relationships and upon the opportunity to experiment and to introduce innovations is considerable.

Because many policies are pursued without regard to their effect upon the general level of employment, the persistence of unemployment cannot be counted upon to produce the changes in policies which are needed to increase employment. If the bargaining power of labor, for example, is too great in relation to the rate of technological discovery, so that the investment function does not permit a satisfactory level of employment, there is no automatic change in policies to reduce the bargaining power of labor, to raise the rate of discovery, or to produce a shift in the propensity to save. These things *may* happen, but they cannot be counted upon to happen. In fact, the response of policies to unemployment may in the main be bad: unemployment may provoke a flood of attempts to protect markets by restrictions which narrow the area of innovation, cut the marginal return on investments, and produce unfavorable shifts in the schedule of liquidity preference. Numerous examples of this kind of response to unemployment can be gathered from the recent depression both in the United States and abroad. The most conspicuous illustrations can be drawn from the field of international economic policy, but many others could be cited.

If the level of employment is unsatisfactory from the standpoint of the community, who is to assume responsibility for seeing that policies are modified or broadened so as to permit the largest amount of employment compatible with the other interests of the community? To some extent the government can assume this responsibility. The government has three principal ways of affecting the general level of employment: (1) the method of correction, (2) the method of compensation, and (3) the method of stimulation.

The method of correction involves making changes in public policies or forcing changes in private policies in order to increase employment or, put in other words, altering the distribution of economic advantages in order to increase the total amount of income. One might visualize as an ideal a central planning agency charged with the responsibility of reviewing the obstacles limiting the amount of enterprise and of estimating how much sacrifice by different groups would produce how much expansion in employment. These reports might be referred to representative agencies to determine which interests to sacrifice for the enlargement of income. Many public policies—tax policies, regulation of security markets, price-pegging schemes—were adopted without an appraisal of their probable effect upon employment and even without a suspicion that there was a problem of maintaining employment. Recognition of the existence of such a problem may lead the community to prefer to revise many of its policies. The policy of correction would also involve the assertion of some public control over private policies. There are various ways by which the government might exercise such control, but on the whole the possibilities are limited because, in many cases, control cannot be accomplished without a large number of detailed regulations which would be impracticable to administer.

The method of compensation involves an attempt by deficit financing to offset the failure of private enterprise to provide a satisfactory amount of employment; note that I do not say "full employment." Strictly speaking, the method of compensation should not be used until the community has gone as far as it is willing to go in applying the policy of correction. Otherwise, the policy may divert the government from thoroughly exploring the possibility of enforcing changes in private policies that would raise the level of employment. In fact, the persistent use of the policy of compensation may stimulate a development of private policies that are unfavorable to employment. Why should an up-and-coming labor movement, for example, permit the demand created by public spending to produce more employment rather than higher wages?

The use of deficits to compensate for a chronic shortage of investment opportunities raises very different economic issues from those involved in the use of deficits in periods of depression when there are idle resources of all sorts. Although the tax expectations aroused by a persistent use of deficits do not necessarily reduce the marginal efficiency of capital, as a practical matter it is very difficult to prevent this effect. There are also likely to be important differences in the economic effects of public and private investment which prevent the former from being merely an offset to the latter. Private investment, being intended to yield a profit, represents an attempt to anticipate trends in consumer demand and thus to keep the pattern of productive capacity adjusted to the pattern of consumer demand.[18] To the extent that this happens, private investment tends to produce a rise in output and employment rather than in prices. Public investment, on the other hand, does not as a rule represent an attempt to adjust productive capacity to consumer demand. Hence, if public spending occurs on a large scale after plant is fairly well employed, its effect will be in the main to raise prices rather than to increase employment. Consequently, the policy of compensation seems to have a much narrower application than most of its proponents have assumed.

The method of stimulation involves expenditures by the government which are designed to produce favorable shifts in the private-investment function. Expenditures on roads or airports and, in some instances at least, on rivers and harbors are an example, but the outlay in fact may take a wide variety of forms. The support of agricultural or industrial research is an example. Note that the efficacy of the method of stimulation does not depend upon the expenditure's being financed by borrowing. The essence of the method is that a public expenditure (or loan) is creating a private-investment

[18] How imperfectly even private investment accomplishes this result is indicated by the jerkiness with which growth occurs. Partly because the pattern of productive capacity does not accurately fit the pattern of consumer demand (and partly because of the nature of costs), the economy during periods of expansion usually presents a mixture of unemployment and inflation.

opportunity which would not otherwise exist. The method is not a new one, but it is susceptible to considerable expansion.

This brief review of the possibilities of public policy leads one to the conclusion that the range within which the government can influence the level of employment is broad but, nevertheless, in a nonregimented economy, limited. Given a fairly rapid rate of technological change, a fairly even balance of power between employers and workers, and a well-organized capital market, the community with the help of the government may maintain a satisfactory level of employment. But we cannot be sure. This brings us to the final and most basic consideration. Both what the government needs to do and what the voters will permit the government to do depend in the last analysis upon the valuations which individuals place upon group interests and common interests.[19] There are two ways in which groups may advance their interests. One is based upon a high valuation of one's special interests and involves improving the bargaining position of the group for the purpose of getting a larger share of an income flow with little regard to the effect upon the size of the total income flow. The other is based upon a high valuation of general interests and involves restraint in pressing special claims which conflict with general interests.

It is not for the economist *qua* economist to quarrel with the valuations which individuals and groups place upon their interests. He is, however, within his scientific rights when he points out that these valuations have profound economic effects. They determine both the methods of production which it is possible to use and the quantity of goods that can be produced. High valuations of special interests can throttle production and render the government and everyone else incapable of providing a satisfactory level of employment. High valuations of common interests will produce public and private policies that will prevent the problem of long-term unemployment.

Is it at all thinkable that groups of workers, employers, and farmers in dealing with one another and in pressing claims for legislation will be limited or guided to a substantial extent by concern for the national income? Or as these groups become more and more highly organized and more and more conscious of their particular interests, will they become less and less disposed to place high valuations on common interests? No one knows. Larger units of decision would help. Wage policy, for example, which is now made by groups too small to feel much responsibility for the general

[19] It is not intended to deny that the valuations of the individual member of a group are molded largely by the leaders of the group. Consequently, the kind of valuations of group and common interests which emerge are determined in large measure by the kind of men who lead groups.

level of employment, might be made by units such as the United States Chamber of Commerce and the National Association of Manufacturers, on the one hand, and the American Federation of Labor and the Congress of Industrial Organizations, on the other.[20] Perhaps new machinery must be invented in order that all groups may agree on the restraints that shall be placed upon their special interests and in order to make possible new ways of promoting common interests.

A lively concern for common interests by well-organized and self-conscious special groups may seem a utopian dream; but in an economy in which the policies of government and of large private groups determine employment, what substitute is there for it? The possibilities of modern technology are tremendous. If these possibilities can be realized, no one can doubt that we are on the threshold of gaining a far better standard of living than man has ever known. Nothing can prevent us from realizing the possibilities of modern technology except unwillingness to place a high valuation upon certain common interests—particularly our interests in enterprise, experimentation, innovation. Never have the rewards of a broad view of common interests been more attractive. Never has the folly of narrowly pressing special claims been greater. The economic future of our country and of the world depends upon the clarity with which this is seen.

[20] In Sweden the recent depression produced rudimentary beginnings of a national wage policy made by the federation of employers and the federations of unions. See P. H. Norgren, *The Swedish Collective Bargaining System* (Cambridge, Mass., 1941), p. 303.

25

Notes on the Structure of Wages

Review of Economics and Statistics, February 1950.

I

NEITHER wage rates nor hourly earnings represent the price of labor—that is, the amount which the employer pays for a given amount and kind of service or the amount which employees receive for doing a given kind of work under given conditions. There are three principle reasons why neither wage rates nor hourly earnings measure the bids of various employers for a given type of labor. In the first place, jobs and occupations which bear the same name do not necessarily involve the same kinds of duties or the same degree of responsibility. Machinists first-class in a candy factory do not necessarily need the same knowledge of the trade as machinists first-class in an oil refinery. Loom fixers may have essentially the same duties in different mills, but the skill required of them may vary greatly depending upon the kind and quality of goods which the mill produces. In the second place, the speed of work varies—particularly between workers paid by the hour and those paid by results. The earnings of piece or bonus workers are likely to run from 15 to 30 per cent above the rates paid time workers on comparable jobs. This does not mean, however, that the variation in speed is the same as the variation in earnings. It may be more or less. In the third place, the quality of labor differs. The plants which pay the highest wages are likely to attract the best men in the occupation in the locality. Hence, it is even possible that the price of labor may be lowest where wages are highest.

There are several principle reasons why the wage rates or the hourly earnings in various plants do not accurately measure the willingness of a given type of labor to accept employment in the several plants. One reason, of course, is the one mentioned above—that jobs and occupations which have the same name in different plants may not in fact be the same and may not in fact use the same kind of labor. A second reason is that the attractiveness of jobs in different plants depends upon conditions other than wages. Hence, two jobs having the same duties, requiring the same skill and responsibility, may have different capacities to attract labor. An important difference between jobs is the steadiness of employment. Another is the length of the standard work week. Does $1.10 an hour on a job with a thirty-five-hour week represent a higher or lower price of labor than $1.00 an hour on a job with a forty-hour week? The answer obviously depends upon the value attached to leisure after thirty-five hours of work. A third reason why wage rates or hourly earnings do not measure the supply price of labor is that the compensation of employees is not always fully reflected in wages. Vacations, sick benefits, and pension provisions vary in different plants. Usually these provisions are most liberal in the plants where hourly earnings are highest. To this extent, differences in hourly earnings understate the differences in the real price of labor.

Consequently, it is not surprising that there are large variations both in the rates paid by different plants within the same locality for jobs nominally at least within the same occupation, and in the hourly earnings of employees doing apparently similar work in different plants. A good illustration of the spread of rates within an occupation in a city is given by the hiring rates for common labor paid by eighty-five plants in Cleveland. In February 1947, these rates were as follows:

Cents an hour	*Number of plants*
50–69	4
70–74	2
75–79	1
80–84	12
85–89	13
90–94	22
95–99	17
$1.00–1.04	6
1.05–1.09	8

(Special interest attaches to these figures because hiring rates for common labor have been compiled for over twenty years by the Cleveland Chamber of Commerce and distributed to various firms throughout the city. Consequently, each enterprise knows reasonably well how its rates compare with those paid by other concerns. The above figures are those compiled and distributed by the Cleveland Chamber of Commerce for February 1947.)

Another illustration of the spread in wages within a locality is provided by a small wage survey made in metropolitan Boston in 1940. The survey covered the hourly earnings in sixteen occupations or occupational classifications in fifteen plants. The survey was made by the staff of the personnel department of one of the enterprises. The staff members were instructed to obtain earnings only from jobs which, in their judgment, corresponded closely in skill and responsibility to the several types of jobs in the plant making the survey. Where properly comparable jobs could not be found, rates were not collected. Consequently, this survey comes closer than most wage surveys to reporting earnings on comparable jobs.[1] The spread between the highest and lowest hourly earnings in sixteen occupations in these plants varied from 87.1 per cent of the average rate in the case of producing and processing employees to 14.9 per cent of the average rate in the case of sheet metal workers. The most usual spread was 40 to 45 per cent of the average hourly earnings in all plants. This was the magnitude of the spread in six out of sixteen occupations. Table 1 shows the unweighted average of hourly

Table 1. Average hourly earnings of sixteen occupations in fifteen plants, 1940

Occupation	*Average hourly earnings in all plants (cents)*	*Average hourly earnings in lowest plant (cents)*	*Average hourly earnings in highest plant (cents)*	*Spread between high and low plants (cents)*	*Per cent of spread to average*
Common labor	57.9	44.8	74.1	29.3	50.6
Janitor	55.3	41.0	70.5	29.5	53.3
Watchman	59.6	45.2	74.0	28.8	48.3
Producing and processing laborers	64.2	44.8	100.7	55.9	87.1
Producing and processing operators	72.0	57.8	88.6	30.8	42.8
Receiving and shipping clerks	68.0	50.0	89.6	39.6	58.2
Machinists	87.5	70.0	105.0	35.0	40.0
Steamfitter	86.4	70.0	105.0	35.0	40.5
Electrician	88.0	67.9	105.0	37.1	42.2
Carpenter	81.5	65.0	99.5	34.5	42.3
Sheet metal workers	85.4	77.8	90.5	12.7	14.9
Millwright	86.1	82.5	95.5	13.0	15.1
Maintenance helper	67.1	50.7	82.0	31.3	46.6
Female producing laborers	45.1	33.8	63.4	29.6	65.6
Female producing operators	47.9	37.7	58.3	20.6	43.0
Firemen	78.4	63.0	90.8	27.8	35.5

The high spread in the case of producing and processing laborers partly reflects the fact that these occupations in some plants were compensated under piece work or bonus plans. It probably also reflects the difficulty in defining jobs in these occupations.

[1] The wage survey, however, did not take account of the fact that there were some variations in the standard work week (one plant had a thirty-five-hour work week but most of the others

earnings in each of the sixteen occupations in the fifteen plants and the spread between the plants with the highest and lowest hourly earnings in each category.

The wide variation in the rates or the hourly earnings within the same locality on jobs normally in the same occupations might lead one to expect to find little regularity in the structure of wage rates or hourly earnings. And yet a surprising amount of regularity can be found. The chaos which *seems* to prevail in the labor market conceals a pattern of order which can be explained and which sheds light on the influences that determine the interindustry wage structure of the community. The purpose of this paper is to report on some of the regularities in the interindustry wage structure, to discuss the light which these regularities shed on the influences determining wages, and to comment briefly on the implications of these influences for wage theory. The figures used in this paper are those of hourly earnings. It is probably a reasonably accurate assumption that at any given time hourly earnings and wage rates in different industries vary together.

II

The search for regularities in the wage structure was made by selecting a number of conditions with which hourly earnings might be expected to vary and computing coefficients of rank correlation between these conditions and the average hourly earnings of male unskilled labor. The conditions selected for study were: (1) Average hourly earnings of semiskilled and skilled workers in the industry; (2) Proportion of women in the industry; (3) Value added by manufacturing per manhour; (4) Value of product per manhour; (5) Ratio of payrolls to income from sales; (6) Ratio of net income after taxes to sales.

Most of the comparisons are for the years 1939 or 1940—the years for which data are available from the census of manufactures or the decennial census. The use of these years, though required by the availability of the data, has two advantages. One is that it avoids the effect of the war upon the wage structure. Since wages were not allowed to move freely during the war, the postwar wage structure may not adequately reflect the influences which normally determine the interindustry wage differences. (As a matter of fact,

a forty-hour work week) or the fact that some plants paid on a straight-time basis and others used piece-work or bonus plans on some jobs. There were some plants in which hourly earnings tended to be high in all occupational classifications. One company, for example, was the highest in eleven out of the fourteen categories in which it had employees and was the second highest in two others. Another company was low in six of the sixteen categories and next to the lowest in two others—although highest in one category.

there is evidence that the war had surprisingly little effect upon the interindustry wage structure.) A second advantage in the use of figures for 1939 or 1940 is that the wage figures for these dates show the wage structure in manufacturing industries before unions and collective bargaining had had time greatly to affect it. Indeed, widespread union organization in manufacturing dates only from 1937. Among the industries included in this survey, only two, namely newspaper and magazine printing and book and job printing, had had a high proportion of union workers prior to 1937. As a basis for judging the effect of unions in the interindustry wage structure, it is desirable to have a clear picture of the influences setting wages before unions became pervasive and powerful.

The wage figures used were the hourly earnings of male unskilled labor. These figures were used because male unskilled labor is the only occupational category for which figures are available in a number of industries. Comparisons of the average hourly earnings of all employees in the several industries could be made. Such comparisons, however, would be unsatisfactory because the proportion of men of a given degree of skill and responsibility varies from industry to industry. In order to show the desirability of studying the interindustry wage structure in terms of more or less precise occupational categories, some analysis was made of the interindustry wage structure for semiskilled and skilled male labor. This category, of course, is a loose one and involves comparing very unlike kinds of jobs and persons in different industries. Hence it is not surprising that the regularities found in the interindustry wage structure for semiskilled and skilled male employees are less pronounced than those found in the wage structure for unskilled male labor.

Even male unskilled labor is not so precise a category as is desirable because there is considerable variation in the kind of common labor hired by different industries. Some firms or industries need in the main to hire strong and vigorous common labor to do heavy work—they are virtually hiring athletes or near athletes. Some industries hire men for light work. The most desirable procedure, of course, would be to study the interindustry wage structure in terms of a series of occupations, such as electrician, machinist, carpenter, steamfitter, shipping clerk. Unfortunately figures for occupations other than common labor are not available. It is reasonable to assume that the regularities found in the structure of earnings of male unskilled labor would be found in the structure of earnings of other more or less homogeneous groups. It would be desirable, however, to test this assumption as soon as data become available.

The wage figures are those collected by the National Industrial Conference Board. The Board did not take steps to assure that its data were representative of the several industries, and there is reason to believe that the larger plants are more heavily represented than the smaller ones. This bias, however, applies to all industries. For that reason it probably does not seriously impair the validity of comparisons among the several industries. Data from plants which are properly representative of each industry would, of course, have been preferable, and it is to be hoped that they will someday become available.

Data on industries were used rather than data on enterprises because only data on industries are available. This also is a matter of regret because comparisons among enterprises would be of more interest and significance provided production and financial data for individual concerns were also available.

Attention in this study is focused upon the wage structure at a given time rather than changes over a period of time. Comparisons of wage movements through time are useful and interesting, and studies of this sort have been made by Dunlop, Ross, and Garbarino. Examination of the wage structure at a given time is also useful. At any moment the wage structure reflects the accumulated influence of various conditions over a considerable period of time. The conditions affecting the movement of wages in an industry during the last decade may not be the same as those affecting the movement in the previous decade. Hence, the analysis of the wage structure at a given time may reveal some of the long-run influences playing upon wages more clearly than the study of changes in the wage structure between two dates. It has seemed desirable, however, to make comparisons of the stability of the interindustry wage structure over periods of time, and this has been done.

The results of the study may be summarized as follows:

1. The average hourly earnings of male unskilled workers tend to vary with the average hourly earnings of semiskilled and skilled workers—that is, where the average hourly earnings of semiskilled and skilled workers are high, the average hourly earnings of common labor are high and vice versa.

2. Where the proportion of women in an industry is high, there is some tendency (not pronounced) for the hourly earnings of male unskilled labor to be low.

3. In industries where value added by manufacturing per wage-earner hour is high, the hourly earnings of male unskilled labor tend to be high.

4. In industries where the value product per wage-earner hour is high, the hourly earnings of male unskilled labor tend to be high.

5. In industries where payrolls are a low percentage of income from sales, the hourly earnings of male unskilled labor tend to be high.

6. In industries where income after taxes is a high percentage of sales, the hourly earnings of male unskilled labor tend to be high.

7. The wage structure changes over time, but the changes are fairly slow and the wage structure between industries within a period of twenty or thirty years exhibits only moderate changes. This conclusion, however, might not hold if the unit of observation were the individual firms in a local labor market.

Let us examine these results briefly.

III

1. *The average hourly earnings of male unskilled labor tend to be high where the average hourly earnings of male semi-skilled and skilled labor are high.* The coefficient of rank correlation among twenty manufacturing industries in 1939 was .7098. Table 2 compares the average hourly earnings of male unskilled labor and male semiskilled and skilled labor in these industries.

The internal wage structures of the several industries more or less appear to be entities—where for any reason the earnings of semiskilled and skilled workers are high the earnings of the unskilled workers also tend to be high. In five cases, however (newspaper and magazine printing, book and job printing, leather tanning, chemicals, and lumber and millwork) the difference in rank is large—6 or more.

Among the industries, it is interesting to compare the spread in the ratios between the average hourly earnings of the unskilled workers and the average hourly earnings of the semiskilled and skilled workers. Since the degree of skill among the skilled and semiskilled workers varies from industry to industry, one has no right to expect an approximate uniformity between industries in this spread. Nevertheless, the variation is not large. For twenty industries in 1939, the unweighted average of the average hourly earnings of common labor was 73.1 per cent of the unweighted average of the average hourly earnings of semiskilled and skilled labor. There was a fairly close concentration around this ratio. In seventeen of the twenty industries, the ratio between the average hourly earnings of common labor and the average hourly earnings of semiskilled or skilled labor was within 10 per cent of the average for the twenty industries; and in eight cases, within 5 per cent of the average.

The wage policies pursued during the war increased the wages of common labor relative to the earnings of semiskilled and skilled workers. An unweighted average of the hourly earnings of male unskilled workers in the

Table 2. Comparison of average hourly earnings of male skilled and semiskilled and male unskilled labor, 1939

Industry	*Average hourly earnings, male semi-skilled and skilled*	*Rank*	*Average hourly earnings, male unskilled*	*Rank*	*Deviation*
Printing, newspaper and magazine	$1.104	1	$.623	10	9
Printing, book and job	1.024	2	.543	12	10
Automobile	.976	3	.797	1	2
Rubber	.967	4	.673	3	1
Iron and steel	.876	5	.638	6	1
Electrical manufacturing	.873	6	.669	4	2
Agricultural implements	.829	7	.654	5	2
Chemicals	.823	8	.694	2	6
Paint and varnish	.786	9	.627	8	1
Foundry and machine shops	.781	10	.629	7	3
Meat packing	.774	11	.624	9	2
Lumber and millwork	.746	12	.479	18	6
Paper products	.735	13	.531	15	2
Hosiery and knit goods	.707	14	.458	19	5
Furniture	.706	15	.536	14	1
Wool	.703	16	.524	16	0
Paper and pulp	.698	17	.540	13	4
Leather tanning	.694	18	.557	11	7
Boot and shoe	.599	19	.434	20	1
Cotton	.566	20	.494	17	3

Source. National Industrial Conference Board, *The Conference Board Economic Record,* vol. II, no. 10 (March 28, 1940), 120–34.

industries reporting to the National Industrial Conference Board shows that in 1923 the earnings of common labor were 71.6 per cent of the earnings of semiskilled and skilled workers; in 1929, 72.8 per cent; in 1933, 72.9 per cent; in 1939, 73.1 per cent; in December 1946, 77.1 per cent.[2] The wage policies of the war, however, had little effect upon the tendency for the average hourly earnings of male unskilled labor to be high in those industries where the average hourly earnings of the semiskilled and skilled are high. In December 1946, the coefficient of rank correlation among the same twenty industries that were compared for 1939 was .6702—only a little less than in 1939.

[2] National Industrial Conference Board, *Wages, Hours, and Employment in the United States, 1914–1936,* computed from tables on pp. 59–159; *Conference Board Record,* II (March 28, 1940), computed from tables on pp. 115–33; *Management Record* (February 1947), pp. 45, 46.

Why should the earnings of common laborers be high where the earnings of semiskilled and skilled workers are high? The explanation undoubtedly is that there are certain common influences, such as wage policies, which tend to affect the entire wage structures of plants and to give them a unity. The effect of common influences upon wages throughout the labor force would be shown more clearly if industries or plants could be classified by the average level of skill and responsibility required by the semiskilled and skilled jobs. As it is, the differences in the average hourly earnings of semiskilled and skilled workers reflect to considerable extent not differences in wage policies but differences in the quality of labor used on the semiskilled and skilled jobs. Nevertheless, the tendency is quite pronounced for hourly earnings of common laborers to be high where the hourly earnings of semiskilled and skilled workers are high.

2. *The hourly earnings of male common labor have some (not pronounced) tendency to be low where the percentage of women among the wage earners is high.* The coefficient of rank correlation among nineteen industries in 1939 was .4491. Table 3 compares the two sets of data.

The tendency for the hourly earnings of common labor to be low where the proportion of women in the industry is high was apparently weakened by the depression. For example, in 1929 the coefficient of rank correlation between the proportion of women among workers and the average hourly earnings of common laborers was .5224, the industries being ranked by the highness of the proportion of women among wage earners and the lowness of the average hourly earnings of male unskilled labor. Possibly the war has still further weakened the relationship, but data on this point are not yet available.

Why is there some tendency for the wages of male common labor to be low in industries where the proportion of women employed is high? Does the employment of women have some more or less direct effect upon either the wages which employers are willing to pay men or the wages which men are willing to accept? Or are the high proportion of women employed and the low wages of men partly the result of common causes?

I believe that each of these last two questions should be answered by "yes." To some extent the wages of women probably do affect the wages of men. Women are available for lower wages than men. Where women are doing skilled or semiskilled work, managements are probably reluctant to pay male employees who are merely doing common labor as much as or more than semiskilled or skilled women workers. Under these conditions, employers may content themselves with rather inferior male common laborers

Table 3. Comparison of the percentage of women among wage earners and average hourly earnings of male unskilled labor, 1939

Industry	*Percentage of women among wage earners* (1)	*Rank* (2)	*Average hourly earnings, male unskilled* (3)	*Rank* (4)	*Deviation* (5)
Hosiery and knit goods	63.9	1	.458	2	1
Boot and shoe	43.9	2	.434	1	1
Paper products	42.7	3	.531	6	3
Cotton	39.0	4	.494	4	0
Wool	38.5	5	.524	5	0
Electrical manufacturing	33.9	6	.669	16	10
Rubber	24.6	7	.673	17	10
Printing, book and job	19.9	8	.543	9	1
Chemicals	19.7	9	.694	18	9
Meat packing	14.9	10	.624	12	2
Leather tanning	8.8	11	.557	10	1
Printing, news and magazine	8.0	12	.623	11	1
Paper and pulp	7.7	13	.540	8	5
Furniture	6.8	14	.536	7	7
Automobiles	6.6	15	.797	19	4
Paint and varnish	5.1	16	.627	13	3
Lumber and millwork	1.8	17	.479	3	14
Agricultural implements	1.0	18	.654	15	3
Iron and steel	.8	19	.638	14	5

Source. Col. 1: U. S. Bureau of the Census, Sixteenth Census of the United States (1940), *Manufactures 1939*, I, 70–87. Col. 3: National Industrial Conference Board, *The Conference Board Economic Record*, vol. II, no. 10 (March 28, 1940), 120–32.

in order to keep the common labor scale below the scale for semiskilled and skilled women. Furthermore, some of the industries which employ a large proportion of women, such as the textile industry, also employ men and are able to offer jobs to both male and female members of families. In such industries the fact that jobs are available for both men and women undoubtedly affects the supply price for male workers.

The industries where a high proportion of workers are women are usually light industries. Some persons are able to accept jobs in either light or heavy industries; others are not strong enough for the heavy industries and must work in the light industries. Consequently, the supply price of labor for the light industries is undoubtedly lower than the supply price for the heavy industries. As a result, the tendency for the hourly earnings of male common labor to be low where the proportion of women workers is high is probably in considerable degree explained by the fact that each of these two conditions is likely to be characteristic of industries turning out light products.

3. *Hourly earnings of male unskilled workers tend to be high where the value added by manufacturing per wage-earner hour is high.* The coefficient of rank correlation in 1939 was .9299. A comparison of the value added per wage-earner hour with the average hourly earnings of male unskilled workers is given in Table 4.

Table 4. Comparison of value added per wage-earner hour and average hourly earnings of male unskilled labor, 1939

Industry	*Value added per wage-earner hour* (1)	*Rank* (2)	*Average hourly earnings, male unskilled* (3)	*Rank* (4)	*Deviation* (5)
Chemicals	$3.48	1	$.694	2	1
Electrical manufacturing	2.00	2	.669	4	2
Automobiles	1.83	3.5	.797	1	2.5
Rubber	1.83	3.5	.673	3	.5
Iron and steel	1.71	5	.638	5	0
Paper and pulp	1.67	6	.540	8	2
Meat packing	1.64	7	.624	6	1
Leather tanning	1.24	8	.557	7	1
Wool	1.12	9	.524	10	1
Furniture	1.04	10	.536	9	1
Lumber and millwork	.88	11	.479	12	1
Hosiery and knit goods	.81	12	.458	13	1
Cotton	.75	13	.494	11	2

Source. Col. 1: U. S. Bureau of the Census and BLS, "Man-Hour Statistics for 171 Selected Industries," *Census of Manufactures: 1939* (March 1942), Table 1, pp. 3–7. Col. 3: National Industrial Conference Board, *The Conference Board Economic Record,* vol. II, no. 10 (March 28, 1940), 120–32.

Some correlation between the value added per wage-earner hour and the average hourly wage of male unskilled workers is to be expected because it is from value added that wages are paid. High wages per hour cannot be paid unless the value added per man hour is high. Of course, the value added per wage-earner hour is the average for *all* employees—not merely for common laborers. If a high value added tends to produce high hourly earnings, however, the unskilled laborers may be expected to feel its effects—and this seems to be the case. Although some correlation between the value added per wage-earner hour and hourly earnings of male unskilled labor is to be expected, a correlation of .9299 is so high that it requires explanation.

"Accepted" wage theory would lead one to expect a high correlation between wages and the *marginal* value added per wage-earner hour. The above high correlation, however, is between hourly earnings and the *average* value added per wage-earner hour. There are two principal explanations for the high figure. One, of course, is that it is correlation of ranks only; it is quite possible that there is a tendency for the average value added to be high where the marginal value added is high. The second explanation is closely related to the first—a high average value added per manhour tends to produce high wages (and high earnings) because it produces liberal wage policies. More specific evidence in support of this conclusion will be given when hourly earnings are compared with the ratio of payrolls to income from sales and to profits per dollar of sales.

4. *Hourly earnings of male unskilled workers tend to be high where the value product per wage-earner hour is high.* The coefficient of rank correlation in 1939 was .8297. The data are compared in Table 5.

Table 5. Comparison of value of product per wage-earner hour and average hourly earnings of male unskilled labor, 1939

Industry	*Value of product per wage-earner hour* (1)	*Rank* (2)	*Average hourly earnings, male unskilled* (3)	*Rank* (4)	*Deviation* (5)
Meat packing	$10.32	1	$.624	6	5
Chemicals	5.73	2	.694	2	0
Automobiles	5.63	3	.797	1	2
Iron and steel	4.39	4	.638	5	1
Rubber	4.08	5	.673	3	2
Paper and pulp	4.02	6	.540	8	2
Leather tanning	3.61	7	.557	7	0
Electrical manufacturing	3.42	8	.669	4	4
Wool	2.65	9	.524	10	1
Furniture	1.94	10	.536	9	1
Lumber and millwork	1.60	11	.479	12	1
Hosiery and knit goods	1.58	12	.458	13	1
Cotton (north)	1.51	13	.494	11	2

Source. Col. 1: U. S. Bureau of the Census and BLS, "Man-Hour Statistics for 171 Selected Industries," *Census of Manufactures: 1939* (March 1942), Table 1, pp. 3–7. Col. 3: National Industrial Conference Board, *The Conference Board Economic Record,* vol. II, no. 10 (March 28, 1940), 120–32.

The high coefficient of rank correlation between value product per wage-earner hour and the average hourly earnings of male unskilled workers may seem surprising. A high value of product per wage-earner hour may be the result of two very different causes—either the application of labor to expensive raw materials or a high productivity of labor. The first cause would not be expected to produce high hourly earnings. The meat-packing industry, where the deviation between the two ranks is large, is an example of an industry in which the value of product per wage-earner hour is high because labor in the industry is applied to expensive raw materials.

5. *Hourly earnings of male unskilled labor tend to be high where payrolls are a low percentage of income from sales.* The coefficient of rank correlation in 1939 was .7228. Table 6 shows the relevant comparisons.

Table 6. Comparison of wage payrolls as a percentage of sales or total receipts, and average hourly earnings of male unskilled labor, 1939

Industry	*Wage (nonsalaried) payrolls as percentage of sales or total compiled receipts* (1)	*Rank* (2)	*Average hourly earnings, male unskilled* (3)	*Rank* (4)	*Deviation* (5)
Meat packing	4.5	1	.624	8	7
Paint and varnish	7.1	2	.627	7	5
Chemicals	8.7	3	.694	2	1
Agricultural implements	14.5	4	.654	5	1
Rubber	15.2	5	.673	3	2
Printing, book and job	15.5	6	.543	11	5
Printing, newspapers and magazines	17.4	7	.623	9	2
Leather tanning	17.7	8	.557	10	2
Automobiles	18.2	9	.797	1	8
Electrical manufacturing	18.3	10	.669	4	6
Paper and pulp	21.0	11	.540	12	1
Iron and steel	22.3	12	.638	6	6
Wool	23.4	13	.524	15	2
Boot and shoe	25.6	14	.434	19	5
Cotton	25.9	15	.494	16	1
Furniture	26.3	16	.536	13	3
Hosiery and knit goods	29.6	17	.458	18	1
Lumber and mill work	34.5	18	.479	17	1
Paper products	41.6	19	.531	14	5

Source. Col. 1: Computed from sales figures in National Industrial Conference Board, *The Conference Board Economic Record,* vol. IV, no. 10 (October 1942), 333–39, and from payrolls, U. S. Bureau of the Census, "General Statistics for Industry Groups," *Census of Manufacturers: 1939* (October 1941), Tables 1 and 2. Col. 3: National Industrial Conference Board, *The Conference Board Economic Record,* vol. II, no. 10 (March 28, 1940), 120–32.

The tendency for the average hourly earnings of male common labor to be high where payrolls are a small percentage of income from sales is quite understandable. Managements naturally are more concerned about the rates which they pay for labor when payrolls are large in relation to the receipts of the enterprise than when payrolls are small. The highness of the correlation is striking and suggests the importance of managerial policy as an influence upon hourly earnings.

There is also some tendency for the average hourly earnings of male semiskilled and skilled workers to be high in those industries where payrolls are a small percentage of sales. Semiskilled and skilled workers, however, are far from a well-defined group of occupations, and the proportion of workers of varying degrees of skill within the entire group of semiskilled and skilled workers may vary considerably between industries. For this group of workers in the same nineteen industries that were used to compare the payrolls as a percentage of sales and the average hourly earnings of male unskilled labor, the coefficient of rank correlation in 1939 was .4930.

6. *The average hourly earnings of male unskilled labor tend to be high where the net income after taxes is a high percentage of sales.* The coefficient of rank correlation in 1939 was .6969. Table 7 presents the comparisons.

The high correlation between sales margins and the average hourly earnings of common labor is not surprising. It reinforces the view that wages, within a considerable range, reflect managerial discretion, that where managements can easily pay high wages they tend to do so, and that where managements are barely breaking even, they tend to keep wages down. It is true that net income per dollar of sales does not indicate the rate of return per dollar of investment and that an enterprise which has a small margin may have a high return on its capital. Nevertheless, if the margin on sales is small, a small rise in costs may wipe out a high return on invested capital. Hence, a small margin puts management under pressure to keep costs down.

Some correlation also exists between sales margins and the average hourly earnings of male semiskilled and skilled workers, but for reasons already given, one must expect the correlation to be substantially less than the correlation between sales margins and the average hourly earnings of male unskilled workers. The correlation in the case of the semiskilled and skilled male workers in 1939 was .5127.

7. *The interindustry structure of wages has considerable stability during short or moderately short periods of time.* When the hourly earnings of male unskilled labor in twenty industries in 1923 and 1946 are compared, a coefficient of rank correlation of .7289 is obtained. When the comparison is

Table 7. Comparison of net income after taxes as a percentage of sales or total receipts, and average hourly earnings of male unskilled labor, 1939

Industry	*Net income after taxes as a percentage of sales or total compiled receipts* (1)	*Rank* (2)	*Average hourly earnings, male unskilled* (3)	*Rank* (4)	*Deviation* (5)
Chemicals	12.6	1	.694	2	1
Automobiles	8.6	2	.797	1	1
Electrical manufacturing	8.1	3	.669	4	1
Printing, newspapers and magazines	6.1	4	.623	9	5
Paint and varnish	5.1	5	.627	7	2
Rubber	4.9	6	.673	3	3
Paper products	4.6	7	.531	14	7
Paper and pulp	4.5	8	.540	12	4
Agricultural implements	4.2	9	.654	5	4
Wool	3.4	10	.524	15	5
Printing, book and job	3.3	11	.543	11	0
Leather tanning	2.9	12	.557	10	2
Iron and steel	2.8	13	.638	6	7
Cotton (north)	2.6	14	.494	16	2
Furniture	2.4	15.5	.536	13	2.5
Boot and shoe	2.4	15.5	.434	19	3.5
Hosiery and knit goods	1.8	17	.459	18	1
Lumber	1.3	18	.479	17	1
Meat packing	0.9	19	.624	8	11

Source. Col. 1: National Industrial Conference Board, *The Conference Board Economic Record*, vol. IV, no. 10 (October 1942), 333–39. Col. 3: *Ibid.*, vol. II, no. 10 (March 28, 1940), 120–132.

between 1923 and 1939, the coefficient is .7154; between 1929 and 1939, .8902; and between 1929 and 1946, .8812.

Table 8 compares the average hourly earnings of male unskilled labor in various industries at the several dates.

IV

What questions or conclusions of theoretical interest are suggested by the results of this examination of the interindustry wage structure? One question is: "How important is managerial policy as a determinant of wages?" Others are: "What are the determinants of managerial wage policy?" "What rela-

Table 8. Comparison of average hourly earnings of male unskilled labor at selected dates

Industry	Earnings										Deviation in rank			
	1923	Rank	1929	Rank	1933	Rank	1939	Rank	July 1946	Rank	1923–1939	1929–1939	1942–1946	1929–1946
Printing, newspapers and magazines	.540	1	.486	7	.419	8	.623	10	1.005	9	9	3	8	2
Rubber	.522	2	.604	1	.475	2	.673	3	1.222	1	1	2	1	0
Automobile	.496	3	.576	2	.505	1	.797	1	1.161	2	2	1	1	0
Paint and varnish	.494	4	.476	10	.441	5	.627	8	.959	11	4	2	7	1
Iron and steel	.484	5	.511	5	.367	15	.638	6	1.080	4	1	1	1	1
Chemical	.477	6	.543	3	.469	3	.694	2	1.082	3	4	1	3	0
Wool	.470	7	.442	17	.373	14	.524	16	.956	12	9	1	5	5
Foundry and machine shops	.469	8	.507	6	.432	6	.629	7	1.068	5	1	1	3	1
Agricultural implements	.450	9	.512	4	.413	9	.654	5	1.055	6	4	1	3	2
Leather and tanning	.442	10	.485	8	.360	16	.557	11	.935	15	0	3	4	7
Paper and pulp	.442	11	.450	15	.375	13	.540	13	.939	14	2	2	3	1
Printing, book and job	.442	12	.479	9	.444	4	.543	12	.998	10	1	3	1	1
Paper products	.435	13	.452	14	.412	10	.531	15	.868	19	2	1	6	5
Electrical manufacturing	.428	14.5	.474	11	.430	7	.669	4	1.036	7	10.5	7	7.5	4
Meat packing	.428	14.5	.471	12	.391	12	.624	9	1.021	8	5.5	3	6.5	4
Cotton (north)	.403	16	.362	20	.341	19	.494	17	.890	17	1	3	1	3
Furniture	.390	17	.447	16	.325	20	.536	14	.900	16	3	2	1	0
Lumber and mill	.369	18	.454	13	.348	17	.479	18	.948	13	0	5	5	0
Boot and shoe	.367	19	.438	18	.397	11	.434	20	.577	20	1	2	1	2
Hosiery and knit goods	.356	20	.385	19	.342	18	.458	19	.872	18	1	0	2	1

Source. National Industrial Conference Board, *Wages and Employment in the United States, 1914–1936*, pp. 56–185; *The Conference Board Economic Record*, vol. II, no. 10 (March 28, 1940), 120–32; *The Conference Board Management Record* (October 1946), p. 339.

tionship is there between hourly earnings and the price of labor?" "Do the several regularities found in the interindustry wage structure require any significant modifications of 'accepted' wage theory?"

The results of this study give strong support to the proposition that managerial policy is important in determining interindustry wage differences. The best evidence in support of this conclusion is supplied by the tendency for the hourly earnings of male unskilled labor to be high where the earnings of semiskilled and skilled labor are high, where payroll costs are low in relation to gross income, and where profit margins per dollar of sales are high. The tendency for the earnings of male unskilled workers to be low in industries where the proportion of women in the labor force is high is consistent with the view that managerial policy is an important determinant of the level of wages. It can hardly be regarded as strong independent proof, partly because the correlation is not high and partly because the correlation may indicate simply two results of a common cause. The very high correlation between value added per wage-earner hour and average hourly earnings of unskilled labor is best explained by the tendency for a high value added per wage-earner hour to produce liberal wage policies and a low value added to produce niggardly wage policies.

The study shows that two important determinants of wage policy are the size of payrolls relative to gross income and profits per dollar of sales. It is not surprising that managements should watch labor costs most carefully in those industries where payrolls are large relative to gross receipts and where profit margins per dollar of sales are low, and that hourly earnings should be lower in these industries than in others where labor costs are less important or where profit margins are higher. There are probably other important determinants of wage policies, but they are not indicated by the results of this study.

May the high correlation between profit margins and the average hourly earnings of unskilled male labor represent, not decisions of wage policy, but rather the varying efforts of different industries to expand? Must one not expect the greatest efforts to expand to be made by the industries with the largest profit margins? Must one not, therefore, expect wages to be highest in those industries which are seeking most vigorously to expand? No correlation, however, seems to exist between the increase in the average hourly earnings of male unskilled workers and the increase in employment. At any rate, in twenty manufacturing industries there was a small negative coefficient of rank correlation between these two series for the period 1923–39.

Had a high negative correlation been found between the average hourly earnings of all workers and the increase in employment, one might have argued that high hourly earnings were an obstacle to expansion. As a matter of fact, when a comparison is made between the increase in employment in the same twenty industries and the average hourly earnings of *all* employees for the period 1923–39, only a low correlation is found—namely, .2812. The conclusion is that the association of high hourly earnings of unskilled common labor with high margins per dollar of sales is explained not by the efforts of enterprises to expand but by wage policy. Furthermore, if margin per dollar of sales is compared with the increase of employment, only a very low correlation is found. Hence, the most satisfactory explanation of the high correlation between hourly earnings and profit margins is that high profit margins tend to make managements liberal and willing to pay more for labor than managements which are having trouble in making ends meet.

The investigation indicates the importance of ascertaining more definitely what relationship there is between hourly earnings and the price of labor. Does the price of labor vary in the same direction as hourly earnings though in smaller degree? If so, is the variation between the price of labor in different plants almost as large as the variation in hourly earnings, or is it considerably less? Or does the price of labor vary inversely with hourly earnings? Do enterprises which pay more-than-average wages usually get a bargain? Are hourly earnings above the average so effective in attracting superior workers and in inducing men to do their best in order to hold desirable high-paying jobs that the price of labor is lowest where wage rates are highest? Are the firms in which hourly earnings (and hence presumably wage rates) are above the average really smart buyers of labor?

Until one knows the answer to these questions, one is not prepared to speculate concerning the effect of the wage structure upon the distribution of resources among places, firms, and industries. Are *firms* with small payrolls in relation to sales or with large profit margins per dollar of sales prevented by their high wage rates from becoming as large as they ought to be? Are the *industries* with small payrolls in relation to sales or with large profit margins prevented by high wages from growing as rapidly as they should?

The fact that the rates which yield the highest hourly earnings occur where labor is not an important item in costs or where profit margins are large indicates that most managements do not regard above-the-average wage rates as economical. Certainly, if most managements believed that a low price of labor is associated with high wage rates, there would not be a pronounced association of high wage rates with a low ratio of payrolls to gross receipts or with high profit margins. The firms in greatest need of low labor costs (those with large payrolls relative to sales or those with low profit margins) would aggressively strive to get themselves a low price for labor by putting up rates.

Hence, the correlations would tend to be the opposite of the observed ones. Of course, it is possible that the majority view among the managers may be wrong. Perhaps the managers are misled, by the immediate effect of an increase in wages upon labor costs, into thinking that high labor costs are associated with high wage rates, and they may overlook the eventual effect of differences in rates or earnings upon the quality of labor attracted to the enterprise.

The need for determining the relationship between wage rates or hourly earnings and the price of labor is indicated again when it is asked whether the results of this inquiry show the need for significant modifications in "accepted" wage theory. This study shows that the models used in accepted wage theory are too simple and need to be supplemented. This is not exactly news. The models used in accepted wage theory assume that wages represent the price of labor. This assumption is untenable. The importance of wage policies indicates the need of an analysis of their economic consequences. Such an analysis must be based upon a determination of the relationship between hourly earnings and the price of labor. If the variations in wages for which existing wage policies are responsible also produce similar but smaller variations in the price of labor, then several highly important consequences must be attributed to wage policies. It follows, for example, that existing wage policies limit to some extent the growth of the most efficient enterprises. It also follows that wage policies tend to raise wages at the expense of profits and, therefore, to produce a slightly higher propensity to consume than would otherwise exist. If the computations of Lubell on the effect of redistribution of income upon consumer spending are correct, however, the effect of existing wage policies upon the marginal propensity to consume is quite limited.[3] If wage policies cause wages to encroach upon net income, they diminish the volume of investment opportunities. If their favorable effect upon the marginal propensity to consume is very small and if they diminish the volume of profit opportunities, wage policies must be unfavorable to employment and expansion. All of these tentative conclusions, however, rest upon the assumption that the price of labor varies directly (though not proportionately) with wage rates, so that the price of labor is highest in those plants or industries where the wage rates for a given type of job are highest. If this assumption is not correct, these conclusions concerning the consequences of wage policies must be reversed.

[3] See Harold Lubell, "Effects of Income Redistribution on Consumers' Expenditures," *American Economic Review* (December 1947), p. 930.

26

Do the Wage-Fixing Arrangements in the American Labor Market Have an Inflationary Bias?

American Economic Review, Proceedings, May 1954.

For more than twenty years the annual average of hourly earning in American industry has risen without a break. This is the longest stretch of unbroken rises on record since the beginning of the Bureau of Labor Statistics' index of the hourly earnings of nonagricultural workers in 1840.[1] There was a twenty-five-year period, from 1895 to 1920, when hourly earnings did not fall, but in four years during that time they did not rise.

Money wages in the United States have always had a strong tendency to rise. Today the average nonagricultural worker earns as many dollars in an hour as his predecessor earned in two eleven-hour days back in 1840. As a result of the rise in prices, the hourly earnings of a worker today will buy only about nine times as much as the earnings of a worker in 1840. Were trends of the last one hundred and thirteen years to continue for another one hundred and thirteen years, the hourly earnings of nonagricultural workers in 2066 would average thirty-five dollars and would have a purchasing power of about fourteen dollars in terms of present dollars, or eighty-four dollars for a six-hour day.

The rise in hourly earnings has not been continuous, but there have been only seventeen years in the last one hundred and thirteen when the annual average of nonagricultural hourly earnings was lower than in the preceding year. In eighteen years there was no change in average hourly earnings, and in seventy-eight there was an increase. The eighteen years in which there

[1] In two periods, from 1860 to 1872 and from 1908 to 1920, the annual averages of hourly earnings increased steadily for twelve years. U. S. Bureau of Labor Statistics, "History of Wages in the United States from Colonial Times to 1928," *Bulletin No. 604*, pp. 521, 574.

was no change reflect the crudity of the early data. Although the data are too crude to provide accurate measurements of the change between any two years, they undoubtedly give an essentially accurate measure of the direction and the magnitude of the trends. The rise of prices, of course, has been much smaller and less continuous than the rise in money wages. The index of the wholesale price level has increased a little more than 130 per cent, while the index of hourly earnings has increased more than sixteen times that amount.

My present examination of some of the influences that have been determining the movement of money wages in the American labor market will be directed in the main to the supply side of the labor market. The shifts in demand curves in the labor market are undoubtedly far greater than the shifts in supply curves. That is probably the reason why there has been a tendency to explain movements in money wages solely by changes in the demand for labor rather than by changes in supply and demand. In particular, the possibility has been neglected that rightward shifts in the demand curve may discourage rightward shifts in the supply curve or may even cause leftward shifts in the supply curve. But if the short-run demand for labor is usually quite inelastic, as it seems to be, influences acting on the supply curve can obviously have considerable influence on the price of labor.

I

Before we look more closely at what has happened to money wages, let us examine briefly some of the specific influences on the supply side of the labor market. The history of wages makes it plain, I think, that the individual, unorganized worker in the American labor market has long possessed the capacity to drive a favorable bargain for himself. Even before trade unionism became important, the gains of technological progress went in the main to people in their capacity as wage earners rather than to people in their capacity as consumers.

The strong bargaining position of unorganized workers is attributable primarily to two conditions: the ability of workers to withhold efficiency when wages or working conditions are unsatisfactory and the unwillingness of employed workers to accept cuts in customary money wages. Workers who feel that their wages are unfair or who fail to receive increases which they regard as fair become less cooperative and more difficult to manage. Employers know that a dissatisfied labor force is inefficient and expensive. That is why there is such a strong tendency for wages in all industries to move up together in spite of differences in conditions.

The unwillingness of employed workers to accept cuts in customary money wages means that as soon as a wage is set, the labor-supply curve changes. A gap appears in the curve to the left of the existing wage. Consequently, in the labor market when demand curves shift to the left, the price is set, not by what the nonsellers will accept, but by the unwillingness of the successful sellers to accept less than the established wage. Hence, there is equilibrium even though the market has not been cleared. The practical result is that only a fairly long and severe depression will make employers willing to risk the strikes that wage cuts might provoke even among unorganized workers. Thus, the mild recessions of 1861, 1867, 1870, 1885, 1888, 1891, 1904, 1908, and 1949 produced no drop in the annual average of hourly earnings, and the mild recessions of 1854, 1900, 1911, 1924, 1927, and 1938 were accompanied by increases in the annual averages of hourly earnings. (An unchanged annual average may conceal a drop and a rise within the year, but the drop would not be a long one and almost certainly not a large one.) Even in the relatively severe depression of the nineties, the drop in average hourly earnings was quite small.

I have referred to the tendency for wages in all industries to move more or less together. Valuable studies have been made by Dunlop, Garbarino, and others of the differences in wage movements in various industries and of the reasons for the differences. These studies should not obscure the fact that even variations in conditions have produced only moderate differences in wage movements. This point is illustrated by comparisons of the movements of hourly earnings and physical output per manhour. Very wide differences in output per manhour are accompanied by much smaller differences in hourly earnings, in spite of the fact that some industries can make wage increases while cutting prices and other industries must raise prices in order to cover the cost of the same wage increases. Garbarino, studying a period (1923 to 1940) when productivity in general was outrunning hourly earnings, found a coefficient of rank correlation of 0.6 between changes in output per manhour and changes in hourly earnings among thirty-four industries. But this coefficient relates to rank only, and there was far more variation in output per manhour than in earnings. The six industries with the largest increases in output per manhour (an average of 226 per cent) had an average increase in hourly earnings of 39 per cent, and the six industries with the smallest increases in productivity (an average of 25 per cent) had an average increase in hourly earnings of 11 per cent.[2] Between 1939 and 1950, a period when

[2] J. W. Garbarino, "A Theory of Interindustry Wage Structure Variation," *Quarterly Journal of Economics* (May 1950), pp. 296–297, 298.

hourly earnings were outrunning productivity, there was no significant relationship between changes in output per manhour and changes in hourly earnings among eighteen industries for which the Bureau of Labor Statistics has estimated increases in productivity. The coefficient of rank correlation was only 0.2. The six industries with the highest increase in output per manhour (an average of 57.4 per cent) had an increase of 116.8 per cent in hourly earnings; the six with the lowest increase in output per manhour (an average of minus 4.1 per cent) had an increase of 111.8 per cent in hourly earnings.

Let us now look briefly at the broad movements of wages and prices since 1840. The time may be conveniently divided into two principal periods of approximately equal length: the first, fifty-six years in length, from 1840 to 1896, and the second, fifty-seven years long, from 1896 to 1953. The first period was in the main a time of falling prices. In thirty-three out of the fifty-six years, the index of wholesale prices was lower than in the preceding year, and in the year 1896 the wholesale price level reached the lowest point in the last one hundred and thirteen years. In that year, the index of wholesale prices was one fourth below the level of 1840.

The second period, from 1896 to the present, has been mainly a time of rising prices. In thirty-eight out of the fifty-seven years, the index of wholesale prices averaged higher than in the preceding year, and today the index of wholesale prices is nearly 3.7 times as high as in 1896.

It has been customary to attribute the downward drift of prices during the second half of the nineteenth century and the upward movement in the twentieth century mainly to monetary influences. Such "explanations" do not tell us much. Money is a medium through which other influences affect the price level, but changes in the supply of money do not in themselves explain the movements of the price level. As a matter of fact, during the latter half of the nineteenth century the supply of money increased far faster in relation to the current dollar value of the national income than during the first half of the twentieth century. Between 1850 and 1896, for example, the money supply increased more than 3 per cent for every 1 per cent increase in the current value of the national income.[3] During the second period, largely

[3] In money supply I include the total deposits of all banks (demand and time) and money in circulation (*Historical Statistics of the United States, 1789–1945*, pp. 262, 263, 274). If figures for demand deposits alone were available for the entire period, it might be preferable to use them rather than total deposits, but the exclusion of time deposits (which include savings deposits) would be debatable. For national income, I have used for 1850 to 1900 Kuznets' estimates of national income as published in "Uses of National Income in Peace and War," *Occasional Paper No. 6* (National Bureau of Economic Research), p. 38; and from 1900 to 1930 Kuznets' estimates published in Dewhurst's *America's Needs and Resources*, Appendix 4, p. 696. An estimate of the national income for the year 1896 was made by assuming that the rate of

because of the rise in prices, the money supply increased less than 1.6 per cent for every 1 per cent increase in the national income. It is evident that the increase in the supply of money had far less effect on prices in the period 1850 to 1896 than in the period 1896 to 1953.

Why did the enormous increase in the supply of money not prevent a drop in prices in the first period, and why did the increase in the supply of money produce a large rise in prices in the second period? The greatest single influence on the price level has been war or absence of war. The absence of important wars during the last quarter of the nineteenth century made it possible for the money supply to grow far faster than output without prices being bid up. It was the great frequency of wars during the last fifty-odd years (the Spanish-American War, the Boer War, the Russo-Japanese War near the turn of the century, the First World War, the Second World War, the Korean War, and the fear of a third world war) which created every now and then strong preferences for goods as compared to money. The strong preference for goods brought about both the creation of money and attempts to shift from holding money to holding goods. I do not assert that there were no other important influences on the demand side of the market. The deliberate use of government fiscal policy after 1933 to create a price rise was a great innovation, but wars have undoubtedly been the strongest influence pushing up prices during the last half century. (The Civil War created a strong preference for goods relative to money, so that the increase in the money supply for a brief period had a far greater effect on prices than during the rest of the latter half of the nineteenth century.)

The differences between the two periods, however, are not solely explained by the demand side of the market. Important changes on the supply side of the labor market have been making wages increasingly sensitive to rises in

---

change in national income between 1890 and 1896 was the same as the rate estimated for the change in the gross national product between those dates in "Basic Facts on Employment and Production," 79th Congress, first session, *Committee Print No. 4,* Table E 1, p. 11. The gross-national-product figures, which are expressed in 1944 dollars, were converted into current dollars by the use of the index of wholesale prices. For the period 1930 to 1950, estimates of the national income by the Department of Commerce were used after adjustment for the difference between these estimates and that of Kuznets for the year 1930. The changes in the money supply and in the national income were as follows:

	Money supply (millions) (June 30)	*National income (billions)*
1850	$ 306	$ 2.2
1896	6,992	12.3
1950	190,926	219.8

prices, so that they move up more promptly and completely in response to advances in the price level. This is indicated in Table 1 by comparing the movements of prices and hourly earnings in periods of rising prices.

Table 1

Period	*Rise in the index of wholesale prices*	*Rise in hourly earnings of nonagricultural employees*	*Rise in hourly earnings as a per cent of the rise in wholesale prices*
1843–47	5.0%	3.0%	60.0%
1849–56	14.6	8.3	56.8
1860–65	116.7	48.7	41.7
1879–82	12.4	6.8	54.8
1896–1907	40.2%	29.0%	72.1%
1915–20	122.2	127.2	104.1
1932–37	33.3	37.8	113.5
1939–48	108.4	104.1	96.0
1949–51	15.7	13.2	84.1

The index of hourly earnings of nonagricultural workers prepared by the Bureau of Labor Statistics terminates in the year 1932. In Table 1 and Table 2, rough estimates of average hourly earnings outside of agriculture have been made as described below. These estimates are crude, but they are undoubtedly sufficiently accurate to show the response of hourly earnings to price changes. For the period 1932–37, nonagricultural hourly earnings were estimated by computing a weighted average of hourly earnings in manufacturing, railroading, and bituminous coal mining. For the period 1937 to 1939, nonagricultural hourly earnings were estimated by computing a weighted average of hourly earnings in manufacturing, bituminous coal mining, building construction, and railroading. For the periods 1939–48, 1948–49, 1949–51, and 1951 to July 1953, the average hourly earnings outside of agriculture were estimated by computing a weighted average of hourly earnings in manufacturing, bituminous coal mining, building construction, railroading, the telephone industry, wholesale trade, and retail trade. In order to eliminate as much as possible the effect of interindustry shifts, constant weights were used for each period. In all cases the weights were based on employment in the terminal year or on the terminal date of the period.

Recent great gains in union membership have made wages more resistant to falling prices, but this cannot be demonstrated statistically. Indeed, a superficial glance at Table 2 showing movements of hourly earnings in periods of falling prices might suggest that wages have become less resistant to a drop in prices.

Such an interpretation of the table would be wrong. The two early periods

Table 2

Period	*Fall in wholesale prices*	*Change in hourly earnings of non-agricultural employees*	*Rise in index of hourly earnings relative to the index of wholesale prices*
		Periods prior to 1896	
1840–43	13.1%	0 %	15.1%
1847–49	7.4	+ 5.9	14.4
1856–60	11.6	0	13.1
1865–71	37.3	+17.2	86.9
1872–79	30.4	−14.5	22.8
1882–96	29.7	+ 9.5	55.8
		Periods subsequent to 1896	
1920–22	37.4%	−11.1%	42.0%
1929–32	32.0	−20.2	17.4
1937–39	10.7	+ 2.1	14.3
1948–49	5.0	+ 4.3	9.8
1951–July 1953	3.4	+11.4	15.3

(1865 to 1871 and 1882 to 1896), when hourly earnings rose most in the face of falling prices, were partly periods of cyclical expansion and partly periods of contraction.[4] Furthermore, in the first of these periods, the rise of wages in the face of falling prices was undoubtedly in part a result of the great lag in wages behind prices during the period of the Civil War. All of the more recent periods of falling prices, except the last, were periods of business contraction, and in all of them the rise of wages relative to prices compares favorably with the great period of contraction in the seventies. As a matter of fact, the rise per year of wages relative to prices in the later periods of contraction (even the Great Depression of the thirties) was greater than in the seventies. It will be observed that neither of the two tables includes the periods 1907 to 1915 or 1922 to 1929. These are best regarded as periods of stability. There was a brief recession in 1908 and a recovery in 1909. Between that year and 1915 the price level moved up and down by small amounts with virtually no net change. The same is true of the period 1922 to 1929.

[4] In the first period there were thirty-four months of expansion and fifty months of contraction; in the second, ninety months of expansion and ninety of contraction. A. F. Burns and W. C. Mitchell, *Measuring Business Cycles* (New York, 1946), p. 78.

II

Five principal influences on the supply side of the market have increased the responsiveness of wages to increases in prices and have built up a tendency for wages to increase fast enough to force an increase in prices. They are: (1) the decline in the proportion of adult population in the labor force; (2) the great drop in the ratio of agricultural employment to nonagricultural employment; (3) the drop in immigration; (4) the rise of trade unionism; and (5) the development of government wage policy. The drop in ratio of agricultural employment to nonagricultural, the drop in immigration, and government wage policy have also been major influences modifying the structure of wages.

1. *The decline in the proportion of adult population in the labor force.* Part of this decline, namely, the withdrawal of many older persons, has been involuntary. Nevertheless, the proportion of population ten years of age or over in the labor force, after climbing considerably from 1870 to 1910, dropped substantially in the next thirty years. Had it not dropped, the labor force in 1940 would have been 5.5 million, or 10 per cent, larger than it actually was. Since 1940, there has been a small rise in the proportion of civilian population of fourteen years of age or over in the civilian labor force. This has been the result of the growing popularity of work among women. Among young men, especially those in the age brackets twenty to thirty-four, the proportion in the labor force has been dropping substantially, at least since 1930. The age group twenty to thirty-four is especially important to industry because its members are at the peak of their strength and vigor. Had the labor-force participation among males twenty to thirty-four years of age been as high in 1950 as in 1930, the labor force in these important age brackets would have been more than a million, or about 7 per cent, greater than it actually was.

2. *The great drop in the ratio of agricultural employment to nonagricultural employment.* In 1840 there were about 2.2 persons employed in agriculture for every worker in nonagricultural employment. By 1880 the ratio was one to one, and by 1930 the number of workers outside of agriculture for every worker in agriculture had risen to 3.9 and by 1950 to 7.6. The sharp drop in the relative size of the agricultural labor force is of great importance in explaining the behavior of wages because agriculture has provided a large reservoir of cheap labor, much of it possessing more than mere rudimentary skill in the mechanical arts.

3. *The drop in immigration.* In the forties and fifties of the last century,

net immigration totaled more than 20 per cent of the average size of the labor force during the decade, in the eighties 18 per cent, and in the sixties and seventies about one seventh. The decade of the nineties was an exception —net immigration was only 9.2 per cent of the average size of the labor force. The first decade of this century, when net immigration was 16.7 per cent of the average labor force, was the last period of large immigration. During the twenties net immigration was only 6.7 per cent of the average labor force, in the thirties there was no net immigration and in the forties immigration was 1.6 per cent of the average labor force. The reason for this drop in immigration is, of course, mainly our immigration law. It means that the economy in periods of expansion can no longer readily attract large quantities of labor from abroad.

4. *The rise of trade unions.* Unions seem to have had considerable influence for brief periods in the nineteenth century, but their sustained influence began with the twentieth century. In 1897, union membership was about 3 per cent of nonagricultural employment other than self-employed, managers, professional workers, and unpaid family workers. The spurt in membership at the turn of the century caused this proportion to rise to over 5 per cent by 1900. By 1910, the proportion was nearly 10 per cent and by 1920 more than 19 per cent. By 1933, however, union membership was down to less than 7 per cent of the nonagricultural labor force exclusive of proprietors, managers, professional workers, and unpaid family workers. It was in 1933, of course, that unions began to come into their own with powerful aid from the government. By 1940 union membership was about 25 per cent of the nonagricultural labor force, exclusive of proprietors, managers, professional workers, and unpaid family workers, and by 1950 about 40 per cent. Around two thirds of the workers in manufacturing and four fifths in construction, transportation, and mining are organized. Only the markets for agricultural products compare with the labor market in the extent of the arrangements for helping sellers gain favorable terms from their point of view.

5. *The development of the wage policy of the government.* Only within the last thirty years can the government be said to have had a wage policy, but in recent years the government has become an important influence in the labor market. The government exerts its influence through the Fair Labor Standards Act, the Bacon-Davis Act, the Walsh-Healey Act, through the direct purchase of labor, and through large construction projects which the government is financing—some of them in areas where wages have been relatively low. Except for the period of the Second World War, the influence

of the government has been designed, in the main, to help the sellers of labor get a better price rather than to help the buyers keep the price down.

III

A number of economists have expressed doubts that trade unions, despite their rapid growth, have had much influence on money wages. Professor Friedman, in his stimulating discussion of "The Significance of Labor Unions for Economic Policy," has expressed the view that "laymen and economists alike tend . . . to exaggerate greatly the extent to which labor unions affect the structure and level of wage rates." [5] He goes so far as to assert that the United Automobile Workers and the United Steel Workers "were responsible for preventing the wages of their members from rising as much as they would in the absence of the union" (pp. 210, 217–228).

Friedman's views are shared by a number of economists, and I wish to examine the evidence for and against them. It would be surprising, I think, if the views of Friedman were correct. It is the principal purpose of the trade-union movement to influence the level of money wages. Unions have demonstrated many times their ability to force employers to accept unwelcome conditions, such as the closed shop or the union shop. Even the automobile workers' and steel workers' unions, which Friedman regards as weak, have established the union shop in their industries, formerly citadels of the open shop. It would be strange if the bargaining ability of unions were so specialized that unions were able to force employers to accept the deeply abominated union or closed shop and yet not force them to pay somewhat higher money wages than they would otherwise pay.

Such a failure of unions to influence money wages would be surprising for another reason—because unions introduce important changes in the methods of buying and selling labor. In the absence of unions, pricing in the labor market is on a take-it-or-leave-it basis, similar in a way to most retail markets except that in the retail market the seller names the take-it-or-leave-it price and in the labor market the buyer names the take-it-or-leave-it price. It is to be expected that negotiated prices would be more responsive to increases in demand than the take-it-or-leave-it price. The quickness of the response is likely to have important long-run consequences because it may determine whether savings in cost are captured by the workers before they are passed on to consumers.

The view that unions have little influence on money wages is supported

[5] In *The Impact of the Labor Union*, David McCord Wright, ed. (New York, 1956), p. 204.

by three principal reasons. In the first place, it is said that managers, realizing that unions will strongly oppose wage cuts, are less willing to raise the wages of union workers than the wages of nonunion workers. In the second place, attention is called to the fact that union contracts in the past have usually run for a year or more. Hence, it is said that unions are unable to press promptly for wage increases when business expands. Finally, it is pointed out that union leaders sometimes seek to discourage stiff wage demands because they believe that the boom will be temporary and that large wage increases will price the union members out of the market.

All of these reasons, it will be observed, relate to the influence of unions during periods of expansion rather than during periods of contraction. I do not believe that the first of these three suggested reasons has been important, but the other two have at times had limited influence on union wages. The possibility of cutting the wages of nonunion workers in case business turns bad has little or no influence on the willingness of employers to increase the wages of nonunion workers. The reason is that wage cuts are likely to cause trouble even when the workers are not union. A notable example of a union contract retarding wage increases was the three-year contract made by the United Mine Workers shortly before the United States entered the First World War. Wages soon rose far above the rates specified in the contract and, in spite of the union's heroic efforts to help employers get labor at the rates agreed to, the market soon compelled the negotiation of new rates. A case where the long-term contract worked in the opposite way was the five-year agreement between the compositors' unions and the commercial printers of New York, effective in January 1928. It provided for annual wage increases. By the time the depression was well advanced the employers were seeking relief, but they did not obtain it. Today unions and employers are well aware of the pitfalls in long-term contracts and rarely freeze wages for more than a year. Many recent contracts have provided for reopening of wages on relatively short notice. There have been times, too, when union leaders have sought to limit the wage demands of their members. This happened in some of the building trades unions during the Second World War. The leaders remembered the difficult adjustments when prices fell after the First World War and they wished to avoid repetition of that experience. And union leaders often warn their members against the danger of getting union rates too much above the rates in competing nonunion plants. But evidence that union leaders do this hardly supports the view that unions have no tendency to accelerate the rise in money wages.

It is plain that unions have a considerable effect upon the structure of money wages. True, many nonunion employers meet the union scale and, now that the threat of unionization is strong, a few deliberately pay more than the union scale, but the most frequent case is the one of higher wage scales in union plants. Furthermore, the history of unionism is full of instances of unions forcing a large part of their employers out of business through enforcing differentials above the nonunion scale. Examples are the coal miners' union, the hosiery workers, the men's-clothing workers (the Chicago market), the potters, the tapestry carpet weavers, the shoe workers, the flint-glass workers, the cotton textile workers, the women's-garment workers, and others.

But the ability of unions to modify the structure of wages does not indicate that unions affect the movement of wages through time. Their influence on the structure of wages may be a once-for-all effect unaccompanied by any tendency of unions to accelerate the rise in money wages. Several attempts have been made to measure the effects of unions on wages through time. Douglas' pioneer attempt, in his *Real Wages in the United States, 1890–1926,* produced ambiguous results because his union figures were in the main time-rate figures and his so-called "payroll" figures (which came from industries in which unions were weak) came mainly from industries (textiles, hosiery, men's clothing, boots and shoes, meat packing, iron and steel) in which piece rates or tonnage rates predominate. Hence, the comparison was as much one of relative movements of day-work and piece-work earnings through time as it was one of the movement of union and nonunion earnings.[6] The investigations of Ross and Goldner lead them to conclude that recently organized unions tend to accelerate the rise in hourly earnings.[7] But Ross and Goldner

[6] Douglas found greater cyclical fluctuations in payroll wages than in union wages, with a tendency for union wages to rise more slowly than payroll wages in periods of expansion and to fall more slowly in periods of recession—or for union wages not to fall at all in periods of recession. But this is the kind of contrast in movement that one would expect to find between hourly earnings based on day rates and hourly earnings based on piece rates. I suspect that the cyclical differences in the wages of the two groups was a result partly of the fact that one group was organized and the other not and partly of the fact that one group was mainly time-workers and the other mainly piece-workers. But the relative influence of these conditions cannot be measured. The fact that in the thirty-six years from 1890 to 1926 the hourly earnings of the union time-workers rose almost as much as the hourly earnings of the other group attests to the influence of unions. The earnings of piece-workers tend to rise faster than the earnings of time-workers because many small changes in materials, equipment, and method do not lead to the rates being reset. Hence, the fact that the hourly earnings of union time-workers rose over the entire period almost as rapidly as the earnings of nonunion piece-workers indicates that unions had a strong influence on wages. On the tendency of the earnings of piece-workers to rise faster than wage rates, see my *Union Policies and Industrial Management,* pp. 255, 256, 293.

[7] "Forces Affecting the Interindustry Wage Structure," *Quarterly Journal of Economics* (May 1950), pp. 254–281.

measure wage changes in absolute rather than relative terms—a procedure which I think is incorrect. Hence, although I believe that this part of their conclusion is correct, their proof is unsatisfactory: they have perhaps demonstrated that unions grew fastest in the industries which happened to have the highest wages in 1933, but they have not shown that unions accelerate the rise in wages. I agree with Ross and Goldner that "the strongest influences on wages seem to have operated throughout the economy rather than affected individual industries differentially" (p. 280). I believe, however, that at least since 1933 unions should be regarded primarily as a general market influence.

The most thorough investigation of the movement of union and nonunion wage rates is that of H. M. Levinson.[8] He divides the period he studied into seven principal parts: 1914–20, 1920–23, 1923–29, 1929–33, 1933–38, 1938–41, and 1941–47. Two of these seven periods (1920–23 and 1929–33) were mainly or entirely times of business contraction. In both of these periods the hourly earnings in the more highly organized industries showed much less tendency to drop than hourly earnings in the less organized industries.[9] There will be little dispute, I think, that unions tend to hold up wages in periods of severe contraction: they widen the gap in the labor-supply curve immediately to the left of the existing wage. As a matter of fact, unions push wages up during the early parts of business contractions. For example, union rates continued to climb for two years after the stock market crash of 1929.[10]

One of the periods covered by Levinson was the time of the Second World War, from 1941 to 1947. Government controls of wages were so complete during this period that it is not surprising to find no relationship between the degree of union organization and the movement of wages. Government policy was devoted in the main to two objectives: (1) to prevent the bargaining power of the strong unions from producing inflationary wage increases, and (2) to concentrate wage increases more or less among the lowest-paid workers in order to give relief from rising prices where it was presumably most needed. Nearly all of the unions cooperated with the government.

Another period studied by Levinson, 1923–29, was a time of prosperity but not of general boom; the speculative buying was limited to the stock market and real estate. It was a time when unions as a whole were not prospering.

[8] *Unionism, Wage Trends, and Income Distribution, 1914–1947* (Ann Arbor, Michigan Business Studies, X).

[9] Levinson, p. 47. The period 1920–23 contained a year of recovery. In all the union industries, wages were generally higher in 1923 than in 1920; in the nonunion, wages were generally lower in 1923 than in 1920. In 1922, however, union wages were below 1920 but the drop was less than the drop in nonunion wages (pp. 34–35).

[10] Bureau of Labor Statistics, "History of Wages in the United States from Colonial Times to 1928," *Bulletin No. 604*, p. 574.

Total union membership remained unchanged at 3.6 million between 1923 and 1929, making no recovery from the 1.4 million drop from the peak in 1920. In this period of weakness, unions influenced the wages of their own members but had little influence on wages outside their union plants. Hence, Levinson found, a comparison of wages in highly unionized industries and poorly organized industries clearly shows wages in the former definitely outrunning wages in the latter between 1923 and 1929 (p. 47).

Of the remaining three periods studied by Levinson, the first, 1914–20, was for the most part a strong sellers' market, and the other two (1933–38 and 1938–41) were times of rapidly rising wages in the face of substantial unemployment. In the first period, 1914–20, nonunion wages rose considerably faster than union wages (p. 33). In the other two periods, union and nonunion wages went up at more or less the same rate (pp. 60–61, 65). And yet despite the fact that during the First World War nonunion wages rose faster than union wages and that during the periods 1933 to 1938 and 1938 to 1941 union and nonunion wages rose at about the same rate, I think that union pressure for higher wages substantially accelerated the rise of all wages in these periods. This assertion requires that I explain the limitations of comparisons of the movements of wages in the well-organized and less-organized industries over more or less extended periods as a method of deducing the influence of unions on money wages and that I adduce specific evidence for believing that unions accelerated the rise in the general level of money wages between 1914 and 1920 and between 1933 and 1941.

IV

The attempt to deduce the influence of unions on money wages by comparing the movements of wages in highly organized industries with the movements in less well-organized industries assumes that the influence of unions on wages is greater in the well-organized industries than in the poorly organized industries. This seems like a reasonable assumption, and it is true much of the time—particularly during severe recessions or other periods, such as 1923 to 1929, when unions are having tough going and gaining few members. But this method of testing the effect of unions breaks down in those times when unions exert great influence on the wages of nonunion workers. Furthermore, the greater the influence of unions on the wages of nonunion workers, the more complete is the breakdown of the method. In periods of strong sellers' markets, when unions are gaining members rapidly and winning large wage increases and thus exerting a powerful influence on wages in nonunion plants, the method of comparing wage changes in union and nonunion plants may show no apparent influence of unions at all. Many unions may be held back a few months in raising the wages of their members by unexpired agreements, and yet the unions which are negotiating may be winning large increases which have immediate repercussions among employers who fear that unionism will spread to their workers. Hence, unions may cause the money wages of nonunion workers to rise faster than the average wages of all union workers. Attempts to detect the influence of unions by comparing the movements of union and nonunion wages through time fail at precisely those periods when the influence of unions is strongest. It is necessary to use methods that enable one to observe more closely the changes in union and nonunion wages and that take account of the circumstances accompanying wage changes.

All three periods, 1914–20, 1933–38, and 1938–41, were times when unions were accentuating the effect of the rightward movements of demand curves by raising the supply price of labor but when the effects of unions on wages were obscured because unions were a general market influence. Let us consider first the period 1914–20 when nonunion wages outran union wages. Unions were not the only important influence on the supply side of the market, because the wage structure was adjusting itself to the sudden stoppage of immigration, but unions were an important influence. Union membership virtually doubled between 1914 and 1920, and labor stoppages increased from 1,204 in 1914 to 4,450 in 1917 and remained well above 3,000 a year for the entire period. During 1919 more than one fifth of so-called "employed wage earners" were at some time engaged in a strike—the largest proportion on record. (By "employed wage earners" the Bureau of Labor Statistics means all wage earners except those in occupations or professions in which strikes rarely, if ever, occur.) It is significant that the rise in hourly earnings between 1919 and 1920, according to the estimates of Douglas, was the largest (23.3 per cent) for any year in the period.

It would be fantastic to argue that the rapid spread of unionism and the great growth in the number of strikes did not alarm nonunion employers and did not lead them to raise wages in an attempt to keep their people satisfied. The efforts of nonunion employers to keep out unions are revealed in the spread of employee-representation plans. Such plans had been quite rare prior to 1914. They were adopted by many companies during the First World War in an effort to keep out unions.[11]

[11] Standard Oil Company of New Jersey, Standard Oil Company of Indiana, International Harvester Company, Goodyear Tire and Rubber Company, Westinghouse Electric and Manu-

The periods 1933–38 and 1938–41 were also times when the influence of unions on wages was so great that it was a general market influence substantially affecting the wages of nonunion workers. The government also, through the National Industrial Recovery Act, the Bacon-Davis Act, the Walsh-Healey Act, and the Fair Labor Standards Act, exerted a powerful influence on wages, especially on the wages of the lowest-paid employees and on wages in the South—wages which unions were least able to influence. Membership in unions almost quadrupled between 1933 and 1941, and work stoppages increased enormously. In 1933, strikes were more than twice as numerous as in 1932, and they were particularly numerous in 1934 and 1937. Employers attempted to halt the spread of unionism by organizing employee-representation plans as well as by making wage concessions. The employees covered by representation plans increased from about 1.3 million in 1932 to about 2.5 million in 1935.

Many employers who endeavored to halt the spread of unions by granting wage increases found themselves having to give a second increase after the first one failed to halt the growth of the union. The United States Steel Corporation is an example. On November 6, 1936, the corporation offered the company unions a 10 per cent wage increase. This was done at a time when more than 8 million people (about one sixth of the labor force) were unemployed, when there had been little movement in the hourly earnings of factory workers for ten months, and when there had been little movement in the consumers' price index for over a year. The increase failed to weaken the interest of the employees in unions. Hence, early in March 1937, U. S. Steel and the Steel Workers' Organizing Committee entered into an agreement by which the company recognized the union as the representative of its own members and granted a second wage increase of ten cents an hour.

About the same time that the Steel Workers' Organizing Committee was winning its important victory over U. S. Steel, the automobile workers were winning important victories over General Motors and Chrysler, and in April 1937 the constitutionality of the Wagner Act was upheld. Under the influence of the Roosevelt victory in November 1936, the steel settlement, the victories of the automobile workers, and the upholding of the Wagner Act, hourly earnings in manufacturing, which had scarcely changed in the face of rising industrial production between January 1936 and October 1936,

---

facturing Company, Bethlehem Steel Corporation, Yale and Towne were among the prominent companies adopting employee-representation plans during this period. Not to be confused with the plans adopted by companies for the purpose of keeping out unions are the plans forced on companies by government agencies such as the National War Labor Board and bitterly resented by the employers.

rose steadily throughout 1937.[12] This increase in hourly earnings during 1937 occurred in the face of only a small rise in the adjusted index of industrial production, from 116 in January to 121 in May, followed by a drop to 87 in December—in the face of falling prices after April, and in the face of a monthly average of 7.7 million unemployed, or about one seventh of the labor force.

What happened to make hourly earnings rise substantially after remaining unchanged for ten months in 1936? Simply the largest gain in union membership in any single year in the history of the United States! The growth in union membership between 1936 and 1937 was in excess of 3 million, or more than the entire trade-union membership of the country at the bottom of the depression in 1933. The spurt in union membership was accompanied by a doubling in the number of strikes, making 1937 the largest year up to then in the number of work stoppages and the next to the largest in number of workers involved. Can anyone contend that the enormous jump in trade-union membership and the doubling of the number of strikes had nothing to do with wages rising in the latter half of 1937 in the face of falling production and rising unemployment?

V

Of particular interest is the period from the end of the Second World War to the present. It is during this period (or most of it) that Friedman asserts that the United Steel Workers and the United Automobile Workers held down the wages of their members. It has been a time when hourly earnings in poorly organized industries have risen almost as rapidly as in well-organized industries. Retailing and wholesaling, which are poorly organized, have lagged behind the better-organized industries, but, in the field of manufacturing, hourly earnings in the poorly organized industries increased as rapidly as in the well-organized ones. Among eight manufacturing industries with less than 40 per cent organization in 1946, straight-time hourly earnings increased by 49.4 per cent between January 1947 and July 1953, and among eighteen manufacturing industries with 60 per cent or more of the employees organized, hourly earnings increased by 48.8 per cent. I believe, however, that the period 1946 to the present is one in which unions have exerted a powerful influence on the wages of nonunion workers. Hence, efforts to test

[12] Hourly earnings of factory workers were 55.3 cents in January 1936 and 55.5 cents in October 1936. In March 1937 they were 59.5 cents and, in December 1937, 64.3 cents. U. S. Bureau of Labor Statistics, *Production-Worker Employment, Payrolls, Hours, and Earnings in Manufacturing Industries, 1914–1938,* LS 55–0902, 9–52, p. 9.

the effects of unions by comparing the movement of union and nonunion wages over fairly extended periods of time are inconclusive. But careful examination of what was going on in the labor market at the time important union settlements were made shows the influence of these important settlements. Let us seek to appraise the contribution of unions to the postwar wage-price spiral by looking at the record.

For some months prior to V-J Day, factory employment had been dropping. It was 1.4 million less in August 1945 than in February 1945. It continued to drop for some months after V-J Day: it was 1.7 million less in December 1945 than in August 1945. Indeed, not until October 1946 did factory employment exceed the level of August 1945. Hours of work were falling also, and with them weekly take-home pay. Average weekly earnings in manufacturing, which had been $47.12 in April 1945, decreased to $41.72 in August and $40.97 in October. The consumers' price index had changed little for a considerable period before and after V-J Day. On January 15, 1945, it was 127.1; in August, 129.3; and in February 1946, 129.6.

The end of the war saw prompt moves by public officials to encourage workers to demand large wage increases. On August 18, 1945, President Truman relaxed wage controls by permitting the War Labor Board and other agencies to allow employers to increase wages without government approval, provided such increases were not used as the basis for raising prices or resisting proper price reductions. In late October, President Truman in a broadcast to the nation urged "substantial" wage increases as "imperative . . . to sustain adequate purchasing power and raise the national income," with the line on prices held to avoid inflation.

Enterprises which were cutting back hours to forty a week (or in some cases to forty-four) saw the necessity of passing on at least part of the saving from the drop in overtime payments. The earliest increases (in Hercules Powder and Du Pont, for example) were 10 per cent, but on September 9, 1945, Standard Oil Company of New Jersey put into effect a 15 per cent increase in pay together with a forty-hour week. The CIO unions were quite generally demanding a 30 per cent rise in base rates to offset cuts in working hours. The first big test came in the oil industry. By the end of September, oil refineries in six states were closed by strikes, and early in October the President seized the plants of eleven oil companies. The key settlement in the oil industry came on December 16, 1945, when the Sinclair Oil Company settled for an 18 per cent wage increase. This settlement was followed in the next month or so by the other oil companies.

The next great test came in the automobile industry. The General Motors strike began on November 21. It was followed by large strikes in the electrical-products industry on January 15, 1946, the meat-packing industry on January 16, the steel industry on January 18, the copper industry, and other industries. The many and large strikes in the latter part of 1945 made the year by far the largest then on record in terms of mandays idle and second only to 1919 in terms of the proportion of employed workers involved. But the year 1946 was destined far to surpass 1945 in time lost. The increase in the number of strikes was small and so was the rise in the proportion of workers involved (though one out of seven of the so-called "employed workers" participated in stoppages), but the longer duration of strikes caused the time lost nearly to treble. No other year comes close to 1946 in the amount of time lost by strikes or lockouts. In the great majority of strikes in 1945 and 1946 the principal issue was wages.

The big strikes in the industries dominated by large and rich corporations (automobile, electrical products, steel, agricultural implements) were settled for about 18 to 18.5 cents an hour. In the steel dispute, after United States Steel Corporation had offered 15 cents, President Truman proposed 18.5 cents. Late in January, while the steel strike was still unsettled, Ford and Chrysler, which had not been struck, settled with the automobile workers for 18 cents and 18.5 cents, respectively, and these figures proved to be the approximate points of settlement of nearly all of the negotiations involving large and prominent enterprises.

The settlements were only several cents more than the employers had offered before the strikes. This fact shows that managements did a good job of estimating the willingness of the unions to fight. But the offers of employers to powerful and aggressive unions do not indicate what employers would have done in the absence of such unions. The so-called pattern settlements in the oil, automobile, steel, and other industries were well above the settlements that were being made by most concerns and had the effect of accelerating the rise in wages generally. This is shown by comparisons of the pattern settlements with the settlements and by comparisons of the movements of wages before and after the pattern-setting settlements.

A special survey by the Bureau of Labor Statistics of general wage changes in six thousand plants between V-J Day (August 18, 1945) and May 1, 1946, showed that most wage increases were far less than the pattern. In manufacturing plants, 21.3 per cent of workers covered by the survey received no general wage increase at all between August 18, 1945, and May 1, 1946; 15.2 per cent received general increases of less than 10 cents an hour; 16.6 per cent increases of 10 to 15 cents; 15.4 per cent increases of 15 to 18 cents; and 23.7

per cent increases of 19 cents and over.[13] In selected nonmanufacturing industries (retailing, wholesaling, finance, services, heat, light and power), where union organization in general was weak, general wage increases were fewer and smaller. Between August 18, 1945, and May 1, 1946, 59.2 per cent of the nonfactory workers received no general wage increase and 25.2 per cent more received increases of less than 10 cents. In other words, among this group of industries only 15.6 per cent of the workers, or less than one sixth, received an increase of 10 cents an hour or more. It seems clear that where unions were strong, wages behaved quite differently from the way in which they behaved where unions were weak.

Comparisons of the movement of hourly earnings before and after the pattern-making settlements in late January and February 1946 show the effects of these settlements in accelerating the upward movement of wages. In the four months from October 1945 to February 1946 "urban wage rates" had increased 4.3 per cent, but in the two months following the pattern settlements, from February to April 1946, they increased more than twice as fast—5.3 per cent.[14]

The above evidence of the lags in wage increases in 1946 in nonmanufacturing industries is of considerable interest. During the entire postwar period, hourly earnings in retailing and wholesaling—two large industries with little union membership—have risen almost as fast as in manufacturing, where two out of three production workers are union members. Between February 1946 and January 1953, straight-time hourly earnings increased by 66.5 per cent in manufacturing and hourly earnings increased 55.9 per cent in wholesaling and 60 per cent in retailing. And yet between August 18, 1945, and May 1, 1946, 48.4 per cent of the employees in wholesaling and 63.6 per cent in retailing among the plants covered by the survey of the Bureau of Labor Statistics had received no increases. The union industries were evidently setting the pace and the less well-organized industries were following suit.

I shall not make extended comment on the other years of the period 1945–53. In 1947 the settlements in the industries composed of wealthy and prominent corporations were on the basis of 15 cents an hour. The year saw

[13] *Monthly Labor Review* (September 1946), p. 344.

[14] *Monthly Labor Review* (November 1946), p. 659. Urban wage rates, it will be recalled, measure changes in basic wage rates resulting from general changes in wage scales and from individual wage-rate adjustments within occupational classifications. They exclude the effects of most changes in the composition of the work force and of shifts in employment between occupations, regions, and industries. They also exclude changes in payments for overtime work, holidays, and vacation.

more people engaged in strikes than usual, but nearly all of these strikes were small ones. After the big strikes of 1946, the large employers and the unions alike were anxious to avoid trouble. A threatened strike of oil workers in seven oil companies in five western states in February was averted by increases equivalent to more than 20 cents an hour.[15] When negotiations in the rubber industry broke down and the union issued a strike call to one hundred thousand men, a tentative settlement was made by a wage advance of 11.5 cents. This settlement, however, was obviously not regarded as a pattern because reopening of the wage issue was permitted after one hundred and twenty days. The pattern was set by the settlement between General Motors and the United Electrical Workers in April for 15 cents. This was quickly followed by the same settlement in the steel, electrical-products, and agricultural-implement industries and in the automobile industry generally. The agreement in the rubber industry was revised to meet the pattern.

The price which the large employers were willing to pay to keep the peace was definitely above the market. This is shown by 310 settlements made just before and after April and during April. Less than 28 per cent of these (86 out of 310) were for 15 cents or more, 83 were for less than 10 cents; and 61 for 10 to 11 cents. Among 180 settlements made in the first three months of 1947, 45, or one fourth, were for 15 cents an hour or more. In the three months before the pattern settlements, January to April 1947, average hourly earnings in manufacturing rose 2.5 cents; in the three months following the settlements, April to July, hourly earnings in manufacturing rose 4.4 cents. Both wholesale prices and the consumers' price index rose more rapidly between January and April 1947 than between April and July.

The year 1948 is difficult to interpret, but I conclude that the union influence in this year in most industries was less than in previous years. The large enterprises, which in 1947 had been primarily concerned with avoiding a repetition of the big strikes of 1946, were in 1948 primarily concerned with halting the wage-price spiral that had been fostered by the large wage increases of the last two years. Consequently, a determined effort was made to hold the line. At the opening of negotiations between the General Electric Company and the United Electrical Workers, the company announced that it did not care to take the responsibility for the inflationary effects of a wage increase. As a result, negotiations were deadlocked for weeks. In April 1948, the United States Steel Corporation refused the demand of steel workers for a "substantial" wage increase. The attempt of employers to hold the line led

[15] *New York Journal of Commerce*, February 20, 1947.

to deadlocks or breaking off of negotiations in the agricultural-implement industry, the rubber industry, and the aluminum industry.

The union in the steel industry was bound by its contract not to strike. It remained to be seen whether any of the other large industrial unions would strike. They were obviously reluctant to do so, each perhaps hoping that some other union would take the lead. In May 1948, however, the United Automobile Workers attempted to break the deadlock by pulling a strike of its seventy-five thousand members in the Chrysler Corporation. Somewhat to the surprise of everyone, the union succeeded in breaking the deadlock, but not in the way that had been foreseen. It was not an agreement between the UAW and Chrysler which set the pattern. While the Chrysler strike was still unsettled, General Motors, instead of taking advantage of the union's preoccupation, offered an increase of 11 cents plus future adjustments for changes in the cost of living and an automatic increase of 3 cents a year for gains in productivity. The offer was accepted and became the basis for settlements in reopened negotiations in the steel, aluminum, rubber, agricultural-implements, and electrical-products industries. These settlements did not contain the cost-of-living or productivity features of the General Motors settlement but were generally for a straight 13 cents. (In rubber the settlement was for 11 cents, in the electrical products industry for 8 per cent, in aluminum for 10 per cent.)

I do not know the motives of General Motors in making its settlement. Perhaps the management thought that wage increases would be good for the economy as a whole; perhaps General Motors feared that Chrysler would not hold out much longer with its rivals making cars and would set a pattern that would be detrimental to the rest of the industry. That the settlement was generous is indicated by the fact that out of 129 wage settlements in March, April, and up to May 20, only 23 were for 13 cents an hour or more and 54 were for less than 10 cents an hour.[16] The effect of the settlement was to quicken the rise in hourly earnings in manufacturing. Between January and May, hourly earnings had increased from $1.302 to $1.324 or 2.2 cents; in the same length of time, May to September, the increase was 6.2 cents.

In 1949, a year of mild contraction, the influence of unions was definite, though limited. In the face of market conditions that would have yielded unorganized workers little or nothing, unions continued to make gains. It

[16] National Industrial Conference Board, *Management Record,* April, 1948, pp. 254–256; May, 1948, pp. 294–296; June, 1948, pp. 382–384. Even in June and July most settlements were below the pattern. Of 87 compiled by the N.I.C.B. made between June 15 and July 15, 1948, only 19 were for 13 cents or more and 29 were for less than 10 cents.

took some striking to win these gains, and the proportion of "employed workers" engaged in work stoppages increased from 5.5 per cent in 1948 to 9.0 per cent in 1949. The most notable gain was the successful strike of the steel workers for noncontributory pensions. This victory led in the following months to a rapid spread of noncontributory pension plans.

In both 1950 and 1951 the influence of unions on money wages was limited and was confined to particular industries. But in 1952 the steel workers won a great victory over the steel industry and the government which had far-reaching effects on wages in other industries and virtually destroyed the wage-stabilization policy of the government.[17] The victory came after the longest strike in recent years in the industry and was equivalent to more than a 21-cent wage increase. How far the settlement was out of line with the market is indicated by the fact that out of 745 settlements in manufacturing industries in the three months, April, May, and June, only 98 were for 15 cents and over and only 5 were for 20 cents or over. Among 520 settlements in nonmanufacturing industries in the same period, 77 were for 20 cents an hour or more and 281 for 15 cents an hour or more.[18] The larger proportion of settlements for 15 cents or better among the nonmanufacturing industries reflects the fact that many nonunion plants outside of manufacturing granted the increases allowed under the government's wage-stabilization policy only after considerable delay.

The steel settlement stimulated rises in wages in many industries. The coal industry was the most notable. The union insisted on a large increase in spite of much short-time work and considerable unemployment in the industry. But straight-time hourly earnings in manufacturing, which had been unchanged since April 1952, began to move up and by November were 5 cents higher than in July.

VI

Let me conclude these remarks with a brief summary and a few observations on matters of theory and policy. Changes in money wages must be explained by influences on the supply side of the market as well as by influences on the demand side. It would be a miracle, no doubt, if the wage-

[17] The real destruction of the wage-stabilization policy of the government was accomplished by the United Mine Workers. The miners were intent on getting more than the steel workers had won, and the miners succeeded.

[18] U. S. Bureau of Labor Statistics, *Current Wage Developments*, May 1952, June 1952, July 1952.

fixing arrangements of the economy had no inflationary or deflationary bias —if they kept the general level of labor costs from rising or falling over the period of the business cycle despite changes in technology and changes in the demand for goods. It looks very much as if the wage-fixing arrangements in the American economy have a small inflationary bias—that they tend to put up wages fast enough to require a slow advance in our price level.

Influences on the supply side of the market (particularly the ability of dissatisfied workers to withhold efficiency) have a strong tendency to keep fairly small the differences in the rates at which wages in most industries rise. Hence, there is a rough similarity in wage movements in most industries, in spite of considerable diversity in conditions in different industries. Various changes on the supply side of the market during the last fifty years have had important influences on both the structure of wages and the movement of wages. The drop in immigration and the great drop in the size of the farm labor force relative to the nonfarm have raised the wages of the unskilled relative to the wages of the skilled. These influences and other influences as well have made wages more responsive to increases in the demand for labor and less responsive to decreases in the demand. Trade unions are among the influences affecting the responsiveness of wages. Within the last twenty years unions have become so pervasive and so powerful that they are a general market influence affecting, usually after short lags, the wages of nonunion workers almost as much as the wages of union workers.

The influence of unions in periods of expansion may be summarized as follows: wages in some occupations or industries increase sooner and faster than elsewhere. Aggressive and powerful unions, such as the miners, the steel workers, or the teamsters, may be partly or largely responsible for the larger than average increase, but there are many reasons. The susceptibility of employers to pressure varies with conditions. These conditions I have not explored. Sometimes managements may yield rather readily because they wish to keep the unions weak and divided. The petroleum industry, in which managements are striving to avert company-wide agreements, is an example.

The pattern-making settlements, though substantially out of line with most settlements at the time, influence the course of wages in industry generally. Hence, over a period of time there is not a great difference in the increase in average hourly earnings in the pattern-setting industries and in industry as a whole. For example, between the years 1947 and the middle of 1953, there was not a great difference in the increase in average hourly earnings in the pattern-setting industries, in manufacturing as a whole, and in retailing and wholesaling, as the following table shows.

	Increase in average straight-time hourly earnings January 1947 to August 1953
Blast furnaces and rolling mills	61.2
Petroleum	58.9
Automobiles	52.3
Coal	59.5
Electrical machinery	48.8
Tires	49.0
All manufacturing	51.0
Retailing	45.7
Wholesaling	46.9

An examination of local labor markets will show a similar influence of settlements by powerful unions, such as the teamsters, building trades, and printers, upon the wages of other unions and upon nonunion wages. Settlements which are out of line with the market accelerate the rise in the market, so that over a period of a few years there are not great differences in wage movements between the pattern-setting industries and other industries.

In periods of contraction the influence of unions is much less than in periods of expansion—though more easily detected. In mild recessions many unions are able to negotiate improvements in wages and fringe benefits in spite of leftward shifts in the demand curve for labor.

The years 1933, 1934, 1937, 1938, 1940, 1941, 1946, 1947, 1948, 1949, and 1952 are recent years in which trade unions seem definitely to have accelerated the rise in money wages. I have made no effort to measure precisely the increase in money wages attributable to trade unions. Since the year 1933, however, the increase attributable to unions is undoubtedly at least 25 cents an hour and probably more.

The largest wage increases considerably exceed the average growth of output per man hour throughout industry as a whole. Hence, when unions tend to spread these increases, they tend to raise wages faster than the average gain in productivity, thus bringing about a rise in labor costs. The advance in labor costs undoubtedly stimulates technological progress, but it is bound also to produce either unemployment or a higher price level.

If our wage-fixing arrangements have an inflationary bias, what should be done about them? From the standpoint of the rest of the world, a slowly rising price level in the United States is greatly to be desired. Certainly it would promote the success of our foreign policy. Furthermore, from the domestic point of view, the inflationary bias in our wage-setting arrangements has advantages as well as disadvantages. But let us assume that for domestic reasons we prefer a stable price level. Some people say we should correct the inflationary bias in wage-fixing arrangements by tight credit policy. The economists of the Swedish trade unions say we should make the employer do a better job of resisting labor's demands by imposing taxes which prevent his passing on higher wages in the form of higher prices. Some distinguished economists, such as Sir William Beveridge and J. M. Clark, say we should build up a sense of responsibility among employers and trade unionists—that an economy such as ours, which does not automatically keep itself in balance, can be satisfactorily operated only when groups are led by public-spirited and responsible persons.

Neither of the first two proposals is satisfactory, and the third is, I fear, too utopian to be promptly achieved. The problem of correct credit policy in an economy with powerful trade unions is extremely difficult. One cannot argue that the monetary authorities should create whatever flow of money is required to keep full employment and also to meet whatever wage demands unions may see fit to press. That would confer intolerable freedom on trade unions. At the same time, correcting an inflationary bias in wage-fixing arrangements by deliberately creating unemployment is wasteful. There must be a better answer.

I do not think that the Swedes have found the answer. It must be possible to stiffen the resistance of employers to excessive wage demands without imposing taxes which are bound to prevent the best use of resources. Clark's analysis of the problem of operating an economy which does not automatically keep itself in balance is admirable. (See his *Alternative to Serfdom,* especially the last chapter.) He is surely correct that such an economy requires that individuals go far in identifying collective interests with their individual interests, so that each individual gets real satisfaction from observing that the community is prospering. The civilized man is one who feels a deep and broad concern for the welfare of large groups, and the struggle to achieve civilization is essentially an effort to make each individual feel an interest in the well-being of an ever-growing number of his fellows. But we cannot wait for the slow progress of the civilization to get better results from the economy. Something quicker is needed.

My belief is that the community must look to employers for help. Certainly, if rising labor costs force a rise in the price level, the community may properly insist that employers do a better job of bargaining. And the community has the means to interest employers in doing a better job of bargaining. The large employers desire and, indeed, need public approval for their principal policies. They have yielded too readily to the claims of labor partly because they did not wish to be shut down while their rivals did business, but partly also because they have felt that a fight on behalf of the consumer would win them less public approval than would the granting of liberal wage concessions. But if the public decides that it must have stable labor costs because it desires a stable price level, it will reserve its approval for the employers who valiantly oppose excessive wage claims and will withhold its approval from the employer who readily accepts higher labor costs rather than risk the costs of a possible shutdown.

Hence, in the last analysis, the answer to the question, "do the wage-fixing arrangements in the American labor market have an inflationary bias?" will be supplied by the public itself. If the public strongly insists that employers hold labor costs stable, employers will attempt to do so. But if the public is indifferent and if the government attempts to maintain full employment, employers will find it easier to accept small increases in labor costs than to risk shutdowns, and the community will have a slowly rising price level.

27

Comments on the Steel Report: Raising the Price of Labor as a Method of Increasing Employment

Review of Economics and Statistics, November 1949.

I

THE Nathan report * raises questions of long-run interest to economists because it argues that raising the price of labor relative to the prices of commodities is an effective way of halting a contraction in business —in other words, that the way to halt a drop in the demand for labor is to raise the price of labor. Students of business cycles have proposed many policies for checking the contraction of business, but more or less general wage increases have not been among them. If raising wages will halt contraction, a long step toward averting business recessions will have been taken and most students of business cycles can shift their activities to other fields.

The Nathan report recognizes that in some plants the immediate effect of higher wage rates relative to commodity prices would be a reduction in the size of payrolls. Hence the report proposes that wages be increased only in those plants where the immediate effect would be an increase in the size of payrolls. The report does not indicate how high wages should be raised—whether up to the point where the immediate demand for labor becomes elastic so that still higher wage rates would mean smaller payrolls, or up to some other point. At any rate, the specific device advocated by the report is raising wages where the immediate effect will be larger payrolls. Hence it is the efficacy of that device which we have to consider.

How would larger payrolls work? Those who get an increase in wages

* The "Nathan report" refers to *A National Economic Policy for 1949: Analysis Prepared for the Congress of Industrial Organization*, by Robert B. Nathan Associates, Inc. (Washington, D. C., July 1949). This report presented arguments for a fourth postwar round of wage increases and argued that further wage increases were necessary to sustain a high level of economic activity.—Ed.

would spend most of the increase. This would increase the demand for consumer goods. This would encourage greater production and would mean more rather than fewer jobs. The increase in production would not be confined to consumer goods. Increased wages and more consumer spending would support greater investment. Hence, the output of investment goods would rise also. It is evident that Mr. Nathan regards wage advances which have the immediate effect of increasing the payrolls of those enterprises making them as an inflationary instrument of great power—though in a period of contraction he apparently believes that the inflationary effect would be on employment, not prices. He does not indicate the limits to the effectiveness of this instrument. Mr. Nathan would undoubtedly agree that above some price the demand for labor would become elastic and that wage increases would produce smaller instead of larger payrolls. Up to this point, however, Mr. Nathan's argument is that wage increases will raise the total amount of spending, the physical volume of sales (since prices will not be increased), the total amount of production, and the total volume of employment in the economy. Mr. Nathan does not discuss whether the inflationary effect of higher wages is so great that it would be dangerous to raise wages during periods of boom.

In view of the broad claims that Mr. Nathan makes for raising wages, it is not clear why he considers it necessary to recommend a positive program for business which includes cutting prices as well as raising wages, and a positive program for government which includes public works projects "on a scale essential to provide work for the unemployed" and changes in fiscal policies "to stimulate greater private demand for the products of industry," or why he should say that "without any doubt, the fiscal policies of government can do more than practically anything else in determining the level of economic activity in the country." Possibly Mr. Nathan lacks faith in his own wage recommendations or possibly he believes that the present price of labor in most plants is not far below the point at which the demand for labor becomes elastic. Otherwise, why should raising wages need to be supplemented by price cuts, public works, and fiscal policy?

II

Let us examine more closely the results of wage advances which have the immediate effect of increasing payrolls in the plants making them. Under some circumstances such wage increases would tend to raise prices and might even accelerate the expansion of employment. Such effects would occur at times when goods are priced too low to equate supply and demand, when expectations are predominantly optimistic, and when enterprises are seeking to increase inventories and are willing to incur short-term debts in order to do so. Quite different, however, would be the effects of wage increases (even if limited to plants where the immediate or short-run effect would be an increase in payrolls) at times when goods in general are priced too high to equate supply and demand, when business concerns are attempting to reduce inventories and debts, and when expectations are far from optimistic.

Wage advances which had the immediate effect of increasing payrolls in the concerns granting higher wages would mean that the income of these enterprises after meeting payrolls would be diminished. Income after meeting payrolls is used for some or all of the following purposes: (1) to increase holdings of cash and securities; (2) to buy raw materials; (3) to buy plant and equipment either for replacement or expansion; (4) to repay debts; (5) to pay dividends and interest. The concerns which were compelled by wage increases to disburse larger payrolls would have to cut some or all of these uses of income or to find new methods of financing some expenditures. Some firms would use some methods of adjusting their operations to larger payrolls; other would use different methods. In some cases the adjustments would be favorable to employment, but in other cases they would be unfavorable.

The nature of the adjustments, as I have suggested, will vary with business conditions. Enterprises will not respond to wage increases in a period of contraction in the same way that they would in a period of expansion. An examination of the probable adjustments to larger payrolls during periods of contraction leads to the conclusion that the adjustments which would be unfavorable to employment would more than offset the adjustments which would be favorable to employment, so that the net effect would be unfavorable. Let us examine in detail the various ways in which managements might adjust their operations to meeting larger payrolls in the face of stationary or contracting income.

1. All enterprises would endeavor to hold the increase in payrolls to a minimum by eliminating men who are not really needed or who are not worth the higher wage. Hence there would be some drop in employment in the plants where payrolls increased. A few of the weaker firms would even temporarily eliminate men who are really needed—putting the protection of their liquidity to some extent above the maintenance of highest operating efficiency.

2. A few concerns are not spending all their income but are increasing

their holdings of securities or cash. These concerns might meet larger payrolls and, at the same time, maintain their dividends and their expenditures on plant and equipment simply by ceasing to buy securities or to increase their holdings of cash or by buying securities and increasing their cash at a slower rate. These effects would be favorable to employment; but they would be small because there are not many concerns which are hoarding at the present time. Corporate industry as a whole is still financing part of its expenditures on plant and equipment by outside capital. Even in 1948, when sales of business concerns were expanding and when there was an increase in the borrowings of enterprises from banks, business holdings of cash, bank deposits, and securities held by business concerns did not increase.

3. A few concerns which are financing part or all of their expenditures on plant and equipment by outside capital would use this method on an even larger scale. This adjustment would also be favorable to employment. It is not a method which is likely to be widely used because enterprises which are experiencing a fairly substantial drop in profits are not in a good position to raise capital in the open market and are usually reluctant to do it anyway. Management does not like to incur new debts when labor costs are rising, and it does not like to sell equities on terms which would be unfavorable to existing stockholders and which would result in a dilution of the equities of present stockholders. The rise in labor costs would particularly increase the difficulty of selling equity issues.

4. Some of the strongest concerns would sell government or other securities or draw down their bank balances in order to avoid curtailing expenditures on plant and equipment. These procedures would be immediately favorable to employment, but they could not continue very long. Eventually the enterprise would have to cut dividends or expenditures on plant and equipment. Weaker concerns would be compelled to sell government or other securities in order to meet maturing bank loans which managements had planned to pay off out of earnings. The immediate effect would be favorable to employment, but later effects would be unfavorable. The weakened financial condition of concerns that were not financially strong to begin with would impair their ability to contribute to the recovery of business.

5. Some concerns which are paying off their debts would do this more slowly. This form of adjustment also would be immediately favorable to employment, except in those cases where the credit of the enterprise was impaired. Although slower payment of debts would tend to diminish the severity of the contraction, it might increase the duration of the contraction.

6. Some concerns would liquidate inventories more rapidly in order to

avoid the necessity of making immediate cuts in expenditures on plant and equipment. This adjustment might on balance be either inflationary or deflationary. It would avert an immediate curtailment of expenditures on plant and equipment and to that extent would be inflationary. On the other hand, filling orders by reducing inventories would mean less employment in the plant for the time being and would be deflationary. Since the depth of recession is partly determined by the extent to which firms carry the reduction of inventories, wage increases which lead enterprises to reduce inventories more drastically than they otherwise would do would aggravate the severity of the recession.

7. Some concerns would pay less for raw materials. In fact, the demand for raw materials in general would be reduced. This is in accordance with the familiar principle that a rise in the supply price of one jointly used factor (in this case labor) reduces the demand price for the other jointly used factor. The smaller expenditures on raw materials would offset in large measure the larger outlays on labor. Urban employees, for example, would gain income at the expense of the farmers, but the total demand for consumer goods would be little changed. This effect would be unfavorable to employment.

8. Some concerns would reduce their expenditures on plant and equipment. This would probably be the most usual adjustment to higher wages and it would be unfavorable to employment. Reduction in expenditures on plant and equipment would not mean abandonment of programs to improve and expand plant and equipment—it would simply mean that these programs would be executed more slowly.

9. Some concerns would cut dividends. This effect would be unfavorable to employment. During recent years the dividends of most companies have been substantially below the net earnings of the company after taxes. Furthermore, dividends have risen since prewar years much less than wages or the income of the self-employed. Hence a drop in profits would be more likely to cause enterprises to make large cuts in their expenditures on plant and equipment rather than in their dividend disbursements.

10. Some concerns would reduce their debts more rapidly. Falling profit margins usually stimulate the desire of management to get its enterprise out of debt. Hence while wage advances which raised payrolls might cause some enterprises to reduce their debts more slowly, these advances would cause other concerns to reduce their debts more rapidly. This would be done either by reducing inventories more drastically or curtailing expenditures on plant and equipment—each deflationary.

The foregoing analysis indicates that raising wages in plants where wage increases will raise payrolls is not likely to be effective in halting a contraction of business. In the first place, the immediate effect of higher wages is to produce some shrinkage of employment in the plants where payrolls increase. In the second place, the increase in payrolls at a time when demand is shrinking and prices are too high to equate supply and demand is more likely to produce deflationary effects (further reduction of inventories, smaller demand for raw materials, postponement of expenditures on plant and equipment, accelerated repayment of debts, reduction of dividend payments) than inflationary effects (reduction in hoarding, greater use of outside funds, liquidation of securities). Indeed, raising the price of labor in a contracting market appears to be a good way of aggravating the contraction. Hence Mr. Nathan is wise to supplement his wage-raising proposal with a program calling for fiscal policy to prevent unemployment, a program calling for public works to absorb the unemployed (does Mr. Nathan not really expect fiscal policy to work either?), and larger unemployment benefits for those who are not absorbed by public works.

III

Not only would Mr. Nathan's wage-raising policy fail to halt contraction but it would limit the effectiveness of other policies which would mitigate the contraction—namely, lower prices. The precise economic problem created by the recession is how to get individuals to spend a larger fraction of their incomes for goods and how to get business concerns to cease from reducing their inventories in order to reduce their debts. The annual rate of personal incomes after taxes in the second quarter of 1949 was nearly $5 billion *above* the annual rate in the second quarter of last year, but personal consumption expenditures were running slightly *below* last year. The biggest increase in personal income was in compensation of employees, which increased about $4.0 billion at an annual rate between the second quarter of 1948 and the second quarter of 1949. If people could be induced to spend as large a proportion of their incomes on consumption as during the second quarter of last year, the level of consumption expenditures (at present prices) would rise by about $4.8 billion a year. The growing reluctance of individuals to spend money has caused business concerns to reduce their inventories and their debts. Filling orders from inventories and using part of income to pay debts rather than to buy goods are the two most immediately deflationary trends in the economy.

The reduction of inventories and the repayment of debts, once started, are not easily and quickly halted. The end of the reduction of inventories and debts will come earlier, however, if consumers can be persuaded to spend a larger fraction of their incomes on goods. The way to induce them to do this is to offer them more attractive goods at more attractive prices. Wage increases would interfere with this process because they would limit both the ability and the willingness of enterprises to cut prices.

Mr. Nathan complains that business has shown little disposition to reduce prices and he does not see much help from this method. I agree that business has not cut prices as quickly or as much as one might desire. By September 1949, wholesale prices had dropped 9.5 per cent, and the consumer price index 2.8 per cent below the peaks in 1948. It should be noted that price cuts have been limited by the fact that the absolute volume of consumer expenditures has held up quite well. In addition, it should be noted that the actual price reductions have been greater than the over-all averages indicate. Different prices reached their peaks at different times. This causes the averages to understate the declines in individual prices. Furthermore, the consumer price index is affected by some artificially repressed prices (such as rents) which are still rising and which need to rise considerably to be in line with other prices. In September 1949, however, food was down 5.8 per cent from the postwar peak, apparel was down 7.1 per cent, and house furnishings, 6.6 per cent. The fact that price cuts have not been so large as one might desire does not excuse a policy of wage increases which would not only aggravate the recession but which would weaken still further the disposition of business concerns to cut prices in order to sell more goods.

Would not price cuts induce the same deflationary policies on the part of business concerns as would wage increases? If wage increases would stimulate management to pay off debts more rapidly or to make expenditures on plant and equipment more slowly, would not price cuts have the same effect? In extreme cases the answer is "yes," but in the usual case the answer is "no." Price cuts may help enterprises convert their inventories into cash more quickly. This would improve the liquidity of the concerns. In this way price cuts may help preserve the demand for goods by making it unnecessary for enterprises to cut postponable expenditures. Price cuts also stimulate business and increase employment by helping the new win out in competition with the old—by helping new houses, new automobiles, new household appliances and furnishings win out in competition with old houses, old automobiles, old appliances and furnishings, and by encouraging people to discard old articles of apparel earlier and replace them with new. To the extent that price cuts preserve the physical volume of business, they discourage enterprises from cutting inventories and from cutting their expenditures on new plant and equipment.

IV

Although an attempt to halt the recession by increasing money wages would be a blunder, one should notice that real wages have been rising, as they ordinarily do during a recession. Furthermore, since the consumers' price index dropped by 2.8 per cent between September 1948 and September 1949, the purchasing power of unchanged wage rates has risen almost as much as one can expect it to rise each year in the long run—because it is hardly likely that output per manhour in industry as a whole can be raised more than 3 per cent. When account is taken of the increases in money wages which have occurred in the last year, real wages have increased far faster than employees can expect them to rise in the long run. In manufacturing, the rise in the purchasing power of hourly earnings between September 1948 and September 1949 was 4.3 per cent. In other fields the latest available figures are July, but in the eleven months ended in July 1949, the purchasing power of hourly earnings in general merchandise stores increased 7.7 per cent; in food and liquor stores, 9.4 per cent; in building construction, 6.2 per cent—all substantially faster than the output per manhour can be expected to rise in the long run.

The greatest immediate need of collective bargaining is to develop principles to guide the adjustment of wages. Thus far, collective bargaining has been largely a process by which the two sides rationalized positions already taken. Employers have invariably had reasons why wages should not be increased; unions have invariably had reasons why wages should be increased. Mr. Nathan says that wage advances are needed in the summer of 1949 because business is contracting. But if business had been booming, Mr. Nathan's clients would still have been demanding higher wages. Likewise, if there were a sudden improvement in business, the unions would not drop their demand for a fourth round of wage increases—they would simply back this demand by different reasons. Nor would an improvement in business cause employers to drop their opposition to wage increases.

It is obvious that collective bargaining will not long command the respect of thinking men if it continues to be a mere attempt of the parties to rationalize positions which are taken without regard to the effect upon the community. And if collective bargaining loses the respect of thinking men, its life will be a limited one. Consequently, unions and employers need to explore the principles which might guide the setting of wages, and to attempt to reach agreement as to how wage settlements should be affected by such basic conditions as changes in the cost of living, changes in productivity, changes in the ability of enterprises to pay, changes in employment, the need of the community for a larger and more efficient industrial plant.

It may be taken for granted that the people of the United States are content to let the results of technological progress continue to be distributed mainly in the form of higher money wages rather than in the form of lower prices to consumers. This is what has happened during the last century or more and it has evoked no serious protest. The chance to raise wages by encroaching upon the income of property is small—even if it were in the interest of employees to attempt to raise wages by the use of this method. Even in 1948 all of the income of all property—dividends, undivided corporate profits, interest, and rent—was only one sixth as large as the compensation of employees and the income of the self-employed. Consequently, the rise in output per manhour will set the approximate rate at which real wages can be increased over a considerable period of time. Output per manhour is likely to increase faster than in the past, when it rose about 2 per cent a year, because industrial research by business and government is growing by leaps and bounds. Output per manhour, however, is hardly likely to grow by much over 3 per cent a year in the long run. Hence, the rate at which real wages can be increased will be in the neighborhood of 3 per cent per year.

Should money wages be raised a little bit every year, or should the increases be bunched in the years when business is expanding? The answer to this question depends upon how good a job the country does in avoiding even moderate ups and downs in business. The recession in 1949 is certainly moderate—in fact, it is likely to set a new record for mildness in recessions because there has thus far been only a very minor drop in retail sales and the decline in output and employment has been pretty largely confined to manufacturing, mining, and transportation. Even a very mild recession such as the recent one, however, calls for lower prices. Hence the conclusion seems to be that increases in money wages should be bunched in those years when the public is willing to buy the entire output of industry at prevailing or at rising prices. This would not mean, however, that increases in *real* wages occurred only in some years. If business did a good job of fighting mild recessions by price cuts, real wages would rise a bit every year.

An increase of 3 per cent in real hourly earnings per year may seem small, but 3 per cent for twenty years is nearly 81 per cent. Whether 3 per cent seems large or small, however, it is high time that all groups in the community realize that real wages are tied to productivity and that collective bargaining cannot raise real wages faster than output per manhour—though by raising money wages too fast it can either create unemployment or force up the price level. Recognition of these basic facts will do much to bring the discussion of wages down from the clouds and to make collective bargaining an informed and sober discussion of economic realities.

28

Economics and Collective Bargaining

Lecture at The Brookings Institution, Washington, D. C., March 5, 1959; Economics and the Policy Maker, Washington, D. C., 1959.

Collective bargaining in the United States today represents the application of the monopoly principle in an economy that is generally committed to the principle of competition. In the case of collective bargaining, the community is not merely tolerating an exception to the general principle of competition; it is giving active encouragement to the formation of powerful monopolies. The central economic question raised by collective bargaining is whether encouragement of the monopolistic principle in the selling of labor is desirable or undesirable. An answer to this question requires a considerably more thorough investigation of the economic consequences of labor monopolies than economic theory has thus far provided.

I

Although the United States actively encourages the selling of labor through monopolies, it never deliberately adopted the policy that labor should be sold through monopolies. The sale of labor through monopolies has been the unplanned and unforeseen result of the policy of encouraging collective bargaining. When public policies in support of collective bargaining were adopted, individual employees were at a disadvantage; they had to sell their labor by accepting or rejecting the standing offers of employers. Thus, it was widely believed that the terms of employment would be fairer if the employees would organize for the purpose of negotiating the terms of the labor contract. No one argued that the government ought to foster monopolistic organizations capable of depriving the country of its steel supply, its coal supply, or its railroad service. Most unions controlled merely a small part of their craft or industry and were growing only slowly. Hence, the community was more concerned about the difficulties that most unions were having in acquiring members than about the possibility that unions might acquire monopoly power. When the government took its most decisive steps to encourage trade-union membership in 1933 (the National Industrial Recovery Act) and in 1935 (the Wagner Act), unemployment was severe and unions were weak.

The transformation of the policy of encouraging collective bargaining into the policy of encouraging labor monopolies was not the result of any decision by the public or the government; it was the natural result of the growth and success of unions. The unions were aided, of course, by the sellers' markets created by the Second World War and the postwar boom. At any rate, in occupation after occupation and in industry after industry unions quickly succeeded in establishing almost complete control of the jobs and the labor supply. Virtually no one works today at production jobs in these industries except on terms agreed to by some union: coal, steel, automobile, paper, rubber, can, flat glass, men's clothing, women's garment, railroad, over-the-road trucking, stevedoring, airplane, air transport, and in many parts of the construction industry, printing, entertainment, and hotel. In some industries, the failure of employers and the union to agree on the terms means that the market is temporarily deprived of newly produced goods. In other industries, however, unions use whipsawing tactics, shutting down only part of the industry at a time. Whipsawing tactics do not completely deprive the public of goods but may increase the ability of unions to raise wages. All in all, labor monopolies are by far the most powerful monopolies to be found anywhere in the economy. Even in industries in which unions fall short of controlling all production jobs, the wage settlements of unions have a substantial effect on the wages of nonunion production workers.[1] Furthermore, the changes negotiated by unions for production workers affect the wages of nonproduction employees. Thus, though only about half of all production employees in private industry are union members, union wage settlements affect the entire wage structure.

[1] Sometimes it is said that trade unions are not monopolies because most of them do not restrict their membership. Hence, it is argued that trade unions lack an essential attribute of the monopoly, namely the restriction of supply. This reasoning is erroneous. Trade unions restrict supply by enforcing a minimum union rate. This rate limits the number of people whom employers can afford to hire, and the number of jobs limits the number of persons who attach themselves to the craft or the industry. There are, of course, differences in the degree of restrictiveness, and the few unions, such as the Die Sinkers' Conference, that restrict their membership are far more restrictive than the unions that use the indirect method of the minimum union rate.

How does the monopoly principle work in the selling of labor? Does it have associated with it the abuses and inequities that are customarily associated with monopoly? The principal objection to monopoly has always been that it produces unfair distribution of incomes, enabling the monopolist to get far more than his fair share. Does this objection to monopoly apply to the monopolistic selling of labor?

The answer is "yes," and it is fairly easy to find examples. The outrageous prices charged by barbers are an example. So also are the wages of photo-engravers or the wages, far above the community level, imposed on can-manufacturing plants in the South. The rapid rise of wages in recent years in such declining industries as coal and railroading illustrates the ability of monopolistic organizations to limit the normal response of wages to market influences. But there are important restrictions on the ability of unions to influence the wage and price structure. The restrictions stem from four important facts.

The first restriction is the result of the fact that unions seek substantially the same terms for all of their members in each given market. This rough uniformity of terms within the same market is a necessary condition of union solidarity, and it limits the ability of the union to extract the best possible terms from the most prosperous employers. Of course, virtually *all* monopolies are restricted by their inability to take advantage of the differing elasticities of demand among different buyers, but this restriction is particularly great in the case of unions. To unions, the loss of sales from the inability of some buyers to pay the monopoly price may be more than simply the loss of sales. Unions must reckon with the possibility that the inability of marginal firms to pay the union wage scale will cause them or some of their employees to become sources of nonunion competition.

The second restriction on the ability of trade unions to influence wages is a result of the fact that the wages of different occupations are linked together so that many skilled workers are limited in their ability to take advantage of the scarcity of their skill. The wages of several occupations may be linked together by custom (each occupation expects to get whatever increases any other occupation obtains), or they may be linked because the members of all occupations are in an industrial union. Certainly the railroad engineers are underpaid in relation to the firemen, and the skilled workers in the automobile industry have been held back by the semiskilled who dominate the union.

The third restriction on the ability of trade unions to gain a monopoly price for labor stems from the fact that stoppages in the labor market can be foreseen and that in most lines of production the customers can protect themselves from lack of goods by accumulating inventories. Thus, imposing large increases in the price of labor may be a fairly costly process to the sellers of labor.

The fourth restriction on the ability of trade unions to influence wages is a result of the broad extent of collective bargaining. In considering the effects of the monopolistic selling of labor we are not thinking of the ability of a single monopoly to extract gain for its owners in a world of competition. Rather we are considering the effects of monopolies in a world of monopolies. In a world of monopolies the inequity is less conspicuous than would be the exploitation by a single monopoly in a world of competition because the fruits of exploitation are so widely distributed. Undoubtedly, the coal miners' union is exploiting the rest of the community by enforcing a monopolistic wage, but in a world of monopolies the coal miners are also being exploited by the steel workers, the automobile workers, the rubber workers, the clothing workers, the barbers, the musicians, and all the other monopolistic sellers of labor.

In this process of mutual exploitation some unions fare better than others. The unions that have the least concern over creating nonunion competition are able to push up their wages faster than the unions that must guard against nonunion competition. Thus, the steel workers, the automobile workers, and the rubber workers have been able to raise their wages faster than the clothing workers have been able to push up theirs.[2] As between members of different unions, however, most of the exploitation cancels out, and the workers, through the process of collective bargaining, are primarily engaged in exploiting one another. The situation would obviously be very different if unionism were less pervasive and if the influence of union wages upon nonunion wages were less pronounced. A few unions ignore the effect of their wage scales upon the extent of nonunion competition and, as a re-

[2] Between 1947 and 1957 hourly earnings in the steel industry, where the union does not have to worry about creating nonunion competition, rose 86.1 per cent. In the automobile industry, where also there is no threat of nonunion competition, hourly earnings rose by 67.3 per cent; in the rubber industry, by 62.6 per cent. On the other hand, in the boot-and-shoe industry, the men's-clothing industry, and the women's-garment industry, where there is danger of creating nonunion competition, hourly earnings went up far less—24.2 per cent in the boot-and-shoe industry, 46.0 per cent in the men's-clothing industry, and 19.6 per cent in the women's-garment industry. Back in the 1920's before unions were established in iron and steel, automobiles, or rubber, the difference between the rise in hourly earnings in these industries and in the boot-and-shoe industry was much less than in the period 1947 to 1957. Thus, between 1922 and 1929 hourly earnings in the steel industry rose 29.8 per cent, in the automobile industry 17.1 per cent, in the rubber industry 13.1 per cent, and in the boot-and-shoe industry 3.5 per cent, according to the National Industrial Conference Board, *Wages in the United States, 1914 to 1929* (1930), p. 39.

sult, may virtually destroy themselves. The full-fashioned hosiery workers' union is an example. It recklessly insisted upon extremely high wages in spite of the fact that it was easy to establish nonunion plants that paid considerably less than the union scale and gave their employees considerably more secure employment than the union plants were able to give. As a result of its short-sighted policy, the hosiery workers' union is now virtually out of existence.

II

More interesting than the effects of collective bargaining upon the structure of wages is its effect upon the creation of money incomes, a topic that has been largely neglected up to now.[3] When collective bargaining becomes as pervasive as it has become in the United States, it introduces a major change into the institutions of capitalism by giving the economy substantial new capacity to generate money incomes. The increase in the economy's capacity to generate money income, for which collective bargaining is responsible, has two effects of great significance: (1) it substantially diminishes the susceptibility of the economy to temporary contractions, and (2) it reinforces the tendency for prices to rise in periods of boom. Such changes in the operation of capitalism are obviously of historic importance. Let me first outline in stark fashion how collective bargaining generates money incomes. Then let me fill in the outline with brief comments on the several points.

The results produced by collective bargaining depend upon the conditions under which it operates and the institutions through which it operates. Both the conditions and the institutions vary from country to country. The following description of collective bargaining and the principal conditions apply to the United States but not necessarily to other countries.

1. The bargains that unions make with employers relate almost exclusively to the price of labor (including fringe benefits) and only to a small extent to the number of workers to be employed. The effects of collective bargaining would be substantially modified if unions were to bargain for a given volume of employment. Not only do unions bargain very little over the number of jobs, but in most circumstances they bargain on the assumption that the demand for labor is perfectly inelastic.

[3] A valuable paper dealing with the income-creating aspects of higher wages was presented at the meeting of the American Econometric Society in December 1958 by Jaroslav Vanek of Harvard University under the title of "The Argument for Higher Wages in Depression Revisited." The paper has not yet been published, but mimeographed copies may be obtained from Mr. Vanek.

2. The unit of bargaining is a small part of the total labor market. Usually it is a small part of the industry. At any rate, it is so small that no union feels any responsibility for the effect of its wage bargain upon the price level.

3. Collective bargaining is sufficiently extensive so that the results of union-employer negotiations in most industries strongly affect the compensation of nonunion employees in those industries and even in other industries.

4. There is considerable rivalry among unions. This rivalry means that a few unions seek to take the lead in getting better conditions for their members. It also means that other unions, which elect to be followers, expect to get promptly about what the leaders obtained.

5. The short-run demand for labor is usually inelastic so that wage increases ordinarily have the immediate effect of raising payrolls, and wage cuts have the immediate effect of reducing payrolls.

These characteristics and conditions have produced the following consequences:

1. The bargaining position of employees is made strong, and the unions have a considerable incentive to take full advantage of their strong bargaining position. The result is that the compensation of employees rises faster than output per manhour and labor costs per unit of output increase.

2. The increased labor costs per unit of output tend to produce smaller output but larger payrolls and larger total expenditures on the part of those enterprises that raise wages.

3. The increased total expenditures by the enterprises raising wages stimulate production in the rest of the economy.

4. The increased production in the part of the economy not raising wages will ordinarily exceed the decreases in production in the firms raising wages, so that the net effect of the wage increases induced by collective bargaining is a rise in output.

5. The higher costs and expenditures produced by collective bargaining tend to increase the demand for money and to stimulate the growth of the banking system.

6. The growth of the banking system limits the tendency for the growing demand for money to raise contractual rates of interest.

7. The strong tendency of collective bargaining to raise money incomes limits the tendency for money incomes to drop when production contracts, but accentuates the rise of incomes in other periods.

8. Since collective bargaining in a closed economy tends to produce rising expenditures and incomes rather than unemployment, the tendency for collective bargaining to push up wages is not self-limiting.

Let us now examine one by one the eight basic propositions that constitute the theory of the effect of collective bargaining upon money incomes.

The conditions of collective bargaining make the bargaining position of employees strong, and the unions have a strong incentive to take advantage of their bargaining position. Behind the strong bargaining position of trade unions is the strong bargaining position of unorganized employees. This strong bargaining position of even the unorganized is a result of the fact that employers have only imperfect direct control over how much men produce. This amount is determined by willingness to work and may be affected by the conscious withholding of efficiency. Striking evidence of the bargaining power of even unorganized workers is the fact that the principal effect of technological progress in preunion days was to raise wages rather than to reduce prices. The explanation is found in the sensitivity of the labor-supply curve to changes of demand for labor. The usual assumption of economic theory that shifts of supply curves are independent of shifts in demand curves cannot be applied in explaining the determination of wages. (As a matter of fact, the assumption is erroneous for most markets; it is a convenient simplification that once made needs to be corrected.) Whenever it becomes evident that there is a rise in the demand for labor—a rightward shift in the demand curve—there is a leftward shift in the labor-supply curve.

What happens among unorganized workers when the labor-supply curve shifts to the left? A leftward shift in the labor-supply curve does not first manifest itself in the form of greater difficulty of recruiting help; the first manifestations occur among workers who are already on the payroll. Let us suppose that the workers feel entitled to more money because the firm is making more. In various ways, the workers in the plant show dissatisfaction—by a generally less cooperative attitude, displays of indifference, or carelessness here and there. There may be a small rise in resignations, and among piece workers and bonus workers a greater disposition to complain about equipment, materials, and shop conditions. If nothing is done to alleviate dissatisfaction, labor turnover and absenteeism will grow; there may be slowdowns or wildcat strikes or refusals to work overtime. Some workers may talk of a union.

Even in the days before unions, most of the gain of technological progress went to employees, but the relationship between output, prices, and hourly earnings was less uniform than it has been during recent years when unions have been strong. There were occasional periods, such as the period 1897 to 1907, which, despite the absence of strong unions, were like the present period, with hourly earnings outrunning both productivity and prices. There were other periods, such as 1922 to 1929, when labor got only a part of the increased output per manhour but in which wages increased faster than prices. Between 1922 and 1929, for example, output per manhour in manufacturing rose 29.2 per cent, hourly earnings in manufacturing 16.2 per cent, and the consumer price level 2.4 per cent.[4] Finally, there were periods such as 1908 to 1913 or 1914 when both productivity and the consumer price index outran wages.

The era of trade unionism that began in the middle of the 1930s has brought a rather stable relationship between hourly earnings and output per manhour and between hourly earnings and prices. In seventeen out of the twenty-five years between 1933 and 1958, the percentage increase in the hourly earnings of factory workers exceeded the rise in output per manhour of factory workers, and in twenty-two out of the last twenty-five years the percentage increase in the hourly earnings of factory workers exceeded the rise in the consumer price level. During the last eleven years the hourly compensation of all employees in private industry has without exception risen faster than the consumer price index and with three exceptions faster than real output per manhour. Furthermore, with the exception of one year in the last eleven, namely 1950–51, the rise in wages has exceeded the rise in the wholesale prices of finished goods.[5] The table below shows the changes in wages in private industry and in prices during the last eleven years.

The increased labor costs per unit of output tend to produce smaller output but larger payrolls and larger total expenditures by the enterprises raising wages. The demand for labor by business enterprises is inelastic, especially in the short run, but not usually completely inelastic. Hence wage increases must be expected to produce some drop in output. But since the demand for most kinds of labor in the short run is inelastic, payrolls in the wage-increasing firms will rise. Larger payroll expenditures will usually

[4] Joint Economic Committee, *Productivity, Prices and Incomes; Materials Prepared for the Joint Economic Committee,* Committee Print, 85th Congress, 1st session, pp. 89, 135.

[5] The difference between the preunion era and the union era is epitomized by the steel industry. In the 1920s there was virtually no unionism in the steel industry. Between 1922 and 1929, output per manhour in the basic steel industry increased by 32.0 per cent, and hourly earnings of production workers increased moderately more, by 39.1 per cent, raising unit labor costs in seven years by 5.6 per cent. By 1948 the steel industry was thoroughly organized. Between that year and 1956, output per manhour increased by 28.0 per cent, or slightly less than the increase in the twenties. Hourly earnings, however, far outdistanced productivity, rising 60.2 per cent in eight years and producing a rise of 25.4 per cent in labor costs per unit of output. See *Productivity, Prices and Incomes,* p. 220.

Changes in wages and prices, 1947–58

Year	*Increases in average hourly compensation of workers in total private economy*	*Change in consumer price index*	*Change in non-farm wholesale prices*	*Change in wholesale prices of finished goods*
1947–48	8.5%	7.6%	8.5%	7.9%
1948–49	2.7	−1.0	−2.0	−2.8
1949–50	5.7	+1.0	3.7	1.8
1950–51	9.3	8.0	10.4	9.5
1951–52	5.8	2.3	−2.3	−0.5
1952–53	5.9	0.8	0.7	−1.0
1953–54	3.5	0.3	0.4	0.3
1954–55	2.9	−0.3	2.2	0.2
1955–56	6.0	1.5	4.4	2.8
1956–57	6.0	3.4	2.8	3.6
1957–58	3.0	2.7	0.3	2.3

The changes in the year-to-year compensation of employees are computed from data in *January 1959 Economic Report of the President,* Hearings before the Joint Economic Committee, 86th Congress, 1st session, p. 782.

mean some drop in nonpayroll expenditures by the firms raising wages—some deferring of repairs, replacements, improvements, expansion, possibly smaller distribution of profits to business owners. But unless the wage increases seriously impair the credit standing of the firm, the drop in nonpayroll expenditures will not fully offset the rise in payroll outlays. Hence, there will be some rise in the total expenditures of the wage-raising firms.

This conclusion that total outlays of the firms raising wages will usually rise follows from the fact that enterprises must be expected to use their resources so that for every use the ratio of marginal cost to marginal advantage is the same as the ratio for every other use. Hence, when payrolls must be increased, it is advantageous for the enterprise to meet the cost, not solely by cutting other expenditures, but partly by drawing on liquid resources, partly by greater use of credit, and partly by greater reliance on outside sources of funds. In addition, the larger payrolls may force some cuts in disbursements to stockholders or owners or a slower rate of repayment of loans and a slower accumulation of depreciation reserves, producing shifts in the saving function that are favorable to spending. Only in a few extreme cases where wage increases are so large as to force the enterprise out of important markets or to impair its credit will payroll increases reduce the total expenditures of the firm.

Will not the rise of wages in the wage-increasing firm produce an offsetting increase in the prices charged by the firm so that the wage increase exerts no general stimulus on the economy? This result is extremely unlikely because the multiplier effect of the increase in spending by the wage-increasing firms is ordinarily large enough to increase spending in the community by more than the rise in labor costs in the wage-increasing firm. This effect is discussed next.

The increased spending by the firms raising wages stimulates spending and production and tends to raise profits in the rest of the economy. The increase in the total outlays by the firms raising wages (payroll plus nonpayroll expenditures) has the same effect on the rest of the economy as any autonomous increase in spending, such as a budget deficit. In this case, however, the increase in autonomous spending is the result of a change in the private sector, of higher expenditures relative to income by the wage-raising firms.

The effect of the increase in spending by the wage-raising firms falls into two parts: the effect on consumption and the effect on investment spending by the firms which do not increase wages. The effect on consumption is determined by the marginal propensity to consume in accordance with the familiar Keynesian multiplier. Thus, if the marginal propensity to consume is three fifths, consumption in the community will ultimately be increased by two and a half times the increase in spending by the wage-raising firms. The effect upon investment in the rest of the economy depends upon the shift in the investment function in the rest of the economy. This function is the result partly of the state of liquidity of business concerns and partly of appraisals of the business outlook that are constantly being made. Increased sales by nonwage-raising firms will improve their liquidity and stimulate investment by them. In addition, the larger volume of consumption induced by increased spending by the wage-raising firms will tend to create greater profits and optimistic expectations in the firms not increasing wages.

The increased production in the part of the economy not raising wages will ordinarily exceed the decreases in production in the firms raising wages so that, in the absence of full employment, wage increases induced by collective bargaining tend to raise output in the economy as a whole. These are not necessary relationships, but they are, I believe, the usual ones. They depend upon the drop of employment in the wage-increasing firms being smaller than the gain in employment in the firms which do not increase wages. The outcome depends upon the elasticity of the demand for labor and for output in the wage-increasing firms, upon the size of the marginal propensity to consume in the nonwage-increasing sector of the economy, and upon the sensitivity of investment functions in the nonwage-increasing part of the economy to changes in demand. Only if employment in the wage-increasing firms were barely inelastic with respect to wage changes, and only if the marginal propensity to consume were low and the investment function in the nonwage-increasing sector of the economy had a low sensitivity to increases in demand, would the net effect of wage increases be to reduce the total volume of employment and production in the economy. In the event that the economy is operating at capacity, the effect of wage increases is solely to raise money incomes.

The higher costs and the higher incomes produced by collective bargaining tend to increase the demand for money. It is true that the speculative demand for money is reduced, not raised, by collective bargaining, since the consequences of collective bargaining make the holding of money a poor speculation. But in the United States the productive uses of money are so attractive that the demand for money to be held as a speculation is not large. On the other hand, collective bargaining, by raising costs and prices, does increase the transactions demand for money—the demand for money for working-capital purposes.

The effect of the increased demand for money is not primarily to raise the rate of interest but to divert more capital into banking and to enlarge the banking system. Only slight advantages are needed to attract capital into any given industry, such as banking, rather than into some competing industry. Hence, from the standpoint of any individual industry, the supply of investment-seeking funds is highly elastic. Shifts in the demand produce only small differences in return. Consequently, the principal effect of the greater transactions demand for funds created by collective bargaining is a larger banking system, not higher rates of interest.[6]

The strong tendency of collective bargaining to raise money incomes of the workers limits the tendency for aggregate money incomes to drop when production contracts and accentuates the rise of aggregate incomes at other periods. Rigorous statistical proof of this proposition cannot be given, but the figures for the recession of 1958, though less than complete proof, are con-

[6] Between December 31, 1947 and December 31, 1957, the capital and surplus of all insured commercial banks in the United States increased from $7.5 billion to $13.4 billion. Member bank reserves increased somewhat less, from a daily average of $16.5 billion in 1947 to $19.0 billion in 1957.

vincing. Total wage and salary payments, seasonally adjusted, reached their low point in April 1958 when they were 2.1 per cent below April 1957. But the hours worked by all wage and salary workers in April 1958 were 4.2 per cent less than in April 1957, indicating a rise of 2.2 per cent in hourly compensation—a rise that exceeded the increase in transfer payments in the same period. Unfortunately, one does not know the elasticity of the demand for labor, though one has good reason for regarding it as small. Hence, one does not know how much the rise in hourly compensation might have reduced employment. But when account is taken of the effect of larger disbursements in the wage-increasing enterprises upon the rest of the economy, one reaches the conclusion that the total effect of the wage increases upon employment was favorable. In that event, wage increases must have been fairly important in mitigating the recession.

Since collective bargaining in a closed economy tends to produce rising expenditures, incomes, and output rather than unemployment, the tendency for collective bargaining to push up wages is not self-limiting. This is a fact of great importance. It requires radical changes in our conception of trade unions and drastic rewriting of wage theory and employment theory. It requires that traditional views of the economic role of unions be discarded and that unions be viewed not simply as redistributors of income but as important generators of money incomes. The fact that rising labor costs tend to produce rising expenditures and incomes throughout the economy means that much of conventional wage theory must be rewritten. Widely accepted beliefs concerning the alleged bad effects of wage increases upon employment must be abandoned. Those bad effects are revealed by the foregoing analysis to be under most circumstances local effects, not general effects. An example of the sort of statement that the foregoing analysis shows to be fallacious is the following excerpt from the *Economic Report of the President* (January 20, 1959): "But this [increasing pay of employed persons] is a factor that works two ways. It may sustain income for the employed; but to the extent that it leads to higher costs and prices, it may induce reductions in the working force and be an obstacle to re-employment" (p. 15). As a description of the effect of wage increases upon employment in the firms raising wages, this statement is correct but, as a description of the *general* effect of wage increases, the statement is incorrect. It overlooks the effect of larger outlays by the wage-increasing firms upon the rest of the economy. The wage increases that are not severe enough to force reductions in total spending by wage-raising firms stimulate spending and the enlargement of employment in the economy as a whole.

III

The picture of trade unionism presented in this paper has far-reaching implications for both economic theory and public policy making. It is not my purpose to discuss these implications, but I wish to indicate their general nature. There are two groups of questions awaiting analysis: (1) the effect of trade unions upon the distribution of incomes, and (2) the possibility and the desirability of controlling the effect of trade unions on expenditures and incomes.

The first question arises because not everyone is fortunate enough to belong to a monopolistic trade union or to work in a nonunion plant that matches the union scale. A broad and searching inquiry into the effects of trade-union monopoly power upon the community is needed. Trade unions, through their monopoly power, have introduced the equivalent of civil rights into industry and have accelerated the growth of orderly management. But unions also have imposed burdensome and wasteful practices upon industry. Unions have had only limited success in altering the distribution of income to their own advantage. Many nonunion workers, for example, have their wages adjusted to changes in union wage scales, though the precise extent to which this happens is not known. Hence, union employers are able to pass on wage increases in the form of higher prices so that union workers are to a large extent exploiting each other. The ability of trade unions to alter the distribution of income to their own advantage is further limited by the fact that collective bargaining tends to raise incomes throughout the economy. Thus owners of business concerns on the whole find that collective bargaining tends to enhance their profits because each wage increase usually raises the demand for the goods of nonwage-increasing concerns by more than it increases the costs of the wage-increasing firms.

The class that one would expect to suffer most from the monopoly power of unions are the self-employed. Unions raise the wage and price structure of the industries using employees relative to the price structure of the industries using primarily self-employed persons. As a result, the number of self-employed is greater than it would otherwise have been, and the increase in their numbers tends to reduce their per capita incomes. But just as collective bargaining tends to increase the total incomes of property owners, so it also tends to increase the total income of the self-employed. The effect on per capita incomes is uncertain. It depends upon which effect of collective bargaining is greater—its tendency to increase the numbers of the self-employed or its tendency to increase the total income of the self-employed. A group that probably suffers on balance from collective bargaining is the farmers. The income-generating effects of trade unions tend to accelerate the movement of men out of agriculture, but the rise of costs in nonfarm industries for which unions are responsible tends to produce terms of trade between agriculture and nonagricultural industries that are unfavorable to the farmers. One is tempted to mention the pensioners as a group that suffers from collective bargaining since the effect of collective bargaining on prices reduces the purchasing power of pensions. But pensioners are a powerful pressure group and thus far have been able to get the average pension raised much faster than the consumer price index has risen. But the day may come when the pensioners will have to be counted as important sufferers from collective bargaining.

Unfortunately, statistical evidence of the influence of collective bargaining upon the distribution of income is lacking. The distribution is affected by changes in technology and in the pattern of demand, and by other influences. All one can say is that the figures appear to indicate that the direct influence of collective bargaining on wages in the unionized firms apparently has been greater than the indirect tendency of collective bargaining to raise profits or to raise the total incomes of the self-employed. For example, if one takes the income originating in all American corporate business and eliminates profits-tax liability (to get rid of the effect of greatly increased profits taxes), one finds that the share of profits after taxes and inventory-valuation adjustment dropped from 19.9 per cent in 1929 to 10.0 per cent in 1956, and that the share of compensation of employees rose from 77.0 per cent to 89.4 per cent. These changes may be partly the result of shifts in the relative importance of different industries. Comparison of the change in median income of male factory workers (most of whom became union members between 1939 and 1951) with the change in median income of male professional workers (a large proportion of whom are self-employed), and with the change in the median income of workers in finance, insurance, and real estate (who include a large proportion of self-employed as well as workers least influenced by unions), shows a faster rise in the wage or salary income of factory workers. In 1939 the median income of factory workers at $1,141 was less than the median income of professional workers, which was $1,235, or of finance, real-estate, and insurance workers, which was $1,487. In 1951, the median income of factory workers at $3,393 was *above* the median of professional workers at $3,004 and almost as large as the median of finance, insurance, and real estate workers, which was $3,462.[7]

IV

Does the capacity of trade unions to generate incomes indicate the need for controlling their activities and, if so, how can control be accomplished? The community has long regarded the process of creating purchasing power as affected with a public interest and as properly subject to public control. The principal creators of purchasing power have been the banks, and the Federal Reserve System was set up to regulate the creation of money by the banks. But now the trade unions have become important sources for the creation of income. Is it not necessary to set up arrangements for controlling the creation of income by the trade unions?

This is a new problem with which economics is not yet prepared to deal for the simple reason that economics has not had an adequate conception of the economic nature of trade unions; it has failed to see that trade unions are income-creating organizations. The suggestion has been made that trade unions be broken up, though the idea behind this suggestion seems to have been to weaken the influence of unions on the structure of wages rather than to reduce the capacity of unions to generate income. But weakening the monopoly power of trade unions would diminish their power to create incomes by raising wages. Hence, two questions arise: (1) Would breaking up unions diminish rather than increase their monopoly power? (2) Does the community desire that the capacity of trade unions to create incomes be changed and, if so, in which direction?

There is good reason to believe that breaking up unions would strengthen rather than weaken the monopolistic principle in the selling of labor. It is true that breaking up unions would lessen the opportunity of a union to strike

[7] Herman P. Miller, *Income of the American People,* Census Monograph Series (1955), p. 99. Confirming data are obtained from analysis of the median incomes by occupation. The craftsmen, foremen, and kindred workers, and the operatives and kindred workers, groups that became strongly organized between 1939 and 1951, made progress relative to the managers, officials, and proprietors except farmers and farm managers. The following are the median wage or salary incomes of males in the several groups (taken from Miller, p. 105):

	1939	*1951*
Craftsmen, foremen, and kindred workers	$1,309	$3,601
Operatives and kindred workers	1,007	3,064
Managers, officials, and proprietors, except farm	2,136	4,143
Farmers and farms managers	373	482

one employer while the members in other plants worked and contributed part of their wages to support the strike. But breaking up unions would remove an important restraint on wage settlements.

Suppose that there were four or five unions in the automobile industry and the same number in the steel industry and the rubber industry. Each principal employer would still be dealing with a monopoly. If he failed to come to terms, his plant would be shut down and he would be cut off completely from alternative sources of labor. Furthermore, an important restraint on wage increases would re removed. No longer would the desire of unions to preserve their solidarity lead them to make more or less the same settlements with all employers, with the most prosperous and the least prosperous alike. The breaking up of unions would introduce rivalries among unions in the same industry. Thus, the union in General Motors, the most profitable maker of automobiles, could push its demands without regard to the ability of Ford, Chrysler, American Motors, or Studebaker to meet those demands. Hence, the breaking up of unions would give them a better opportunity to practice the monopoly principle than they now possess and would strengthen the tendency of unions to raise wages and to generate increases in money incomes.

Would the public interest be served by reducing the ability of unions to increase incomes? Or should the public seek to increase the ability of unions to raise money incomes? Unions at present do not raise incomes fast enough to prevent occasional recessions, but, by their influence on costs and incomes, they are a principal cause of creeping inflation. By encouraging trade unions to raise wages a little faster than they now do, the public can accelerate the growth of incomes and pretty much get rid of business recessions—provided, of course, that rising prices in periods of boom do not foster speculative accumulation of inventories. In addition, by encouraging the creation of income by trade unions, the public can accelerate the growth of productive capacity and of physical production since the pressure of demand upon resources (at least up to a certain point) stimulates the expansion of the economy. But the price that the public must pay for a faster and steadier growth of money incomes is a slightly faster rise in the price level. Hence, the public must decide whether it wishes faster income creation by trade unions in order to have fewer and milder recessions and faster growth of physical production or slower income creation in order to have a more stable price level.

When the public has made up its mind, will economists be prepared to tell the public what to do? I have said that today economists are not prepared. Certainly one of the first questions to be answered is whether breaking up unions would increase or diminish their monopoly power. Only experience will give reliable answers, and there is little experience that is in point. Nevertheless, careful studies of dual or rival unionism may shed some light on the matter.

The toughest problems for the economists will arise in the event that the public desires to weaken the capacity of the trade unions to generate incomes. Up to the present the economists have little to offer except general policies, such as credit restraint, which are too costly to be feasible, or decentralized action, such as more capital-saving inventions or plant-wide wage incentive systems of the Scanlon type, which are not subject to central control and which come into effect only as individual firms are persuaded to become interested in the general problem of cutting costs. Something less costly than credit restraint and quicker and more effective than a call for more capital-saving inventions is needed. A special tax on all wage settlements, including fringes, in excess of a given percentage would probably not be feasible. At any rate, since economists do not know whether the community is likely to demand more income creation or less income creation by trade unions, they should be ready to suggest ways of implementing either demand.

One concluding observation is of importance alike to trade union members and to all citizens. The discovery that trade unions are income generating organizations means that capitalism is stronger than we had suspected: it has greater capacity for expansion than we had realized. But it also means that trade unions are affected with a public interest to a considerably greater extent than had previously been evident. Union members must expect the community to assert considerable control over union activities, and the community will be well within its rights in exercising such control.

THE WRITINGS OF SUMNER H. SLICHTER

The Writings of Sumner H. Slichter

1912–1915

"The Concentrators of Control," in Interlocking Directorates. Reports of the U. S. Commission on Industrial Relations, 1912–1915 (4 vols., microfilm, hf + 1425).

1916

"The Cream of Wheat Case," *Political Science Quarterly*, 31:392–412 (September).

1917

"The Legality of the Combination of Competitors under the Sherman Act," *Journal of Political Economy*, 25:761–804 (October).

1919

The Turnover of Factory Labor (New York and London, D. Appleton & Co.).

"The Management of Labor," *Journal of Political Economy*, 27:813–839 (December).

1920

"The Scope and Nature of the Labor Turnover Problem," *Quarterly Journal of Economics*, 34:329–345 (February).

"Industrial Morale," *Quarterly Journal of Economics*, 35:36–60 (November).

1921

Review of A. M. Simons, *Personnel Relations in Industry*, in *Administration*, vol. 2 (August).

1923

Review of P. F. Brissenden and E. Frankel, *Labor Turnover in Industry*, in *Quarterly Publication of the American Statistical Association*, 18:809–816 (June).

"Labor Problems," review of C. R. Walker, *Steel;* H. Robbins, *The Labor Movement and the Farmer;* and W. L. Huggins, *Labor and Democracy*, in *Yale Review*, 13:193–196 (October).

1924

"The Organization and Control of Economic Activity," in *The Trend of Economics*, edited by Rexford Guy Tugwell (New York, Alfred A. Knopf), pp. 303–355.

1925

"Competitive Exchange as a Method of of Interesting Workmen in Output and Cost," *American Economic Review, Supplement,* 15:92–100 (March).

1926

"The Worker in Modern Economic Society," review of Douglas, Hitchcock, and Atkins, *The Worker in Modern Economic Society,* in *Journal of Political Economy,* 34:100–124 (February).

1927

"Some Ways in Which Trade Unions Can Help Reduce Unemployment," *American Federationist,* 34:1202–1207 (October).

1928

"What is the Labor Problem?" in *American Labor Dynamics in the Light of Post-War Developments,* edited by Hardman, pp. 287–291 (New York, Harcourt Brace & Co.).

"The Price of Industrial Progress," *New Republic,* 53:316–318 (February 8).

"Economic and Social Aspects of Increased Productive Efficiency: Discussion," *American Economic Review, Supplement,* 18:166–170 (March).

"The Secret of High Wages," *New Republic,* 54:183–185 (March 28).

"The Problem of Unemployment," *Catholic Charities Review,* 12:107–111 (April).

1929

"Market Shifts, Price Movements, and Employment," *American Economic Review, Supplement,* 19:5–22 (March).

"Recent Employment Movements," *Survey,* 62:16–18 (April 1).

"The Current Labor Policies of American Industries," *Quarterly Journal of Economics,* 43:393–435 (May).

"Labor's Share in the Control of Industry," *American Federationist,* 36:598–602 (May).

"Do Manufacturers Need Relief?" *New Republic,* 60:35–37 (August 28).

"Der Wandel in der Arbeiterpolitik der nordamerikanischen Industriellen," *Zeitschrift für Völkerpsychologie und Soziologie,* Heft 3, 5 jahrgang:267–302 (September).

1930

"Orderly Marketing for Labor," *New Republic,* 63:342–344 (August 6).

"Doles for Employers," *New Republic,* 65:181–183 (December 31).

1931

Modern Economic Society (New York, Henry Holt & Co., Inc.).

"The Significance of Trade Unionism," *Harvard Business School Alumni Bulletin,* May 15.

"Misleading Attack on the Wagner Bill," *American Labor Legislation Review,* 21:192 (June).

"Pharaoh Dreams Again—Fat Years Must Take Care of the Lean," *Atlantic Monthly*, 148:248–252 (August).

"Unemployment Relief by Business," *New Republic*, 69:181–184 (December 30).

Letter to the editor. "Criticizing Secretary Doak's Attack on Senator Wagner's Employment Exchange," *New York Times*, April 10, p. 24.

1932

"Is the Tariff a Cause of Depression?" *Current History*, 35:519–524 (January).

"The Federal Labor Board," *American Federationist*, 39:170–175 (February).

"Technological Unemployment—Lines of Action, Adaptation, and Control," *American Economic Review, Supplement*, 22:41–54 (March).

"Should the Budget Be Balanced?" *New Republic*, 70:262–264 (April 20).

"Modern Economic Society—Further Considered," with F. H. Knight, *Journal of Political Economy*, 40:814–820ff (December).

"Underlying Causes and Historical Background of the Depression," *Teachers College Record*, 34:212–227 (December).

Letter to the editor. "Says States Are Delinquent in Providing Relief," *New York Times*, November 20, section II, p. 2.

Radio address. "The Limitations of Planning," National Council on Radio in Education, National Broadcasting Co., March 12; published by the University of Chicago, Economic Series Lecture No. 20.

1933

"The Immediate Unemployment Problem," *Annals of the American Academy of Political and Social Science*, 165:1–12 (January).

"Making Booms Bear the Burden of Relief—Some Financial Implications of Unemployment Reserves," *Harvard Business Review*, 11:327–335 (April).

"Should We Deflate Labor?" *New Republic*, 74:329–331 (May 3).

1934

"Labor Aspects of the National Recovery Administration," in *Current Economic Policies, Selected Discussions*, edited by Joseph B. Hubbard, pp. 295–362 (New York, Henry Holt & Co., Inc.).

Towards Stability (New York, Henry Holt & Co., Inc.).

"Implications of the Shorter Hour Movement," *Proceedings of the Academy of Political Science*, 15:431–443 (January).

"The Economics of Public Works," *American Economic Review, Supplement*, 24:174–185 (March).

1935

"The Government and Collective Bargaining," *Annals of the American Academy of Political and Social Science*, 178:107–122 (March).

"The Government as an Economic Manager," *Proceedings of the Academy of Political Science*, 16:391–401 (June).

"Trends in the Labor Situation," *Bulletin of the Harvard Business School Alumni Association*, 11:269–276 (July).

"The Outlook for Labor Relations under the Wagner Industrial Disputes Act," *The Annalist,* 46:78 (July 19).
"Labor and the Government," *Yale Review,* 25:258–274 (December).

1936

"The Adjustment to Instability," *American Economic Review, Supplement,* 26:196–213 (March 1936).
"Economic Planning in Recent Literature," *Harvard Business Review,* 14:502–508 (Summer).
"Selling More Labor," *Atlantic Monthly,* 158:321–330 (September).

1937

"The Period 1919–1936 in the United States: Its Significance for Business-Cycle Theory," *Review of Economic Statistics,* 19:1–19 (February).
"Labor Faces the Future," *Christian Science Monitor Weekly Magazine Section,* March 3, pp. 3ff.
"Must We Have Another Boom?" *Atlantic Monthly,* 159:600–607 (May).
Review of Dale Yoder and G. R. Davies, *Depression and Recovery,* in *Weltwirtschaftliches Archiv,* 45. Band, Heft 1:8–10 (January).
Address. "Current Trends in Labor Relations," New England Council, Providence, Rhode Island, March 19.
Address. "Safeguards Against Depressions," Address No. 4, Special Session for Business Executives, Department of Economics and Business Administration, Westminster College, New Wilmington, Pennsylvania, November 19.

1938

"Collective Bargaining at Work," *Atlantic Monthly,* 161:20–27 (January).
"The Contents of Collective Agreements—The Wisdom of Hindsight," *Society for the Advancement of Management Journal,* 3:13–21ff (January).
"Risks—The Key to Recovery," *Nation,* 146:294–297 (March 12).
"The Downturn of 1937," *Review of Economic Statistics,* 20:97–110 (August).
"Profits and Prosperity," *Atlantic Monthly,* 162:635–642 (November).
Address. "An Economic Analysis of Our Major Industries," Lecture No. 4, Business Executives, Westminster College, New Wilmington, Pennsylvania, November 17.
"The Adjustment to Instability," in *Business and Modern Society,* edited by Malcolm P. McNair and Howard T. Lewis (Cambridge, Harvard University Press), pp. 235–356.

1939

Economic Factors Affecting Industrial Relations Policy in the War Period, Industrial Relations Monograph No. 3 (New York, Industrial Relations Counselors, Inc.).
"Corporate Price Policies as a Factor in the Recent Business Recession," *Proceedings of the Academy of Political Science,* 18:142–155 (January).
"The Changing Character of American Industrial Relations," *American Economic Review, Supplement,* 29:121–137 (March).
Et al., "The Effects of Government Spending upon Private Enterprise," First Fortune Roundtable, *Fortune,* 19:59ff (March).

"The Great American Experiment," *Atlantic Monthly,* 163:470–477 (April).
"Budget and Tax Increases," *Fortune,* 19:123 (May).
Et al., "Taxation and Recovery," Second Fortune Roundtable, *Fortune,* 19:67ff (May).
Et al., "How Can America Put Its Unemployed Back to Work?" Fourth Fortune Roundtable, *Fortune,* 20:41ff (October).
"Business Looks Ahead," *Atlantic Monthly,* 164:592–600 (November).
Letter to the editor. "On His Statement on Long-Term Investments," *New York Times,* November 18, p. 16.
Address. "Layoff Policy," Ninth Annual Conference on Industrial Relations, University of Michigan, Ann Arbor, Michigan, April 12–15.

1940

"Labor Economics in a Period of Change," Personnel Series No. 41 (New York, American Management Association).
"The Present Nature of the Recovery Problem," *Proceedings of the Academy of Political Science,* 18:380–393 (January).
"Impact of Social Security Legislation upon Mobility and Enterprise," *American Economic Review, Supplement,* 30:44–60 (March).
"Paying for Armaments," *Atlantic Monthly,* 166:12–16 (July).
"The Economics of National Defense," *New England News Letter, Supplement,* pp. 1–4 (December).
Address. "The Significance of Collective Bargaining," Business Lectures No. 1, Allegheny College, Meadville, Pennsylvania.
Address. "Labor Policies in View of Current Economic Conditions," Tenth Annual Conference on Industrial Relations, University of Michigan, Ann Arbor, Michigan, April 10–12.
Address. "Union Management Co-Operative Movement," Mechanical Section System Co-Operative Committee Meeting, Canadian National Railways, Montreal, Canada, May 16.

1941

Union Policies and Industrial Management (Washington, D. C., The Brookings Institution).
"The Development of National Labor Policy," in *Studies in Economics and Industrial Relations,* Bicentennial Conference, pp. 141–160 (Philadelphia, University of Pennsylvania).
Economic Factors Affecting Industrial Relations Policy in National Defense, Industrial Relations Monograph No. 6 (New York, Industrial Relations Counselors, Inc.).
"Good Bargains and Bad Bargains," in *Collective Bargaining Contracts,* pp. 43–66 (Washington, D. C.: Bureau of National Affairs, Inc.).
"National Labor and Production Policies," *Proceedings of the Academy of Political Science,* 19:179–196 (January).
"Labor and the War," *Atlantic Monthly,* 167:555–563 (May).
Foreword. Paul H. Norgren, *The Swedish Collective Bargaining System,* pp. v–vi (Cambridge, Harvard University Press).
Address. "Economic Problems Generated by the Defense Program," Eleventh

Annual Conference on Industrial Relations, University of Michigan, Ann Arbor, Michigan, April 17–18; published in *Addresses on Industrial Relations,* Bureau of Industrial Relations Bulletin No. 13 (Ann Arbor, University of Michigan Press).

Address. "The Outlook for Private Enterprise in America," Thirtieth Annual Convention of the Investment Bankers Association of America, Chicago, December 2.

1942

"Summary of American Economic Objectives," in *American Economic Objectives,* pp. 19–40 (New Wilmington, Pennsylvania, The Economic and Business Foundation).

"The Conditions of Expansion," *American Economic Review,* 32:1–21 (March).

"Postwar Boom or Collapse," *Harvard Business Review,* 21:5–42 (Autumn).

"Harvard Trade Union Fellowships," *Harvard Alumni Bulletin,* 45:48–49 (October 10).

Introduction. S. E. Hill, *Teamsters and Transportation,* pp. vii–viii (Washington, D. C., American Council on Public Affairs).

Address. "The Economic World of Tomorrow," Radcliffe College, Cambridge, Massachusetts, March.

1943

Present Savings and Postwar Markets (New York, McGraw-Hill Book Company).

"Labor after the War," in *Postwar Economic Problems,* edited by S. E. Harris, pp. 241–262 (New York, McGraw-Hill Book Company).

"How Much Trade-Unionism as Usual?" *Atlantic Monthly,* 171:74–82 (January).

"Some Problems of a 'Catching-up' Economy," *The Seminar Bulletin,* 3:1–8 (April).

"Postwar Business Outlook," *Trusts and Estates,* 76:416–418 (May).

"A Summary View of American Economic Policies," with R. D. Calkins and J. F. Ebersole, *Proceedings of a Forum Meeting* (New Wilmington, Pennsylvania, The Economic and Business Foundation, May 13).

"Foreign Trade and Postwar Stability," *Foreign Affairs,* 21:674–689 (July).

Address. "Enterprise in Postwar America," National Association of Investment Companies, New York, January 25.

Address. "Social Security after the War," Radcliffe College, Cambridge, Massachusetts, April 4.

Address. "Labor and Management," International Ladies' Garment Workers' Union Officer Institute, New York, December 10.

Address. "Labor and Management," International Ladies' Garment Workers' Union Officer Institute, New York, December 17.

1944

"Postwar Labor Stability," Personnel Series No. 79 (New York, American Management Association).

"Inflation and Wages," *Proceedings of the Academy of Political Science,* 20:336–359 (January).

"Runaway Inflation? Economist Says No," *Christian Science Monitor Weekly Magazine Section*, January 8, p. 5.

"Labor Crisis," *Atlantic Monthly*, 173:37–41 (February).

"A New Outlook Needed for Postwar Labor-Industry Relations," *Commerce*, pp. 13–14ff (April).

"Problems of Wage Policy after the War," *Proceedings of the Academy of Political Science*, 21:64–88 (May).

"Economic Aspects of American Business Policies," with E. P. Beatty, L. Jackson, and C. W. Ullman, *Proceedings of Conference* (New Wilmington, Pennsylvania, The Economic and Business Foundation, May 11).

"The Role of Business Policies in America's Economic Future," with J. E. Bennett, A. Upgren, and A. B. Wolfe, *Proceedings of a Panel Forum* (New Wilmington, Pennsylvania, The Economic and Business Foundation, May 11).

"Postwar Outlook for Business," *Supervision*, 6:12–13 (September).

"Wanted: A National Labor Policy for Industry and Labor," *Public Opinion Quarterly*, 8:407–415 (Fall).

"Jobs after the War," *Atlantic Monthly*, 174:87–91 (October).

"Fitting the Veteran into Industry," *State Government*, 17:462–464 (December).

"What You Should Know about Taxes," *Saturday Evening Post*, pp. 217–223ff (December 23).

Foreword. H. R. Northrup, *Organized Labor and the Negro*, pp. xi–xiii (New York, Harper & Brothers).

Address. "Postwar Jobs or Bread Lines?" International Ladies' Garment Workers' Union Officer Institute, New York, January 7.

Address. "The Role of Unemployment Compensation in Social Security," Postwar Forum of the American Federation of Labor, New York, April 12–13.

Address. "Business and Labor's Postwar Outlook," Annual Meeting of the Committee for Economic Development, July 13.

Address. "The Postwar Outlook for Business and Labor," New York City Committee for Economic Development, New York, October 10.

Radio address. "The Postwar Outlook for Business and Labor," Columbia Broadcasting System, October 31.

Address. "Postwar Jobs, Taxes and Debt," American Pharmaceutical Manufacturers Association, New York, December 12.

1945

"Public Policies and Postwar Employment," in *Financing American Prosperity*, pp. 266–336 (New York, Twentieth Century Fund).

"Report and Findings of Panel of the National War Labor Board in Certain Disputes Involving Supervisors," with R. D. Calkins and W. H. Spohn (Washington, D. C., National War Labor Board).

"How to Stimulate Postwar Employment," *Annals of the American Academy of Political and Social Science*, 238:158–166 (March).

"Removal of War-Time Controls with Special Reference to Price Policy and Wage Policy," *Proceedings of Conference* (New Wilmington, Pennsylvania, The Economic and Business Foundation, March 8).

"An Orderly Rise in Prices," *Greater Pittsburgh*, pp. 14–15 (April).
"The Postwar Outlook for Business and Labor," *Mail Order Journal*, 61:11–14 (May–June).
"Issue of the Annual Wage," *Fortune*, 31:25ff (June).
"Formula for Avoiding a Tailspin," *New York Times Magazine*, June 17, pp. 5ff.
"Comments on the Murray Bill," *Review of Economic Statistics*, 27:109–112 (August).
"Adjustment of Wages During Conversion," *Harvard Business Review*, 24:57–74 (Autumn).
"More Job Givers Wanted," *Fortune*, 32:160–161ff (October).
"Stimulating Peacetime Employment," *Dun's Review & Modern Industry*, 53: 11–13ff (October).
"Seven Surprises in Our Economic Picture," *New York Times Magazine*, November 25, pp. 5ff.
"American Tariff and World Trade," *Atlantic Monthly*, 176:61–65 (December).
"The Changing Position of Foremen in American Industry," *Advanced Management*, section I, 10:155–161 (December).
"Strikes and the Public Interest," *Yale Review*, 35:207–221 (December).
Letter to the editor. "On Article on U. S. Post-War Economy," *New York Times*, July 8, section VI, p. 4.
The Lowell Lectures, The Lowell Institute, Boston Public Library, Boston, Massachusetts, February–March.
1. "The Supply of Enterprise," February 1.
2. "The Problem of Economic Stability," February 4.
3. "Wage Policy, Production, and Employment," February 8.
4. "The Relations Between Business and Labor," February 11.
5. "The Responsibility of Business for Employment," February 15.
6. "The Responsibility of Government for Employment," February 18.
7. "The World Economic Position of the United States," February 25.
8. "The Conditions of Expansion," March 1.
Address. "The Postwar Outlook for Business and Labor," Associated Industries of Minneapolis, Minneapolis, Minnesota, April 30.
Address. "After the War: Prosperity or Depression," Institute of Business and Economic Problems in a Private Enterprise Economy, University of Pittsburgh and the Pittsburgh Chamber of Commerce, Pittsburgh, Pennsylvania.

1946

"The Place of Labor Unions in the Social Framework," *Labor Relations Reference Manual*, 18:152–164.
"Wage Policies and Problems in the Months Ahead," Bureau of Industrial Relations Bulletin No. 17, pp. 43–47 (Ann Arbor, University of Michigan Press).
"What to Do about the Labor Mess," in *Factory Management and Maintenance* (New York: McGraw-Hill Book Company).
"Business Outlook for 1946," *Commercial and Financial Chronicle*, 163:121ff (January 10).

"We Can Avoid Inflation If —," *New York Times Magazine*, February 3, pp. 5ff.
"Organized Labor and the Public Interest: The Responsibility of Organized Labor for Employment," *American Economic Review Proceedings*, 36:193–208 (May).
"Wage Policies," *Proceedings of the Academy of Political Science*, 22:3–15 (May).
"Wage-Price Policy and Employment," *American Economic Review Proceedings*, 36:304–318 (May).
"The Threat of Inflation," *Commercial and Financial Chronicle*, 163:2349ff (May 2).
"A Bill of Rights for the Public—Proposals for Preventing Strikes in Essential Industries," *Christian Science Monitor*, May 20, section II, p. 9.
"What Do the Strikes Teach Us?" *Atlantic Monthly*, 177:35–40 (May).
"Some Long-Range Trends," *Bulletin of the Robert Morris Associates*, 29:1–8 (June).
"Needed: A Basic Labor Policy," *New York Times Magazine*, June 9, pp. 10ff.
"To Avoid a Boom—and Then a Bust," *New York Times Magazine*, July 21, pp. 5ff.
"Higher Salaries for Professors," *Bulletin of the American Association of University Professors*, 32:438–442 (Autumn).
"Still the Danger: Not Collapse But Boom," *New York Times Magazine*, September 29, pp. 7ff.
"Mutual Understanding Is the Best Way to Prevent Industrial Strife," *Boston Sunday Herald Industrial Peace Supplement*, October 6, pp. 14–15.
"How Stable Is the American Economy?" *Commercial and Financial Chronicle*, 164:1925ff (October 17).
"Holding Labor at Arm's Length," *Trade Union Courier Magazine Section*, October 28, pp. 15f.
"The Economic Outlook," *Manufacturers' News*, pp. 7–8ff (December).
"The Nathan Report on Wage Policy," *New York Herald Tribune*, December 19, p. 34, and December 20, p. 26.
"What Has Happened to Professors' Salaries since 1940?" *Bulletin of the American Association of University Professors*, 32:718–723 (Winter).
Address. "The Economic Outlook," Forty-first Annual Meeting of the American Life Convention, Chicago, October 7–11.

1947

Basic Criteria Used in Wage Negotiations (Chicago, Chicago Association of Commerce and Industry).
The Challenge of Industrial Relations (Ithaca, Cornell University Press).
Trade Unions in a Free Society (Cambridge, Harvard University Press).
When Are Wages Too Low? (New York, Bank of New York).
"Some Economic Consequences of Science," *Annals of the American Academy of Political and Social Science*, 249:99–110 (January).
"To End Strikes in Essential Industries," *New York Times Magazine*, January 12, pp. 7ff.

"Professor Slichter X-rays Mr. Nathan's Report," *Industry*, 12:15–16ff (February).
"The Governor's Labor Management Committee Report," *House Bill No. 1875*, Commonwealth of Massachusetts (March).
"Prices Must Come Down," *New York Times Magazine*, April 13, pp. 7ff.
"The Great Question in Industrial Relations," *New York Times Magazine*, April 27, pp. 5ff.
"The Business Outlook," *Commercial and Financial Chronicle*, 165:2469ff (May 8).
"The Business Outlook," *Appraisal Journal*, 15:310–316 (July).
"Is a Recession Necessary?" *Dun's Review & Modern Industry*, 55:11–14ff (August).
"Problems of Wage Policy in the Spring of 1947," *Review of Economic Statistics*, 29:139–145 (August).
"Is the United States Unionized for Conflict or Cooperation?" *The Commonwealth* (California), 23:148–153 (August 4).
"Eight Errors in Our Economic Thinking," *New York Times Magazine*, August 10, pp. 7ff.
"The Danger of Spiraling Prices," *New York Times Magazine*, September 14, pp. 12ff.
"The Business Outlook," *Commercial and Financial Chronicle*, 166:1307ff (October 2).
"Is America's Industrial Plant Too Small?" *New York Times Magazine*, November 30, pp. 8ff.
"Wages, Prices and Business Outlook," *Commercial and Financial Chronicle*, 166:2474ff (December 18).
Letter to the editor. "Assailing Proposed Cut in U. S. Conciliation Service Budget," *New York Times*, March 26, p. 24.
Review of *The American Individual Enterprise System*, The Economic Principles Commission of the National Association of Manufacturers, in *The Management Review*, 36:445–446 (August).
Address. "Collective Bargaining and the National Economy," Industrial College of the Armed Forces, Washington, D. C., February 12.
Address. "Some Current Problems in Industrial Relations," Wisconsin Manufacturers' Association, April 15.
Address. "Trends in Labor Relations," Boston Chamber of Commerce Retail Trade Board, October 20–21, published in *19th Boston Conference on Distribution*, pp. 68–71.

1948

The American Economy: Its Problems and Prospects (New York, Alfred A. Knopf, Inc.).
"The State of Business," *Commercial and Financial Chronicle*, 167:99ff (January 8).
"The Long-Range Demand for Capital," *Commercial and Financial Chronicle*, 167:302ff (January 22).
"Tax Formula: For Savers, Lower Levies," *New York Times Magazine*, January 25, pp. 13ff.

"The Problem of Inflation," *Review of Economics and Statistics,* 30:3–5 (February).

"Commends Taft-Hartley Act, But Warns of Abuse," *Commercial and Financial Chronicle,* 167:610ff (February 5).

"Survey of Our Economy: Pluses and Minuses," *New York Times Magazine,* February 29, pp. 11ff.

"Wages and Prices," *Proceedings of the Academy of Political Science,* 23:47–63 (May).

"Are We Becoming a 'Laboristic' State?" *New York Times Magazine,* May 16, pp. 11ff.

"Are Profits Too High?" *Atlantic Monthly,* 182:31–35 (July).

"Some Basic Issues Raised by Trade Unions," *Proceedings of the American Philosophical Society,* 92:203–209 (July).

"The Business Outlook," *Commercial and Financial Chronicle,* 168:1197ff (September 23).

"Our Economy Was Never More Stable," *New York Times Magazine,* October 17, pp. 7ff.

"The Business Outlook," *Commercial and Financial Chronicle,* 168:2061ff (November 18).

"Business Profits Exaggerated," *Commercial and Financial Chronicle,* 168:2381ff (December 9).

Address. "Economic Trends—Short Run and Long Run," Savings Bank Association of Connecticut, October 9.

1949

"Collective Bargaining and Productivity," *Report of the First Industrial Relations Conference,* Montreal University Industrial Relations Section, pp. 15–41.

"The Economics of Collective Bargaining," in *The Economics of Collective Bargaining,* edited by Charlotte Knight, *Proceedings of the California Institute of Industrial Relations, 1948–1949,* pp. 30–45.

"The Problems of Business Leadership in a Laboristic Economy," in *Development of Executive Leadership,* edited by Marvin Bower, pp. 3–27 (Cambridge, Harvard University Press).

"Trends in Prices, Demand for Capital, and Supply of Capital," *Appraisal Journal,* 17:25–35 (January).

"Can Stability Be Maintained?" *Commercial and Financial Chronicle,* 169:254ff (January 20).

"A Tax Increase Now Would Be Dangerous," *New York Times Magazine,* January 23, pp. 7ff.

"The Taft-Hartley Act: Summary," *Quarterly Journal of Economics,* 63:1–31 (February).

"Industry's Real Need: More Expansion," *Commerce,* pp. 17ff (March).

"Economic Outlook for Construction," *Commercial and Financial Chronicle,* 169:957ff (March 3).

"Deflation Tips Balance of Economy, Says Slichter," *Harbus News,* March 17, p. 13.

"Can Industry Produce Enough?" *Harvard Business School Alumni Bulletin,* 25:6–7ff (Spring).
"Less Spending, Threat to Stability," *Commercial and Financial Chronicle,* 169:1613ff (April 14).
"Profits in a Laboristic Society," *Harvard Business Review,* 27:346–361 (May).
"The Readjustment of Business," *Commercial and Financial Chronicle,* 169:2158ff (May 19).
"The Economic Picture: More White Than Black," *New York Times Magazine,* May 23, pp. 7ff.
"Today's Economic Danger Signals," *Management Review,* 38:298–300 (June).
"The Changing American Economy," *Commercial and Financial Chronicle,* 169:2374ff (June 2).
"The Upturn in Business Is Not Far Away," *New York Times Magazine,* July 17, pp. 7ff.
"The Outlook for Recovery," *Commercial and Financial Chronicle,* 170:645ff (August 18).
"Business Forecast, Fair: Upturn Likely Before Christmas," *Commerce,* pp. 16–17ff (September).
"The Businessman in a Laboristic Economy," *Fortune,* 40:108–110ff (September).
"The State of Economics," *Social Science Research Council Items,* 3:25–28 (September).
"Near-Term Business Prospects," *Commercial and Financial Chronicle,* 170:1245ff (September 29).
"The Pressing Problem of Old-Age Security," *New York Times Magazine,* October 16, pp. 9ff.
"Will Business Recovery Continue?" *Commercial and Financial Chronicle,* 170:1649ff (October 27).
"Comments on the Steel Report: Raising the Price of Labor as a Method of Increasing Employment," *Review of Economics and Statistics,* 31:283–288 (November).
"How Big in 1980?" *Atlantic Monthly,* 184:39–43 (November).
"Business Prospects in First Half of 1950," *Commercial and Financial Chronicle,* 170:2277ff (December 8).
Foreword. Walter Galenson, *Labor in Norway,* pp. ix–x (Cambridge, Harvard University Press).
Address. "The Responsibility of Business for Employment in 1949," New Haven Chamber of Commerce, New Haven, Connecticut, March 7.
Address. "American Business in a Changing World," American Association of Collegiate Schools of Business, Madison, Wisconsin, April 22.
Address. "Debits and Credits—Some Observations on Current Social Trends," Honors Convocation, University of Wisconsin, Madison, Wisconsin, June 16.
Address. "What's Ahead? Recession or Boom?" Fortieth Annual Meeting of the Grocery Manufacturers of America, Inc., New York, November 16.
Address. "The Business Outlook," Toy Manufacturers of the United States, New York, December 5.

1950

Social and Economic Impact of the Pension Trend, Personnel Series No. 133 (New York, American Management Association).

"Better Than We Think," *Atlantic Monthly,* 185:46–49 (January).

"What is America's Short-Term Business Outlook?" *Dun's Review & Modern Industry,* 58:11–12ff (January).

"A Long Look Ahead at Economic Trends," *Commercial and Financial Chronicle,* 171:53ff (January 5).

"The Social Control of Industrial Relations," *Commercial and Financial Chronicle,* 171:419ff (January 26).

"Comment on the Papers on Employment and Unemployment Figures," *Review of Economics and Statistics,* 32:74–77 (February).

"Notes on the Structure of Wages," *Review of Economics and Statistics,* 32:80–91 (February).

"Economic Problems of the Year Ahead," *New York Times Magazine,* February 5, pp. 11ff.

"The High Cost of Low Incomes," *New York Times Magazine,* March 5, pp. 10ff.

"The Problem of Old Age Security," *Commercial and Financial Chronicle,* 171: 1200ff (March 23).

"Affirmation of Faith in Our Economy," *New York Times Magazine,* March 26, pp. 9ff.

"Where Are We and Where Are We Going?" *Commercial and Financial Chronicle,* 171:1309ff (March 30).

"Further Drop in Production and Employment Predicted This Year," *Milk Plant Monthly,* April, pp. 85–88.

"Long-Term Economic Trends," *American Economic Review Papers and Proceedings,* 40:457–469 (May).

"How Stable Is the American Economy?" *Yale Review,* 39:577–590 (June).

"Our Best Defense," *Atlantic Monthly,* 185:21–25 (June).

"Factors in Next Decade's Business," *Commercial and Financial Chronicle,* 171: 2249ff (June 1).

"How Long Can Business Boom Last?" *Commercial and Financial Chronicle,* 171:2463ff. (June 15).

"Factors Molding the Course of Business in the Next Decade," *Harvard Business Review,* 28:129ff (July).

"No More Big Depressions," *Coronet,* 28:28–31 (July).

"American Economy Now and Its Growth Capacity," *Commercial and Financial Chronicle,* 172:429ff (August 3).

"We Can Win the Economic 'Cold War,' Too," *New York Times Magazine,* August 13, pp. 7ff.

"Likely Characteristics of Our Defense Economy," *Commercial and Financial Chronicle,* 172:801ff (August 31).

"Some Major Questions on Current Economic Trends," *Investment Fund Section: Investment Dealers' Digest,* Report on the Second Annual Mutual Fund Sales Conference, pp. 20–25 (September 11).

"Economic Problems of a Defense Economy," *Commercial and Financial Chronicle,* 172:1485ff (October 19).
"Business and Armament," *Atlantic Monthly,* 186:38–41 (November).
"Our Economic Problems," *National Savings and Loan Journal,* 5:8–18 (November).
"Today's Greatest Need," *Commerce,* pp. 13–14ff (November).
"Problems in Production Race with Russia," *Commercial and Financial Chronicle,* 172:1681ff (November 2).
"The Changing American Economy and Its Significance for Banking," *U. S. Investor,* 61:22–26 (November 4).
"Some Current Economic Misconceptions," *Commercial and Financial Chronicle,* 172:1881ff (November 16).
"Retirement Age and Social Policy," in *The Aged and Society,* Industrial Relations Research Association Publication No. 5, pp. 106–114 (Champaign, Illinois, Industrial Relations Research Association, December).
"Economic Implications of Korean Crisis," *Commercial and Financial Chronicle,* 172:2179ff (December 7).
"To Curb Inflation and Equalize Its Burden," *New York Times Magazine,* December 17, pp. 13ff.
Address. "Stampede for Pensions: The Problem of Old-Age Security," Twenty-ninth Annual Business and Professional Men's Group, University of Cincinnati, Cincinnati, Ohio, March 10.
Address. "The Economic Position of the United States," Magazine Advertising Bureau, New York, April 6.
Address. "The Business Outlook," Sixty-seventh Annual Convention of the National Confectioners' Association, New York, June 7.
Address. "How Much Will Social Security Cost Us?" American Meat Institute, Chicago, October 2.

1951

What's Ahead for American Business? (Boston, Little, Brown & Co.).
"The Need for More Employment of Older Workers," *Wisconsin Labor 1951,* published by the Wisconsin State Federation of Labor.
"Armed America," *Nation's Business,* 39:29–30ff (February).
"The Economic Outlook," *Savings and Loans News,* 71:30ff (February).
"Should We Pay as We Go?" *New York Times Magazine,* February 4, pp. 10ff.
"Curb Inflation with a Purchasing-Power Bond," *Commercial and Financial Chronicle,* 173:1121ff (March 15).
"Can We Hold Down Prices?" *Atlantic Monthly,* 187:46–49 (April).
"Wage Policy and Inflation, Control of Costs is Essential to Control of Prices," *Barron's,* April 23, 1951, pp. 23–26.
"What Next, Mr. Business Man?" *Commercial and Financial Chronicle,* 173:1756ff (April 26).
"The Integrity of the Dollar," *Proceedings of the Academy of Political Science,* 24:385–402 (May).
"What to Expect from the Defense Economy," *Commercial and Financial Chronicle,* 173:1942ff (May 10).

"Hails Industrial Research as Vital to U. S. Economy," *The Julius Klein Newsletter,* 3:1 (June).

"The Past Year and the Next in Our Economy," *New York Times Magazine,* June 10, pp. 9ff.

"Near-Term Prospects and Their Policy Implications," *Commercial and Financial Chronicle,* 174:414ff (August 2).

"Why Is United States Industry So Productive?" *Commercial and Financial Chronicle,* 174:862ff (September 6).

"A Balance Sheet on Foreign Aid," *New York Times Magazine,* September 9.

"Personal Saving in an Inflationary Economy," *Commercial and Financial Chronicle,* 174:1149ff (September 27).

"What Makes the Economy Tick?" *The General Electric Review,* 54:14–18 (October).

"What Have We Learned from Our Experience with Inflation?" *Commercial and Financial Chronicle,* 174:1557ff (October 25).

"Slichter Says Wage Controls Urgent Now," *The Christian Science Monitor,* December 22, p. 2.

Address. "Education in a Value-Creating Age," University of Wisconsin, Madison, Wisconsin, May 15.

Address. "History of the Labor Movement," Industrial College of the Armed Forces, Washington, D. C., October 12.

Address. "Labor Relations in the Light of the Current Economic Situation and Stabilization Program," Joint Association of the Master Printers' Section and the Union Employers' Section of the Printing Industry of America at Boston, October 25.

Address. "The Impact of Economic Groups on American Industry," Northwestern University, Chicago, November 15.

1952

"Can the Economy Afford the Loss of Production of Its Older Workers or the Financial Burden of Maintaining Them? What is the Effect of Changes of the Business Cycle on Employment and Retirement Practices?" in *Retirement of Older Workers* (New York, National Committee on the Aging of the National Social Welfare Assembly).

"Rearmament: Too Much, Too Soon," *Atlantic Monthly,* 189:49–51 (January).

"Is Inflation Still a Threat?" *Commercial and Financial Chronicle,* 175:969ff (March 6).

"Prospects for Growth in the American Economy," *Commercial and Financial Chronicle,* 175:1383ff (April 3).

Wage Stabilization and Emergency Disputes," *Commercial and Financial Chronicle,* 175:1699ff (April 24).

"Conflicting Trends in the American Economy," *Commercial and Financial Chronicle,* 175:1809ff (May 1).

"Productivity: Still Going Up," *Atlantic Monthly,* 190:64–68 (July).

"How Bad Is Inflation?" *Harper's Magazine,* 205:53–57 (August).

"Professor Slichter Defends Need for Rising Price Level," *Journal of Commerce,* September 2, p. 4.

"The Short-Term Economic Outlook," *Commercial and Financial Chronicle,* 176:1109ff (September 25).
"A Look at the Economy," *Commercial and Financial Chronicle,* 176:1215ff (October 2).
"How Stable Is the Economy?" *Commercial and Financial Chronicle,* 176:1520ff (October 23).
"Current Labor Trends and Labor Problems," *Commercial and Financial Chronicle,* 176:1619ff (October 30).
"Wage Policies since World War II," *Commercial and Financial Chronicle,* 176: 2122ff (December 4).
"Slichter—No Recession in Late '53," *Harbus News,* December 12, p. 6.
Compilation. "What Every Executive Should Read," *Saturday Review,* 35:55 (January 19).
Foreword. Walter Galenson, *The Danish System of Labor Relations,* pp. vii–viii (Cambridge, Harvard University Press).
Address. "What Is the Possibility of Increasing the Employment of Persons of 65 Years of Age or More?" Conference on Aging, Boston, March 14.
Address. "Discussion of Economic Trends," Revenue Requirements Conference, New York, March 22.
Address. "Key Factors in Increasing the Standard of Living in the United States," Harvard Business School Club of Chicago, March 29.
Address. "Current Business Trends," Farmers and Merchants Bank of Long Beach, California, April 14.
Address. "Current Business Trends," Boys' Apparel Buyers' Association, New York, May 6.
Address. "Savings and Inflation: Long-Run Prospects and Policies," Minneapolis Club, Minneapolis, Minnesota, May 17.
Address. "Role of Management in Industrial Relations," Thirty-fourth Annual American Gas Association Convention, Atlantic City, New Jersey, October 27.

1953

"Labor and the National Economy," *Connecticut Federationist,* published by the Connecticut American Federation of Labor.
"More Imports Needed," *Atlantic Monthly,* 191:37–40 (January).
"The U. S. Economy," *Barron's National Financial Weekly,* 33:5ff (January 26).
"Are We Headed for a Depression?" *Harper's Magazine,* 206:25–30 (February).
"A Slowly Rising Price Level the Lesser of Two Evils," *Michigan Business Review,* 5:6–8 (March).
"Business Outlook for Next Several Years," *Commercial and Financial Chronicle,* 177:1205ff (March 19).
"Reconciling a Defense Economy with Private Enterprise," *Commercial and Financial Chronicle,* 177:1317ff (March 26).
"Slichter Looks Ahead," *Commerce,* 50:20–22ff (April).
"Economics," *Saturday Review,* 36:24–25ff (April 4).
"Coming Developments in Labor Relations," *Commercial and Financial Chronicle,* 177:1642ff (April 16).

"We Can Have Peace *and* Prosperity," *New York Times Magazine*, April 26.
"Revision of the Taft-Hartley Act," *Quarterly Journal of Economics*, 67:149–180 (May).
"Must We Have a Recession?" *Commercial and Financial Chronicle*, 177:1959ff (May 7).
"Scheme of a Conversion," *Saturday Review*, 36:33–34 (May 9).
"Strong Points and Weak Points in the American Economy," *New York Public Library Bulletin*, 57:335–348 (July).
"Recession Psychology and the Boom," *New York Times Magazine*, August 23.
"The New Outlook for Business," *Commercial and Financial Chronicle*, 178: 1325ff (October 8).
"Can Business Check an Economic Slump?" *Commerce*, 50:13–14ff (November).
"Growth and Stability," *Review of Economics and Statistics*, 35:260–262 (November).
"The Growth of Competition," *Atlantic Monthly*, 192:66–70 (November).
"A Recession Can Be Prevented," *Purchasing*, 35:109–110 (November).
Foreword. Theodore V. Purcell, *The Worker Speaks His Mind on Company and Union*, pp. ix–xi (Cambridge, Harvard University Press).
Compilation. "Recommended Reading for Executives," *Saturday Review*, 36:48 (January 24).
Address. "What Lies Ahead?" Management Conference, University of Chicago, March 28.
Address. "Economic Trends and Influences," Personnel Association of Toronto, Ontario, Canada, April 30.
Address. "How Strong Is the American Economy?" Business Executives Conference, University of Omaha, May 15.

1954

"Slichter on the Slump," *Mortgage Banker*, pp. 12–15 (January).
"Top Economists See Slight Decline in '54. Six Month Drop to Precede Year-End Revival," *Harbus News*, January 8, pp. 3–4.
"Personal Check-List," *Saturday Review*, 37:40 (January 23).
"Slichter Sees Upturn in Business by Fall," *Boston Globe Annual Business Review*, January 24, p. A27.
"How Much Contraction?" *Commercial and Financial Chronicle*, 179:663ff (February 11).
"Reflections on the Guaranteed Annual Wage," *Commercial and Financial Chronicle*, 179:782ff (February 18).
"Industrial Relations in the United States," *Commercial and Financial Chronicle*, 179:1225ff (March 18).
"Can We Stabilize Price Levels and Have Full Employment?" *The Rotarian*, 84:14–15ff (March 19).
"The Business Outlook," *Journal of Business of the University of Chicago*, 27, no. 2, part 2:5–15 (April).
"A Noted Economist Looks Carefully at Conditions, Then States the Case for the Mild Readjustment," *Mortgage Banker*, pp. 10–15 (April).

"Business Upturn Should Come Soon," *New York Times Magazine,* April 11, pp. 13ff.

"The Business Decline and Prospects for Early Upturn," *Commercial and Financial Chronicle,* 179:1773ff (April 22).

"Do the Wage-Fixing Arrangements in the American Labor Market Have an Inflationary Bias?" *American Economic Review,* 44:322–346 (May).

"Slichter Speaks Up Again," *Business Week,* p. 162 (May 15).

"Has the Bottom of the Recession Been Reached?" *Commercial and Financial Chronicle,* 179:2301ff (May 27).

"The Prospects Are Bright," *Atlantic Monthly,* 193:31–33 (June).

"Is the Recession Over?" *Mortgage Banker,* pp. 11–13 (July).

"The Danger of Severe Recession Seems Over," *New York Times Magazine,* July 18, pp. 5ff.

"Undermining the Foundations," *Atlantic Monthly,* 194:50–54 (September).

"Wall Street as a Barometer: An Analysis," *New York Times Magazine,* October 3, pp. 9ff.

"U. S. Economic Foreign Policy," *Naval War College Review,* 7:13–28 (November).

"Prospective Changes in the Economic Trend," *Commercial and Financial Chronicle,* 180:1827ff (November 4).

Foreword. Philip Taft, *The Structure and Government of Labor Unions,* pp. ix–xi (Cambridge, Harvard University Press).

Address. "The Present State of Industrial Relations in the United States," Associated Industries of Cleveland, Ohio, March 12.

Address. "The Prospects for a Business Upturn," Executive Development Program of Drake University at Des Moines, Iowa, March 23.

Address. "The Short-Run Business Outlook," Fifty-first Annual Convention, National Paper Trade Association, Inc., New York, March 29.

The Merrill Lectures, Tulane University, New Orleans, Louisiana, April 2–9.

1. "Some Speculations on Economic Growth and Evolution."
2. "The Growth in Output per Manhour in the United States."
3. "Some Elements in a General Theory of Private Demand."
4. "Conditions and Institutions that Affect the Capacity of the Economy to Increase the Demand for Goods."
5. "The Future of Economic Institutions in the United States."

Address. "Supplementary Unemployment Compensation Plans—Some Problems and Issues," Industrial Relations Association of Buffalo, New York, April 19.

1955

The Most Competitive Country in the World (New York, Alumni Publications).

"Second Half of 1955 is Big Question," *Boston Sunday Globe Annual Business Review,* January 16, pp. C3–C5.

"Breakup of the Business Cycle," *Harvard Business Review,* 33:19ff (January–February).

"The American System of Industrial Relations: Some Contrasts with Foreign Systems," *Arbitration Today* (Washington, BNA Incorporated, 1955).

"Big Business: When Is It Too Big?" *New York Times Magazine,* March 20, pp. 13ff.

"Guaranteed Annual Wage," *Barron's National Financial Weekly,* 35:3ff (April 11).

"Have We Conquered the Business Cycle?" *Atlantic Monthly,* 195:51–55 (May).

"Some Features of the American System of Industrial Relations," *Société Belge d'Etudes & d'Expansion,* Bulletin Bimestriel, 166:518–525 (March–April).

"What's the Long-Term Outlook for Machine Tools?" *Iron Age,* 176:201–204 (August 25).

"Labor's New Victory: Threat or Promise?," *Atlantic Monthly,* 196:63–66 (September).

"Outlook for the Business Boom," *New York Times Magazine,* October 23, pp. 15ff.

"Guaranteed Annual Wage—The Future," *Challenge Magazine,* 4:16–19 (November).

"A $570 Billion Economy in 1965," *Sales Management Magazine,* 75:26–30 (November 10).

"Our Economy—Is It Politics-Proof?" *New York Times Magazine,* December 4, 1955, pp. 9ff.

"Slichter Shows Optimism About 1956 Prospects. Sees $410 Billion Last Quarter G. N. P." *Harbus News,* December 16, 1955, pp. 1ff.

Foreword. Lloyd Ulman, *The Rise of the National Trade Union,* pp. ix–x (Cambridge, Massachusetts: Harvard University Press, 1955).

Compilation. "Reading for Executives," *Saturday Review,* 38:50–51 (January 22).

Address. "The Ford-General Motors Supplementary Unemployment Compensation Plans," Interstate Conference on Labor Statistics, Madison, Wisconsin, July 5–8.

The Stanford Lectures, 14th Stanford Business Conference, Palo Alto, California, July 25–29.

1. "Some Distinctive Features of American Management."
2. "Is Bigness in Business a Problem?"
3. "Our Growing Capacity to Make Innovations."
4. "Are Business and the Government Succeeding in Breaking up the Business Cycle?"
5. "Some Unsettled Problems Ahead."

Address. "Our Expanding Economy," Executive Staff of the Port of New York Authority, New York, October 28.

1956

Economics and Men's Hopes for the Future (Washington, D. C., U. S. Information Agency).

"Slichter Says '56 2nd Half May Surpass 1st Half," *Boston Sunday Globe Annual Business Review,* January 1, pp. 53ff.

Summary of address. "SUB Plans—Their Economic Impact," *Management Record,* 18:45–47 (February).

"Short-and-Medium Term Economic Outlook," *Commercial and Financial Chronicle,* 183:829ff (February 16).

"Underlying Economic Trends and Labor Relations Outlook," *Commercial and Financial Chronicle,* 183:1292ff (March 15).
"Nearing Boom's Peak?" *Commercial and Financial Chronicle,* 183:2237ff (May 10).
"Economy's Current State: Output, Steel and Inflation," *Commercial and Financial Chronicle,* 184:165ff (July 12).
"The Growth of Moderation," *Atlantic Monthly,* 198:61–64 (October).
"Why I Am for Eisenhower," *New Republic,* 135:15 (October 22).
Et al., "The Economics of Eisenhower: A Symposium," *Review of Economics and Statistics,* 38:365–371 (November).
"A Look into Our Economic Future," *New York Times Magazine,* November 4, pp. 15ff.
"Basic Trends in the Economy and Effect upon Securities," *Commercial and Financial Chronicle,* 184:2065ff (November 15).
"Slichter Is Optimistic about 1957 Prospects," *Harbus News,* December 21, pp. 1ff.
Compilation. "Books for Top Executives," *Saturday Review,* 39:38–39 (January 21).
Address. "The Impact of Unions," University of Illinois, Urbana, Illinois, February 22.

1957

Creeping Inflation: A Debate, with Dr. Heinz Luedicke (New York, *The Journal of Commerce*).
"Slichter Sees Price Rises Checked in '57," *Boston Sunday Globe Annual Business Review,* January 6, pp. B21ff.
"5 Trends Shape Business Future," *Nation's Business,* 45:29–31 (February).
"Current Business Trends and the Wage Outlook," *Commercial and Financial Chronicle,* 185:1101ff (March 7).
"Government Expansion in a Dynamic Society," *Commercial and Financial Chronicle,* 185:1943ff (April 25).
"Business Trends in the Next Six Months," *Business Scope,* 1:1–3 (May 4).
"Why We Have Big Government and Why It Will Remain Big," *Mortgage Banker,* June, pp. 19–23ff.
"Government Spending Can Reduce Taxes," *Harvard Business Review,* 35:100–108 (July–August).
"A Defense of Bigness in Business," *New York Times Magazine,* August 4, pp. 10ff.
"Too Much Credit Restraint May Force Congress to Block It, Slichter Warns," *American Banker,* 122:184 (September 23).
"On the Side of Inflation," *Harvard Business Review,* 35:15ff (September–October).
"Slichter Traces Inflation in a Strong U. S. Economy," *Christian Science Monitor,* October 5, p. 18.
"The Economic Outlook," *Commercial and Financial Chronicle,* 186:1559ff (October 10).

"Inflation: Two Views," *The Rotarian,* 91:9ff (November).

"The Passing of Keynesian Economics," *Atlantic Monthly,* 200:141–144ff (November).

"The Rediscount Rate and the Recession," *New Republic,* 137:6 (November 25).

"What's Ahead for 1958?" *Business Scope,* 1:1–3 (December 28).

Address. "An Outlook on International Trade," Executive Staff of the Port of New York Authority, New York, February 15.

Address. "Technology and the Great American Experiment," Annual Engineers' Day Dinner, University of Wisconsin, May 3 (Madison, University of Wisconsin Press, 1957).

Address. "Reconciling Expansion with a Stable Price Level," Committee for Economic Development, October 31.

1958

"Slichter Predicts Slow Upturn in Business," *The Boston Globe 1958 Business Review,* January 5, p. A33.

"Year of Expansion Seen," *Detroit Free Press,* January 12.

"How Serious Is the Recession?" *Harvard Business School Bulletin,* 34:15–17 (February).

"How Long Will the Recession Last?" *New Republic,* 138:8–10 (March 3).

"Current Outlook for Business and Industrial Relations," *Commercial and Financial Chronicle,* 187:1041ff (March 6).

"The Financial Condition of the United States," statement before the Finance Committee of the U.S. Senate, April 18, 1958.

"The American Economy—Trends, Problems and Prospects," *Commercial and Financial Chronicle,* 187:2391ff (May 29).

"American Wage System: Its Effect upon Economy," *Commercial and Financial Chronicle,* 188:401ff (July 31).

"The American Economy—Problems and Prospects," *Commercial and Financial Chronicle,* 188:2085ff (November 20).

"New Goals for the Unions," *Atlantic Monthly,* 202:54–58 (December).

"The Power Holders in the American Economy," *Saturday Evening Post,* 231:34–35ff (December 13).

"American Economy on the Threshold of 1959," *Commercial and Financial Chronicle,* 188:2697ff (December 25).

"The Industry of Discovery," *Science,* 128:1610–1613 (December 26).

Foreword. William Haber, John J. Carroll, Mark L. Kahn, and Merton J. Peck, *Maintenance of Way Employment on U. S. Railroads,* pp. iii–iv (Detroit, Brotherhood of Maintenance of Way Employes).

Letter to the editor. "Consumer Confidence Reported by Slichter," *Boston Herald,* February 13, p. 18.

Interview. "A Noted Economist Tells What's Ahead in Business," *U. S. News and World Report,* 44:42–47 (April 4).

Address. "Technological Research as Related to the Growth and Stability of the Economy," Conference on Research and Development and Its Impact on the Economy, National Science Foundation, Washington, D. C., May 20.

Address. "The American Wage System—An Instrument of Stability in Times of Mild Recession and of Creeping Inflation in Times of Expansion," Economics-in-Action Group, University of Wisconsin, Madison, Wisconsin, July 1.

1959

"Economics and Collective Bargaining," in *Economics and the Policy Maker: Brookings Lectures, 1958–1959*, pp. 117–139 (Washington, D. C., The Brookings Institution).

"Labor Costs and Prices," in *Wages, Prices, Profits, and Productivity*, American Assembly, pp. 167–180 (New York, Columbia University Press).

"The Position of Trade Unions in the American Economy," in *Labor in a Free Society*, edited by Michael Harrington and Paul Jacobs, pp. 17–44 (Berkeley and Los Angeles, University of California Press).

"New Factors to Aid Recovery, Says Slichter," *Boston Globe 1959 Business Review*, January 4, p. A19.

"Sumner Slichter Gives the Outlook for '59," *Harbus News*, January 16, pp. 1ff.

"Forecast for 1959," *Harvard Business School Bulletin*, 35:37 (February).

"Current Trends, Problems and Prospects in the American Economy," *Commercial and Financial Chronicle*, 189:867ff (February 19).

"Argument for 'Creeping' Inflation," *New York Times Magazine*, March 8, pp. 23ff.

"Slow Inflation: An Inescapable Cost of Maximum Growth Rate," *Commercial and Financial Chronicle*, 189:1410ff (March 26).

"Inflation: A Problem of Shrinking Importance," *Commercial and Financial Chronicle*, 189:1854ff (April 23).

"Is U. S. Inflation Inevitable?" *Financial Times* (London), June 8.

"Straightforward Reporting on Economy and Prospects," *Commercial and Financial Chronicle*, 190:313ff (July 23).

"Observations on the American Economy," *Daedalus*, 88:499–504 (Summer).

"Influence of Bargained Wage Increases on Prices," *Monthly Labor Review*, 82:868–871 (August).

"How the Four-Day Week Would Affect U. S. Marketing," *Printers' Ink*, 269:68–69 (October 9).

Foreword. Mark W. Leiserson, *Wages and Economic Control in Norway*, pp. vii–x (Cambridge, Harvard University Press).

Foreword. William M. Leiserson, *American Trade Union Democracy*, pp. v–xiii (New York, Columbia University Press).

Radio and television interview. "Meet the Press," National Broadcasting Company, February 22.

Interview. "Don't Throttle Growth to Fight Inflation," *U. S. News and World Report*, 46:106–107 (March 9).

INDEX

INDEX

WERTHEIM PUBLICATIONS IN INDUSTRIAL RELATIONS

J. D. Houser, *What the Employer Thinks*, 1927
Wertheim Lectures on Industrial Relations, 1929
William Haber, *Industrial Relations in the Building Industry*, 1930
Johnson O'Connor, *Psychometrics*, 1934
Paul H. Norgren, *The Swedish Collective Bargaining System*, 1941
Leo C. Brown, S.J., *Union Policies in the Leather Industry*, 1947
Walter Galenson, *Labor in Norway*, 1949
Dorothea de Schweinitz, *Labor and Management in a Common Enterprise*, 1949
Ralph Altman, *Availability for Work: A Study in Unemployment Compensation*, 1950
John T. Dunlop and Arthur D. Hill, *The Wage Adjustment Board: Wartime Stabilization in the Building and Construction Industry*, 1950
Walter Galenson, *The Danish System of Labor Relations: A Study in Industrial Peace*, 1952
Lloyd H. Fisher, *The Harvest Labor Market in California*, 1953
Theodore V. Purcell, S.J., *The Worker Speaks His Mind on Company and Union*, 1953
Donald J. White, *The New England Fishing Industry*, 1954
Val R. Lorwin, *The French Labor Movement*, 1954
Philip Taft, *The Structure and Government of Labor Unions*, 1954
George B. Baldwin, *Beyond Nationalization: The Labor Problems of British Coal*, 1955
Kenneth F. Walker, *Industrial Relations in Australia*, 1956
Charles A. Myers, *Labor Problems in the Industrialization of India*, 1958
Herbert J. Spiro, *The Politics of German Codetermination*, 1958
Mark W. Leiserson, *Wages and Economic Control in Norway, 1945–1947*, 1959
J. Pen, *The Wage Rate under Collective Bargaining*, 1959
Jack Stieber, *The Steel Industry Wage Structure*, 1959
Theodore V. Purcell, S.J., *Blue Collar Man: Patterns of Dual Allegiance in Industry*, 1960
Carl Erik Knoellinger, *Labor in Finland*, 1960
Sumner H. Slichter, *Potentials of the American Economy: Selected Essays*, edited by John T. Dunlop, 1961

STUDIES IN LABOR-MANAGEMENT HISTORY

Lloyd Ulman, *The Rise of the National Trade Union: The Development and Significance of Its Structure, Governing Institutions and Economic Policies*, 1955

WERTHEIM PUBLICATIONS IN INDUSTRIAL RELATIONS

STUDIES IN LABOR-MANAGEMENT HISTORY, CONTINUED

Joseph P. Goldberg, *The Maritime Story: A Study in Labor-Management Relations*, 1957, 1958

Walter Galenson, *The CIO Challenge to the AFL: A History of the American Labor Movement, 1935–1941*, 1960

Morris A. Horowitz, *The New York Hotel Industry: A Labor Relations Study*, 1960

Bei Fragen zur Produktsicherheit wenden Sie sich bitte an:
If you have any questions regarding product safety,
please contact:

Walter de Gruyter GmbH
Genthiner Straße 13
10785 Berlin
productsafety@degruyterbrill.com